GOOD HOUSEKEEPING

ALL COLOUR

PARTY
COOK BOOK

GOOD HOUSEKEEPING
ALL COLOUR
PARTY
COOK BOOK

EBURY PRESS
LONDON

Published in 1992 by Ebury Press
an imprint of Random House UK Ltd
Random House
20 Vauxhall Bridge Road
London SW1V 2SA

First impression 1992
Text copyright © 1992 by The National Magazine Company Ltd
Illustrations copyright © 1992 by The National Magazine Company Ltd

The Good Housekeeping Institute is the food and consumer research centre of
Good Housekeeping magazine.

ISBN 0 09 175384 8

Photography by Jan Baldwin, Martin Brigdale, Laurie Evans, John Heseltine,
James Jackson, David Johnson, Paul Kemp

Drawings by Kate Simunek, John Woodcock, Bill le Fever

Printed and bound in Italy by New Interlitho S.p.a., Milan

CONTENTS

COOKERY NOTES

Follow either metric or imperial measures for the recipes in this book as they are not inter-changeable. Sets of spoon measures are available in both metric and imperial size to give accurate measurement of small quantities. All spoon measures are level unless otherwise stated. When measuring milk we have used the exact conversion of 568 ml (1 pint).

* Size 4 eggs should be used except when otherwise stated.
† Granulated sugar is used un-less otherwise stated.
● Plain flour is used unless otherwise stated.

OVEN TEMPERATURE CHART

°C	°F	Gas mark
110	225	$\frac{1}{4}$
130	250	$\frac{1}{2}$
140	275	1
150	300	2
170	325	3
180	350	4
190	375	5
200	400	6
220	425	7
230	450	8
240	475	9

KEY TO SYMBOLS

1.00* Indicates minimum preparation and cooking times in hours and minutes. They do not include prepared items in the list of ingredients; calcu-lated times apply only to the method. An asterisk * indicates extra time should be allowed, so check the note below symbols.

Chef's hats indicate degree of difficulty of a recipe: no hat means it is straightforward; one hat slightly more complicated; two hats indicates that it is for more advanced cooks.

✳ Indicates that a recipe will freeze. If there is no symbol, the recipe is unsuitable for freezing. An asterisk * indicates special freezer instructions so check the note immediately below the symbols.

309 cals Indicates calories per serving, including any sugges-tions (e.g. cream, to serve) given in the ingredients.

METRIC CONVERSION SCALE

LIQUID				SOLID		
Imperial	*Exact conversion*	*Recommended ml*		*Imperial*	*Exact conversion*	*Recommended g*
$\frac{1}{4}$ pint	142 ml	150 ml		1 oz	28.35 g	25 g
$\frac{1}{2}$ pint	284 ml	300 ml		2 oz	56.7 g	50 g
1 pint	568 ml	600 ml		4 oz	113.4 g	100 g
$1\frac{1}{2}$ pints	851 ml	900 ml		8 oz	226.8 g	225 g
$1\frac{3}{4}$ pints	992 ml	1 litre		12 oz	340.2 g	350 g
For quantities of $1\frac{3}{4}$ pints and over, litres and fractions of a litre have been used.				14 oz	397.0 g	400 g
				16 oz (1 lb)	453.6 g	450 g
				1 kilogram (kg) equals 2.2 lb.		

INTRODUCTION

This bumper cookbook is packed with imaginative dishes that all the family will enjoy. In addition to recipes for everyday meals there are recipes for all those special family occasions. Every possible mealtime is covered—from snacks and suppers to main courses, desserts and barbecues.

Every one of the 327 recipes in the main section of the book is illustrated with a colour photograph so that you can see at a glance the finished dishes. There are also helpful step-by-step illustrations to guide you smoothly through the method, ensuring that all the recipes are simple to follow. Special symbols indicate how long each recipe takes to make, the degree of difficulty involved, whether it will freeze and the calorie count. What's more, all the recipes have been double-tested so you can be absolutely sure of achieving successful results every time.

We hope very much that you enjoy these recipes and feel sure that they will become all-time family favourites.

Soups and Starters

CHESTNUT AND ORANGE SOUP

| 1.00 | £ | ✳ | 199 cals |

Serves 6

450 g (1 lb) whole chestnuts

40 g (1½ oz) butter

125 g (4 oz) carrots, peeled and finely chopped

2 onions, skinned and finely chopped

125 g (4 oz) mushrooms, wiped and finely chopped

5 ml (1 tsp) plain flour

1.4 litres (2½ pints) beef stock

salt and freshly ground pepper

15 ml (1 tbsp) finely grated orange rind

3 Melt the butter in a large saucepan, add the vegetables and fry together until lightly browned. Add the flour and cook, stirring, for a further 3–4 minutes or until the flour begins to colour.

4 Off the heat, stir in the stock, prepared chestnuts and seasoning. Bring slowly to the boil, stirring. Simmer, covered, for 40–45 minutes or until the chestnuts are quite tender.

5 Cool a little, then purée in a blender or a food processor, a small quantity at a time. Add half the orange rind and reheat for serving. Adjust seasoning and garnish with the remaining orange rind.

Menu Suggestion
Serve with Boned Stuffed Poussins (page 172) and Fresh Pear Short-cake (page 298).

1 Nick the brown outer skins of the chestnuts with a pair of sharp kitchen scissors, or the tip of a sharp knife.

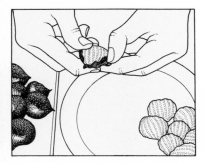

2 Cook the chestnuts in boiling water for 3–5 minutes, then lift out, a few at a time, using a slotted spoon. Peel off both the outer and inner skins and discard.

SWEET CHESTNUTS
These grow prolifically all over the Mediterranean, and are a common feature of many of the local cuisines – the Italians and the French have so many of them they even grind them into flour. Sweet chestnuts are grown in Britain, but most of the ones we see in the shops come from Spain and France – the French ones called *marrons* being the most highly prized.

CREAM OF JERUSALEM ARTICHOKE SOUP

| 0.45 | 🔲 | £ £ | ✳ | 278 cals |

Serves 4

900 g (2 lb) Jerusalem artichokes

2 slices of lemon

25 g (1 oz) butter or margarine

100 g (4 oz) onion, skinned and chopped

450 ml (¾ pint) milk

25 ml (1½ tbsp) lemon juice

30 ml (2 tbsp) chopped fresh parsley

150 ml (¼ pint) single cream

salt and freshly ground white pepper

croûtons, to garnish

1 Wash the artichokes well and put them in a large saucepan with the lemon slices. Cover with 900 ml (1½ pints) cold water. Bring to the boil and cook until tender, about 20 minutes.

2 Drain off the water, reserving 600 ml (1 pint). Leave the artichokes to cool.

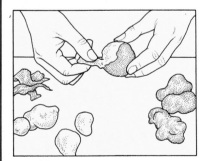

3 Peel the artichokes with your fingers, then mash them roughly.

4 Melt the butter in a clean saucepan, add the onion and cook gently for 10 minutes until soft but not coloured. Stir in the reserved artichoke water, artichokes and milk. Bring the soup to the boil, stirring, then simmer for 2–3 minutes.

5 Sieve or purée the soup in a blender or food processor. Return to the rinsed-out pan and stir in the lemon juice, parsley, cream and plenty of salt and pepper. Reheat gently, without boiling. Serve hot, garnished with croûtons.

Menu Suggestion

Creamy soups such as this one make elegant dinner party starters. Serve with warm bread rolls and a chilled dry white wine, and follow with a main course of roast poultry or game.

CREAM OF JERUSALEM ARTICHOKE SOUP

Jerusalem artichokes are strange-looking vegetables with an even stranger-sounding name! No-one really knows for sure how they got their name, but one theory is that it comes from the Italian word for sunflower —*girasole* — because the vegetable is a member of the sunflower family.

Another theory is that the name derives from Ter Heusen in Holland, the town from where the vegetable originally came. Street vendors are said to have corrupted 'Artichoke na Ter Heusen' to 'Artichokes of Jerusalem'.

CREAM OF PARSLEY SOUP

| 0.55 | £ | ✳ | 125 cals |

Serves 8

225 g (8 oz) parsley

225 g (8 oz) onions, skinned

125 g (4 oz) celery, washed and trimmed

50 g (2 oz) butter or margarine

45 ml (3 tbsp) plain flour

2 litres (3½ pints) chicken stock, preferably jellied homemade (see page 442)

salt and freshly ground pepper

150 ml (¼ pint) single cream

parsley sprigs, to garnish

1 Wash the parsley, drain and chop roughly. Slice the onions and celery.

2 Melt the fat in a large saucepan and add the parsley, onions and celery. Cover the pan and cook gently for about 10 minutes until the vegetables are quite soft. Shake the pan from time to time.

3 Stir in the flour until smooth, then mix in the stock. Add seasoning to taste and bring to the boil.

4 Cover the pan and simmer for 25–30 minutes. Cool a little, then purée in a blender or food processor. Leave to cool completely, then chill in the refrigerator until required.

5 Reheat until bubbling, taste and adjust seasoning and swirl in the cream. Serve immediately, garnished with the parsley.

Menu Suggestion

Serve this creamy soup in summer when there is plenty of fresh parsley in the garden. Hot French bread or garlic bread would make the perfect accompaniment.

CREAM OF PARSLEY SOUP

This soup can be made in next to no time if you have a food processor. Simply put the parsley, onions and celery in together and chop finely, then add the butter or margarine, flour and stock and work to a smooth purée. Transfer to a saucepan and bring to the boil, stirring constantly until thickened. Lower the heat and simmer as in the recipe. If you like, you can work the soup in the machine again before serving, for a really velvety smooth texture.

CURRIED PARSNIP AND ORANGE SOUP

| 0.55* | £ | ✳* | 276 cals |

* plus cooling and overnight standing;
freeze after blending in step 3

Serves 4

50 g (2 oz) butter or margarine

2 medium parsnips, peeled and
    diced

1 medium onion, skinned and
    chopped

1 garlic clove, skinned and crushed

5 ml (1 tsp) curry powder

5 ml (1 tsp) ground cumin

15 ml (1 tbsp) flour

1.1 litres (2 pints) chicken stock
    (see page 442)

finely grated rind and juice of 2
    large oranges

salt and freshly ground pepper

150 ml ($\frac{1}{4}$ pint) single cream, to
    serve

1 Melt the butter or margarine
in a large heavy-based
saucepan. Add the parsnips and
onion, cover the pan and fry gently
for about 10 minutes until
softened, shaking the pan
frequently.

2 Add the garlic and spices and
fry, uncovered, for 2 minutes,
stirring constantly to prevent
burning. Stir in the flour and cook
for a further 2 minutes, then pour
in the stock and the orange juice.
Bring to the boil, stirring, then
add seasoning to taste. Lower the
heat, cover and simmer for about
20 minutes until the parsnips are
tender.

3 Work the soup in a blender or
food processor until smooth,
then turn into a bowl, cover and
leave overnight in a cool place or
the refrigerator until cold, to allow
the flavours to develop.

4 Reheat the soup until
bubbling, then lower the heat,
stir in half the cream and heat
through without boiling. Taste
and adjust the seasoning.

5 Pour the hot soup into a
warmed tureen or individual
bowls, swirl with the remaining
cream and sprinkle with the grated
orange rind. Serve immediately.

Menu Suggestion
This soup makes an unusual
dinner party starter served with
crisp poppadoms. Follow with
Pork with Cider and Coriander
(page 118) for the main course and
Orange water ice (page 282) for
the dessert.

ICED COURGETTE SOUP

0.40*	✳*	260 cals

* plus cooling and overnight chilling;
freeze at the end of step 3

Serves 4

50 g (2 oz) butter or margarine

**450 g (1 lb) courgettes, trimmed
and chopped**

1 medium potato, peeled and diced

**750 ml (1¼ pints) vegetable stock or
water**

**5 ml (1 tsp) chopped fresh basil or
2.5 ml (½ tsp) dried basil**

salt and freshly ground pepper

100 g (4 oz) ripe Blue Brie

sliced courgette, to serve (optional)

1 Melt the butter or margarine
in a large heavy-based
saucepan. Add the courgettes and
potato, cover the pan and fry
gently for about 10 minutes until
softened, shaking frequently.

2 Add the stock or water with
the basil and seasoning to
taste. Bring to the boil, stirring,
then lower the heat and simmer
for 20 minutes until the vegetables
are tender.

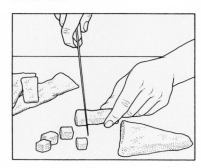

3 Remove the rind from the Brie
and chop the cheese into small
dice. Put into a blender or food
processor, then pour in the soup.
Blend until smooth, then turn into
a bowl, cover and leave until cold.
Chill in the refrigerator overnight.

4 Whisk the soup vigorously to
ensure an even consistency,
then taste and adjust seasoning.
Pour into a chilled soup tureen or
individual bowls and float the
courgette slices on the top if liked.

Menu Suggestion
The perfect starter for a summer
dinner party or barbecue.

15

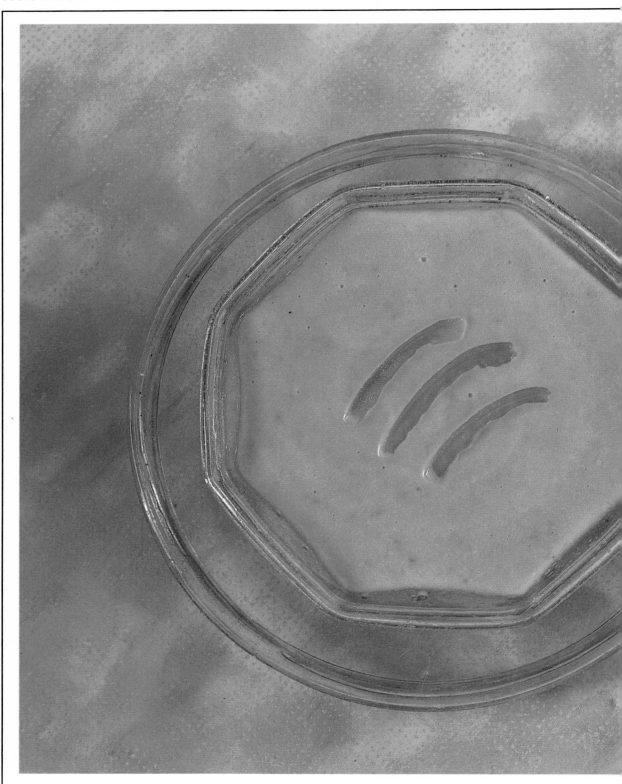

AVOCADO SOUP

| 0.15* | 🍴 | £ | 183 cals |

* plus 2 hours chilling

Serves 4

1 avocado

450 ml (¾ pint) chicken stock

30 ml (2 tbsp) lemon juice

200 ml (7 fl oz) milk

5 ml (1 tsp) golden syrup

a pinch of cayenne

salt and freshly ground pepper

2 ripe tomatoes, to garnish

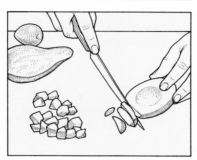

1 Halve the avocado, discard the stone and peel and roughly chop the flesh.

2 Put the avocado into a blender or food processor with the chicken stock, lemon juice, milk, golden syrup and cayenne and blend until smooth. Season to taste with salt and pepper. Pour into a bowl, cover with cling film and chill in the refrigerator for no longer than 2 hours. (The soup will begin to discolour if you leave it for longer.)

3 Meanwhile, plunge the tomatoes into boiling water for 10 seconds, remove from the water and peel off the skin. Halve the tomatoes, remove the seeds, then cut each half into thin slivers.

4 Taste and adjust the seasoning of the soup. Garnish with the tomato slivers just before serving.

Menu Suggestion

Chilled avocado soup has a delicate, lemony flavour. Serve for a special dinner party starter.

AVOCADO SOUP

Avocados are becoming increasingly popular, and prices are dropping accordingly, so that they are no longer the luxury 'fruit' they were a few years ago. The Mexicans were the first people to discover just how delicious this fruit could be if used as a vegetable. They called it *ahuacatl*, then the Spaniards brought it back to Europe and called it *aguacate*, which was translated into English as avocado. Nowadays, avocados are grown all over the world, and there are said to be over 500 varieties, ranging from the tiny 'cocktail' or salad avocados which have no stone, to the large Ettinger avocados which can weigh as much as 225 g (8 oz) each.

CHILLED ASPARAGUS SOUP

1.00* £ £ ✳ 310 cals

* plus refrigeration time

Serves 6

700 g (1½ lb) stalks of asparagus

salt and freshly ground pepper

50 g (2 oz) butter or margarine

225 g (8 oz) onions, skinned and thinly sliced

1.4 litres (2½ pints) chicken stock

30 ml (2 tbsp) chopped fresh parsley

150 ml (5 fl oz) single cream

small brown uncut loaf, fresh butter, for spreading

lemon slices, to garnish

1 Rinse the asparagus. Cut off the heads and simmer very gently in salted water until just tender. Drain carefully and cool; cover and refrigerate until required to make asparagus rolls.

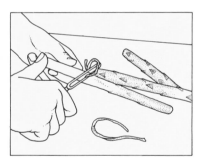

2 Scrape the asparagus stalks with a potato peeler or knife to remove any scales; cut off the woody ends. Thinly slice the asparagus stalks.

3 Melt the butter or margarine in a large saucepan. Add the asparagus and onions, cover and cook over a moderate heat for 5–10 minutes or until the vegetables are beginning to soften.

4 Add the stock and parsley, season and bring to the boil. Cover and simmer for 30 minutes, or until the asparagus and onion are quite tender. Cool slightly.

5 Purée in a blender or food processor until smooth. Sieve if necessary. Cool, then stir in the cream and adjust seasoning. Cover and chill well before serving.

6 Cut six thin slices of brown bread and butter them. Cut off the crusts and halve lengthwise. Roll asparagus heads inside each piece of bread; place on a serving plate, cover with cling film and refrigerate until required.

7 Serve the soup well chilled, garnished with wafer thin lemon slices and accompanied by the asparagus rolls.

Menu Suggestion
Serve with Rump Steak in Whisky (page 37) and Raspberry Pavlova (page 90).

ASPARAGUS
This vegetable is sold graded according to the thickness of its stems, usually in bundles, but sometimes by the kg/lb. The thicker the stems the more expensive the asparagus; for making soups it is not essential to buy the best grades. For use in cooked dishes or soups, look for the small, thin green asparagus called 'sprue', which is the least expensive grade.

CHILLED MELON SOUP

| 1.10* | ☐ | £ £ | ✳ | 159 cals |

* plus at least 4 hours chilling

Serves 4

1 ripe honeydew or cantaloupe melon, weighing about 700 g (1½ lb)

25 g (1 oz) butter or margarine

5 ml (1 tsp) ground ginger

900 ml (1½ pints) vegetable stock

salt and freshly ground white pepper

1 egg yolk

60 ml (4 tbsp) double cream

very thin slices of preserved (stem) ginger, to garnish (optional)

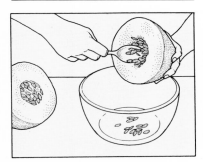

1 Cut the melon in half and scoop out the seeds with a sharp-edged teaspoon.

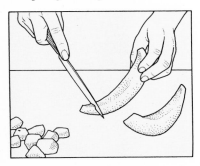

2 Remove the flesh from the skin of the melon. Cut the melon halves into sections, then release the flesh by cutting between the skin and underside of the flesh. Cut the flesh into small chunks.

3 Melt the butter in a large saucepan, add the cubes of melon and cook very gently for 5 minutes until softened and coated in butter.

4 Sprinkle in the ginger and cook for a further 1–2 minutes, stirring constantly. Pour in the stock, add salt and pepper to taste and bring to the boil. Lower the heat, cover the pan and simmer for 30 minutes.

5 Sieve or purée the soup in a blender or food processor. Mix the egg yolk and cream together in a bowl, then stir in a little of the soup.

6 Return the soup to the rinsed-out pan and stir in the egg yolk liaison. Heat through gently without boiling, stirring constantly until thickened. Leave to cool, then chill in the refrigerator for at least 4 hours. Taste and adjust seasoning before serving garnished with ginger slices, if liked.

CHILLED MELON SOUP

Both honeydew and cantaloupe melons are widely available in the summer months. Honeydew melons have green flesh and a delicate flavour, whereas cantaloupes have yellow flesh and are sweeter, with a scented flesh. Both types of melon are suitable for making soup, as long as they are ripe and juicy. To test for ripeness, press gently with your thumbs at both ends — the melon should give slightly if it is ripe.

21

MEXICAN AVOCADO DIP

| 0.15 | £ £ | 383 cals |

Serves 6

30 ml (2 tbsp) vegetable oil

1 small onion, skinned and finely chopped

2 garlic cloves, skinned and crushed

2.5 ml ($\frac{1}{2}$ tsp) chilli powder

4 tomatoes, skinned and chopped

2 ripe avocados

juice of $\frac{1}{2}$ lemon

142 ml (5 fl oz) soured cream

salt and freshly ground black pepper

tomato slices, to garnish

1 Heat oil in a small pan, add the onion, garlic and chilli and fry gently, stirring, until onion is soft. Add the tomatoes and fry for a further 5 minutes, breaking them up with a wooden spoon.

2 Put the tomato mixture into a blender or food processor and blend until smooth. Turn into a bowl and leave to cool.

3 Halve and stone the avocados, then peel three halves. Add to the tomato mixture with the lemon juice and mash to a purée. Blend in half the soured cream, then taste and add salt and pepper and more chilli powder, if liked.

4 Transfer the dip to a shallow serving bowl. Peel and slice the remaining avocado half. Arrange avocado slices on top of dip, alternating with tomato slices.

5 To serve, spoon the remaining cream into the centre and sprinkle with a little chilli powder. Serve immediately.

PERE AL GORGONZOLA
(GORGONZOLA STUFFED PEARS)

| 0.30 | 607 cals |

Serves 4

100 g (4 oz) Gorgonzola cheese, at room temperature

25 g (1 oz) unsalted butter, softened

50 g (2 oz) shelled walnuts, finely chopped

salt and freshly ground pepper

150 ml ($\frac{1}{4}$ pint) thick homemade mayonnaise (see page 443)

about 15 ml (1 tbsp) tarragon vinegar

2 ripe firm pears (e.g. Packham)

juice of $\frac{1}{2}$ a lemon

lettuce leaves, to serve

1 Make the stuffing mixture. Work half the cheese and the butter together with a fork. Add half of the walnuts and pepper to taste and mix together until well combined. (Do not add salt as the cheese is quite salty enough.)

2 Soften the remaining cheese and work it into the mayonnaise. Stir the tarragon vinegar into the mayonnaise mixture to thin it down to a light coating consistency. If too thick, add a little more vinegar. Taste and adjust seasoning.

3 Peel the two pears and, using a sharp knife, cut each one in half lengthways.

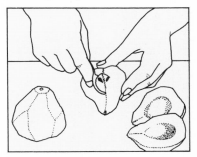

4 Scoop out the cores and a little of the surrounding flesh with a sharp-edged teaspoon. Immediately brush lemon juice over the exposed flesh to prevent discoloration.

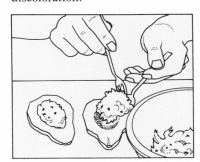

5 Fill the scooped-out centres of the pears with the Gorgonzola stuffing mixture.

6 To serve, place 1–2 lettuce leaves in the centre of each individual serving plate. Place one pear half, cut side down, on the lettuce. Coat the pears with the mayonnaise, then sprinkle with the remaining chopped walnuts. Serve immediately.

Menu Suggestion
Serve as a dinner party starter followed by Osso Buco (page 83) and Granita di Caffé (page 124).

STUFFED MUSHROOMS

1.05* ⬚ ✳* 642 cals

* plus 1 hour or overnight chilling; freeze mushrooms and the dip separately in step 6

Serves 4

30 ml (2 tbsp) olive oil

1 small onion, skinned and chopped

2 garlic cloves, skinned and crushed

396 g (14 oz) can tomatoes

5 ml (1 tsp) dried oregano

5 ml (1 tsp) dried basil

30 ml (2 tbsp) chopped fresh parsley

1.25 ml (¼ tsp) sugar

salt and freshly ground pepper

32 even-sized button mushrooms, wiped

175 g (6 oz) unsalted butter, softened

50 g (2 oz) can anchovies in olive oil, drained and chopped

finely grated rind of 1 lemon

2 eggs, beaten

75 g (3 oz) dried breadcrumbs

vegetable oil for deep frying

1 Make the tomato dip. Heat the oil in a saucepan, add the onion and half the garlic and fry gently for 5 minutes until soft but not coloured.

2 Add the tomatoes, dried herbs, half the parsley, the sugar and seasoning to taste. Bring to the boil, stirring constantly with a wooden spoon to break up the tomatoes. Lower the heat and simmer, covered, for 30 minutes, stirring occasionally.

3 Meanwhile pull the stalks carefully from the mushrooms with your fingers. Chop the stalks finely, then place in a bowl with the butter, anchovies, lemon rind, remaining garlic and parsley. Beat the ingredients together until well combined, then add pepper to taste (do not add salt because of the saltiness of the anchovies).

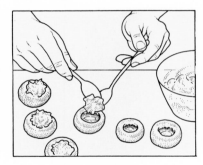

4 Spoon the butter mixture into the cavities of each of the mushrooms.

5 Sandwich the mushrooms together in pairs and pierce through the centre of each pair with a wooden cocktail stick. Dip the mushrooms in the beaten eggs, then in the breadcrumbs until evenly coated.

6 Chill in the refrigerator for 1 hour, or overnight if more convenient. Remove the tomato dip from the heat, leave to cool, then chill in the refrigerator at the same time as the mushrooms.

7 Work the tomato dip in a blender or food processor, then sieve to remove the tomato seeds. Taste and adjust seasoning, then pour into a serving bowl or jug. Return to the refrigerator while frying the mushrooms.

8 Heat the oil in a deep frier to 190°C (375°F) and deep fry the mushrooms in batches for about 5 minutes until golden brown and crisp on all sides. Drain quickly on absorbent kitchen paper, then remove the cocktail sticks. Serve immediately, with the chilled tomato dip handed separately.

Menu Suggestion
This dinner party starter is so substantial that it needs no accompaniment other than chilled dry white wine.

ASPARAGUS MALTAISE

| 0.30 | f f | 220 cals |

Serves 6

450 g (1 lb) asparagus, washed and trimmed

3 egg yolks

grated rind and juice of 1 orange

salt and freshly ground white pepper

100 g (4 oz) unsalted butter, softened

15 ml (1 tbsp) lemon juice

30–45 ml (2–3 tbsp) double cream

orange twists, to garnish

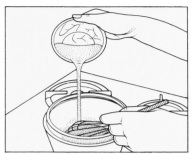

1 Tie the asparagus in bundles of six to eight stalks. Standing them upright in a pan of boiling water, cook for 10–15 minutes until tender.

2 Meanwhile, make the sauce. Beat together the egg yolks, orange rind and seasoning in a bowl with a knob of the softened butter.

3 Place the bowl over a pan of hot water and whisk in the orange and lemon juice. Cook over a gentle heat and gradually beat in remaining butter, a little at a time.

4 Once the sauce begins to thicken, remove from the heat and continue beating for 1 minute. Adjust seasoning to taste. Stir in the cream.

5 Remove the asparagus from the pan and drain well. To serve, remove the string, garnish and serve immediately with the orange butter sauce handed separately.

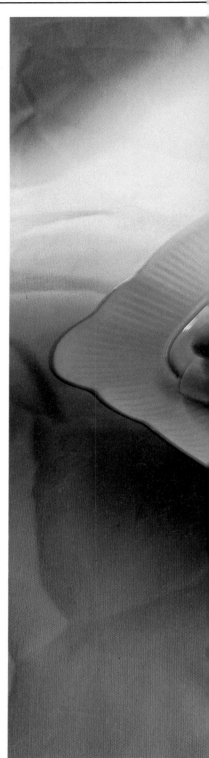

SAUCE MALTAISE

This simple recipe for fresh asparagus served with sauce maltaise is a version of a classic French dish. Sauce maltaise is in fact a variation of hollandaise sauce – grated orange rind and juice is added to make the sauce a delicate shade of pink. Traditionally, a blood orange should be used, but this is not absolutely essential. This sauce can also be served with broccoli or fish.

Hollandaise sauce is not difficult to make, but it does require patience – if you want to make a perfect sauce there are no cutting corners! From the same family of sauces as mayonnaise – it is in fact a cooked emulsion of egg yolks and butter as opposed to the uncooked emulsion of egg yolks and oil – the skill lies in the whisking in of the butter. This should be added a little at a time: if you rush this stage and whisk in more butter before the first amount has emulsified, the resulting sauce will be curdled.

STUFFED GLOBE ARTICHOKES

1.30	⬒	f f	518 cals

Serves 6

6 medium globe artichokes
45 ml (3 tbsp) lemon juice
salt and freshly ground pepper
2 onions, skinned and finely chopped
350 g (12 oz) rindless streaky bacon, finely sliced
75 g (3 oz) butter
700 g (1½ lb) ripe tomatoes, skinned
175 g (6 oz) fresh white breadcrumbs
finely grated rind and juice of 2 medium oranges
90 ml (6 tbsp) chopped fresh parsley
2 eggs
melted butter, to serve

1 Strip away discoloured leaves. Slice off stem of artichoke as close as possible to the base of leaves. Level up so artichokes stand upright.

2 Using scissors, snip off the leaf tips. Soak the artichokes in cold water acidulated with 15 ml (1 tbsp) lemon juice for about 30 minutes while preparing the rest.

3 Drain artichokes and place them in a large pan of boiling salted water with the remaining lemon juice.

4 Cover and boil gently for 30–45 minutes, depending on size. The artichokes will float, so turn them during cooking and keep covered, to steam the leaves above the water.

5 Meanwhile, make the stuffing. Fry the onions and bacon in the butter until onions are soft and bacon golden. Quarter, seed and roughly chop tomatoes.

6 Add the tomatoes to the pan, cook for a few minutes, then stir in the crumbs, grated orange rind, parsley, eggs and seasoning, beating well to mix.

7 Test whether the artichokes are cooked. To do this, gently pull an outer leaf; if cooked, it will come out easily.

8 Drain the cooked artichokes upside down in a colander and hold briefly under cold tap. This helps to bring out and set the green colour and cools down the leaves for handling.

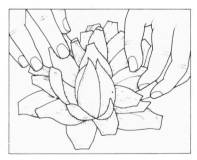

9 Gradually peel back leaves, working from the outside inwards (be careful not to snap any off). Continue peeling back the leaves until the hairy choke of the artichoke is exposed.

10 With a teaspoon, scrape away and discard hairs. Hollow out heart slightly.

11 Spoon stuffing generously over hearts; divide it evenly between the six artichokes.

12 Gently fold the leaves back around the stuffing. Tie string around each one to hold it together.

13 Pack artichokes into a well-buttered deep ovenproof dish or shallow casserole. Pour over strained orange juice and cover tightly with buttered grease-proof paper or foil and the lid. Bake in the oven at 190°C (375°F) mark 5 for 25 minutes. To serve, remove string and offer melted butter separately.

AVOCADO WITH PARMA HAM

| 0.10 | £ £ | 401 cals |

Serves 6

50 g (2 oz) Parma ham
90 ml (6 tbsp) vegetable oil
45 ml (3 tbsp) lemon juice
5 ml (1 tsp) Dijon mustard
salt and freshly ground pepper
3 spring onions, finely chopped
3 ripe avocados
hot French bread, to serve

1 With lightly oiled kitchen scissors, cut the ham into fine shreds. Whisk the oil, lemon juice, mustard and seasoning together.

2 Stir in the spring onions and the ham. Cut the avocados in half and twist to remove the stones; put each half on a plate. If necessary, cut a thin slice off the base of each one so that it stands level on the serving plate.

3 Spoon the ham mixture into the avocados. Serve at once with hot French bread, if wished.

Menu Suggestion
Serve with Baked Trout with Lemon (page 182) and Walnut Meringue Cake (page 284).

FETA CHEESE SOUFFLÉ

| 1.00 | £ | 207 cals |

Serves 6

butter, for greasing
grated Parmesan cheese
25 g (1 oz) butter
30 ml (2 tbsp) plain flour
200 ml (7 fl oz) milk
salt and freshly ground pepper
225 g (8 oz) Feta cheese, grated
50 g (2 oz) stuffed olives, chopped
4 eggs, separated

1 Lightly butter a 1.7-litre (3-pint) soufflé dish and dust out with the grated Parmesan.

2 Melt the butter in a saucepan, add the flour and cook for 1 minute, stirring. Off the heat, gradually stir in the milk and black pepper. Bring to the boil; cook for 2–3 minutes, stirring. Allow to cool slightly, then beat in the Feta, olives and egg yolks. Season.

3 Whisk the egg whites until stiff and beat a large spoonful into the sauce. Lightly fold in the rest and pour the mixture into the dish.

4 Bake in the oven at 180°C (350°F) mark 4 for about 40 minutes or until the soufflé is golden. Serve immediately.

ITALIAN SQUID SALAD

2.00*	🍳🍳 f f	394 cals

*including 1 hour standing time

Serves 6

1.25–1.5-kg (2½–3-lb) squid

6 garlic cloves, skinned and crushed with 5 ml (1 tsp) salt

300 ml (½ pint) full-bodied Italian red wine

300 ml (½ pint) water

½ onion, skinned and finely sliced

1 red pepper, cored, seeded and thinly sliced

1 green pepper, cored, seeded and thinly sliced

135 ml (9 tbsp) olive oil

juice of 1 lemon

700 g (1½ lb) prawns in their sheels or 225 g (8 oz) peeled prawns and 12 whole prawns to garnish

one 50-g (2-oz) can anchovies in oil, drained and soaked in milk 20 minutes

15 ml (1 tbsp) chopped fresh basil, or 10 ml (2 tsp) dried

freshly ground pepper

few large lettuce leaves

fresh basil sprigs and black olives, to garnish

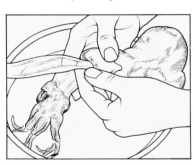

1 Clean the squid. Hold under cold running water to rinse thoroughly. Pull back the edge of the body pouch to expose the translucent quill or pen.

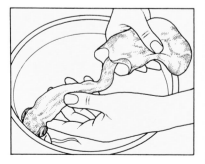

2 Holding the body pouch firmly with one hand, take hold of the end of the exposed quill with the other and pull it free. Then discard the quill.

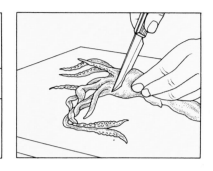

3 Separate the tentacles from the body pouch. Holding the body pouch in one hand, pull out the head and tentacles with the other.

4 Cut through the head, just above the eyes. Discard the eyes and ink sac and reserve the tentacles until required.

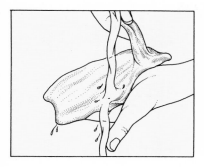
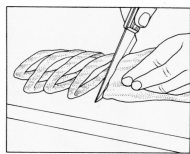
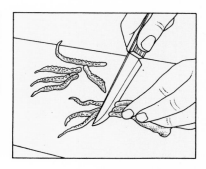

5 Rub the purplish skin off the body pouch and tentacles, holding them under cold running water. Discard the skin.

6 Using a sharp knife, carefully cut the triangular fins off the body pouch. Discard the fins and cut the body into thin rings.

7 Cut the reserved tentacles into small pieces. If they are very small, leave some whole.

8 Put all the squid pieces in an earthenware baking dish. Add half the garlic. Pour over the wine and water, then cover and cook in the oven at 180°C (350°F) mark 4 for $1\frac{1}{2}$–2 hours until tender. Cool.

9 Drain the squid, then rinse quickly under cold running water and drain again thoroughly. Put into a bowl with the remaining garlic, the onion, red and green peppers, olive oil and lemon juice. Stir well to mix.

10 Peel the prawns, if using whole prawns, reserving twelve whole ones for the garnish. Drain the anchovies, rinse and pat dry on absorbent kitchen paper, then chop them roughly.

11 Add the peeled prawns to the salad with the anchovies, basil and pepper to taste. Fold gently to mix, then cover and leave to stand for about 1 hour.

12 To serve, line a bowl with lettuce leaves and pile the squid into the centre. Garnish with the reserved whole prawns, and basil sprigs and black olives.

ANTIPASTO MISTO
(ITALIAN MIXED SALAD)

0.30* £ £ 347 cals*

* plus 2 hours refrigeration and 20 minutes standing time; 394 cals with optional ingredients

Serves 6

1 head radicchio or a small lettuce

12 thin slices of Italian salami

6 thin slices of Mortadella sausage

6 thin slices of Parma ham

170 g (6 oz) Mozzarella cheese

3 hard-boiled eggs, quartered

3 tomatoes, sliced

160 g (5½ oz) can of mussels in oil (optional)

280 g (10 oz) jar of artichoke hearts in oil (optional)

280 g (10 oz) jar of sweet and sour peppers (optional)

olives and anchovies, to garnish

bread sticks, to serve

1 Wash the radicchio or lettuce leaves; drain well and pat dry with kitchen paper. Coarsely shred the leaves.

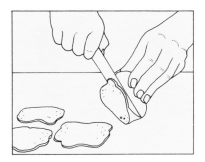

2 Using a sharp knife, carefully cut the Mozzarella cheese into thin slices.

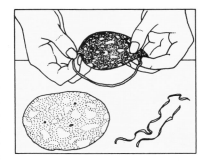

3 Ease any skin or rind off the salami and the Mortadella sausage with your fingers.

4 Place a bed of radicchio or lettuce on a large serving platter. Arrange the slices of salami, Mortadella, Parma ham, Mozzarella, hard-boiled eggs, tomatoes, mussels, artichoke hearts, and peppers on top. Garnish with black olives and anchovies.

5 Cover tightly with cling film and refrigerate for at least 2 hours. Leave at cool room temperature for about 20 minutes before serving.

ANTIPASTO MISTO

The word 'antipasto' means 'before the meal', and it can be anything from one or two slices of salami to a huge selection of cold meats, fish, eggs, vegetables and salads. For everyday meals, most Italian families have the simplest of antipasto, say a slice or two of cold meat and hard-boiled eggs with some olives and fresh bread—just enough to whet the appetite before the pasta course.

NUTTY CAMEMBERT PÂTÉ

0.20*	✳*	315–475 cals

* plus overnight chilling; freeze at the
end of step 3

Serves 4–6

175 g (6 oz) soft ripe Camembert
    cheese

225 g (8 oz) full-fat soft cheese

2.5 ml (½ tsp) paprika

salt and freshly ground pepper

75 g (3 oz) finely chopped blanched
    almonds

extra paprika, to serve

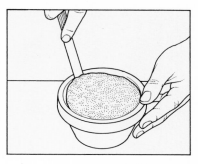

1 Cut the rind off the
Camembert, then work the
cheese through a sieve into a bowl,
or mix in a food processor until
smooth.

2 Add the soft cheese, paprika
and seasoning to taste. Beat
vigorously with a wooden spoon to
combine the ingredients well
together.

3 Spoon the pâté into a greased
and base-lined 300 ml (½ pint)
dish or mould. Press down well
and smooth the surface with the
back of the spoon. Cover the dish
and freeze for 1 hour.

4 Loosen the pâté from the dish
by running a palette knife
between the two. Turn the pâté
out upside down on to a serving
plate and peel off the lining paper.
Chill overnight.

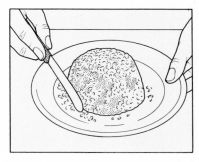

5 Sprinkle the nuts over the
pâté, then press evenly over
the top and around the sides with
the palette knife. Sprinkle with
paprika. Serve chilled.

Menu Suggestion

Cheese makes an unusual starter.
Serve this creamy pâté with
wholemeal toast, crispbreads or
crackers.

LAYERED TURKEY AND HAM TERRINE

2.40*	✳	266–399 cals

* plus cooling and overnight chilling
Serves 8–12

12 streaky bacon rashers, rinded

450 g (1 lb) boneless pork sparerib

225 g (8 oz) pig's liver

100 g (4 oz) fresh white (crustless) bread

50 g (2 oz) can anchovy fillets, soaked in milk for 20 minutes and drained

finely grated rind and juice of 1 lemon

60 ml (4 tbsp) brandy

50 g (2 oz) shelled pistachio nuts, chopped

1 egg, beaten

salt and freshly ground pepper

225 g (8 oz) boiled ham, thickly sliced

225 g (8 oz) turkey breast fillet, skinned and thickly sliced

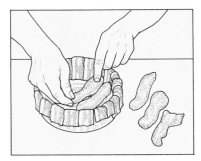

1 Stretch the bacon rashers with the flat of the blade of a large cook's knife.

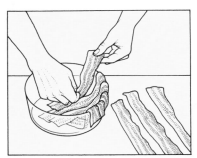

2 Use the bacon rashers to line the base and sides of a 1.2 litre (2 pint) soufflé dish or mould. Set aside.

3 Mince the pork, liver, bread and anchovies together (or work in a food processor for a finer-textured terrine). Turn into a bowl and add the lemon rind and juice, the brandy, pistachio nuts, egg and salt and pepper to taste. Mix well to combine all the ingredients evenly together.

4 Put one-third of the minced mixture in the bottom of the lined soufflé dish and press down well. Cover with a layer of half of the ham and turkey slices. Put another third of the minced mixture in the dish and press down well, then cover with a layer of the remaining ham and turkey slices. Top with the remaining minced mixture and press down well.

5 Cover the dish with foil, place in a bain marie (page 39) and bake in the oven at 170°C (325°F) mark 3 for 2 hours.

6 Carefully drain off the fat and cooking juices, then cover with a plate or saucer and put heavy weights on top. Leave to cool, then chill in the refrigerator overnight.

7 Turn the terrine out of the dish onto a board or serving plate and cut into slices to serve, to expose the layers.

Menu Suggestion
This is a spectacular-looking terrine for a special dinner party. Serve with chilled champagne or sparkling dry white wine.

DANISH LIVER PÂTÉ

2.15*	✳	468–701 cals

* plus cooling and overnight chilling

Serves 4–6

450 g (1 lb) unsmoked streaky bacon rashers, rinded

50 g (2 oz) butter or margarine

1 small onion, skinned and chopped

225 g (8 oz) chicken livers, cleaned and dried

50 g (2 oz) can anchovy fillets, soaked in milk for 20 minutes and drained

10 ml (2 tsp) whole allspice berries, crushed or 5 ml (1 tsp) ground allspice

25 g (1 oz) plain flour

300 ml (½ pint) milk

1 egg, beaten

freshly ground pepper

3 Melt the remaining butter in a saucepan, add the flour and cook gently, stirring, for 1–2 minutes. Remove from the heat and gradually blend in the milk. Bring to the boil, stirring constantly, then simmer for 3 minutes until thick and smooth. Add the egg, ground allspice, if using, and pepper to taste.

4 Work the chicken liver mixture in a blender or food processor until smooth, then add the white sauce and work again until evenly combined.

5 Turn the mixture into the lined loaf tin, smooth the surface and cover with greased foil. Place in a bain marie (see page 59) and bake at 170°C (325°F) mark 3 for 1½ hours or until set.

6 Remove the tin from the bain marie and place heavy weights on top of the foil covering. Leave until cold, then refrigerate overnight. Turn out and slice.

Menu Suggestion
This pâté has a strong flavour of bacon. Serve with granary or wholemeal toast and unsalted butter.

1 With the flat of the blade of a large cook's knife, stretch enough of the bacon rashers to line the base and sides of a 450 g (1 lb) loaf tin.

2 Chop the remaining bacon rashers roughly. Melt half of the butter in a frying pan, add the onion and fry gently until soft. Add the chopped bacon, the chicken livers, anchovies and allspice berries, if using. Fry, stirring constantly, until the chicken livers change colour. Remove from the heat and set aside.

VEAL, WINE AND APRICOT PÂTÉ

2.20* £ ✳	481 cals

* plus 2 nights chilling and 30 minutes standing

Serves 6

700 g (1½ lb) pie veal

25 g (1 oz) dried apricots

100 ml (4 fl oz) dry white wine

225 g (8 oz) pork fat

½ small bunch of watercress, washed and trimmed

2 garlic cloves, skinned and crushed

2 eggs

50 g (2 oz) fresh white breadcrumbs

2.5 ml (½ tsp) ground allspice

7.5 ml (1½ tsp) salt

freshly ground pepper

1 Cut the pie veal into pieces and put in a shallow dish with the apricots. Pour over the wine, cover and chill in the refrigerator overnight.

2 The next day, drain the veal and apricots, reserving the marinade. Finely mince the veal and apricots with the pork fat. Chop half of the watercress; reserve the rest for garnish.

3 Put the minced mixture in a large bowl with the reserved marinade and the remaining ingredients. Mix well together.

4 Spoon the mixture into a 1.4 litre (2½ pint) terrine or loaf tin and press down well. Cover and place in a roasting tin.

5 Pour boiling water into the tin to come halfway up the sides of the terrine. Cook in the oven at 170°C (325°F) mark 3 for about 1¾ hours until firm.

6 When the pâté is cooked, remove from the roasting tin, uncover and spoon off the excess fat. Leave to cool slightly, then place a piece of greaseproof paper on top. Place heavy weights on top, then chill in the refrigerator overnight.

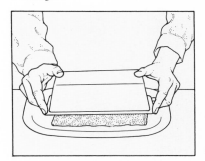

7 The next day, turn the pâté out of the tin and allow to stand at room temperature for 30 minutes. Garnish with the reserved watercress sprigs before serving.

Menu Suggestion
This unusual pâté would make a delicious dinner party starter. Serve with Melba toast and a chilled dry white wine such as a Muscadet.

VEAL, WINE AND APRICOT PÂTÉ

To make Melba toast to serve with this pâté, simply remove the crusts from thin slices of white or brown bread (from a packet), then toast the bread lightly on both sides. Place the toast on a board and split through the middle, working carefully with a sharp knife and using a sawing action. Pop the bread back under the grill, untoasted side facing upwards, and grill until the toast becomes crisp and the edges curl up. Remove from the heat, leave until cold, then store in an airtight tin.

DUCK PÂTÉ EN CROÛTE BIGARADE

3.45* ▢ ▢ £ £ ✳ 485 cals

* plus 1 hour standing time plus overnight chilling

Serves 12

450 g (1 lb) pork belly
3-kg (6-lb) duckling
225 g (8 oz) chicken livers
100 g (4 oz) white breadcrumbs
grated rind and juice of orange
60 ml (4 tbsp) brandy
2 garlic cloves
6 black peppercorns
6 juniper berries
6 coriander seeds
5 ml (1 tsp) salt
275 g (10 oz) streaky bacon, rinded
225 g (8 oz) middle-cut bacon rashers, rinds removed
453-g (16-oz) can cherries, drained
225 g (8 oz) packet frozen puff pastry or 100 g (4 oz) home-made (see page 439)
1 egg, beaten

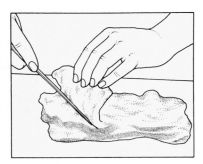

1 Remove skin from pork and cut meat and fat into small pieces. Bone the duckling (see page 158) and cut all the meat into small pieces except the breast.

2 Mince duck and pork pieces in a food processor with livers. Turn into a bowl, add bread-crumbs, orange rind and juice and half the brandy and stir well. Pound garlic and spices to a paste. Add to duck mixture with salt and mix. Cover; set aside for 1 hour.

3 Meanwhile, place the duck breasts in a shallow dish and pour over the remaining brandy. Cover; set aside for 1 hour.

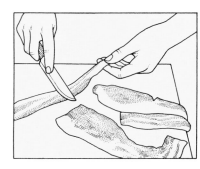

4 With the flat of a large knife, stretch the streaky bacon rashers and the streaky end of the middle-cut bacon. Use about three-quarters to line the base and sides of a 20-cm (8-inch) round cake tin.

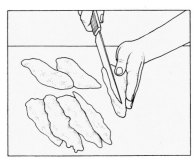

5 Put half the duck mixture in the tin. Drain the suprêmes and cut horizontally into thin slices. Cover the duck mixture with half the duck slices and half of remaining middle-cut bacon.

6 Arrange the cherries in a single layer over the top, then cover with the remaining duck slices and middle-cut bacon.

7 Put the remaining duck mix-ture on top, pressing it down firmly, then top with the remaining stretched bacon.

8 Cover the tin with foil, then place in a roasting dish half filled with hot water. Bake in the oven at 180°C (350°F) mark 4 for 2½ hours or until the juices run clear when the pâté is tested with a skewer.

9 Carefully drain off the fat and cooking juices, then cover with a plate and place heavy weights on top. Cool overnight.

10 The next day, roll out the pastry on a lightly floured surface into a circle large enough to enclose the pâté completely. Reserve pastry trimmings.

11 Turn the pâté out of the tin and scrape off any jelly or sediment. Brush the pastry lightly with beaten egg, then place the pâté in the centre.

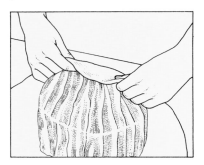

12 Wrap in the pastry, then place join side down on a dampened baking sheet. Brush with beaten egg, then decorate with pastry trimmings and brush these with egg.

13 Bake in the oven at 200°C (400°F) mark 6 for 25 minutes until golden. Leave to cool before serving.

POTTED PRAWN PÂTÉ ▶

| 0.20* | ✳ | 100 cals |

* plus 1 hour chilling

Serves 8

175 g (6 oz) peeled prawns
75 g (3 oz) butter, softened
10 ml (2 tsp) lemon juice
20 ml (4 tsp) chopped fresh parsley
salt and freshly ground pepper
prawn and lemon, to garnish
French bread, to serve

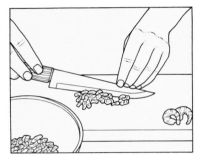

1 Finely chop the prawns. Beat into 50 g (2 oz) butter with the lemon juice, parsley and seasoning.

2 Spoon into a serving dish and level the surface. Melt the remaining butter and pour over the prawn mixture. Refrigerate for 1 hour. Garnish with prawn and lemon. Serve with French bread.

POTTED SHRIMPS

0.10*	✳	520 cals

* plus 1 hour chilling

Serves 4

150 g (5 oz) peeled shrimps

225 g (8 oz) butter

pinch of ground mace

pinch of cayenne pepper

pinch of ground nutmeg

lemon wedges, to garnish

brown bread or melba toast

1 Melt half the butter in a sauce-pan. Add the shrimps and heat very gently without boiling. Add the seasonings.

2 Pour the shrimps into ramekin dishes or small pots. Leave them to cool.

3 Gently heat the remaining butter in a pan until it melts, then continue to heat slowly, without browning. Remove from the heat and leave to stand for a few minutes for the salt and sediment to settle, then carefully pour a little clarified butter over the shrimps to cover. Leave until set.

4 Unless the pots are really attractive, turn the shrimps out on to individual plates lined with a few lettuce leaves, but try to retain the shape of the pot. Before serving, remove from the re-frigerator and leave at room tem-perature for about 30 minutes. Serve with lemon wedges and brown bread or melba toast.

CLARIFIED BUTTER

Cooked fish or meat will keep for a longer period if stored under a seal of clarified butter. The seal excludes air and moisture which encourage the growth of bacteria.

Store in the refrigerator and use within 2–3 days. Once the seal has been broken, the fish or meat should be eaten within 7 days.

SALMON MOUSSE

1.10*	🍳 🍳 £ £ ✳*	290 cals

* plus 2 hours refrigeration; freeze
without aspic and garnish

Serves 8

350 g (12 oz) salmon steaks
1 onion, skinned and sliced
75 g (3 oz) carrots, peeled and sliced
2 bay leaves
10 black peppercorns
salt and freshly ground pepper
150 ml ($\frac{1}{4}$ pint) white wine
240 ml (16 tbsp) water
22.5 ml ($4\frac{1}{2}$ tsp) gelatine
300 ml ($\frac{1}{2}$ pint) milk
25 g (1 oz) butter or margarine
30 ml (2 tbsp) plain flour
75 ml (5 tbsp) lemon mayonnaise (see page 145)
150 ml (5 fl oz) whipping cream
red food colouring (optional)
1 egg white
15 ml (1 tbsp) medium sherry
5 ml (1 tsp) rosemary vinegar
10-cm (4-inch) piece of cucumber
Melba toast, to serve

1 Place the salmon steaks in a small shallow pan. Add half the onions and carrots, one bay leaf, five peppercorns and a good pinch of salt.

2 Spoon over 75 ml (5 tbsp) wine with 75 ml (5 tbsp) water and bring slowly to the boil. Cover and simmer gently for 10–15 minutes.

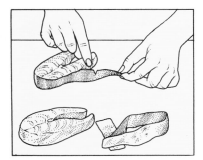

3 Remove salmon pieces (reserve the liquor). Carefully ease off the skin.

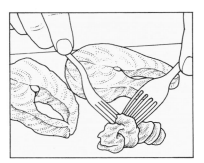

4 Using two forks, roughly flake the fish, being careful to remove any bones. Place the fish in a small bowl and keep on one side. Bubble down the cooking liquor until reduced by half, strain off and reserve.

5 Make the mousse. Spoon 45 ml (3 tbsp) water into a small basin or cup. Carefully sprinkle 15 ml (3 tsp) gelatine over the surface; leave for 10 minutes.

6 Prod any dry grains gently to submerge. Don't stir violently or grains of gelatine will stick to the sides of the bowl and won't soak properly.

7 Bring the milk to the boil with the remaining sliced onion, carrot, bay leaf and peppercorns; pour into a jug and leave to infuse for 10 minutes. Melt butter and off the heat blend in the flour and strained milk. Season, bring to the boil, bubble for 2–3 minutes, stirring. Pour into a bowl and while still warm stir in the soaked gelatine until dissolved.

8 Stir the fish into the cool sauce with the reserved cooking juices. Spoon half at a time into a blender or food processor and switch on for a few seconds only; the fish should retain a little of its texture. Pour into a large mixing bowl.

9 Stir the mayonnaise gently into the salmon mixture. Lightly whip the cream and fold through the mousse, adjust seasoning and add a little red food colouring if necessary.

10 Lastly, whisk the egg white until stiff but not dry, and fold lightly through mousse until no traces of white are visible.

11 Pour the mousse into an oiled 18-cm (7-inch) soufflé dish, smooth the surface, cover and refrigerate for about 2 hours to set.

12 Meanwhile, make aspic by soaking the remaining gelatine in 30 ml (2 tbsp) water and dissolving it in the usual way. Stir in the remaining white wine, the sherry, vinegar, 90 ml (6 tbsp) water and seasoning. Refrigerate for 1 hour to set.

13 Turn mousse out on to a flat platter and gently dab with absorbent kitchen paper to absorb any oil. Turn the aspic out on to a sheet of damp greaseproof or non-stick paper and chop roughly.

14 Run a fork down cucumber to form grooves, slice thinly. Garnish mousse with a cucumber twist and aspic; serve with Melba toast.

—————— VARIATION ——————

To make this mousse slightly less expensive, ask your fishmonger for the end or tail pieces of salmon – these are usually sold cheaper than salmon steaks, and as long as you have the same weight of salmon flesh as specified in the recipe you will not notice any difference. End pieces of salmon are a good buy for dishes such as mousses.

LAYERED FISH TERRINE

2.00* 🔲🔲 £ £ ✱

393–524 cals

* plus at least 5 hours chilling and
2 hours cooling

Serves 6–8

700 g (1½ lb) whiting, sole, plaice or
    hake, skinned and chilled

3 egg whites, chilled

salt and freshly ground white
    pepper

15 ml (1 tbsp) lemon juice

30 ml (2 tbsp) chopped fresh
    tarragon or 10 ml (2 tsp) dried

30 ml (2 tbsp) chopped fresh dill or
    10 ml (2 tsp) dried

300 ml (½ pint) double cream,
    chilled

25 g (1 oz) butter, for greasing tin

450 g (1 lb) piece of fresh salmon
    tail, filleted and skinned

15 ml (1 tbsp) green peppercorns,
    drained

300 ml (½ pint) smetana or soured
    cream

a little milk

30 ml (2 tbsp) snipped chives
    (optional)

sprigs of dill, to garnish

1 Trim the fish, remove any
bones and cut into small
pieces. Work in a blender or food
processor until finely minced.
Alternatively, put the fish through
a mincer and mince finely.

2 Add the egg whites and pepper
to the fish and process or beat
until completely incorporated.
Turn into a bowl, cover with cling
film and chill in the refrigerator
for at least 30 minutes.

3 Stir in the lemon juice,
tarragon and dill and process
or beat again, gradually adding the
double cream. Add salt to taste,
cover and refrigerate again for at
least 30 minutes.

4 Meanwhile, grease a 1.2 litre
(2 pint) terrine or loaf tin with
the butter and line the bottom
with greaseproof paper.

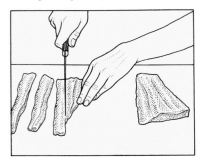

5 Cut the salmon into chunky
strips, about 1 cm (½ inch)
square and the length of the loaf
tin or terrine. Cover and chill in
the refrigerator until required.

6 Carefully stir the green
peppercorns into the fish
mixture. Spoon a third of the fish
mixture into the terrine and
spread out evenly to cover the
bottom. Lay half of the salmon
strips on top, leaving a 1 cm
(½ inch) border all the way round.
Cover this with half of the remaining fish mixture, levelling it
carefully.

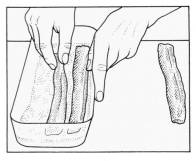

7 Repeat the salmon layer, using
the remaining salmon strips.
Finally cover with the remaining
fish mixture and smooth the top.

8 Cover the terrine with
buttered foil and place in a
bain marie (page 59). Bake in the
oven at 180°C (350°F) mark 4 for
45 minutes or until a skewer
inserted into the centre comes out
clean.

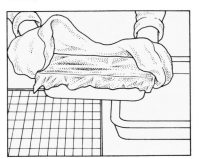

9 Transfer the terrine to a wire
rack and leave to cool for 2
hours at room temperature.
Remove from the rack, cover with
cling film and chill in the
refrigerator for at least 4 hours.

10 When ready to serve the
terrine, mix the smetana
or soured cream with a little milk
to make a thin sauce. Add the
chives, if using, and salt and
pepper to taste.

Menu Suggestion
This beautiful fish terrine makes
an impressive first course for a
dinner party. Serve with a chilled
dry white wine such as a French
Muscadet or an Italian Orvieto
Secco.

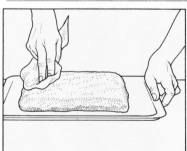

11 Turn the terrine out onto a
plate and wipe with
absorbent kitchen paper to remove
any butter or liquid. Slice thickly.
Flood individual serving plates
with the sauce, and place a slice
of terrine in the centre. Garnish
with dill.

LAYERED FISH TERRINE
Red lumpfish roe is sometimes
used in this terrine. It is
often referred to as 'mock
caviar'. Real caviar is the salted
hard roe of the sturgeon, and is
extremely expensive because it is
so rare, and mostly fished in the
Caspian Sea. Lumpfish, which
are found in the waters off
Iceland and Greenland, are more
common, and so the roe is far
less expensive. It is available in
jars at most supermarkets and
delicatessens, coloured either red
or black, and is useful as a tasty
and unusual garnish.

SMOKED HADDOCK PÂTÉ EN CROÛTE

1.00* 🎩 f 380–506 cals

* plus 1½ hours cooling, 2 hours chilling and 30 minutes to come to room temperature

Serves 6–8

50 g (2 oz) butter

350 g (12 oz) smoked haddock fillet, skinned

30 ml (2 tbsp) lemon juice

175 g (6 oz) cream cheese

2 eggs

freshly ground pepper

175 g (6 oz) shortcrust pastry made with 175 g (6 oz) plain flour (page 439)

2 caps canned pimiento, well drained and dried

50 g (2 oz) capers

chopped fresh parsley

1 Melt the butter in a saucepan, add the haddock and cook gently for about 5 minutes, or until beginning to flake; turn once.

2 Transfer the fish and cooking juices to a bowl and leave to cool slightly. Flake the flesh, discarding any bones, then beat in lemon juice, cheese, 1 egg and pepper to taste. (It is unlikely that salt will be needed as smoked fish is salty.) Cool completely for at least 30 minutes.

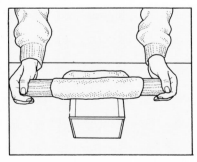

3 Meanwhile, roll out the pastry thinly and use three-quarters to line a 450 g (1 lb) loaf tin.

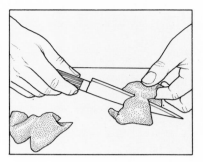

4 Split open the pimiento caps and place half over the pastry base. Sprinkle the capers on top.

5 Spoon half the fish mixture into the pastry case and place the remaining pimiento caps over the fish. Cover with the remaining fish mixture and sprinkle over a thick layer of parsley. Top with the remaining pastry, sealing the edges well with water. Chill in the refrigerator for 30 minutes.

6 Beat the remaining egg and use to glaze the top of the pie. Stand the dish on a preheated baking sheet and bake in the oven at 200°C (400°F) mark 6 for about 40 minutes, or until well browned.

7 Cool for at least 1 hour, then chill in the refrigerator for at least 2 hours. Leave at cool room temperature for 30 minutes before serving.

Menu Suggestion
Serve this delicately flavoured pâté as a dinner party starter, with a light dry white wine such as an Italian Frascati. If liked, a lightly dressed green salad can be served as an accompaniment. For a summer lunch party, the pâté would make a pretty addition to a cold table; it is also excellent for buffets.

SMOKED TROUT MOUSSE IN LEMON SHELLS

1.00* ⬜ ✳* 197 cals

* plus cooling, and chilling for at least
4 hours or overnight; freeze at the end
of step 7

Serves 6

one 225 g (8 oz) smoked trout

6 large, even-sized lemons

300 ml (½ pint) milk

**few slices each of onion and
    carrot**

1 bay leaf

4–6 peppercorns

7.5 ml (1½ tsp) powdered gelatine

25 g (1 oz) butter or margarine

30 ml (2 tbsp) flour

15 ml (1 tbsp) creamed horseradish

**90 ml (6 tbsp) double or whipping
    cream, whipped**

1 egg white

salt and freshly ground pepper

**chopped fresh parsley and sprigs
    of fresh herbs, to serve**

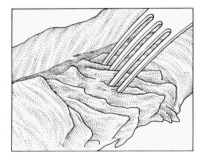

1 Skin the trout and flake the
flesh, discarding any bones.
Cover and set aside.

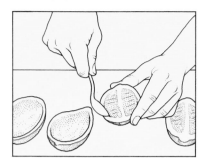

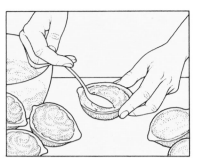

2 Cut the lemons in half
lengthways and scoop out all
the flesh and membranes with a
sharp-edged teaspoon; reserve the
shells. Measure 60 ml (4 tbsp)
lemon juice, pour into a small
heatproof bowl and reserve.

3 Bring the milk to the boil in a
saucepan with the onion,
carrot, bay leaf and peppercorns.
Remove from the heat, cover and
leave to infuse while preparing the
mousse mixture.

4 Sprinkle the gelatine over the
reserved measured lemon
juice. Leave for 5 minutes until
spongy, then stand the bowl in a
pan of gently simmering water and
heat until dissolved.

5 Melt the butter or margarine
in a separate saucepan.
Sprinkle in the flour and cook,
stirring, for 1–2 minutes. Strain in
the infused milk a little at a time,
whisking vigorously until smooth.
Simmer gently for 2 minutes, then
turn into a bowl and stir in the
liquid gelatine. Leave to cool.

6 Fold the flaked fish into the
cold sauce with the horseradish and whipped cream. Whisk
the egg white until stiff, then fold
in until evenly incorporated. Add
seasoning, taking care not to add
too much salt because the trout
may be quite salty.

7 Spoon the mousse into the
hollowed-out lemon shells,
then chill in the refrigerator for at
least 4 hours, or overnight if more
convenient.

8 Arrange 2 lemon shells on each
of 6 serving plates garnished
with chopped parsley and a sprig
of herbs. Serve chilled.

SMOKED TROUT MOUSSE IN LEMON SHELLS

If you are short of time and
prefer not to serve this
deliciously rich and creamy
mousse in the lemon shells, it
can be served simply in a large
soufflé dish or individual
ramekins. White china looks very
pretty with the pale colour of the
mousse, and you can garnish the
tops with delicate 'butterflies' of
sliced lemon. Cut a lemon into
thin slices, then cut out
opposite quarters, leaving the
flesh intact in the middle. Press a
small sprig of parsley or other
herb into the centre.

PUFFTOP SCALLOPS WITH MUSHROOMS AND CREAM

| 1.00 | 🍞 | £ £ | ✷* | 579 cals |

* freeze at step 8 before glazing

Serves 4

4 scallops, with their shells

175 g (6 oz) button mushrooms, wiped

25 g (1 oz) butter

150 ml (¼ pint) dry cider

150 ml (¼ pint) double cream

10 ml (2 tsp) chopped fresh tarragon or 5 ml (1 tsp) dried

2.5 ml (½ tsp) mustard powder

salt and freshly ground pepper

200 g (7 oz) packet frozen puff pastry, thawed

1 egg, beaten

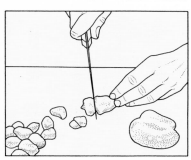

1 Chop the scallops roughly, including the coral. Slice the mushrooms finely.

2 Melt the butter in a frying pan, add the mushrooms and fry over moderate heat for 5 minutes. Remove with a slotted spoon and set aside in a bowl. Add the scallops and fry for 5 minutes, stirring frequently, then pour in the cider and cook for a further 5 minutes until the scallops are just tender. (Do not cook for longer or the scallops will toughen.)

3 Remove the scallops with a slotted spoon and set aside with the mushrooms. Add the cream to the pan and boil, whisking constantly with a balloon whisk or wooden spoon, until a thick sauce is formed.

4 Add the sauce to the scallops and mushrooms with the tarragon, mustard and salt and pepper to taste. Fold gently to mix, then leave to cool.

5 Meanwhile, roll out the pastry on a lightly floured surface and cut out 4 'lids' to fit the scallop shells.

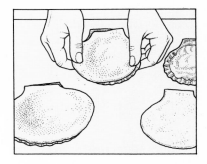

6 Divide the cold filling equally between the scallop shells. Brush the edges of the shells with beaten egg, then place the pastry lids on top and press firmly to seal. Brush all over the pastry with beaten egg. Decorate, if liked, then brush with egg.

7 Bake in the oven at 220°C (425°F) mark 7 for 15 minutes or until puffed up and golden. Serve hot.

Menu Suggestion

Scallops in their shells are an attractive starter for a special dinner party. Serve with sparkling dry white wine or champagne.

FISH IN FILO PARCELS

`0.40` 🖐 £ £ `464 cals`

Serves 4

25 g (1 oz) butter

30 ml (2 tbsp) vegetable oil

450 g (1 lb) monkfish fillets, skinned and finely diced

100 g (4 oz) peeled prawns, defrosted and thoroughly dried if frozen

pinch of saffron powder or saffron threads

15 ml (1 tbsp) finely sliced stem or preserved ginger, with the syrup

8 sheets of filo pastry (see box)

melted butter, for brushing

15 ml (1 tbsp) plain flour

10 ml (2 tsp) ground coriander

300 ml ($\frac{1}{2}$ pint) ginger ale

salt and freshly ground pepper

90 ml (6 tbsp) single cream

unpeeled prawns, lime twists and sliced stem ginger, to garnish

1 Melt the butter with the oil in a frying pan, add the cubes of monkfish and cook over moderate heat, stirring for 5 minutes. Add the prawns, saffron and half of the ginger and cook for a further 5 minutes until the fish is tender. Remove with a slotted spoon and set aside.

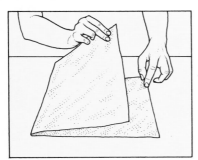

2 Cut one sheet of pastry to measure 40.5 × 20.5 cm (16 × 8 inches). Brush half of the sheet with a little melted butter, then fold the plain half over to make a 20 cm (8 inch) square.

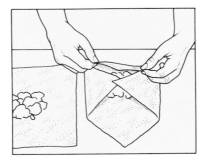

3 Put the fish mixture in the centre of the square and fold over the opposite corners of the pastry to make an envelope-shaped parcel. Seal the points of the envelope with a little melted butter.

4 Place the parcel seam side down on a lightly greased baking sheet. Repeat with the remaining pastry and fish mixture to make 8 parcels altogether. Brush the parcels with melted butter. Bake in the oven at 200°C (400°F) mark 6 for 15 minutes until golden brown and crisp.

5 Meanwhile, make the sauce. Sprinkle the flour and coriander into the juices in the frying pan and stir for 1–2 minutes over gentle heat. Gradually stir in the ginger ale, then add salt and pepper to taste.

6 Bring to the boil, stirring, then simmer for 3 minutes. Stir in the cream and remaining stem ginger and heat through without boiling.

7 Serve the filo parcels hot on individual plates, with the sauce poured around them. Garnish with unpeeled prawns, lime twists and stem ginger, if liked.

Menu Suggestion

Pretty parcels of filo pastry stuffed with monkfish and prawns make a luxurious starter for a dinner party meal. Follow with a meaty main course such as a boned stuffed duck, or a boned, stuffed and rolled loin of pork.

FISH IN FILO PARCELS

Filo pastry, sometimes spelt *phyllo*, is a paper-thin pastry made of flour and water—like the Austrian and German strudel pastry used for making *apfelstrudel*. It is possible to make filo at home, but it is a laborious task because of the amount of rolling and stretching. Commercial filo, available in boxes at Greek and Cypriot delicatessens and in some specialist food shops, is well worth buying to save time and trouble. Filo pastry is used extensively in the cuisines of these two countries, and in the cooking of the Middle East, both for sweet and savoury dishes. The Greek sticky honey and nut pastries known as *baklava* are made with filo pastry, and so too is the spinach and cheese savoury called *spanakopittes*.

Frozen filo is excellent, but take care to buy it from a shop with a fast turnover. If the pastry has been stored in the freezer for too long, it will be brittle and therefore crack easily. Cracking is often a problem when handling filo. Once the pastry is exposed to the air, it quickly dries out and becomes difficult to handle. For this reason, thaw for the time recommended on the packet, use immediately and always keep the pastry wrapped in a damp cloth as you work.

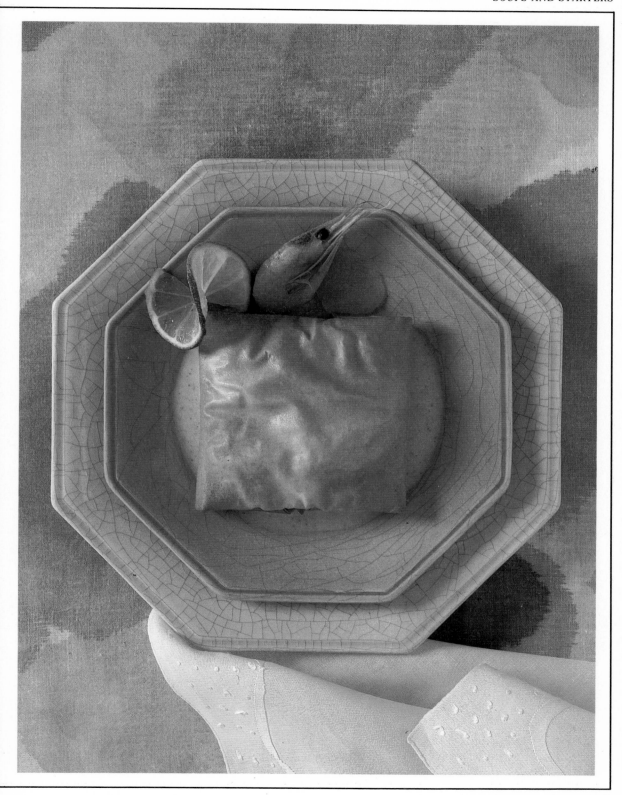

LA MOUCLADE (MUSSELS IN CREAM AND GARLIC SAUCE)

| 0.40* | 🍴 | £ £ | 344 cals |

* plus 20 minutes soaking

Serves 4

| 2.3 litres (4 pints) or 1.1–1.4 kg (2½–3 lb) live mussels |
| 150 ml (¼ pint) dry white wine |
| ½ small onion, skinned and finely chopped |
| 25 g (1 oz) butter |
| 2 garlic cloves, skinned and crushed |
| 15 g (½ oz) plain flour |
| 300 ml (½ pint) double cream |
| pinch of saffron or turmeric powder |
| 30 ml (2 tbsp) lemon juice |
| freshly ground pepper |
| 1 egg yolk |
| chopped fresh parsley, to garnish |

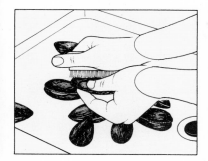

1 To clean the mussels, put them in a sink or basin and scrub them thoroughly with a hard brush in several changes of water.

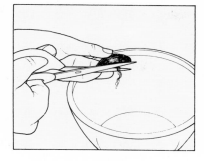

2 With scissors or a very sharp knife, take off any beards or tufts protruding from the shell.

3 Leave the mussels to soak in a bowl of cold water for 20 minutes, then discard any that are not tightly closed or do not close when given a sharp tap against the work surface.

4 Drain the mussels and place in a large saucepan. Pour in the wine and add the chopped onion, cover and cook over high heat for 5–10 minutes until the mussels are open, shaking the pan frequently.

5 Pour through a sieve, reserving the cooking liquid. Discard one half shell from each mussel. Keep the mussels warm while making the sauce.

6 Make the sauce. Boil the cooking liquid rapidly until reduced by half. Melt the butter in a saucepan, add the garlic and fry gently for 1 minute. Add the flour and cook gently, stirring, for 1–2 minutes. Gradually blend in the reduced cooking liquid. Bring to the boil, stirring constantly, add the cream and saffron or turmeric and simmer for 3 minutes until slightly thickened and smooth. Add the lemon juice and pepper to taste.

7 Remove the pan from the heat and stir in the egg yolk. Pour the sauce over the mussels, sprinkle with chopped parsley and serve immediately.

Menu Suggestion
Serve as a first course for a French-style dinner party, with chunks of fresh French bread to mop up the garlic juices.

LA MOUCLADE
There is never any need to worry about mussels these days, as long as you buy them from a reputable fishmonger. All mussels offered for sale must, by law, undergo a special cleaning process, so there is absolutely no risk of shellfish poisoning. Always be sure to cook the mussels on the day of purchase, however, and to clean and cook them correctly. If after soaking in cold water for 20 minutes you find that a few of the mussel shells are not closed, these must be thrown away. The same goes for any mussels that have not opened after cooking. Recipes always allow for this wastage in the quantity of mussels specified.

DEEP-FRIED WHITEBAIT

| 0.15 | 🍳 | £ | 596 cals |

Serves 4

450 g (1 lb) whitebait
90 ml (6 tbsp) plain flour
salt and freshly ground pepper
vegetable oil, for deep frying
15 ml (1 tbsp) chopped fresh
   parsley
lemon wedges, to garnish

1 Rinse the whitebait thoroughly in a colander, drain well and dry on absorbent kitchen paper. Toss in the flour seasoned with salt and pepper.

2 Heat the oil in a deep-fat frier to 180°C (350°F). Deep fry the whitebait, in 4 batches, allowing 2–3 minutes for each batch until crisp. Drain on absorbent kitchen paper. Keep warm, uncovered, in the oven at 200°C (400°F) mark 6 until all the fish are cooked.

3 Sprinkle with salt and parsley and garnish with lemon wedges. Serve hot.

Menu Suggestion
Serve this crisp, fishy starter with triangles of thinly sliced brown bread and butter. An Italian-style main course such as chicken sautéed in white wine and rosemary would make a good main course to follow, with baked peaches stuffed with crushed macaroons for dessert.

DEEP-FRIED WHITEBAIT
Whitebait are available frozen in 450 g (1 lb) bags at most super-markets and freezer centres. They must always be thawed before coating and deep-frying, otherwise the tiny fish stick together and are difficult to serve. Drain them thoroughly after thawing and pat dry with absorbent kitchen paper.

CHICKEN AND GRUYÈRE CRÊPES

1.00* £ £ ✳*	870–435 cals

* freeze at step 8, before baking

Serves 4–8

140 g (5½ oz) plain flour
salt and freshly ground pepper
1 egg, beaten
300 ml (½ pint) milk
225 g (8 oz) frozen chopped spinach
350 g (12 oz) boneless cooked chicken
175 g (6 oz) Gruyère, grated
150 ml (¼ pint) double cream
2.5 ml (½ tsp) ground mace or grated nutmeg
50 g (2 oz) butter
300 ml (½ pint) dry white wine

1 Make the batter for the crêpes. Mix 100 g (4 oz) of the flour in a bowl with a pinch of salt. Make a well in the centre and add the egg. Gradually whisk in the milk until a smooth batter is formed. Leave to stand while preparing the filling and sauce.

2 Make the filling. Put the frozen spinach in a heavy-based saucepan and heat gently until thawed, stirring frequently. Meanwhile, chop the chicken into small dice, discarding any skin and gristle.

3 Put the chicken and spinach in a bowl with 50 g (2 oz) of the Gruyère, 30 ml (2 tbsp) of the cream, half the mace or nutmeg and salt and pepper to taste. Stir well to mix.

4 Make the sauce. Melt the butter in a saucepan, add the remaining flour and cook gently, stirring, for 1–2 minutes. Remove from the heat and gradually blend in the wine. Bring to the boil, stirring constantly, then add the remaining cream and simmer for 3 minutes until thick and smooth. Add 75 g (3 oz) of the cheese, the remaining mace or nutmeg and salt and pepper to taste. Stir until the cheese has melted, then remove from the heat.

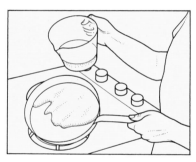

5 Make the crêpes. Heat a little oil in a pancake pan until very hot. Whisk the batter well, then swirl one-eighth into the pan. Cook over high heat for 1–2 minutes until set and golden on the underside.

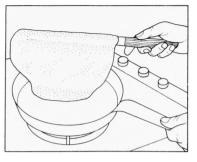

6 Toss or turn the crêpe over and cook for a further 30 seconds, then slide out of the pan. Repeat with the remaining batter to make 8 crêpes altogether.

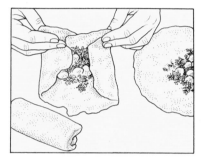

7 Spoon the chicken and spinach filling onto the crêpes, dividing it equally between them. Roll or fold the crêpes up around the filling, then place seam side down in individual gratin dishes.

8 Pour the sauce over the crêpes and sprinkle with the remaining cheese. Bake in the oven at 180°C (350°F) mark 4 for 15 minutes until golden and bubbling. Serve hot.

Menu Suggestion

Crêpes filled with chicken and spinach make a filling starter. Serve 1 crêpe per person if you are planning a substantial main course. Alternatively, serve 2 crêpes per person and follow with a light main dish and fresh fruit instead of dessert.

SALADE TIÈDE AUX LARDONS

| 0.20 | £ | 526 cals |

Serves 4

135 ml (9 tbsp) olive oil

30 ml (2 tbsp) wine vinegar

2 garlic cloves, skinned and
   crushed

5 ml (1 tsp) French mustard

salt and freshly ground pepper

8 streaky bacon rashers, rinded

4 thick slices of white bread, crusts
   removed

30 ml (2 tbsp) single or double
   cream

1 small head of curly endive,
   leaves separated

1 Put 90 ml (6 tbsp) of the oil in
a large salad bowl with the
wine vinegar, garlic, mustard and
salt and pepper to taste. Whisk
with a fork until thick.

2 Cut the bacon and bread into
small dice. Heat the remaining
oil in a frying pan, add the bacon
and bread and fry over brisk heat
until crisp and golden brown on
all sides. Remove with a slotted
spoon and drain on absorbent
kitchen paper.

3 Stir the cream into the
dressing, then add the endive
and warm bacon and croûtons.
Toss quickly to combine and serve
immediately.

Menu Suggestion

Salade Tiède aux Lardons is a very
popular first course in France,
served with crusty French bread
and red or white wine.

MEAT AND VEGETABLE SAMOSAS

1.20* 🔲 £ ✳ 135 cals

* plus 45 minutes chilling and 1 hour
cooling
Makes 20

275 g (10 oz) self-raising flour
7.5 ml (1½ tsp) salt
75 g (3 oz) margarine
2 carrots, peeled and finely diced
1 medium onion, skinned and finely chopped
2.5 cm (1 inch) fresh root ginger, peeled and finely chopped
2.5 ml (½ tsp) ground turmeric
1 small garlic clove, crushed
15 ml (1 tbsp) hot curry powder
350 g (12 oz) lean minced pork
a little milk, for brushing
vegetable oil, for deep frying

1 Make the pastry. Mix the flour
and 2.5 ml (½ tsp) of the salt
in a bowl. Rub in 50 g (2 oz) of the
margarine. Bind with a little
water. Knead for 5 minutes until
elastic. Refrigerate for 15 minutes.

2 Melt the remaining margarine
in a heavy-based saucepan.
Add the carrots, onion and ginger
and fry gently for 2–3 minutes.
Stir in the spices and pork. Fry for
15 minutes, remove from the heat
and cool for about 1 hour.

3 Divide the pastry into 20
pieces. Roll each one into a
10 cm (4 inch) circle. Brush with
milk.

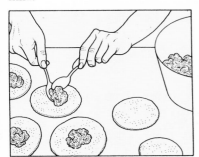

4 Place 7.5 ml (1½ tsp) of the
meat and vegetable filling onto
each pastry circle.

5 Fold the circles in half, then
fold again to form triangles.
Seal the edges well. Chill in the
refrigerator for 15–20 minutes.

6 Heat the oil in a deep-fat frier
to 180°C (350°F) and deep fry
the samosas a few at a time, for
2–3 minutes. Drain well on
absorbent kitchen paper and serve
immediately.

STUFFED VINE LEAVES

3.00* ☐ £ £ 361–542 cals

* plus cooling and chilling

Serves 4–6

175 g (6 oz) burghul (cracked wheat)

4 tomatoes, skinned and finely chopped

2 garlic cloves, skinned and crushed

100 g (4 oz) shelled pine nuts or almonds, finely chopped

30 ml (2 tbsp) chopped fresh mint

5 ml (1 tsp) ground cinnamon

2.5 ml ($\frac{1}{2}$ tsp) ground allspice

salt and freshly ground pepper

225 g (8 oz) packet vine leaves preserved in brine, soaked and drained (see box)

150 ml ($\frac{1}{4}$ pint) olive oil

juice of 1 lemon

lemon slices, to garnish

1 Put the burghul in a bowl, pour in boiling water to cover, stir and leave to soak for 10 minutes until all the water is absorbed.

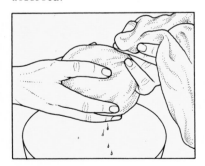

2 Transfer the burghul to a clean tea towel, wrap tightly and ring out as much moisture as possible.

3 Put the burghul in a bowl with the remaining ingredients, except the vine leaves, olive oil and lemon juice. Add salt sparingly, but plenty of pepper.

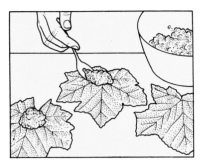

4 Place 1 vine leaf, vein side upwards, flat on a board or work surface. Put a little filling on the edge of it.

5 Fold the opposite sides of the leaf into the centre, then roll the leaf up around the filling like a cigar.

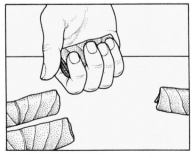

6 Squeeze the vine leaves gently in the palm of your hand to seal the parcel. Continue filling and rolling the vine leaves until all the ingredients are used up, putting any ragged or torn vine leaves in the base of a large heavy-based saucepan or flameproof casserole.

7 Put the stuffed vine leaves in the pan, packing them in layers as close together as possible to prevent them from opening.

8 Mix the olive oil and lemon juice with 150 ml ($\frac{1}{4}$ pint) water and pour slowly into the pan. Put a plate immediately on top of the vine leaves, then cover the pan with a lid. Simmer very gently for 2 hours, then leave the vine leaves to cool in the liquid. Serve chilled garnished with lemon slices.

Menu Suggestion

Serve this Greek starter with hot wholemeal pitta bread and a dry white Retsina wine. Follow with a main course of grilled or barbecued lamb kebabs which have been marinated in olive oil, lemon juice, garlic and fresh coriander.

STUFFED VINE LEAVES

To prepare the leaves for stuffing, place them in a bowl, pour over boiling water and leave to soak for 20 minutes. Drain, soak for the same length of time in cold water, then drain again. A 225 g (8 oz) packet of vine leaves should contain about 40 leaves. Don't worry if this isn't the case—the leaves vary in size and number from packet to packet. If you have large leaves, but less than 40, simply use more stuffing for each one.

HOT MUSHROOM MOUSSE

2.30*	390 cals

* plus 15 minutes cooling

Serves 6

50 g (2 oz) butter or margarine

1 small onion, skinned and chopped

450 g (1 lb) mushrooms, wiped and finely chopped

10 ml (2 tsp) ground coriander

225 g (8 oz) curd cheese

4 eggs, separated

salt and freshly ground pepper

125 g (5 oz) unsalted butter

2 egg yolks

15 ml (1 tbsp) lemon juice

pinch of cayenne or fresh coriander, to garnish

1 Melt the butter in a large saucepan, add the onion and fry gently for 5 minutes until soft. Add the mushrooms and coriander and cook, stirring, for about 20 minutes until dry. Leave for 15 minutes.

2 Turn the mushrooms into a bowl. Add the cheese, egg yolks and season to taste. Mix well, then blend or process in batches.

3 Whisk the egg whites until stiff, then fold into the mushroom mixture. Pour into a well-buttered and base-lined 1 kg (2 lb) loaf tin and cover with well-buttered foil.

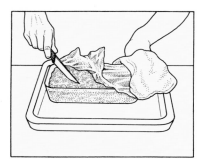

4 Place in a bain marie (page 59) and bake in the oven at 180°C (350°F) mark 4 for 1½ hours or until firm. Remove from the bain marie.

5 Meanwhile, make a hollandaise sauce. Melt the butter gently in a heavy-based saucepan, then pour into a jug. Put the egg yolks in the warmed goblet of a blender and turn to low speed.

6 Pour in 25 ml (1½ tbsp) boiling water, then add the warm melted butter very slowly in a thin steady stream. Add the lemon juice and cayenne with salt to taste and continue blending until smooth and creamy.

7 Turn the mushroom terrine out onto a serving dish and peel off the lining paper. Cut into slices and coat with the hollandaise sauce. Garnish with cayenne or coriander.

Menu Suggestion

Although light in texture, this mushroom mousse has a coating of hollandaise sauce, and therefore makes a very rich and filling starter. It needs no accompaniment other than a chilled dry white or rosé wine.

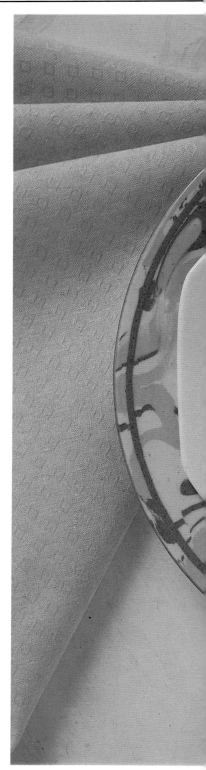

STUFFED VEGETABLE PLATTER

2.20* 🗏 🗏 f f 852 cals

* plus cooling and overnight chilling

Serves 4

200 ml (7 fl oz) olive oil

1 large Spanish onion, skinned and very finely chopped

2 garlic cloves, skinned and crushed

1 bunch of fresh parsley

225 g (8 oz) Italian risotto rice, cooked

20 ml (4 tsp) tomato purée

50 g (2 oz) pine nuts

75 g (3 oz) raisins

2.5 ml (½ tsp) ground allspice

salt and freshly ground pepper

4 medium courgettes

4 small squat peppers (preferably different colours)

4 small very firm continental or beefsteak tomatoes

1 First prepare the stuffing. Heat 60 ml (4 tbsp) of the oil in a heavy-based saucepan, add the onion and garlic and fry gently for about 10 minutes until very soft.

2 Trim the parsley stalks, then chop the parsley very finely. Add the rice to the onion with the tomato purée, chopped parsley, nuts, raisins, allspice and salt and pepper to taste. Stir well to mix all the ingredients together, then remove the pan from the heat and set aside.

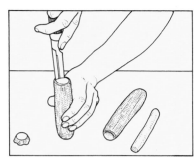

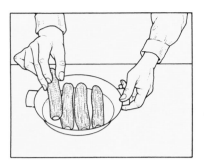

3 Using an apple corer, scoop out the flesh from the courgettes. Work from the stalk end, taking care not to break the skin of the courgettes and to leave the opposite ends intact. Mix the courgette flesh into the stuffing. Sprinkle salt inside the courgettes and leave to drain while preparing the other vegetables.

4 Cut a slice off the top of each pepper and reserve. Remove the cores and seeds and discard, then wash the peppers and pat dry with absorbent kitchen paper.

5 Cut the tops off the tomatoes and reserve. With a sharp-edged teaspoon, scoop out the flesh. Mix the flesh with the stuffing. Sprinkle the insides of the tomatoes with salt and stand upside down to drain.

6 Stuff the vegetables with the filling. Wrap the open ends of the courgettes with foil. Replace the tops on the peppers and tomatoes.

7 Brush the inside of a flame-proof gratin dish liberally with some of the remaining olive oil. Arrange the courgettes side by side in the dish. Brush 2 heavy-based saucepans liberally with oil; stand the peppers and tomatoes in them, keeping them separate.

8 Sprinkle with the remaining oil and salt and pepper to taste, then pour in enough cold water to come halfway up the vegetables. Bring slowly to the boil, then cover and simmer very gently. Allow 30 minutes for the tomatoes, 45 minutes for the courgettes and peppers. Leave to cool in the pans, then chill in the refrigerator overnight.

9 To serve, lift the vegetables carefully out of the cooking liquid and arrange attractively on a large serving platter. Moisten with a little of the cooking liquid, if liked. Serve chilled.

Menu Suggestion

Stuffed mixed vegetables are a favourite starter in the Middle East, but this quantity is ample to serve 4 people for a main course, and would make an impressive cold lunch dish in summer, when courgettes, peppers and tomatoes are at their best. Serve with French bread or warm pitta bread, to mop up the juices.

VEGETABLE TERRINE

2.30	⊟ ⊟ £	250–334 cals

Serves 6–8

900 g (2 lb) turnips, peeled and cut into chunks

450 g (1 lb) carrots, peeled and sliced

450 g (1 lb) fresh spinach, trimmed or 300 g (10.6 oz) packet frozen spinach

50 g (2 oz) butter or margarine

1 medium onion, skinned and thinly sliced

350 g (12 oz) flat mushrooms, sliced

finely grated rind and juice of $\frac{1}{2}$ lemon

4 eggs

salt and freshly ground white pepper

1.25 ml ($\frac{1}{4}$ tsp) ground coriander

1.25 ml ($\frac{1}{4}$ tsp) freshly grated nutmeg

30 ml (2 tbsp) chopped fresh parsley

2 ripe tomatoes, skinned

300 ml ($\frac{1}{2}$ pint) Vinaigrette (page 441)

1 Put the turnips into a medium saucepan, cover with cold water and bring to the boil. Lower the heat and simmer for 10–15 minutes, until completely tender.

2 Meanwhile, put the carrots in a separate saucepan and cover with cold water. Bring to the boil and cook for 10 minutes or until completely tender. Drain both turnips and carrots.

3 Wash the fresh spinach in several changes of cold water. Place in a saucepan with only the water that clings to the leaves. Cook gently for 5 minutes until wilted, 7–10 minutes if using frozen spinach. Drain well.

4 Melt 40 g ($1\frac{1}{2}$ oz) of the butter in a frying pan, add the onion and fry gently for about 10 minutes until very soft. Add the mushrooms and fry, stirring constantly, for a further 5 minutes. Stir in the lemon rind and juice.

5 Put the mushroom mixture in a blender or food processor and work until smooth. Transfer to a small heavy-based pan. Cook over moderate heat, stirring constantly, until all the liquid has evaporated and the purée is fairly thick and dry. Watch that the mixture does not catch and burn.

6 Purée and dry the turnips, carrots and spinach in the same way and place each purée in a separate bowl. Add 1 egg to each purée and mix well. Season each with salt and pepper to taste. Stir the coriander into the carrot purée, the grated nutmeg into the spinach and the chopped parsley into the mushroom.

7 Brush a 1.1 litre (2 pint) terrine or loaf tin with the remaining butter. Put a layer of turnip purée in the bottom, making sure it is quite level. Cover with a layer of carrot, followed by spinach and finally mushroom. Cover the tin tightly with foil.

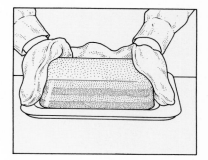

8 Place the terrine in a roasting tin and pour in enough hot water to come three-quarters of the way up the sides of the terrine. Bake in the oven at 180°C (350°F) mark 4 for 1 hour 20 minutes or until firm. Remove and allow to cool slightly, then turn out carefully on to a serving plate.

9 Just before serving, put the tomatoes and vinaigrette in a blender or food processor and work until smooth. Do not let the dressing stand before serving or it will separate.

10 Serve the terrine hot or cold, cut into slices, on top of the tomato vinaigrette.

Note Other vegetables may be used when in season, such as cauliflower, fennel, watercress, parsnips and even peas. Try to balance colour and flavour.

Menu Suggestion
Vegetable Terrine can be served as a dinner party starter or for a light lunch dish. In either case, it is delicious served with a crusty French stick or granary bread.

MAIN COURSES
Meat

BEEF WELLINGTON

| 1.35 | 🥘 🥘 £ £ | 850 cals |

1.4 kg (3 lb) fillet of beef

freshly ground pepper

100 g (4 oz) butter

225 g (8 oz) button mushrooms sliced

175 g (6 oz) smooth liver pâté

368-g (13-oz) packet frozen puff pastry, thawed, or 225 g (8 oz) homemade (see page 439)

beaten egg, to seal and glaze

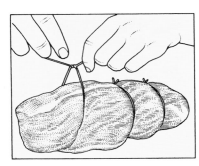

1 Trim and tie up the fillet of beef at regular intervals to retain its shape, and season with freshly ground pepper. Melt 50 g (2 oz) butter in a large frying pan. When the butter is foaming, add the meat and fry briskly on all sides to colour. Press down with a wooden spoon while frying, to seal the surface well.

2 Place the fried fillet of beef in the oven and roast at 220°C (425°F) mark 7 for 20 minutes. Leave beef to cool and remove the string.

3 Meanwhile, sauté the mushrooms in remaining butter until soft; leave until cold, then mix with the pâté.

4 Roll the pastry out to a large rectangle about 33 × 28 cm (13 × 11 inches) and 0.5 cm ($\frac{1}{4}$ inch) thick.

5 Spread the pâté mixture down the centre of the pastry. Place the meat in the centre. Brush the edges of the pastry with egg.

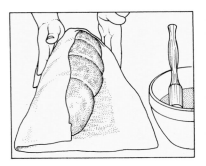

6 Fold the pastry edges over lengthways and turn the parcel over so that the join is underneath. Fold the ends under the meat on a baking sheet.

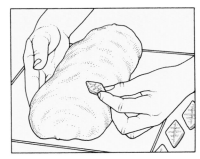

7 Decorate with leaves cut from the pastry trimmings. Chill until pastry is firm; just before baking, brush with egg. Cook at 220°C (425°F) mark 7 for 50 minutes, covering with foil after 25 minutes.

Menu Suggestion
Serve with Avocado with Parma Ham (page 32) and Gooseberry Charlotte (page 262).

DAUBE DE BOEUF *(BRAISED BEEF WITH OLIVES)*

3.15*	✳*	564 cals

* plus 4–6 hours marinating; freeze in marinade before cooking

Serves 6

1.1 kg (2½ lb) rolled top rump of beef

50 g (2 oz) stuffed green olives, sliced

salt and freshly ground pepper

300 ml (½ pint) red wine

30 ml (2 tbsp) olive oil

30 ml (2 tbsp) beef dripping or lard

75 ml (3 fl oz) brandy

1 large onion, skinned and sliced

3 carrots, peeled and sliced

4 tomatoes, skinned and roughly chopped

6 rashers of smoked streaky bacon, rinded

2 garlic cloves, skinned and halved

bouquet garni

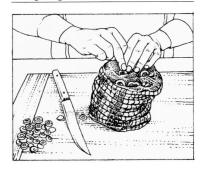

1 Make several deep incisions in the joint of beef and insert the slices of olive.

2 Put the beef in a bowl and sprinkle with salt and pepper. Mix together the wine and olive oil and pour over the beef. Cover the bowl and leave to marinate for 4–6 hours.

3 Remove the beef from the marinade and pat dry with absorbent kitchen paper. Reserve the marinade. Melt the dripping or lard in a large flameproof casserole, add the beef and brown quickly on all sides over high heat.

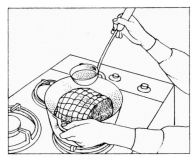

4 Heat the brandy gently in a separate small pan or a ladle. Turn off the heat under the casserole, pour in the brandy and set it alight. When the flames have died down, remove the beef from the casserole and set it aside.

5 Add the onion and carrots to the casserole and fry gently for 5 minutes until onion is soft but not coloured. Add the tomatoes and stir well to mix, then remove the vegetables with a slotted spoon.

6 Put the bacon rashers in the bottom of the casserole, then cover with the vegetables. Bury the garlic and bouquet garni in the vegetables, then place the beef on top and pour over the reserved marinade mixed with enough water to come halfway up the meat. Add salt and pepper to taste and bring slowly to boiling point.

7 Cover the casserole with foil or greaseproof paper, then the lid. Cook in the oven at 150°C (300°F) mark 2 for 2½ hours or until the beef is tender.

8 Blot the surface of the sauce with absorbent kitchen paper to remove as much fat as possible and remove the bouquet garni. Taste and adjust the seasoning of the sauce before serving.

Menu Suggestion

An informal main course, Daube de Boeuf is traditionally served in France with boiled potatoes or noodles and a tossed green salad.

DAUBE DE BOEUF

Almost every region of France has its own version of Daube de Boeuf. The word *daube* comes from *daubière*, which is the French word for a covered casserole. This recipe is for a joint of beef, which the French sometimes lard with strips of fat to make more moist. Bite-sized pieces of chuck steak can be used instead of one large piece of meat, whichever you prefer.

SPICED SILVERSIDE

5.00* £ 618 cals

* plus soaking overnight and 3–4 hours cooling

Serves 6

1.8 kg (4 lb) piece of salted rolled silverside

1 medium onion, skinned and sliced

4 medium carrots, peeled and sliced

1 small turnip, peeled and sliced

1–2 celery sticks, trimmed and chopped

8 cloves

100 g (4 oz) soft brown sugar

2.5 ml ($\frac{1}{2}$ tsp) mustard powder

5 ml (1 tsp) ground cinnamon

juice of 1 orange

1 Soak the meat in cold water for several hours or overnight, then rinse. Tie up the meat to form a neat joint and put in a large pan with the vegetables. Cover with water and bring slowly to the boil. Remove any scum, cover with a lid and simmer for 3–4 hours until tender. Allow to cool completely in the liquid for 3–4 hours.

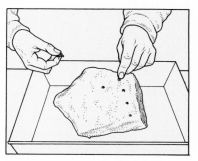

2 Drain the meat well, then put into a roasting tin and stick the cloves into the fat. Mix together the remaining ingredients and spread over the meat.

3 Bake the joint in the oven at 180°C (350°F) mark 4 for 45 minutes to 1 hour until tender, basting from time to time. Serve hot or cold.

Menu Suggestion

Spiced Silverside can be served hot like any other joint of beef and makes a welcome change from the usual Sunday roast. Served cold, it can be sliced very thinly and would be excellent for a buffet party arranged on a platter with other cold meats.

SPICED SILVERSIDE

Salted silverside can be bought at family butchers and some large supermarkets, but it is not always available. To salt beef at home, bring 700 g (1½ lb) salt, 175 g (6 oz) brown sugar, 25 g (1 oz) saltpetre and 4.8 litres (8 pints) water to the boil in a large saucepan. Strain through muslin into a large earthenware bowl and leave until cold. Submerge the fresh meat to completely cover it in the liquid, then cover the meat with a plate and place heavy weights on top if necessary. Leave for 5–10 days, turning it daily. Soak in fresh cold water for 3 hours or overnight before using.

If you wish, you can press the meat after cooking. Fit it snugly into a casserole or foil-lined tin and pour over a few spoonfuls of the cooking liquid. Cover with a board or plate, then place a heavy weight on top. Leave in a cold place for several hours.

MANZO STUFATO AL VINO ROSSO
(BEEF STEWED IN RED WINE)

| 3.45* | ✳* | 441 cals |

* plus 4–5 hours marinating; freeze after step 2

Serves 6

1.4 kg (3 lb) piece top rump or chuck steak, trimmed

450 ml (¾ pint) red wine

1 onion, skinned and finely sliced

3 garlic cloves, skinned and sliced

3 parsley stalks, lightly crushed

8 peppercorns

sprig of fresh thyme or 2.5 ml (½ tsp) dried

30 ml (2 tbsp) olive oil

about 150 ml (¼ pint) beef stock

100 g (4 oz) lean gammon, cut into cubes

salt and freshly ground pepper

1 Place the piece of beef in a plastic bag or bowl, pour in the wine and add the onion, garlic, parsley stalks, peppercorns and thyme. Mix well to combine. Alternatively, the beef can be cut into large pieces first.

2 Seal the bag or cover the bowl and leave in a cool place to marinate for 4–5 hours.

3 Remove the beef from the marinade. Set aside. Strain the marinade and set aside. Reserve the onion slices.

4 Heat the oil in a heavy flame-proof casserole, add the reserved onion slices and fry gently for 5 minutes until soft but not coloured. Add the beef and fry it for about 10 minutes until brown on all sides.

5 Pour over the marinade and the 150 ml (¼ pint) stock, then add the cubes of gammon. Season with salt and pepper. Bring to the boil and boil rapidly for about 2–3 minutes.

6 Cover tightly and cook in the oven at 180°C (350°F) mark 4 for 2½–3 hours until the beef is tender. Check every 30 minutes, turning the beef and making sure that the liquid has not evaporated. If necessary, top up with a little stock or water.

7 To serve, remove the cooked beef from the casserole and slice neatly. Arrange the slices overlapping on a warmed serving platter. Taste and adjust the seasoning of the sauce, then serve immediately, with the sliced beef.

FILLET STEAK EN CROÛTE WITH MUSHROOMS

| 1.30 | 🍱 🍱 £ £ ✳* | 763 cals |

* freeze at end of step 9

Serves 8

350 g (12 oz) medium flat
   mushrooms

50 g (2 oz) butter or margarine

1 medium onion, skinned and
   finely chopped

100 g (4 oz) fresh breadcrumbs

2.5 ml ($\frac{1}{2}$ tsp) chopped fresh thyme
   or 1.25 ml ($\frac{1}{4}$ tsp) dried

salt and freshly ground pepper

1.4 kg (3 lb) fillet of beef, trimmed
   of all fat and gristle

two 368 g (13 oz) packets frozen
   puff pastry, thawed

1 egg separated

600 ml (1 pint) Quick Tomato
   Sauce (page 440)

parsley sprigs, to garnish

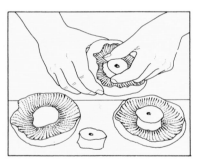

1 Remove the stems from 8
mushrooms and reserve the
caps. Chop the stems and the
remaining mushrooms finely.

2 Melt the butter in a large
frying pan, add the chopped
mushrooms and onion and cook
gently for about 10 minutes until
the onion is soft but not coloured.

3 Stir in the breadcrumbs and
thyme and season with salt and
pepper. Mix well and remove from
the heat.

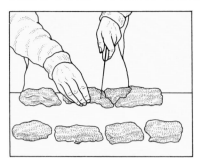

4 Cut the meat in half
lengthways, then slice each
half crossways into 4 equal pieces.
Dry the pieces of meat with
absorbent kitchen paper.

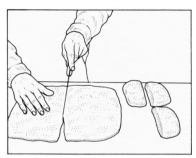

5 Cut each piece of pastry in
half. Roll out 1 piece to a
35.5 × 28 cm (14 × 11 inch)
rectangle, then cut in half. Roll
each half to 25.5 × 16 cm (10 × 6$\frac{1}{2}$
inches). Repeat with the remaining
pieces of pastry to make 8
rectangles altogether.

6 Put 60 ml (4 tbsp) of the
mushroom mixture in the
middle of 1 pastry rectangle. Place
a piece of beef on top and sprinkle
it with salt.

7 Top the beef with a whole
mushroom cap. Beat the egg
white with 10 ml (2 tsp) water and
brush this along the edges of the
pastry rectangle.

8 Fold the pastry over the meat
and mushroom, overlapping
the edges. Press lightly to seal.
Place seam-side down on a baking
sheet. Prepare the remaining
parcels in the same way.

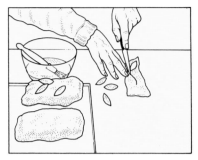

9 Roll out the pastry trimmings
and cut out decorative shapes.
Brush 1 side with the egg white
mixture and stick on to the pastry
parcels.

10 Chill the parcels in the
refrigerator until you are
ready to cook. Beat the egg yolk
with 10 ml (2 tsp) water and brush
this glaze over the pastry. Bake in
the oven at 200°C (400°F) mark 6,
allowing 25 minutes for rare beef
or 27 minutes for medium-cooked
beef. Transfer the parcels to a
large warmed serving dish or
individual plates. Serve
immediately garnished with the
parsley sprigs, with hot tomato
sauce.

Menu Suggestion
Serve these individual steak and
mushroom parcels with seasonal
vegetables such as broccoli and
mange-touts.

BLADE BEEF WITH BRANDY

2.45 | ✳* | 340 cals

* freeze after step 5

Serves 6

**6 thick slices of blade of beef,
each weighing 150 g (5 oz)**

30 ml (2 tbsp) vegetable oil

25 g (1 oz) butter or margarine

**175 g (6 oz) onions, skinned and
thickly sliced**

**225 g (8 oz) carrots, peeled and
thickly sliced**

45 ml (3 tbsp) brandy

150 ml ($\frac{1}{4}$ pint) beef stock

1 garlic clove, skinned and crushed

salt and freshly ground pepper

**175 g (6 oz) button mushrooms,
sliced**

**chopped fresh parsley, to garnish
(optional)**

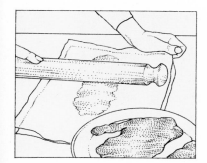

1 Trim any fat or skin off the
meat and bat out the pieces of
meat between sheets of greaseproof paper.

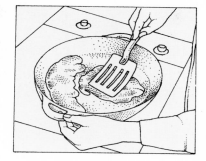

2 Heat the oil and fat in a
medium flameproof casserole
and fry the pieces of meat, one or
two at a time, pressing the meat on
to the hot surface of the pan with a
fish slice until browned. Remove
from the casserole.

3 Add the onions and carrots
and fry for 5 minutes until
lightly browned. Replace the
meat.

4 Heat the brandy in a ladle,
ignite and pour over the meat.
When the flames have subsided,
add the stock, garlic and
seasoning to the casserole.

5 Bring to the boil, cover and
cook in the oven at 170°C
(325°F) mark 3 for 1$\frac{1}{2}$–1$\frac{3}{4}$ hours or
until the meat is almost tender.

6 Strain the juices, then return
to the meat with the sliced
mushrooms. Cover the casserole
and continue to cook for a further
15 minutes.

7 Lift the meat out of the cooking liquor and arrange in a
warmed shallow serving dish.

8 Bring the liquor to the boil
and reduce slightly by cooking
for 1–2 minutes, stirring con-
tinuously. Adjust the seasoning.

9 To serve. Spoon the juices
over the meat. Garnish with
chopped fresh parsley.

Menu Suggestion
An excellent main course dish for
an informal dinner party. Serve
with creamed or jacket baked
potatoes and a seasonal green
vegetable such as broccoli.

**BLADE BEEF WITH
BRANDY**
Blade of beef is an excellent cut
for long, slow cooking in the
oven. From the shoulder of the
cow, it is sold with the blade
bone removed, usually cut into
thick slices rather than cubed as
other stewing meats. Blade is
always fairly lean, but don't
worry if you notice a thick seam
or two of fat running through
it—this will break down during
the long, slow cooking and give
the finished meat a moist, tender
quality.

CELERIAC AND MUSTARD BEEF

| 2.00 | £ | 562 cals |

Serves 4

8 thin slices of silverside, about
  900 g (2 lb) total weight

175 g (6 oz) celeriac, peeled and
  grated

3 medium carrots, peeled and
  grated

1 medium onion, skinned and
  thinly sliced

75 ml (5 tbsp) wholegrain mustard

75 ml (5 tbsp) chopped fresh
  parsley

salt and freshly ground pepper

45 ml (3 tbsp) vegetable oil

30 ml (2 tbsp) plain flour

300 ml ($\frac{1}{2}$ pint) beef stock

60 ml (4 tbsp) Madeira or medium
  sherry

extra chopped fresh parsley, to
  garnish

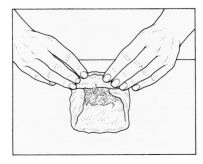

1 Place the beef slices between 2 sheets of dampened greaseproof paper. Bat out thinly with a rolling pin.

2 Place all the vegetables in a saucepan. Cover with cold water and bring to the boil. Drain immediately.

3 Stir half of the wholegrain mustard and half of the parsley into the vegetable mixture with salt and pepper to taste.

4 Spoon a little of the vegetable mixture on to each slice of beef. Fold in the edges and roll up to enclose the filling. Secure with wooden cocktail sticks or tie neatly with fine string.

5 Heat the oil in a large frying pan, add the beef rolls and brown quickly. Transfer to a 2 litre ($3\frac{1}{2}$ pint) ovenproof casserole with a slotted spoon.

6 Stir the flour into the frying pan. Cook, stirring, for 1–2 minutes, then add the stock, Madeira and the remaining mustard. Bring to the boil.

7 Pour the sauce over the beef, cover the casserole tightly and bake in the oven at 180°C (350°F) mark 4 for about $1\frac{1}{2}$ hours or until the beef is tender. Garnish with chopped parsley and serve hot.

Menu Suggestion

Rolls of stuffed silverside make an economical main course for an informal dinner party. Serve on a bed of nutty brown rice, with side dishes of seasonal vegetables.

CELERIAC AND MUSTARD BEEF

Madeira is a wine which has been fortified with brandy. It comes from the island of the same name, which is off the coast of Morocco in the Atlantic. In Victorian times, Madeira was immensely popular in England, both as an after-dinner drink, and as a mid-morning 'pick-me-up' served with the plain cake of the same name. Nowadays it is drunk less often, and most homes are more likely to have sherry than Madeira. If you do happen to have a bottle of Madeira in the house, however, it will add body and a distinctive caramel flavour to the sauce in this dish.

BOEUF BOURGUIGNON *(BEEF IN WINE)*

2.30	£ £ ✳	585 cals

Serves 4

50 g (2 oz) butter

30 ml (2 tbsp) vegetable oil

100 g (4 oz) bacon in a piece, rinded and diced

900 g (2 lb) braising steak or topside, cubed

1 garlic clove, skinned and crushed

45 ml (3 tbsp) plain flour

salt and freshly ground pepper

bouquet garni

150 ml (¼ pint) beef stock

300 ml (½ pint) red Burgundy

12 small onions, skinned

175 g (6 oz) button mushrooms

chopped fresh parsley, to garnish

1 Heat half the butter and oil in a flameproof casserole and fry the bacon for 5 minutes. Drain.

2 Reheat the fat and fry the meat in small amounts for about 8 minutes until browned.

3 Return the bacon to the casserole with the garlic. Sprinkle the flour over and stir in.

4 Add seasoning, the bouquet garni, stock and wine, then bring to the boil, stirring. Cover and cook in the oven at 170°C (325°F) mark 3 for 1½ hours.

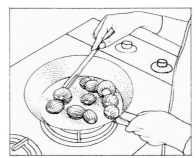

5 Meanwhile, heat the remaining butter and oil together and sauté the whole onions for about 10 minutes until glazed and golden brown. Remove from the pan. Add the mushrooms to the pan and fry for 5 minutes.

6 Add the mushrooms and onions to the casserole and cook for a further 30 minutes until the meat is tender.

7 Remove the bouquet garni. Skim off the surface fat. Serve garnished with chopped parsley.

Menu Suggestion

Serve this classic French dish for a dinner party with new potatoes tossed in melted butter and chopped fresh parsley, followed by a green salad tossed in vinaigrette dressing.

BEEF AND CHESTNUT CASSEROLE

2.45* ✳* 763 cals

* plus overnight cooling; freeze at the
end of step 4

Serves 4

45 ml (3 tbsp) vegetable oil

1.1 kg (2½ lb) chuck steak, trimmed
   of fat and cubed

1 medium onion, skinned and
   sliced

1 garlic clove, skinned and crushed

30 ml (2 tbsp) plain wholewheat
   flour

300 ml (½ pint) dry cider

300 ml (½ pint) beef stock

30 ml (2 tbsp) mushroom ketchup

5 ml (1 tsp) dried mixed herbs

salt and freshly ground pepper

439 g (15½ oz) can whole chestnuts
   in salted water, drained

30 ml (2 tbsp) chopped fresh
   parsley, to garnish

1 Heat the oil in a large
flameproof casserole, add the
beef in batches and fry over brisk
heat until browned on all sides.
Remove with a slotted spoon and
set aside.

2 Add the onion and garlic to
the casserole, lower the heat
and fry gently for 5 minutes until
soft but not coloured.

3 Return the meat to the
casserole and stir in the flour.
Cook, stirring, for 1–2 minutes,
then stir in the cider, stock and
mushroom ketchup. Bring slowly
to the boil, then add the herbs and
seasoning to taste.

4 Cover the casserole and cook
in the oven at 170°C (325°F)
mark 3 for 2 hours or until the
beef is tender. Leave in a cool
place overnight.

5 Reheat the casserole on top of
the cooker until bubbling, then
add the chestnuts and heat
through for a further 10 minutes.
Taste and adjust seasoning and
sprinkle with the parsley before
serving.

Menu Suggestion
This is a hearty casserole, suitable
for a winter dinner party.

BEEF AND CHESTNUT CASSEROLE

Cans of whole chestnuts in
salted water (brine) are available
at most large supermarkets and
delicatessens, imported from
France. They are very
convenient to use and have a
good flavour. Their texture is
rather soft, however, due to the
canning process. If you prefer
crunchier chestnuts, then fresh
chestnuts can be used, but it is
best to cook them beforehand and
add them to the casserole just to
heat through, otherwise you run
the risk of overcooking them. To
cook fresh chestnuts: first make a
small cut in the rounded part of
each shell with the point of a
small sharp knife. Put the
chestnuts in a saucepan and
cover with cold water. Bring
to the boil and simmer for 10
minutes, then drain. While the
chestnuts are still warm, peel off
both the outer shells and the
inner skins.
   Cook the chestnuts in stock or
water to cover for about 20
minutes until tender, then drain
before use.

BEEF IN BRANDY AND MUSTARD

| 2.00 | £ £ * * | 477 cals |

* freeze before step 4

Serves 6

1.1-kg (2½-lb) piece chuck steak

30 ml (2 tbsp) vegetable oil

50 g (2 oz) butter

2 onions, skinned and chopped

60 ml (4 tbsp) brandy

1 garlic clove, skinned and crushed

15 ml (1 tbsp) whole grain mustard

300 ml (½ pint) beef stock

salt and freshly ground pepper

225 g (8 oz) celery, trimmed

50 g (2 oz) walnut halves

75 ml (5 tbsp) single cream

1 Cut the piece of chuck steak into thin strips about 0.5 cm (¼ inch) wide and 3.5 cm (1½ inches) long.

2 Heat the oil with 25 g (1 oz) butter in a medium flameproof casserole and brown the meat well; take out and drain.

3 Add the onion to the reheated pan juices and fry until golden; return the meat to the casserole and flame with the brandy. Stir in garlic with mustard, stock and seasoning and bring to the boil.

4 Cover the dish tightly and cook in the oven at 150°C (300°F) mark 2 for about 1½ hours or until the meat is quite tender.

5 Cut the celery diagonally into fine strips and, just before serving time, sauté with the walnuts in the remaining butter until golden.

6 Add the walnut mixture to the meat and bring to the boil, stirring; simmer for 2–3 minutes and drizzle cream over the top before serving.

RUMP STEAK IN WHISKY

| 0.20* | £ £ | 309 cals |

*plus 12 hours marinating

Serves 6

1.1-kg (2½-lb) piece rump steak, about 2 cm (¾ inch) thick

1 small onion, skinned and thinly sliced

2 garlic cloves, skinned

90 ml (6 tbsp) whisky

30 ml (2tbsp) vegetable oil

freshly ground pepper

salt

watercress sprigs, to garnish

1 Trim off any excess fat from the steak, then place the meat in an edged dish into which it will just fit comfortably.

2 Scatter onion over meat. To make the marinade, crush the garlic and mix with the whisky, oil and pepper. Pour over meat. Cover tightly with cling film and refrigerate for at least 12 hours, turning and basting once.

3 Preheat the grill. Lift the meat out of the marinade and pat the surface dry with absorbent kitchen paper, then place on the rack of the grill pan.

4 Grill the rump steak under a high heat for about 6 minutes each side, depending on how rare you like it.

5 Meanwhile, strain the marinade into a small saucepan and warm gently; adjust seasoning, adding salt at this stage if necessary.

6 Lift the steak on to a serving plate and spoon over the warmed liquid. To serve, garnish the steak with watercress sprigs.

MARINATED SPICED BEEF

2.15* ✳* 340 cals

* plus 3 days marinating and at least
8 hours cooling and refrigeration before
serving; freeze in marinade before
cooking
Serves 6

450 ml (¾ pint) red wine
150 ml (¼ pint) red wine vinegar
1 onion, skinned and sliced
10 ml (2 tsp) ground allspice
50 g (2 oz) soft brown sugar
1.1 kg (2½ lb) rolled topside of beef
15 ml (1 tbsp) whole cloves
salt and freshly ground pepper
30 ml (2 tbsp) vegetable oil
mustard and horseradish sauce, to
  serve

1 Make the marinade. In a large
bowl, mix together the wine,
vinegar, onion, allspice and sugar.

2 Stud the beef with the cloves.
Sprinkle all over with salt and
pepper, then place the joint in
the marinade.

3 Cover the bowl with cling film
and marinate in the refrigerator
for 3 days, turning it each day.

4 When ready to cook the beef,
remove it from the marinade
and pat dry with absorbent
kitchen paper.

5 Heat the oil in a large flameproof casserole, add the beef
and brown quickly on all sides
over high heat. Pour in the
marinade, bring slowly to boiling
point, then lower the heat, cover
and simmer for 2 hours or until
the beef is tender.

6 Remove the casserole from the
heat and leave to cool. Refrigerate for at least 8 hours, turning the beef occasionally during
this time.

7 To serve. Remove the meat
from the liquid and slice
neatly. Serve cold, with mustard
and horseradish sauce.

Menu Suggestion
Serve this sliced cold beef as part
of a buffet party spread or summer
luncheon with a selection of
salads—potato and beetroot salads
would go especially well.

MARINATED SPICED BEEF
Try not to skimp on the
marinating time in this recipe.
Three days may seem rather a
long time, but you will find it
helps enormously to tenderise
topside, which can sometimes be
a rather dry, tough joint of meat.

The acid in the wine and the
wine vinegar in the marinade
helps break down the connective
tissue in the topside, and the
longer the beef is left, the more
tender it will be after cooking.

ABBACHIO ALLA ROMANA
(ROAST LAMB ROMAN-STYLE)

2.20	310–465 cals

Serves 4–6

30 ml (2 tbsp) olive oil

1.4 kg (3 lb) leg of lamb

50 g (2 oz) can anchovy fillets

2 garlic cloves, skinned and crushed

10 ml (2 tsp) chopped fresh rosemary or 5 ml (1 tsp) dried

30 ml (2 tbsp) wine vinegar

salt and freshly ground pepper

150 ml (¼ pint) dry white wine

1 Heat the olive oil in a flame-proof casserole, add the lamb and fry over moderate heat for about 10 minutes until browned and sealed on all sides. Remove from the casserole and leave to cool for about 30 minutes.

2 Meanwhile, make the anchovy paste. Crush the anchovies with their oil in a mortar and pestle. Add the garlic, rosemary and wine vinegar and mix to a smooth paste.

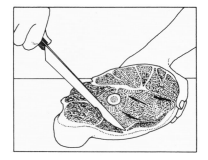

3 Make random incisions all over the leg of lamb with a sharp, pointed knife.

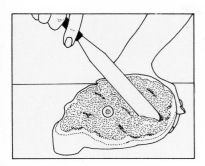

5 Return the lamb to the casserole and roast in the oven at 220°C (425°F) mark 7 for 15 minutes. Lower the oven temperature to 180°C (350°F) mark 4 and roast for a further 1½ hours or until the juices run clear when the thickest part of the meat is pierced with a skewer.

6 Transfer the lamb to a warmed serving platter and keep warm. To serve. Pour the wine into the casserole and stir to dislodge the sediment. Bring to the boil, then simmer, stirring, until the sauce reduces slightly. Serve the lamb carved into slices, with the sauce handed separately.

4 Spread the anchovy paste all over the lamb, working it into the incisions as much as possible. Sprinkle with salt and pepper.

MARINATED LEG OF LAMB

2.15* £ £ ✳* | 430–645 cals

* plus 24 hours marinating; freeze in
the marinade

Serves 4–6

1.8 kg (4 lb) leg of lamb

**2 garlic cloves, skinned and cut
into slivers**

few rosemary sprigs

salt and freshly ground pepper

90 ml (6 tbsp) olive oil

30 ml (2 tbsp) lemon juice

30 ml (2 tbsp) white wine vinegar

**150 ml (¼ pint) dry white wine or
water**

extra rosemary sprigs, to garnish

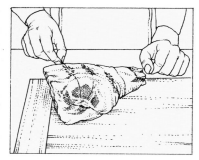

1 Make deep incisions in the
lamb with a sharp, pointed
knife. Insert the slivers of garlic
and the sprigs of rosemary into
the incisions.

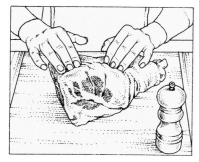

2 Rub the outside of the joint all
over with plenty of salt and
freshly ground pepper.

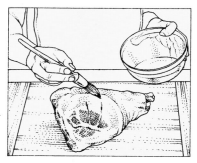

3 Mix together the oil, lemon
juice and wine vinegar, then
brush all over the joint. Place the
joint in a flameproof casserole
and leave to marinate for 24 hours.

4 Put the casserole on top of the
cooker and fry the joint over
moderate heat until browned on
all sides. Pour in the wine or
water, bring slowly to boiling
point, then cover and simmer
gently for 2 hours or until the
lamb is very tender, basting
occasionally. Serve hot, garnished
with fresh rosemary sprigs.

Menu Suggestion
This French-style casserole makes
an unusual Sunday lunch. Serve
with new potatoes tossed in
melted butter and chopped fresh
mint, and a selection of fresh
seasonal vegetables such as
carrots, courgettes and beans.

**MARINATED LEG
OF LAMB**

Freezing meat in a marinade
is a convenient way to impart
flavour, which involves little or
no effort on your part! Simply
place the leg of lamb in a rigid
container and follow the recipe
instructions above up to step 3.
Instead of leaving to marinate in
a cool place for 24 hours, seal the
container and freeze for up to 6
months. Defrost at room temperature overnight, then continue from the beginning of step
4—nothing could be simpler!

LAMB CHOPS RATATOUILLE

| 1.00 | £ £ ✳* | 558 cals |

* freeze the ratatouille only

Serves 4

1 small aubergine

salt and freshly ground pepper

45 ml (3 tbsp) olive oil

1 large onion, skinned and roughly chopped

2 garlic cloves, skinned and crushed

1 small red pepper, cored, seeded and thinly sliced

1 small green pepper, cored, seeded and thinly sliced

3 medium courgettes, trimmed and sliced

450 g (1 lb) ripe tomatoes, skinned and roughly chopped

150 ml ($\frac{1}{4}$ pint) dry white wine

15 ml (1 tbsp) chopped fresh basil or 7.5 ml ($1\frac{1}{2}$ tsp) dried basil

12 loin chops

50 g (2 oz) butter

1 Slice the aubergine thinly and place in a colander, sprinkling salt between each layer. Cover with a plate, place heavy weights on top, then leave to dégorge for 20 minutes.

2 Meanwhile, heat the oil in a large, heavy-based saucepan, add the onion and garlic and fry gently for about 5 minutes until soft and lightly coloured.

3 Add the peppers to the pan and fry gently for a few minutes, stirring, then stir in the courgettes. Rinse the aubergine slices under cold running water, then add to the pan with the tomatoes, wine, basil and salt and pepper to taste.

4 Stir well to mix and bring to the boil, then lower the heat, cover and simmer very gently for 30 minutes. At the end of cooking time the vegetables should be soft and juicy, stir frequently during cooking and add a few spoonfuls of water if there is not enough liquid in the pan.

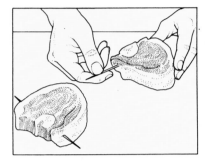

5 Meanwhile, trim as much fat as possible off the lamb chops. Curl the 'apron' around the eye of the meat and secure with wooden cocktail sticks.

6 Melt the butter in 1 or 2 heavy-based frying pans. Add the chops and fry over high heat until seared on both sides, then lower the heat and cook for a further 5 minutes on each side until the meat is tender, but still pink on the inside.

7 Taste and adjust the seasoning of the ratatouille, then transfer to a warmed serving dish. Arrange the chops on top and serve immediately.

Menu Suggestion

These lamb chops come with their own mixed vegetables, and are very quick to prepare and easy to serve—ideal for an informal mid-week dinner party. The French potato dish Gratin Dauphinois (see page 443), rich with cream and Gruyere cheese, would complement the flavour of the lamb and vegetables, and could be prepared the night before.

NAVARIN D'AGNEAU
(SPRING LAMB CASSEROLE)

2.10 £ ✳* 771 cals

* freeze after step 4 without adding the potatoes

Serves 4

30 ml (2 tbsp) vegetable oil
1 kg (2¼ lb) best end of neck of lamb, divided into cutlets
5 ml (1 tsp) sugar plus a little extra
15 ml (1 tbsp) plain flour
900 ml (1½ pints) chicken stock
30 ml (2 tbsp) tomato purée
salt and freshly ground pepper
bouquet garni
225 g (8 oz) button onions, skinned
4 carrots, peeled and sliced
1–2 turnips, peeled and quartered
8 small even-sized potatoes, peeled
225 g (8 oz) fresh peas, shelled, or 112 g (4 oz) packet frozen peas
chopped fresh parsley, to garnish

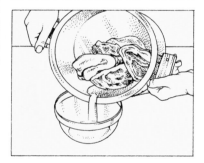

1 Heat the oil in a saucepan and fry the cutlets for about 5 minutes on both sides until lightly browned. If there is too much fat at this stage, pour off a little to leave 15–30 ml (1–2 tbsp).

2 Stir in 5 ml (1 tsp) sugar and heat until it browns slightly, then add the flour, stirring all the time until cooked and browned.

3 Remove from the heat, stir in the stock gradually, then bring to the boil and add the tomato purée, seasoning, a pinch of sugar and the bouquet garni. Cover, reduce the heat and simmer for about 1 hour.

4 Remove the bouquet garni, add the onions, carrots and turnips and continue cooking for 30 minutes. Add the potatoes and cook for 10 minutes more.

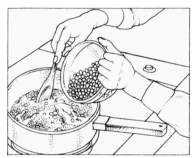

5 Stir in the peas and cook for a further 10 minutes or until the meat and potatoes are tender.

6 To serve, place the meat on a warmed serving dish and surround with the vegetables. Garnish with parsley.

Menu Suggestion
Hot French bread is the traditional accompaniment to this classic French stew of meat and vegetables cooked together.

NAVARIN D'AGNEAU
This French casserole was originally made with mutton — and so called Navarin de Mouton. These days, mutton is almost impossible to come by, and so lamb is invariably used instead. It is a classic springtime dish, which should be made with freshly picked, young spring vegetables, although frozen peas and beans are often used for convenience at other times of year.

LAMB WITH ALMONDS

| 1.45 | ££ | 597 cals |

Serves 6

2-kg (4½-lb) leg of lamb on the bone
60 ml (4 tbsp) vegetable oil
2 onions, skinned and finely chopped
15 ml (1 tbsp) ground ginger
5 ml (1 tsp) paprika
75 g (3 oz) ground almonds
75 ml (3 fl oz) chicken stock
300 ml (10 fl oz) single cream
1 garlic clove, skinned and crushed
salt and freshly ground pepper
25 g (1 oz) fresh root ginger
chopped fresh parsley, to garnish

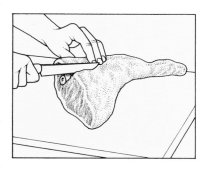

1 Using a sharp knife, carefully remove the meat from the bone of the leg of lamb, scraping the meat until the entire bone of the leg is exposed.

2 Cut the meat into 2.5-cm (1-inch) pieces, making sure to thoroughly discard the skin and any excess fat.

3 Heat the oil in a medium flameproof casserole and brown the meat a little at a time. Remove meat from the casserole using draining spoons and set aside.

4 Add the onion to the residual oil and sprinkle over the ground ginger and paprika. Cook gently for 1 minute, stirring.

5 Mix in the almonds, stock, cream, garlic and seasoning and bring to the boil. Replace the meat, stir well, cover tightly and cook in oven at 170°C (325°F) mark 3 for 1¼ hours.

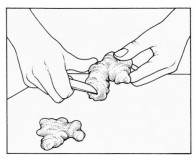

6 Peel root ginger and chop finely; stir into the lamb dish, re-cover and return to the oven for a further 20 minutes, or until the meat is quite tender. Skim well, adjust seasoning and serve garnished with chopped parsley.

--- VARIATION ---

This recipe requires about 1.1 kg (2½ lb) lean boned meat. If you want to use shoulder of lamb instead of leg, buy 2.5 kg (5½ lb) to allow for wastage when boning and trimming off fat.

For a Middle Eastern flavour, use **ground allspice** instead of ground ginger, omit the root ginger, and use **50 g (2 oz) pine nuts** instead of the almonds. Add these nuts 20 minutes before the end of cooking time.

MISHMISHIYA
(PERSIAN LAMB AND APRICOT STEW)

| 1.55* | £ £ ✳ | 782 cals |

* plus 2 hours soaking

Serves 4

225 g (8 oz) dried apricots

2.3 kg (5 lb) leg of lamb, boned and trimmed of fat

15 ml (1 tbsp) vegetable oil

1 large onion, skinned and chopped

5 ml (1 tsp) ground coriander

5 ml (1 tsp) ground cumin

2.5 ml ($\frac{1}{2}$ tsp) ground cinnamon

25 g (1 oz) ground almonds

salt and freshly ground pepper

1 Put the apricots in a bowl, cover with 300 ml ($\frac{1}{2}$ pint) boiling water and leave to soak for 2 hours. Cut the meat into 2.5 cm (1 inch) cubes.

2 Drain the apricots, reserving the liquid. Heat the oil in a large saucepan, add the lamb and onion and cook for 10 minutes, stirring, until lightly browned. Add the spices, almonds and salt and pepper to taste, then add the reserved apricot soaking liquid.

3 Cut the apricots in half and stir them into the lamb. Cover and simmer gently for 1$\frac{1}{2}$ hours, or until the lamb is tender, stirring occasionally. Serve hot.

Menu Suggestion
This Persian dish is rich and spicy. Serve with a nutty rice pilaf and okra (ladies' fingers) or courgettes tossed in grated lime rind, lime juice and chopped fresh coriander.

MARINATED LAMB CUTLETS

1.45* ☐ £ £ 714 cals

* plus 12 hours marinating and 1 hour cooling

Serves 6

two 1.1 kg (2½ lb) best end necks of lamb, chined

450 ml (¾ pint) dry white wine

200 ml (7 fl oz) vegetable oil

60 ml (4 tbsp) chopped fresh rosemary or 20 ml (4 tsp) dried

5 ml (1 tsp) salt

freshly ground pepper

1 large garlic clove, crushed

700 g (1½ lb) pickling onions, skinned

30 ml (2 tbsp) soft brown sugar

30 ml (2 tbsp) red wine

30 ml (2 tbsp) tomato purée

1 Trim away any excess fat, and remove the flesh between each cutlet bone. Place the meat in a glass or china dish.

2 Mix the white wine, 120 ml (8 tbsp) oil, rosemary, seasoning and crushed garlic together and pour over the meat. Cover and marinate for 12 hours, turning once.

3 While the meat is marinating, heat the remaining vegetable oil in a large frying pan, add the onions with the sugar and stir well. Cook over moderate heat for about 15 minutes until well-browned, shaking the pan occasionally.

4 Add the red wine and tomato purée and bring to the boil. Lower the heat and cook gently, uncovered, for 5–10 minutes until the onions are glazed. Remove from the heat, cool and chill.

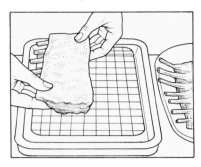

5 Lift the meat out of the marinade and place on a rack standing over a roasting tin.

6 Cook in the oven at 180°C (350°F) mark 4 for about 1½ hours or until the meat is tender, basting occasionally.

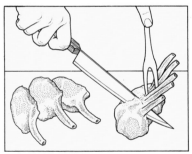

7 While still warm, divide the meat into cutlets and spoon over the marinade. Baste and turn from time to time until cold, about 1 hour. Cover and leave in a cool place until serving time.

8 Arrange the cutlets on a serving plate and garnish with the onions. Serve chilled.

Menu Suggestion
Serve this as a main course for a dinner party. Start with Iced Courgette Soup (page 15); finish with Pommes Bristol (page 254).

PORK LOIN WITH CIDER

| 2.40 | 🍳🍳🍳 £ £ | 926 cals |

Serves 6

600 ml (1 pint) dry cider

1.8 kg (4 lb) loin of pork, boned, with rind on

salt

2 onions, skinned

125 g (4 oz) rindless streaky bacon

50 g (2 oz) butter

225 g (8 oz) button or cup mushrooms, wiped and chopped

5 ml (1 tsp) dried rubbed sage

125 g (4 oz) fresh white breadcrumbs

1 egg, beaten

freshly ground pepper

30 ml (2 tbsp) vegetable oil

175 g (6 oz) carrots, peeled and cut into matchsticks

2 bay leaves

15 ml (1 tbsp) cornflour

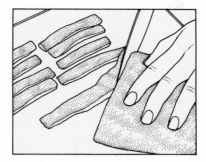

1 Pour the cider into a small pan and boil to reduce by half. Remove the rind and most of the fat from the pork and cut into thin fingers. Place these in a small roasting tin. Add salt; set aside.

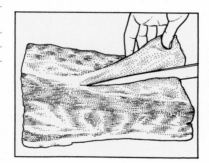

2 Slit the loin of pork along the eye of the meat three-quarters of the way through, from the centre outwards. Open out so that it forms a long roll.

3 To make the stuffing, chop one of the onions and snip the bacon into small pieces.

4 Melt half the butter in a medium frying pan, add the bacon and onion and cook slowly until the bacon fat runs and the ingredients begin to brown. Increase the heat, add the mushrooms and cook until all excess moisture has evaporated.

5 Turn out into a large bowl and stir in the sage, breadcrumbs and enough egg to bind. Season, mix well and cool.

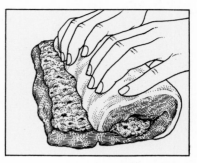

6 Spread the cold stuffing over the pork, roll up and tie at regular intervals. Slice the remaining onion. Heat the oil in a flameproof casserole, add the remaining butter and brown the joint. Remove from pan.

7 Add the sliced onion and carrots to the residual fat and lightly brown. Replace the meat and pour the reduced cider around. Stir in the bay leaves and seasoning and bring to the boil.

8 Cover tightly and place on a low shelf in the oven at 170°C (325°F) mark 3. Place the roasting tin of pork rind and fat above and cook both for about 2 hours.

9 Lift the pork out of the casserole with any stuffing that has oozed out and slice, discarding string. Remove vegetables from casserole and arrange on the serving plate with the sliced pork, cover and keep warm.

10 Mix the cornflour to a smooth paste with a little water and stir into the pan juices. Bring to the boil, stirring. Cook for 2 minutes. To serve, garnish with the crackling strips. Serve the gravy separately.

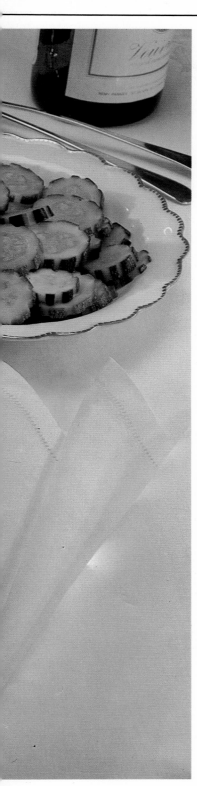

Noisettes de Porc Touraine
(FRENCH PORK NOISETTES WITH WINE, PRUNES AND CREAM)

| 1.00* | 🍞 | £ £ | 670 cals |

* plus soaking time for the prunes

Serves 4

12–16 large, plump prunes

300 ml ($\frac{1}{2}$ pint) dry white wine

700 g ($1\frac{1}{2}$ lb) pork fillet or tenderloin

25 ml ($1\frac{1}{2}$ tbsp) plain flour

salt and freshly ground pepper

25 g (1 oz) butter

15 ml (1 tbsp) olive oil

30 ml (2 tbsp) port

15 ml (1 tbsp) redcurrant jelly

150 ml ($\frac{1}{4}$ pint) double cream

1 Put the prunes in a bowl, pour in the wine, cover and leave to soak overnight, or according to packet instructions.

2 The next day, when ready to cook, lift the prunes out of the liquid with a slotted spoon and set aside. Reserve the soaking liquid.

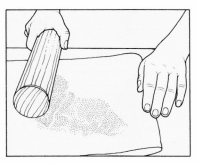

3 Cut the pork fillet into 0.5 cm ($\frac{1}{4}$ inch) slices. Place the slices in a single layer between 2 sheets of greaseproof paper. Using a meat cleaver, mallet or rolling pin, bat the meat out thinly.

4 Coat the slices of pork in the flour seasoned with salt and pepper. Heat the butter and oil in a large, flameproof casserole, add as many pork slices as the pan will hold in a single layer and fry over moderate heat until golden brown on both sides. Remove and drain on absorbent kitchen paper while frying the remaining slices.

5 Pour the soaking liquid from the prunes into the casserole and stir to scrape up any sediment from the base and sides of the pan. Add the prunes and simmer for 20 minutes or until just tender, then return the pork to the pan and simmer for 8–10 minutes or until the meat is tender.

6 Arrange the pork slices overlapping on a warmed serving dish and surround with the prunes. Cover loosely with foil and keep hot in a low oven. Stir the port and redcurrant jelly into the cooking liquid and boil rapidly until reduced. Lower the heat, slowly stir in the cream and heat through gently. Taste and adjust seasoning, then drizzle over the pork. Serve immediately.

Menu Suggestion
Pork fillet with prunes, wine, port and cream is a sumptuously rich dinner party dish. Serve with the plainest of accompaniments such as new potatoes, and a green vegetable or a dressed salad. To be authentic, use a white Vouvray wine in the sauce, then serve the same wine to drink, well chilled.

NORMANDY PORK

1.30 £ £ 688 cals

Serves 4

8 thinly cut lean pork loin chops,
    trimmed of rind and excess fat
15 ml (1 tbsp) plain flour
salt and freshly ground pepper
50 g (2 oz) butter
30 ml (2 tbsp) olive oil
300 ml ($\frac{1}{2}$ pint) dry French cider
30 ml (2 tbsp) finely chopped fresh
    parsley
3 crisp eating apples
45 ml (3 tbsp) apple brandy or
    brandy
60 ml (4 tbsp) double cream

1 Coat the chops lightly in the
flour seasoned with salt and
pepper. Heat 25 g (1 oz) of the
butter and 15 ml (1 tbsp) of the oil
in a flameproof casserole, add the
chops, a few at a time, and fry over
moderate heat until browned on
both sides.

2 Return all the chops to the pan
and pour in the cider. Bring to
the boil, then lower the heat and
add the parsley. Cover and
simmer gently for 30–40 minutes,
or until the chops are tender.

3 Remove the chops from the
pan and arrange, overlapping,
on a warmed serving platter.
Cover loosely with foil and keep
hot in a low oven. Pour the
cooking liquid into a jug.

4 Quarter and core the apples,
but do not peel them. Slice
the quarters thickly. Heat the
remaining butter and the remaining
oil in the casserole. Add the
apple slices and toss over moderate
heat for a few minutes until golden
but still crisp.

5 Heat the brandy very gently
in a small saucepan or ladle.
Remove the casserole from the
heat. Ignite the brandy, then
pour flaming over the apple slices
in the casserole.

6 Arrange the apple slices
around the pork. Pour the
cooking liquid back into the pan
and reheat. Stir in the cream and
heat through gently, then taste
and adjust seasoning. Pour the
sauce over the chops and serve
immediately.

Menu Suggestion
Normandy Pork is a very rich and
satisfying dinner party dish. Serve
with plain accompaniments such
as new potatoes cooked in their
skins, and a chicory, endive or
radicchio salad.

PORK WITH CIDER AND CORIANDER

| 0.30 | £ £ | 418 cals |

Serves 4

450 g (1 lb) pork fillet (tenderloin)

1 green pepper

225 g (8 oz) celery

125 g (4 oz) onion, skinned

30 ml (2 tbsp) oil

50 g (2 oz) butter

15 ml (1 tbsp) ground coriander

15 ml (1 tbsp) plain flour

150 ml ($\frac{1}{4}$ pint) dry cider

150 ml ($\frac{1}{4}$ pint) chicken or vegetable stock

salt and freshly ground pepper

1 Trim and slice the pork fillet into 5 mm ($\frac{1}{4}$ inch) thick pieces. Place between sheets of cling film and bat out thinly. Cover and chill until required.

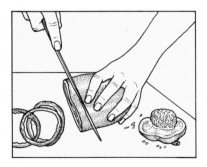

2 Cut the pepper into rings, discarding the core and seeds. Slice the celery into 5 mm ($\frac{1}{4}$ inch) pieces. Chop the onion. Cover the vegetables and chill in the refrigerator until required.

3 Heat the oil with half the butter in a large frying pan. Add the green pepper and celery and fry gently for 2–3 minutes. Lift out with a slotted spoon and keep warm on a serving plate.

4 Add the remaining butter, increase the heat to high, then add the pork, a few pieces at a time. Brown the pork on all sides, then remove from the pan.

5 Add the onion to the residual fat and fry until golden brown. Stir in the coriander and flour and cook for 1 minute. Add the cider and stock and bring quickly to the boil, stirring constantly. Return the pork to the pan, add seasoning to taste and simmer for about 5 minutes. Serve hot, with the green pepper and celery.

Menu Suggestion
This dinner party main course would go well with Stuffed Mushrooms (page 27) to start and Pommes Bristol (page 254) to finish.

PORK WITH CIDER AND CORIANDER

Fillet or tenderloin of pork is a luxury cut of meat, but well worth the expense when you are entertaining, because you can rely on it being beautifully moist and tender, and there are no wasteful bones and fat. The fillet or tenderloin comes from beneath the middle loin and the chump end of the pig—the butcher detaches it and sells it separately rather than including it with middle loin or chump chops. It is an excellent cut for quick pan-frying as in the recipe; it also makes a good roasting joint if two fillets are tied together with a stuffing in between.

CIDER PORK SAUTÉ

1.45	536 cals

Serves 4

450 g (1 lb) green dessert apples

450 g (1 lb) floury old potatoes
(eg King Edwards)

salt and freshly ground pepper

50 g (2 oz) butter

450 g (1 lb) pork escalope

15 ml (1 tbsp) vegetable oil

1 small onion, skinned and finely
chopped

15 ml (1 tbsp) plain flour

300 ml (½ pint) dry cider

30 ml (2 tbsp) capers

beaten egg, to glaze

1 Peel half of the apples. Halve, core and slice thickly. Peel the potatoes, then cut them into small chunks.

2 Cook the prepared apples and potatoes together in a sauce-pan of salted water for 20 minutes or until the potatoes are tender. Drain well.

3 Press the apples and potatoes through a sieve into a bowl. Beat in 25 g (1 oz) of the butter, then add salt and pepper to taste.

4 Spoon or pipe the mixture down both ends of a 1.4 litre (2½ pint) shallow ovenproof dish.

5 Meanwhile, cut the pork escalope into fine strips. Quarter and core the remaining apples (but do not peel them). Slice them thickly into a bowl of cold water.

6 Heat the remaining butter and the oil in a large frying pan, add the pork strips, a few at a time, and fry until browned. Remove with a slotted spoon.

7 Add the onion to the pan and fry for 2–3 minutes. Return all the pork strips and stir in the flour. Cook, stirring, for 1–2 minutes, then blend in the cider and bring to the boil.

8 Drain the apple slices and stir into the pork. Simmer gently for 4–5 minutes, or until the pork is tender but the apple still holds its shape. Stir in the capers, with salt and pepper to taste.

9 Spoon the mixture into the centre of the dish. Brush the potato with beaten egg. Bake in the oven at 200°C (400°F) mark 6 for 25–30 minutes until golden. Serve hot, straight from the dish.

Menu Suggestion
Cider Pork Sauté is ideal for mid-week entertaining. Potatoes are included, so all you need is a seasonal vegetable like creamed spinach or a purée of sprouts.

PORK ESCALOPES WITH JUNIPER

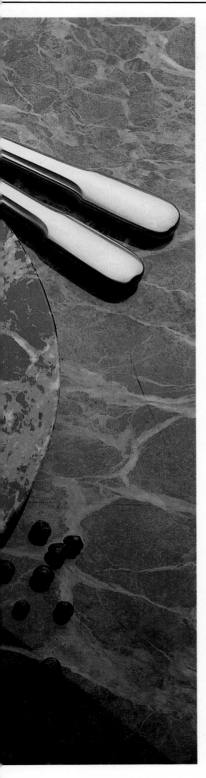

| 0.20 | £ £ | 646 cals |

Serves 4

450 g (1 lb) pork fillet (tenderloin)
40 g (1¼ oz) seasoned flour
25 g (1 oz) butter
75 ml (5 tbsp) dry white wine
4 juniper berries, lightly crushed
150 ml (¼ pint) double cream
salt and freshly ground pepper
chopped fresh parsley, to garnish

1 Trim any fat from the pork fillet and cut the meat into 5 mm (¼ inch) slices. Bat out into even thinner slices between two sheets of dampened greaseproof paper, using a meat cleaver or a wooden rolling pin.

2 Dip the pork escalopes in the seasoned flour and shake off any excess.

3 Heat the butter in a large frying pan and fry the escalopes briskly for 2 minutes on each side. Remove and keep warm in a low oven while making the wine and cream sauce.

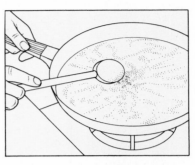

4 Add the wine and juniper berries to the pan and boil rapidly, scraping the bottom of the pan to loosen any sediment, until reduced by half. Pour in the cream, season to taste and bring to the boil. Boil rapidly for 1 minute, stirring. Pour over the escalopes and serve immediately, garnished with chopped parsley.

PORK ESCALOPES WITH JUNIPER

Juniper berries are round, purple-brown berries which look similar to peppercorns except that they are slightly larger and have smooth skin. They are not always easy to obtain in jars in supermarkets, so look for them in a health food shop or continental delicatessen. In the Mediterranean, they are a favourite spice to flavour pork and game dishes, and are often used in pâtés and terrines made with these meats.

WILTSHIRE GAMMON CASSEROLE

| 1.30* | 378–504 cals |

* plus 4 hours marinating and several
hours cooling time if serving cold

Serves 6–8

**1.4 kg (3 lb) unsmoked middle
gammon joint, soaked for 4
hours in cold water (see box)**

½ bottle rosé wine

10 ml (2 tsp) demerara sugar

few whole cloves

bouquet garni

1 Drain the joint, rinse under
cold running water and then
put into a casserole or saucepan
into which it just fits. Mix together the wine, sugar and cloves
in a separate pan and bring to just
below boiling point.

2 Pour the hot liquid over the
gammon, then tuck in the
bouquet garni. Cover with a tight-
fitting lid and leave to marinate
for 4 hours. Turn the gammon in
the marinade occasionally during
this time.

3 Place the casserole on top of
the cooker and bring slowly to
boiling point. Lower the heat and
simmer, covered, for 1 hour 20
minutes until the gammon is
tender. Remove bouquet garni.

4 Cut into slices and serve hot,
with a little of the cooking
liquid spooned over. Alternatively,
to serve cold, remove the gammon
from the liquid and leave to cool
for several hours before slicing.
Serve with Cumberland sauce.

Menu Suggestion
If serving hot, sauté potatoes and a
green salad would make ideal
accompaniments. If serving cold,
serve with a selection of salads.

WILTSHIRE GAMMON

Gammon is the name given to
whole hind legs of bacon, cut
after curing. The middle
gammon specified in this recipe
is the prime, central cut — whole
middle gammons can weigh as
much as 4 kg (9 lb), but these are
usually cut into smaller joints
which are of a more manageable
size. For this recipe, try to get a
mild Wiltshire or a tendersweet
cure. Wiltshire cure means that
the pork will have been injected
with a brine solution, then
immersed in brine for 2–4 days
and afterwards left to hang in a
maturing room if it is to be sold
as unsmoked. With such mild
cures of bacon, soaking in cold
water before cooking is now considered unnecessary because the
salt content is so low, but if you
feel happier soaking the joint
beforehand then by all means do
so. Do not soak for longer than 4
hours, however, or the soaking
will have the opposite of the de-
sired effect — the salt which has
come out of the joint into the
soaking water will work its way
back into the gammon, making it
saltier than it was originally!

CATALAN VEAL

| 1.20 | 🗋 £ £ | 393 cals |

Serves 4

2 whole fillets of veal (see box)
salt and freshly ground pepper
6 rashers of smoked streaky bacon
30 ml (2 tbsp) olive oil
juice of 2 oranges
150 ml ($\frac{1}{4}$ pint) dry white wine
**orange slices and coriander leaves,
   to garnish**

1 Trim any fat off the veal, then sprinkle liberally with pepper. Place the fillets one on top of another.

2 Wrap the bacon rashers around the 2 fillets, then tie with fine string to hold them securely together.

3 Heat the oil in a flameproof casserole which is long enough to contain the veal. Add the veal and fry over moderate heat until the bacon is golden brown on all sides, turning frequently.

4 Pour in the orange juice and white wine. Sprinkle with a little salt and plenty of pepper. Cover the casserole and simmer for 1 hour or until the veal feels tender when pierced in the centre with a fine skewer.

5 Remove the veal from the cooking liquid and place on a board. Leave to stand in a warm place for 10 minutes. Meanwhile, bring the cooking liquid to the boil and boil rapidly to reduce and slightly thicken the sauce

6 Slice the veal fillets neatly and arrange on a warmed serving platter. Reheat the cooking liquid until bubbling, then drizzle a little over the veal. Garnish with the orange slices and coriander leaves. Serve immediately, with the remaining cooking liquid handed separately in a sauceboat.

Menu Suggestion
Catalan Veal is very quick to prepare; perfect for last-minute entertaining, yet sure to impress. Serve a selection of charcuterie (cold meats) to start the meal, then finish simply with fresh ripe melon, figs or other seasonal fruit.

CATALAN VEAL

This recipe comes from Catalonia in north-eastern Spain, where meat is often cooked with wine and fruit juice to give it a sweet succulence. In Catalonia, the veal would be cooked in an earthenware dish, but a flameproof casserole can also be used.

Whole fillets of veal cut from the loin of the calf can be bought from large supermarkets and butchers specialising in 'continental cuts'. They are similar to tenderloins of pork, which can also be used if wished.

Swiss Veal

| 3.00 | £ £ | 479–719 cals |

Serves 4–6

1.4 kg (3 lb) boned and rolled loin or shoulder of veal

45 ml (3 tbsp) plain flour

salt and freshly ground pepper

175 g (6 oz) streaky bacon, rinded and roughly chopped

1 medium onion, skinned and roughly chopped

2 medium carrots, peeled and sliced

30 ml (2 tbsp) vegetable oil

150 ml ($\frac{1}{4}$ pint) dry white wine

150 ml ($\frac{1}{4}$ pint) chicken stock

finely grated rind and juice of 1 lemon

15 ml (1 tbsp) tomato purée

10 ml (2 tsp) chopped fresh thyme or 5 ml (1 tsp) dried

2 bay leaves

90 ml (6 tbsp) single cream (optional)

fresh thyme sprigs, to garnish

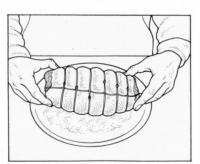

1 Coat the joint of veal in the flour seasoned with salt and pepper. Set aside.

2 Put the chopped bacon in a heavy flameproof casserole and heat gently until the fat runs. Increase the heat to moderate, add the onion and carrots and fry until the bacon turns colour, stirring frequently. Remove from the casserole with a slotted spoon and drain on absorbent kitchen paper.

3 Heat the oil in the casserole, then add the veal and fry over moderate heat until browned on all sides.

4 Return the bacon and vegetables to the casserole, then pour in the wine and stock. Add the lemon rind and juice, the tomato purée, thyme and bay leaves. Bring to the boil, stirring the liquid to combine the flavouring ingredients.

5 Cover the casserole and cook in the oven at 170°C (325°F) mark 3 for 2–2$\frac{1}{2}$ hours until the joint is really tender. Remove the veal from the casserole, place on a carving dish and set aside to 'rest' in a warm place.

6 Meanwhile, strain the cooking liquid through a sieve into a clean saucepan. Discard the bay leaves and press the vegetables with the back of a spoon to work them through the sieve.

7 Reheat the sauce gently, then taste and adjust seasoning. Stir in the cream, if using, and heat through very gently, without boiling. Pour into a sauceboat. Serve the veal carved into neat slices, garnished with fresh thyme sprigs.

Menu Suggestion
Reserve this veal dish for a special occasion such as Sunday lunch when entertaining friends. Serve with new potatoes and a seasonal green vegetable.

PAUPIETTES DE VEAU
(STUFFED AND ROLLED VEAL ESCALOPES)

1.00	£ £ ✳*	454 cals

* freeze at end of step 3

Serves 4

4 veal escalopes, about 100 g (4 oz) each

100 g (4 oz) butter

1 medium onion, skinned and finely chopped

175 g (6 oz) cooked ham, chopped

finely grated rind and juice of ½ lemon

50 g (2 oz) fresh breadcrumbs

15 ml (1 tbsp) chopped fresh parsley and marjoram or 5 ml (1 tsp) dried

salt and freshly ground pepper

1 egg, beaten

150 ml (¼ pint) dry white wine

15 ml (1 tbsp) plain flour

chopped fresh parsley, to garnish

1 Place each veal escalope between 2 sheets of damp greaseproof paper and bat out thinly with a rolling pin.

2 Melt 40 g (1½ oz) of the butter in a frying pan, add the onion and cook over gentle heat for about 10 minutes until soft but not coloured. In a bowl, mix together the ham, half of the lemon rind and juice, the breadcrumbs, herbs and salt and pepper to taste. Mix in the onion and beaten egg.

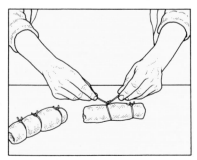

3 Spread the stuffing over the pieces of veal and roll up. Tie each roll with thin string.

4 Melt another 40 g (1½ oz) of the butter in a shallow ovenproof casserole. When foaming, add the paupiettes and brown them quickly all over. Pour in the wine and 150 ml (¼ pint) water, the remaining lemon rind and juice and salt and pepper to taste. Cover and simmer gently for 25–30 minutes, until the meat is tender.

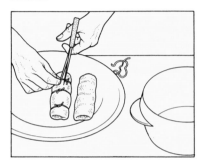

5 When the paupiettes are cooked, lift them out of the casserole and place on a serving dish. Carefully remove the string, cover and keep warm while making the sauce.

6 Put the flour and the remaining butter on a small plate and work to a paste (beurre manié). Bring the liquid in the casserole to the boil, then gradually whisk in the beurre manié to thicken the sauce slightly. Taste and adjust seasoning.

7 Pour the sauce over the paupiettes and garnish with the chopped parsley. Serve immediately.

Menu Suggestion
Paupiettes de Veau are good for a dinner party main course because they can be prepared up to the cooking stage (step 4) up to 24 hours in advance. Serve them with a special potato dish such as the French Gratin Dauphinois (page 443).

ROQUEFORT AND WALNUT VEAL

| 1.45* | £ £ | 570 cals |

* plus 30 minutes chilling

Serves 4

50 g (2 oz) butter or margarine

1 small onion, skinned and chopped

100 g (4 oz) walnuts, chopped

100 g (4 oz) Roquefort or Danish Blue cheese, crumbled

75 ml (5 tbsp) soured cream

30 ml (2 tbsp) chopped fresh parsley

225 g (8 oz) minced veal

2 large veal escalopes, about 225 g (8 oz) each

10 ml (2 tsp) plain flour, plus extra for dusting

1 egg, beaten

50 g (2 oz) dried breadcrumbs

150 ml (¼ pint) veal stock

salt and freshly ground pepper

1 Melt half of the butter in a small frying pan, add the onion and walnuts and fry gently for 2–3 minutes. Cool for 15 minutes.

2 In a bowl, beat together the cheese, 30 ml (2 tbsp) of the soured cream and the parsley. Add the minced veal, onions and walnuts and mix well.

3 Place the escalopes between 2 sheets of dampened greaseproof paper and bat out thinly with a rolling pin.

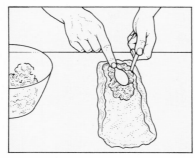

4 Lay the escalopes on a work surface with 2 of the longest edges overlapping slightly. Spoon the cheese filling evenly down the centre of the escalopes.

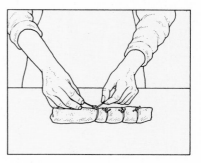

5 Fold the veal over the filling and carefully roll up into a long 'log' shape. Tie at regular intervals with fine string.

6 Dust the veal lightly all over with flour. Coat in beaten egg, then roll until coated in the breadcrumbs. Place in a small shallow roasting tin and chill in the refrigerator for 30 minutes.

7 Melt the remaining butter and pour over the veal. Cook in the oven at 220°C (425°F) mark 7 for 15 minutes, then lower the oven temperature to 190°C (375°F) mark 5 and cook for a further 45 minutes.

8 Pour the pan juices into a small saucepan—there should be about 50 ml (2 fl oz). Cover the veal loosely with foil and return to a low oven to keep warm.

9 Bring the pan juices to the boil and whisk in the stock. Mix the remaining soured cream with 10 ml (2 tsp) flour and whisk into the pan juices. Bring to the boil and add more stock to thin the sauce if necessary. Taste and adjust seasoning, then pour into a sauceboat. Slice the veal into thick slices and serve hot, with the sauce handed separately.

Menu Suggestion
Serve this rich main course for a dinner party with simple vegetables such as buttered new potatoes and broccoli, French beans or mange-touts.

FRICASSEE OF VEAL

1.45	£ £ ✳*	441 cals

* freeze before step 8

Serves 6

900 g (2 lb) stewing veal
450 g (1 lb) carrots, peeled
1 onion, skinned
15 ml (1 tbsp) chopped fresh thyme or 2.5 ml ($\frac{1}{2}$ tsp), dried
150 ml ($\frac{1}{4}$ pint) dry white wine
900 ml ($1\frac{1}{2}$ pints) water
salt and freshly ground pepper
50 g (2 oz) butter
50 g (2 oz) plain flour
6 rashers streaky bacon
2 egg yolks
150 ml (5 fl oz) single cream

1 Cut the veal into 4-cm ($1\frac{1}{2}$-inch) squares. Cover the meat with cold water, bring to the boil and bubble for 1 minute.

2 Strain the veal through a colander and clean. Rinse out the pan thoroughly and replace the pieces of meat.

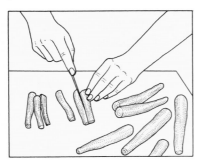

3 Cut the carrots into finger-sized pieces and slice the onion. Add to the pan with the thyme, wine, water and seasoning.

4 Bring slowly to the boil, cover and simmer gently for about $1\frac{1}{4}$ hours or until the veal is quite tender.

5 Strain off the cooking liquid, make up to 750 ml ($1\frac{1}{4}$ pints), with water or stock if necessary, and reserve; keep the veal and vegetables warm in a covered serving dish.

6 Melt the butter and stir in the flour, cook gently for 1 minute. Off the heat, stir in the strained cooking liquid, season well and bring to the boil, stirring all the time. Cook the sauce gently for 5 minutes.

7 Carefully remove the rinds from the streaky bacon and roll up the rashers. Then grill the bacon rolls.

8 Mix the egg yolks with the cream; take the sauce off the heat and stir in the cream mixture. Return to the heat and warm gently – without boiling – until the sauce becomes slightly thicker.

9 To serve, adjust seasoning. Pour the cream sauce over the meat and serve garnished with the bacon rolls.

FRICASSEE

This recipe for Fricassee of Veal is very typically French – the word *fricassée* is used for any dish which is cooked in a white sauce or stock (often made with white wine). Usually white meats such as veal and chicken are cooked in *fricassées*, although other meats and fish and vegetables are also sometimes cooked this way. *Blanquette* is another French term which means virtually the same as *fricassée*.

LIAISON

The thickening of the sauce with egg yolks and cream just before serving is also typically French. Known as a *liaison*, it is used in *fricassées* and *blanquettes* rather than the other methods of thickening with *beurre manié* (a paste of butter and flour) or cornflour, to give a richer, creamier result.

Osso Bucco
(VEAL BRAISED WITH WHITE WINE)

| 2.40 | £ £ ✳ | 451 cals |

Serves 4

| 1.75 kg (3½ lb) veal knuckle (veal shin, hind cut), sawn into 5 cm (2 inch) lengths |
| 50 g (2 oz) plain flour |
| salt and freshly ground pepper |
| 25 g (1 oz) butter |
| 30 ml (2 tbsp) olive oil |
| 1 medium onion, skinned and very finely chopped |
| 1 medium carrot, peeled and very finely chopped |
| 1 celery stick, trimmed and very finely chopped |
| 2 garlic cloves, skinned and crushed |
| 2 canned anchovy fillets |
| 300 ml (½ pint) dry white wine |
| 300 ml (½ pint) Veal Stock (page 144) |
| 30 ml (2 tbsp) tomato purée |
| thinly pared rind and juice of 1 lemon |
| 10 ml (2 tsp) chopped fresh marjoram or 5 ml (1 tsp) dried |
| 1 bay leaf |
| 45 ml (3 tbsp) chopped fresh continental parsley |
| finely grated rind of 1 lemon |

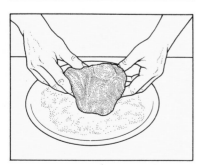

1 Coat the pieces of veal in the flour seasoned with salt and pepper. Melt the butter with the oil in a large flameproof casserole, add the veal a few pieces at a time and fry over moderate heat until browned on all sides. Remove with a slotted spoon and set aside to drain on absorbent kitchen paper.

2 Lower the heat, add the chopped vegetables to the casserole with half of the garlic and fry gently for about 10 minutes, stirring frequently. Add the anchovies and stir to combine.

3 Add the wine, stock, tomato purée, pared lemon zest and juice, marjoram and bay leaf. Bring to the boil, stirring, then return the veal to the casserole.

4 Cover the pan tightly and simmer for 1½–2 hours, turning the veal occasionally and basting with the sauce.

5 Remove the veal with a slotted spoon and arrange on a warmed serving dish or plate. Discard the pared lemon zest and bay leaf and taste and adjust seasoning.

6 Mix the remaining garlic with the parsley and grated lemon rind. Spoon the sauce over the pieces of veal and sprinkle each one with the garlic, parsley and lemon mixture. Serve immediately.

Menu Suggestion
Serve Osso Bucco for an informal supper party. Italian antipasto would make a good first course, with a fresh fruit salad, macerated in an Italian liqueur such as Amaretto or Strega to finish the meal. In Milan, Osso Bucco itself is traditionally accompanied by *risotto alla Milanese*, a deliciously creamy rice dish made from Italian arborio rice, beef stock, butter, onion and grated Parmesan cheese. Follow with a crisp green salad to refresh the palate before serving the dessert.

Saltimbocca Alla Romana
(VEAL ESCALOPES WITH HAM AND MARSALA)

| 0.25 | £ £ | 311 cals |

Serves 6

| 6 veal escalopes, about 100 g (4 oz) each |
| lemon juice |
| freshly ground pepper |
| 6 fresh sage or basil leaves or sprigs of marjoram |
| 6 thin slices of Parma ham (prosciutto) |
| 50 g (2 oz) butter or margarine |
| 15 ml (1 tbsp) vegetable oil |
| 30 ml (2 tbsp) Marsala |
| 3 slices of white bread, crusts removed |
| extra vegetable oil, for frying |

1 Place each escalope between 2 sheets of dampened greaseproof paper and bat out thinly with a rolling pin. Remove the paper and sprinkle the veal with lemon juice and pepper to taste.

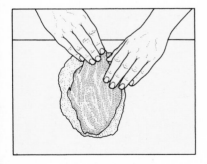

2 Place a sage or basil leaf or a sprig of marjoram in the centre of each escalope and cover with a slice of ham cut to fit.

3 Roll up the escalopes and fix firmly with wooden cocktail sticks. Melt the butter with the oil in a frying pan, add the veal and fry gently until golden brown.

4 Stir in the Marsala and bring to simmering point. Cover the pan and simmer gently for about 10 minutes, or until the veal is tender when pierced with a fine skewer.

5 Meanwhile, cut each slice of bread into 4 triangles. Heat about 1 cm ($\frac{1}{2}$ inch) of oil in a frying pan, add the bread and fry until golden on both sides. Drain on absorbent kitchen paper.

6 Serve the veal with the juices poured over and surround with fried bread.

Menu Suggestion
Serve for an Italian-style dinner party. Start the meal with antipasto, then serve a pasta course—or a risotto. In Italy, the veal would be served on its own, followed by a green vegetable in season, or a salad.

VEAL ESCALOPES IN WHITE WINE WITH FENNEL

| 0.25 | £ £ | 301 cals |

Serves 8

8 veal escalopes, about 175 g (6 oz) each

30 ml (2 tbsp) plain flour

salt and freshly ground pepper

450 g (1 lb) fennel

1 large onion, skinned

700 g (1½ lb) tomatoes, skinned

50 g (2 oz) butter

45 ml (3 tbsp) vegetable oil

150 ml (¼ pint) dry white wine

30 ml (2 tbsp) tomato purée

1 Cut each escalope into 3 equal pieces. Place between 2 sheets of dampened greaseproof paper and bat out thinly with a rolling pin or meat mallet.

2 Spread the flour out on a plate and mix with salt and pepper. Use to coat the pieces of meat.

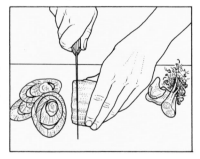

3 Trim the fennel, reserving the feathery tops for garnish. Slice the fennel and onion thinly. Skin the tomatoes, then cut each one into 8 pieces.

4 Melt the butter with the oil in a large frying pan. When foaming, brown the veal, a few pieces at a time. Remove from the pan with a slotted spoon and transfer to a plate.

5 Add the fennel and onion to the butter and oil remaining in the pan and brown lightly. Stir in the white wine, tomato purée and tomatoes, with salt and pepper to taste. Bring to the boil and replace the meat.

6 Cover the pan and simmer for about 5 minutes or until the meat is tender. Taste and adjust seasoning, then transfer to a warmed serving dish and garnish with the reserved fennel tops. Serve immediately.

Menu Suggestion
Serve this Italian-style dish for a dinner party main course with a risotto, and a salad of radicchio, lamb's lettuce and basil leaves.

MEDALLIONS OF VEAL WITH GINGER

| 0.35 | £ £ | 525 cals |

Serves 4

22.5 ml (1½ tbsp) plain flour
5 ml (1 tsp) ground ginger
salt and freshly ground pepper
8 veal medallions (see box)
40 g (1½ oz) butter
15 ml (1 tbsp) olive oil
3 pieces of stem ginger, with syrup
100 ml (4 fl oz) dry white wine
150 ml (¼ pint) double cream

1 Mix the flour on a plate with the ground ginger and salt and pepper to taste. Coat the veal in the flour.

2 Melt 25 g (1 oz) of the butter with the oil in 1 or 2 large, heavy-based frying pans. Add the veal and fry over moderate heat until lightly coloured, turning once.

3 Meanwhile, chop 1 of the pieces of stem ginger very finely. Mix with the syrup from all the pieces of ginger. Add the white wine, then pour over the veal.

4 Bring the wine to the boil, then lower the heat, cover the pan tightly and simmer the veal very gently for 15 minutes or until just tender. Turn once during cooking.

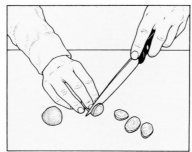

5 Meanwhile, slice the remaining 2 pieces of stem ginger into neat, thin rings with a sharp knife.

6 When the veal is tender, transfer to a warmed dish, cover and keep hot in a low oven. Stir the cream into the sauce (combining them in 1 pan if 2 were used to cook the veal). Simmer until reduced, stirring constantly, then whisk in the remaining butter. Taste and adjust seasoning.

7 Place 2 medallions on each of 4 warmed dinner plates and spoon over the sauce to coat the veal. Arrange a few slices of stem ginger on top of each piece of veal and serve immediately.

Menu Suggestion

This rich dinner party main course has a spicy-hot 'kick' to it from the ginger. Serve nouvelle cuisine style with plain accompaniments such as individual side dishes of mange-touts, French beans or broccoli, and steamed new potatoes tossed lightly in butter and finely chopped herbs.

MEDALLIONS OF VEAL WITH GINGER

Large supermarkets and some high-class butchers now specialise in 'continental cuts'. Medallions of veal, or *médaillons de veau* to give them their proper French title, are cut from the rump end of the fillet or the loin, and are usually sold tied into a neat shape with string, sometimes with fat around them to keep them moist during cooking. This fat should be removed before serving.

VEAL CHOPS WITH SPINACH PURÉE

| 1.30* | 🍳 | £ £ | 320 cals |

*plus overnight marinating

Serves 6

6 veal chops, weighing about 175 g (6 oz) each, trimmed

finely grated rind of 2 lemons

90 ml (6 tbsp) lemon juice

150 ml (¼ pint) dry Vermouth

1 large garlic clove, skinned and crushed

salt and freshly ground pepper

225 g (8 oz) fresh spinach, trimmed

50 g (2 oz) butter or margarine

freshly grated nutmeg

45 ml (3 tbsp) vegetable oil

bunch of spring onions, trimmed and cut into 2.5 cm (1 inch) strips

1 egg, hard-boiled and finely chopped

1 Place the chops in a large shallow dish. Whisk together the lemon rind and juice, Vermouth, garlic and salt and pepper to taste. Pour over the chops. Cover and leave to marinate in the refrigerator overnight.

2 Wash the spinach well in several changes of cold water. Put in a saucepan with just the water that clings to the leaves, cover and cook for 3–4 minutes.

3 Drain the spinach well in a colander, pressing with the back of a wooden spoon to extract as much liquid as possible. Chop finely.

4 Melt 25 g (1 oz) of the butter in the rinsed-out pan, add the chopped spinach and the nutmeg and cook for 1–2 minutes to dry off any excess moisture. Transfer to a bowl, cool and cover.

5 Remove the chops from the marinade (reserving the marinade), drain and pat dry with absorbent kitchen paper. Melt the remaining butter with the oil in a large frying pan. When foaming, add the chops 1 or 2 at a time and brown well on both sides. Place in a single layer in a shallow ovenproof dish.

6 Pour the reserved marinade into the frying pan. Bring to the boil, stirring any sediment from the base. Strain over the chops. Cover tightly and cook in the oven at 180°C (350°F) mark 4 for about 50 minutes, or until the chops are tender.

7 Transfer the chops to a warmed serving dish and keep hot. Pour the pan juices into a blender or food processor, add the spinach mixture and work until smooth. Pour into a small saucepan and simmer gently for 5–10 minutes until hot.

8 Garnish the chops with the spring onions and chopped egg. Serve immediately, with the spinach purée handed separately.

HOT VEAL AND HAM TERRINE

| 2.15 | 🍳 | £ | 346–519 cals |

Serves 4–6

700 g (1½ lb) minced veal
2 eggs, size 2
300 ml (½ pint) single cream
30 ml (2 tbsp) dry sherry
1.25 ml (¼ tsp) grated nutmeg
salt and freshly ground pepper
1 bunch watercress
40 g (1½ oz) butter
1 garlic clove, skinned and crushed
100 g (4 oz) button mushrooms, thinly sliced
100 g (4 oz) sliced cooked ham
1 bay leaf
5 ml (1 tsp) arrowroot

1 Put the veal in a blender or food processor with the eggs, cream, sherry, nutmeg, 2.5 ml (½ tsp) salt and pepper to taste. Work together until smooth.

2 Wash, drain and trim the watercress, then chop finely. Melt half of the butter in a saucepan, add the watercress and garlic and cook gently for 2–3 minutes until softened. Remove from the pan with a slotted spoon and leave to cool for 15 minutes.

3 Melt the remaining butter in the same pan, add the mushrooms and fry gently for 3 minutes. Set aside to cool.

4 Cut 1 slice of ham into fine shreds, cover and reserve. Cut the remaining slices of ham into wide strips.

5 Line the base of a 1.4 litre (2½ pint) terrine or dish with greaseproof paper. Divide the veal mixture into four. Place alternate layers of veal, watercress, ham strips and mushrooms in the terrine, beginning and ending with a layer of veal.

6 Place the bay leaf on top, then cover tightly with foil. Place the terrine in a roasting tin and pour in enough hot water to come halfway up the sides of the terrine. Bake in the oven at 180°C (350°F) mark 4 for about 1½ hours, or until just firm to the touch.

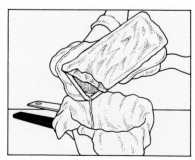

7 When the terrine is cooked, drain the juices into a saucepan through a sieve lined with muslin.

8 Turn the terrine on to a serving dish and gently scrape away the creamy curd from the sides. Rub this through the muslin and add to the juices. Re-cover the terrine and keep warm in a low oven.

9 Mix the arrowroot to a smooth paste with a little water. Bring the juices to the boil, then stir in the arrowroot paste. Simmer until slightly thickened, whisking all the time. Add the reserved shreds of ham and spoon over the terrine. Serve hot.

Menu Suggestion
Hot Veal and Ham Terrine makes an unusual main course for a dinner party. Serve with new potatoes, seasonal vegetables and chilled dry white wine.

HOT VEAL AND HAM TERRINE

It is essential to cook this terrine on a bain marie (roasting tin of hot water) as described in step 6. Minced veal is lean and can easily dry out if not cooked correctly. The bain marie creates a steamy atmosphere inside the oven, which helps to keep the meat moist and succulent.

VITELLO TONNATO
(VEAL WITH TUNA FISH MAYONNAISE)

| 2.15* | 🍳 | £ £ | 651–977 cals |

* plus several hours cooling,
24–48 hours chilling and 1 hour
standing

Serves 4–6

**900 g (2 lb) boned, rolled and tied
leg or loin of veal**

300 ml ($\frac{1}{2}$ pint) dry white wine

1 carrot, peeled and sliced

1 celery stick, trimmed and sliced

**1 small onion, skinned and stuck
with 2 cloves**

few sprigs of parsley

2 bay leaves

few black peppercorns

salt and freshly ground pepper

200 g (7 oz) can tuna in oil

**4 canned anchovy fillets, soaked in
milk for 20 minutes and drained**

**300 ml ($\frac{1}{2}$ pint) thick homemade
mayonnaise (page 441)**

**15 ml (1 tbsp) capers, roughly
chopped**

**lemon slices, black olives and
parsley sprigs, to garnish**

1 Put the veal in a large
saucepan and add the wine,
carrot, celery, onion, parsley, bay
leaves, peppercorns and 5 ml
(1 tsp) salt. Add enough water to
just cover the veal, then bring
slowly to the boil.

2 Lower the heat, cover the pan
and simmer gently for 1–1$\frac{1}{4}$
hours, until the veal is tender.
Remove the pan from the heat and
leave the veal to cool in the liquid.

3 When the meat is cold, remove
from the pan, reserving the
cooking liquid, and pat dry with
absorbent kitchen paper.

4 Untie the meat, then slice
neatly and arrange,
overlapping, on a large serving
platter. Cover with cling film.

5 Pound the tuna and anchovies
together with a pestle and
mortar, then stir into the
mayonnaise with the capers and
pepper to taste. (Alternatively, put
all the ingredients in a blender or
food processor and work until
evenly combined.)

6 Thin the mayonnaise mixture
down to a coating consistency
with a few spoonfuls of the
reserved cooking liquid, then taste
and adjust seasoning (it is unlikely
that you will need to add salt
because of the saltiness of the
anchovies and capers).

7 Spoon the mayonnaise
carefully and evenly over the
veal, then cover loosely with foil.
Chill in the refrigerator for
24–48 hours.

8 To serve, remove the veal from
the refrigerator and leave to
stand at room temperature for
about 1 hour. Uncover, then
garnish with the lemon slices,
olives and parsley.

Menu Suggestion
Vitello Tonnato is a very special
dish, best reserved for
entertaining. It is delicious in
summer, and would make an eye-
catching centrepiece for a cold
table, surrounded by a selection of
colourful and crunchy salads.

VITELLO TONNATO
Vitello Tonnato, slices of boned
and rolled veal masked in a
creamy tuna fish mayonnaise,
must be one of Italy's most
famous dishes. The combination
of tender, delicate veal and a
strong 'fishy' sauce is most
unusual—and absolutely
delicious. Try not to skimp on
the chilling time at the end of
step 7; this really improves the
flavour of the finished dish—the
tuna mayonnaise matures and
seeps into the meat during
chilling.

MAIN COURSES
Poultry and Game

CHICKEN SUPREMES IN WINE AND CREAM

| 1.00 | £ £ | 411 cals |

Serves 6

45 ml (3 tbsp) red wine vinegar

50 g (2 oz) unsalted butter

6 French-style chicken supremes (with the wing bone attached), about 175 g (6 oz) each, wiped and trimmed of excess skin

1 small onion, skinned and roughly chopped

225 g (8 oz) tomatoes, skinned and roughly chopped

15 ml (1 tsp) tomato purée

1 large garlic clove, skinned and crushed

150 ml (¼ pint) dry white wine

300 ml (½ pint) chicken stock

salt and freshly ground pepper

150 ml (5 fl oz) double cream

chopped fresh parsley, to garnish

1 Place the vinegar in a small saucepan and boil to reduce by half. Heat the butter in a large sauté or deep frying pan. Add the chicken pieces and brown well on all sides. Remove from the pan with a slotted spoon.

2 Add the onion, tomatoes, tomato purée and crushed garlic, cover and cook gently for about 5 minutes.

3 Add the wine and cook, uncovered, over a high heat for 5–10 minutes until the wine reduces by half. Add the vinegar, stock and seasoning and bring to the boil.

4 Replace the chicken, covering it with the sauce. Simmer gently, covered, for about 25 minutes or until the chicken is quite tender. Lift the chicken out of the pan with a slotted spoon and keep warm.

5 Boil the sauce until it is reduced by half, then stir in the cream. Continue reducing the sauce until a thin pouring consistency is obtained.

6 Adjust the seasoning, pass the sauce through a strainer and spoon over the chicken for serving. Garnish with chopped parsley.

———— VARIATION ————

Chicken breast fillets can be used instead of the French-style chicken supremes and, when in season, **75 g (3 oz) shallots** substituted for the onion.

Buying poultry
When buying fresh or chilled (non-frozen) chickens, feel the tip of the breast-bone with the thumb and finger. In a young bird this is soft and flexible; if it is hard and rigid the bird is probably too old to roast satisfactorily and will have to be steamed or boiled. Look at the feet also – in a young bird they are smooth with small (not coarse) scales and with short spurs.

COQ AU VIN BLANC
(CHICKEN IN WHITE WINE)

| 1.45 | £ £ ✳* | 621–829 cals |

* freeze after step 7

Serves 6–8

175 g (6 oz) lean bacon, rinded and diced

75 g (3 oz) butter

450 g (1 lb) button onions, skinned

225 g (8 oz) button mushrooms

2.7 kg (6 lb) roasting chicken, jointed into 8 pieces

75 g (3 oz) plain flour

salt and freshly ground pepper

vegetable oil for frying

60 ml (4 tbsp) brandy

600 ml (1 pint) dry white wine

chicken stock

1 garlic clove, skinned and crushed

sprigs of fresh thyme or 2.5 ml ($\frac{1}{2}$ tsp) dried

2 bay leaves

6–8 pieces of French bread, in 1 cm ($\frac{1}{2}$ inch) slices, or 3 slices of white bread, crusts removed

chopped fresh parsley, to garnish

1 Blanch the bacon by dropping it into boiling water for 30 seconds. Lift out and dry on absorbent kitchen paper.

2 Melt 25 g (1 oz) of the butter in a large frying pan until foaming. Add the bacon and fry gently for 1 minute. Add the onions, increase the heat and fry until evenly browned. Lastly, add the mushrooms and fry for 2 minutes. Transfer the bacon and vegetables to a plate with a slotted spoon.

3 Coat the chicken joints with 50 g (2 oz) of the flour, seasoned with salt and pepper. Heat another 25 g (1 oz) butter and 30 ml (2 tbsp) oil in the frying pan, add the chicken, and fry until browned all over. Transfer the bacon, vegetables and chicken to an overproof casserole.

4 Warm the brandy, ignite and pour it over the chicken joints. Let the flames die down.

5 Pour 150 ml ($\frac{1}{4}$ pint) of the white wine into the frying pan. Bring to the boil, scraping any sediment from the bottom of the pan, then pour over the chicken joints in the casserole.

6 Add the bacon and vegetables to the casserole with the remaining wine and enough chicken stock to cover the joints. Add the garlic, herbs and seasoning to taste.

7 Bring to the boil, then cover and cook in the oven at 170°C (325°F) mark 3 for 1 hour, or until chicken is tender.

8 Meanwhile, fry the French bread or bread slices on each side in oil until golden brown. Drain well on absorbent kitchen paper. Cut each bread slice into triangles.

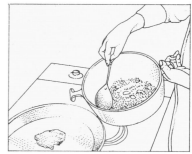

9 When cooked, remove the chicken and vegetables from the liquid, arrange on a serving dish, cover and keep warm. Skim the fat from the cooking liquid, then bring it to the boil.

10 Knead the remaining butter and remaining flour to a smooth paste (beurre manié). Add to the liquid in small amounts and bring to the boil, whisking all the time. Simmer for 2 minutes until thickened. Taste and adjust the seasoning.

11 Garnish with the French bread croûtes or white bread triangles and lots of chopped parsley.

Menu Suggestion
A classic French dish, Coq au Vin is traditionally served with steamed or boiled potatoes tossed in melted butter and finely chopped fresh parsley. A green vegetable such as petits pois, courgettes or mange-touts is also sometimes served.

COQ AU VIN BLANC

Coq au Vin Blanc—Chicken in White Wine—is simply a variation of the classic French dish Coq au Vin Rouge—Chicken in Red Wine. To be sure of the success of this dish, which makes an excellent dinner party main course, buy a good-quality French wine. It is a mistake to think that any inferior wine can be used for cooking, and any wine that is labelled 'cooking wine' should be treated with suspicion. Muscadet, Sancerre, Graves or white Burgundy are all suitable for this dish.

CHICKEN VÉRONIQUE

1.45	342 cals

Serves 4

50 g (2 oz) butter

15 ml (1 tbsp) chopped fresh
   tarragon or 10 ml (2 tsp) dried
   tarragon

finely grated rind of 1 lemon

1 garlic clove, skinned and crushed

salt and freshly ground pepper

1.5 kg (3 lb) chicken

300 ml ($\frac{1}{2}$ pint) homemade chicken
   stock (see page 440)

150 ml ($\frac{1}{4}$ pint) dry white wine

150 ml (5 fl oz) double cream

175 g (6 oz) green grapes, halved
   and seeded

1 Soften the butter in a bowl
with the tarragon, lemon rind,
garlic and salt and pepper to taste.
Put half the mixture in the cavity
of the bird.

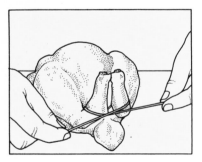

2 Truss the chicken with thread
or fine string. Spread the remainder of the mixture over the
outside of the bird (especially the
legs), then stand on a rack in a
roasting tin. Pour the chicken
stock under the rack.

3 Roast the chicken in the oven
at 200°C (400°F) mark 6 for
about 1$\frac{1}{4}$ hours or until the juices
run clear when the thickest part of
the thigh is pierced with a skewer.
Turn the bird and baste every 15
minutes or so during roasting.

4 Carve the chicken into neat
portions, then arrange on a
warmed serving platter, cover and
keep warm.

5 Make the sauce. Blot off any
excess fat from the roasting tin
with absorbent kitchen paper, then
place the tin on top of the cooker.
Pour in the wine, then boil to
reduce to about half the original
volume, stirring and scraping the
tin to dislodge sediment.

6 Stir in the cream and continue
simmering and stirring until
thick, smooth and glossy. Add the
grapes and heat through, then
taste and adjust seasoning.

7 Pour a little of the sauce over
the chicken, arranging the
grapes as attractively as possible
on each portion. Serve immediately, with the remaining
sauce and grapes handed
separately in a sauceboat.

Menu Suggestion
A rich and creamy main course for
a dinner party, Chicken Véronique
needs an accompaniment which
contrasts in flavour and texture.
Crisply cooked mange-touts or
French beans are ideal, with a
simple dish of plain boiled rice.
Serve with chilled dry white wine.

PÂTÉ CHICKEN

| 0.50 | £ | 419 cals |

Serves 4

15 g (½ oz) butter

10 ml (2 tsp) vegetable oil

4 chicken portions

5 ml (1 tsp) chopped fresh rosemary or 2.5 ml (½ tsp) dried rosemary

salt and freshly ground pepper

60 ml (4 tbsp) dry white wine

90 ml (6 tbsp) homemade chicken stock (see page 440)

50 g (2 oz) fine liver pâté

45 ml (3 tbsp) single cream

few sautéed sliced button mushrooms, to garnish

1 Heat the butter with the oil in a large frying pan. Add the chicken portions, sprinkle with the rosemary and salt and pepper to taste, then fry over moderate heat for 15–20 minutes until well coloured on all sides.

2 Pour in half the wine and half the stock, bring to the boil, then lower the heat, cover the pan and continue cooking a further 10–15 minutes until the chicken is tender. Remove the chicken from the pan with a slotted spoon.

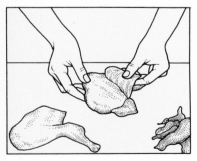

3 Strip the skin off the chicken portions and discard. Place the chicken on a serving platter, cover and keep hot while making sauce.

4 Add the remaining wine and stock to the pan and stir to combine with the cooking juices. Boil vigorously for a few minutes to reduce the liquid slightly.

5 Meanwhile, beat the pâté and cream together until they are smooth and well combined.

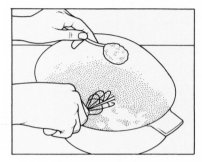

6 Gradually whisk the pâté mixture into the pan over low heat. Cook gently for 1–2 minutes, stirring constantly, then taste and adjust seasoning. Pour over the chicken, garnish with a few sautéed mushrooms and serve immediately.

Menu Suggestion

Quick to make, this chicken dish is perfect for last-minute entertaining. Serve with buttered noodles and finely sliced courgettes tossed in butter and lime or lemon juice.

CHICKEN MARENGO

1.25	✳	757 cals

Serves 4

4 chicken portions

50 g (2 oz) flour

100 ml (4 fl oz) olive oil

50 g (2 oz) butter

1 medium onion, skinned and sliced

30 ml (2 tbsp) brandy

salt and freshly ground pepper

450 g (1 lb) tomatoes, skinned, or 397-g (14-oz) can tomatoes, with their juice

1 garlic clove, skinned and crushed

150 ml (¼ pint) chicken stock

100 g (4 oz) button mushrooms

chopped fresh parsley, to garnish

1 Coat the chicken portions in the flour. Heat the oil in a large frying pan and fry the chicken on both sides, until golden brown, about 5–10 minutes. Remove from the frying pan and place, skin side up, in a large saucepan or flameproof casserole together with 25 g (1 oz) butter.

2 Add the onion to the oil in the frying pan and cook for 5 minutes until soft.

3 Sprinkle the chicken joints with the brandy and salt and pepper and turn the joints over.

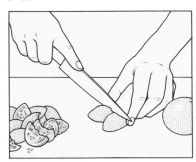

4 Roughly chop the tomatoes. Add them to the chicken with the onion, garlic and stock. Cover and simmer gently for about 1 hour, until the chicken is tender.

5 Ten minutes before serving, melt the remaining butter in a pan and cook the mushrooms for about 5 minutes, until soft. Drain and add to the chicken.

6 When the chicken joints are cooked, remove to a warmed serving dish. If the sauce is too thin, boil briskly to reduce. Spoon the sauce over the chicken and serve garnished with parsley.

Menu Suggestion
A classic French dish with its own sauce, Chicken Marengo should be served with steamed or boiled new potatoes and a green salad to follow.

MIDDLE EASTERN STUFFED CHICKEN

2.40	415 cals

Serves 6

75 g (3 oz) butter

1 small onion, skinned and finely chopped

1–2 garlic cloves, skinned and crushed

50 g (2 oz) blanched almonds, roughly chopped

50 g (2 oz) long grain rice

150 ml (¼ pint) water

salt and freshly ground pepper

50 g (2 oz) stoned prunes, chopped

50 g (2 oz) dried apricots, chopped

2.5 ml (½ tsp) ground cinnamon

1.8 kg (4 lb) chicken

1 Melt one third of the butter in a heavy-based saucepan, add the onion and garlic and fry gently until soft and lightly coloured. Add the almonds and fry until turning colour, then add the rice and stir-fry until the grains begin to swell and burst.

2 Pour the water over the rice (it will bubble furiously), then add salt and pepper to taste. Cover and simmer for 15 minutes or until all the water has been absorbed by the rice.

3 Remove the pan from the heat and stir in 25 g (1 oz) butter with the dried fruit and cinnamon. Taste and adjust the seasoning.

4 Stuff the chicken with the rice mixture, then truss with thread or fine string. Place on a large sheet of foil and brush with the remaining butter. Sprinkle liberally with salt and pepper, then wrap tightly in the foil.

5 Roast in the oven at 200°C (400°F) mark 6 for 1½ hours, then unwrap and roast for a further 30 minutes until the chicken is brown and the juices run clear when the thickest part of the thigh is pierced with a skewer. Serve hot.

Menu Suggestion
Serve with saffron rice.

CHICKEN WITH TARRAGON MAYONNAISE

| 1.50* | £ £ | 645 cals |

* plus 3–4 hours marinating

Serves 6

6 chicken leg joints

2 sticks of celery, washed, trimmed and sliced

200 ml (7 fl oz) medium dry white wine

30 ml (2 tbsp) chopped fresh tarragon or 10 ml (2 tsp) dried

salt and freshly ground pepper

300 ml ($\frac{1}{2}$ pint) mayonnaise (see page 155)

fresh tarragon sprigs or slices of lemon, to garnish

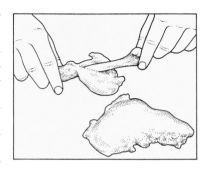

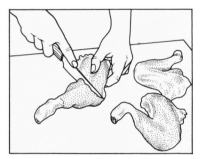

1 Skin the chicken leg joints and divide each one into a leg and thigh portion, making sure to trim away any excess fat.

2 Place the joints in a shallow ovenproof dish into which they will just fit. Scatter the celery over the chicken.

3 To make the marinade, mix the wine, chopped tarragon and seasoning together. Pour the marinade over the chicken.

4 Cover the dish and leave the chicken to marinate in a cool place for 3–4 hours, turning once. Cook, covered, in the oven at 180°C (350°F) mark 4 for about 1$\frac{1}{4}$ hours, or until chicken is tender.

5 Leave the chicken to cool, covered. Strain off the cooking liquid and boil down until only 90 ml (6 tbsp) remains. Cool and set aside. Ease the bones out of the chicken pieces and arrange the joints on a serving plate.

6 Stir the reduced cooking liquid into the mayonnaise and spoon over the chicken just before serving. Garnish with fresh tarragon sprigs or lemon slices.

— VARIATION —

Chicken breasts can be used instead of leg joints and when fresh tarragon is not in season use **slices of fresh lemon** to garnish.

TURKEY SCALOPPINE WITH ALMOND CREAM

| 0.30 | 🍲 £ £ | 418 cals |

Serves 4

4 turkey steaks

30 ml (2 tbsp) lemon juice

salt and freshly ground pepper

30 ml (2 tbsp) vegetable oil

50 g (2 oz) blanched almonds, roughly chopped

30 ml (2 tbsp) brandy

150 ml (5 fl oz) single cream

1 garlic clove, skinned and crushed

snipped fresh chives, to garnish

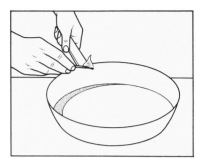

1 Bat out each turkey steak thinly between sheets of damp greaseproof paper or cling film. Divide each steak into three pieces. Place in a shallow dish and sprinkle over the lemon juice. Season and leave aside for 15 minutes to marinate.

2 Heat the oil in a sauté pan, add the almonds and fry until brown. Remove from the pan.

3 Add the turkey pieces and sauté for about 3 minutes on each side or until golden brown. Remove from the pan using a slotted spoon and keep warm.

4 Add the brandy to the pan, heat gently, then remove from the heat and ignite the brandy.

5 When the flames have died down, stir in the single cream, crushed garlic and the browned almonds. Return to the heat and warm through—do not boil. Pour the sauce over the turkey steaks and snip fresh chives over the top. Serve immediately.

Menu Suggestion

Quick and easy to make if you have to entertain unexpected guests, this dish contains a rich combination of turkey, almonds, brandy and cream. A lightly cooked vegetable such as broccoli would provide the perfect crisp contrast, with buttered new potatoes as an additional accompaniment.

—————— VARIATIONS ——————

Try using **chopped skinned hazelnuts** in place of the blanched almonds.

Replace the brandy with the same quantity of **dry sherry**.

Omit the crushed garlic clove and add a little **finely chopped fresh ginger root** to the pan instead.

MARINATED TURKEY WITH ASPARAGUS

| 0.50* | 🔔 🔔 | £ £ | 433 cals |

* plus 3–4 hours marinating

900 g (2 lb) turkey fillets

900 ml (1½ pints) chicken stock

salt and freshly ground pepper

**30 ml (2 tbsp) chopped fresh
    parsley**

50 g (2 oz) walnuts, chopped

1 garlic clove, skinned and crushed

20 ml (4 tsp) ground ginger

**450 ml (¾ pint) Vinaigrette (see
    page 441)**

**450 g (1 lb) fresh asparagus,
    scraped and trimmed**

5 ml (1 tsp) salt

celery leaves to, garnish

1 Put the turkey fillets in a large saucepan and add enough well-seasoned chicken stock to cover. Poach for about 20 minutes until tender. Leave to cool in the liquid.

2 Meanwhile, make the marinade. Stir the parsley, walnuts, crushed garlic and ginger into the French dressing.

3 Tie the asparagus stalks into two neat bundles. Wedge upright in a large deep saucepan, cover tips with foil.

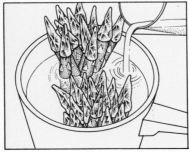

4 Pour in enough boiling water to come three-quarters of the way up the asparagus stalks. Add salt, return to the boil and simmer gently for about 10 minutes.

5 Lift the bundles carefully out of the water, place in a dish and remove the string. While still hot, stir in half the dressing. Leave the asparagus to cool.

6 Cut the turkey into 0.5 cm (¼ inch) wide strips. Marinate in the remaining dressing for 3–4 hours.

7 To serve, arrange the turkey strips and asparagus in a serving dish. Garnish with celery leaves. Serve chilled.

PREPARING AND COOKING ASPARAGUS

Asparagus is a delicate vegetable and needs careful preparation. Rinse each stalk very gently to wash away any dirt. Scrape or shave the length of each stalk, starting just below the tip. Cut off any ends if they are very woody (don't throw them away, they can be used in soup for extra flavour). Trim the stalks to roughly the same length and tie them into neat bundles of six to eight stalks of an even thickness (heads all at one end). Secure each bundle under the tips and near the base.

Cook asparagus with care. Use a special asparagus pan or wedge bundles upright in a deep sauce-pan containing enough boiling salted water to come three-quarters of the way up the stalks. Cover the tips with foil and simmer gently for about 10 minutes, until tender. This way the stalks are poached while the delicate tips are gently steamed.

ITALIAN STUFFED CAPON

4.20* 🍴🍴 £ £ 378–504 cals

* plus 3–4 hours cooling and overnight chilling

Serves 12–16

100 g (4 oz) butter

1 medium onion, skinned and finely chopped

45 ml (3 tbsp) Marsala

50 g (2 oz) green olives

450 g (1 lb) minced pork

100 g (4 oz) fresh white breadcrumbs

50 g (2 oz) pine nuts, roughly chopped

15 ml (1 tbsp) chopped fresh marjoram or 5 ml (1 tsp) dried marjoram

pinch of grated nutmeg

salt and freshly ground pepper

1 egg, beaten

3 kg (6½ lb) capon, boned

450 g (1 lb) piece Italian salami, skinned

sprigs of watercress, to garnish

1 Melt 50 g (2 oz) of the butter in a frying pan and cook the onion for 5 minutes until soft but not brown. Add the Marsala and boil rapidly for 2 minutes. Cool slightly for 5 minutes.

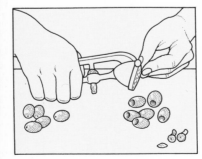

2 Stone the olives, then roughly chop the flesh. Add to the onion with the minced pork, breadcrumbs, pine nuts, marjoram, nutmeg and salt and pepper to taste. Bind with the egg.

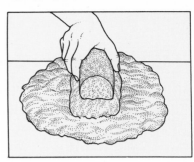

3 Place the capon, skin side down, on a large board or work surface. Push the legs and wings inside and bat out with a rolling pin to evenly distribute the flesh. Spread one half of the stuffing mixture over the centre of the capon, then place the salami on top. Cover with the remaining stuffing mixture.

4 Sew up the capon with fine string or strong thread, reshaping the bird. Weigh the bird.

5 Place the bird in a roasting tin. Sprinkle with salt and pepper, then spread with remaining butter. Roast in the oven at 190°C (375°F) mark 5, basting occasionally, allowing 25 minutes per 450 g (1 lb).

6 Cool completely for 3–4 hours, then refrigerate overnight. Remove string before slicing. Garnish with watercress.

Menu Suggestion

Serve this cold dish for a festive occasion with a rice salad and a tomato and basil salad.

DUCKLING WITH BRANDY AND GREEN PEPPERCORN SAUCE

2.10 £ £ ✳ 715 cals

Serves 6

6 duckling portions

salt

3 large oranges

45 ml (3 tbsp) vegetable oil

1 onion, skinned and chopped

30 ml (2 tbsp) green peppercorns,
   lightly crushed

30 ml (2 tbsp) plain flour

300 ml ($\frac{1}{2}$ pint) chicken stock

freshly ground pepper

30 ml (2 tbsp) brandy

dash of gravy browning

1 Wipe the duckling portions all over and pat dry with absorbent kitchen paper; place on a wire rack over a roasting tin.

2 Prick the skin well with a fork and sprinkle with salt. Roast in the oven at 180°C (350°F) mark 4 for about 1 hour or until the juices run clear, basting occasionally.

3 Meanwhile, make the sauce. Remove the peel from one orange and cut it into fine shreds.

4 Blanch in boiling water for 1 minute. Drain. Squeeze out juice and reserve. Slice the remaining oranges.

5 Heat the oil in a medium saucepan, add the chopped onion and fry gently until golden.

6 Then stir in the lightly crushed peppercorns and flour and cook gently, stirring, for 1–2 minutes.

7 Blend in the stock with the orange juice. Season and bring to the boil, stirring all the time; simmer for about 4 minutes.

8 Separately, ignite the brandy and add to the sauce with a dash of gravy browning and a few orange shreds. Adjust seasoning.

9 Heat the sauce to boiling point and serve separately. Garnish the duck portions with orange slices and remaining shreds.

GREEN PEPPERCORNS
Green peppercorns sold in cans are preserved in brine; fresh green peppercorns are available from the vegetable sections of some large supermarkets. Both are suitable for this recipe.

Green peppercorns are in fact the unripe berries of the *Piper nigrum* tree, from which come the more familiar white and green peppercorns. (White peppercorns are the fully ripened berries, black peppercorns come from the berries which were picked when green then left to dry in the sun.)

The fresh pungent flavour of green peppercorns is totally different from the dried varieties, and their unusual tang adds interest to most grilled meats and poultry; it goes especially well with duckling as it helps offset the natural richness of the meat.

DUCKLING ROULADES WITH PEACHES

`2.00` 🍴 f f ✳* `742 cals`

Serves 6

6 duckling wing portions, about 350 g (12 oz) each

slices of onion and carrot, for flavouring

bay leaf

salt and freshly ground pepper

small onion, skinned and finely chopped

25 g (1 oz) hazelnuts, roughly chopped

2 firm, ripe peaches, skinned and chopped

65 g (2½ oz) butter

30 ml (2 tbsp) brandy

50 g (2 oz) fresh brown breadcrumbs

30 ml (2 tbsp) plain flour

bay leaves and peach slices, to garnish

1 Using a small sharp knife, carefully ease the skin and fat together off each of the six duckling wing portions.

2 Carefully fillet the duckling flesh in one piece away from the breastbone. Place the breast meat between sheets of cling film and bat out thinly with a meat mallet or rolling pin; cover and refrigerate until required. Cut any remaining duckling flesh off the wing bones. Chop finely and set aside until required.

3 To make the stock, place the wing bones in a saucepan together with the slices of onion and carrot, bay leaf and seasoning. Just cover with water and bring to the boil.

4 Simmer, uncovered, for 30–40 minutes or until about 300 ml (½ pint) stock remains. Strain off the stock and reserve.

5 Meanwhile, make the stuffing. Melt 25 g (1 oz) butter and fry the onion, chopped duckling flesh and hazelnuts for 3–4 minutes, turning frequently.

6 Stir in the peaches and fry for a few minutes longer or until the peaches are beginning to soften. Remove from the heat, stir in the brandy, breadcrumbs and seasoning, and cool.

7 Divide the cold stuffing between the duckling fillets and roll them up tightly. Secure each one with two wooden cocktail sticks. Sprinkle the flour over the rolls.

8 Melt the remaining butter in a large shallow flameproof casserole. Add the duckling rolls and brown lightly all over. Sprinkle in any remaining flour and then pour in 300 ml (½ pint) duckling stock. Season.

9 Bring to the boil, cover and bake in the oven at 180°C (350°F) mark 4 for about 40 minutes. Adjust seasoning and skim the juices before serving, garnished with peach slices and bay leaves.

Menu Suggestion
Serve with Avocado with Parma Ham (page 10) and Walnut Meringue Cake (page 284).

Buying duckling
Duckling portions can be found in most supermarkets and many butchers' shops. Alternatively, you could joint three duckling yourself, using the breast portions for this recipe and the legs for a pâté or casserole. Bat out the flesh thinly otherwise it's hard to make neat roulades.

SWEET AND SOUR DUCK JOINTS

1.00	458 cals

Serves 4

4 duck portions
salt and freshly ground pepper
60 ml (4 tbsp) soy sauce
45 ml (3 tbsp) soft brown sugar
45 ml (3 tbsp) honey
45 ml (3 tbsp) wine or cider vinegar
30 ml (2 tbsp) dry sherry
juice of 1 orange
150 ml (¼ pint) water
2.5 ml (½ tsp) ground ginger
few orange slices and watercress
**   sprigs, to garnish**

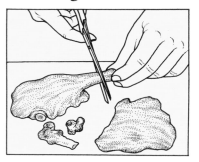

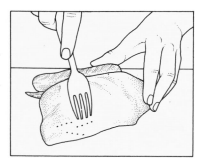

4 Trim the duck joints neatly by cutting off any knuckles or wing joints. Arrange the duck on a warmed serving platter and coat with some of the sauce. Garnish with orange and watercress. Hand remaining sauce separately.

Menu Suggestion
For an unusual Chinese-style meal, serve these duck joints with Chinese egg noodles and a stir-fried dish of finely sliced celery, onion and fresh root ginger with beansprouts, grated carrot and broccoli or cauliflower florets.

1 Prick the duck portions all over with a fork, then sprinkle the skin liberally with salt and freshly ground pepper.

2 Place on a rack in a roasting tin and roast in the oven at 190°C (375°F) mark 5 for 45–60 minutes until the skin is crisp and the juices run clear when the thickest part of each joint is pierced with a skewer.

3 Meanwhile, make the sauce. Mix together all the remaining ingredients in a saucepan and bring to the boil. Simmer, stirring constantly, for about 5 minutes to allow the flavours to blend and the sauce to thicken slightly. Add salt and pepper to taste.

ROAST DUCK WITH GRAPEFRUIT

| 2.00* | 🏠 🏠 £ £ ✳ | 524 cals |

* plus 3–4 hours cooling and overnight chilling

Serves 8

125 g (4 oz) fresh white breadcrumbs
225 g (8 oz) minced pork
225 g (8 oz) minced veal
100 g (4 oz) cooked ham
8 stuffed green olives
1 small grapefruit
2.5 ml (½ tsp) dried sage or 5 ml (1 tsp) chopped fresh sage
salt and freshly ground pepper
1 egg
2 kg (4½ lb) duckling, boned
grapefruit slices, to garnish

1 Place the breadcrumbs, minced pork and veal in a large mixing bowl. Roughly chop the ham and olives and add to the mixture. Grate the rind of the grapefruit and chop the flesh. Add to the mixture with the sage, plenty of seasoning and the egg. Stir well until evenly blended.

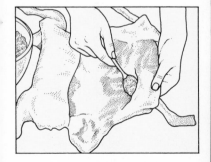

2 Spoon a little stuffing into each of the leg cavities of the duck, pressing in firmly.

3 Mound the remaining stuffing in the centre of the body section. Using a needle and fine string or cotton, sew up the body and wing cavities.

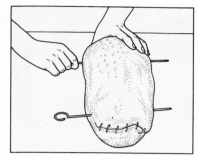

4 Turn the bird over, breast side up, then push it back into shape and secure with skewers.

5 Weigh the duckling and put on a wire rack placed over a roasting tin. Sprinkle with salt. Roast at 180°C (350°F) mark 4, allowing 25 minutes per 450 g (1 lb), basting occasionally. Pierce the duckling leg with a fine skewer; the juices should run clear when the bird is cooked. Leave for 3–4 hours until cool, then refrigerate overnight.

6 To serve, carefully ease out the string and slice. Garnish with the grapefruit slices.

Menu Suggestion
Serve with a selection of salads and chilled dry white wine or Champagne.

DEVILLED DUCKLING SALAD

2.15*	£ £	390 cals

* plus 2–3 hours chilling

Serves 6

two 1.4-kg (3-lb) oven-ready
　ducklings

salt

142 ml (5 fl oz) soured cream

90 ml (6 tbsp) mayonnaise (see
　page 441)

15 ml (1 tbsp) clear honey

15 ml (1 tbsp) mild curry paste

salt and freshly ground pepper

50 g (2 oz) cashew nuts

350 g (12 oz) fresh apricots, stoned
　and thickly sliced

endive leaves, to serve

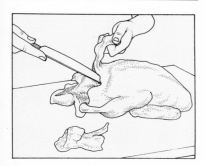

1 Cut away any surplus fat from
the ducklings, then wipe them
with a damp cloth. Pat dry.

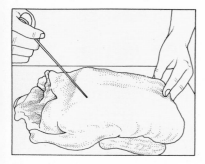

2 Prick the birds all over with
a sharp fork or skewer and
sprinkle generously with salt. Place
the ducklings, breast-side down,
side by side on a wire rack or trivet
in a large roasting tin.

3 Roast in the oven at 180°C
(350°F) mark 4 for about 1¾
hours, or until the birds are really
tender, basting occasionally. Halfway through the cooking time, turn
the birds over so they are standing
breast-side up.

4 Meanwhile, prepare the dressing. In a large bowl, mix
together the soured cream, mayonnaise, honey and curry paste.
Season and stir in the cashew nuts
and apricots.

5 While the ducklings are still
warm, strip off the crisp breast
skin and reserve. Remove the meat
from the bones.

6 Coarsely shred the meat, discarding all the remaining skin,
fat and bones. Fold the shredded
duckling meat into the dressing,
cover and chill well for 2–3 hours
in the refrigerator.

7 Using a pair of kitchen scissors,
cut the reserved duckling skin
into strips and quickly crisp it
further under a hot grill.

8 To serve, spoon the duckling
salad down the centre of a large
flat platter, then arrange the crisp
duck skin over the top. Serve on a
bed of endive leaves.

DUCKLINGS

The Chinese were the first to eat
ducklings – as long ago as 168
BC! The nobles of the Han
dynasty used to breed domestic
white ducks for the table – especially for banquets and royal
feasts, and they also enjoyed wild
duck in stews for more humble
occasions. In those days duck
meat was served completely un-
seasoned, and was recommended
as a sacrificial offering to appease
the gods. Duck soup was also recommended as a remedy for
estranged husband and wives – a
drop of duck soup was supposed
to bring the couple back together
again!

　Henry the Eighth had a passion for duck, and was said to retire to bed at night on a supper of
roast duckling – not the ideal
food for a good night's sleep, but
certainly rich enough to satisfy
his notoriously large appetite!

SPATCHCOCKED GUINEA FOWL WITH PLUM AND GINGER SAUCE

| 1.00 | ⊟ | £ £ | 286 cals |

Serves 4

2 guinea fowl

50 g (2 oz) butter or margarine

1 shallot or 2 spring onions, skinned or trimmed and finely chopped

100 ml (4 fl oz) red wine

30 ml (2 tbsp) thick plum or damson jam

1.25 ml–2.5 ml ($\frac{1}{4}$–$\frac{1}{2}$ tsp) ground ginger, according to taste

salt and freshly ground pepper

30 ml (2 tbsp) crushed juniper berries

watercress sprigs, to garnish

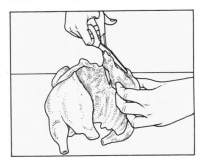

1 Prepare each guinea fowl for grilling. Cut off the wing tips. Remove the backbone by cutting down each side of it with scissors, then easing it out without cutting the bird in half.

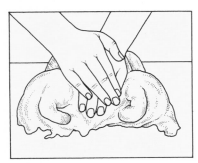

2 Turn the bird over and open it out. Snip the wishbone from the underside so that the bird can lie completely flat.

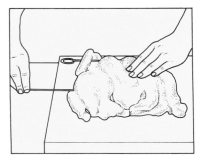

3 Push 2 skewers crossways into each bird, one through both legs and one through both wings.

4 Make the plum sauce. Melt half the fat in a small pan, add the shallot or spring onions and fry gently for 5 minutes until soft. Pour in the wine, then add the jam, ginger and salt and pepper to taste. Heat gently until the jam melts, then bring to the boil and simmer for a few minutes until thickened slightly. Remove from the heat.

5 Melt the remaining fat in a small pan with the juniper berries and salt and pepper to taste. Place the guinea fowl on an oiled grill and brush with half of the juniper berry mixture. Grill for 7 minutes, then turn the guinea fowl over and brush with the remaining mixture. Grill for a further 7 minutes.

6 To make sure the insides of the legs are cooked through, remove the skewers from the legs and fold the legs back so that they are exposed to the heat underneath. Grill for a further few minutes, covering the rest of the birds with foil if they are becoming too well browned.

7 Just before the guinea fowl are ready to serve, pour the cooking juices into the plum sauce and reheat. Taste and adjust seasoning. Remove the remaining skewers from the birds, then arrange them on a serving platter and garnish with watercress. Serve sauce separately in a sauceboat.

Menu Suggestion

Rich and very different, this main course game dish is best served with traditional vegetables such as creamed potatoes, and Brussels sprouts tossed with chestnuts and chopped thyme. A full-bodied red wine is the most suitable drink.

SPATCHCOCKED GUINEA FOWL

Nowadays guinea fowl are bred for the table, so these smallish birds are plumper than the wild guinea fowl. The tender flesh has a delicious flavour rather like gamy chicken, but it must be kept moist during cooking as it has a tendency to dry out.

Guinea fowl are available all year round and make an excellent choice for a special occasion. They can be roasted in the traditional way, or used in almost any recipe for pheasant, partridge or young chicken.

Older, slightly tougher birds may be casseroled successfully, to tenderise them.

BONED STUFFED POUSSINS

2.05 | 695 cals

Serves 6

3 double poussins, about 700 g
  (1½ lb each)

2 large onions, skinned

carrot, peeled

bay leaf

6 black peppercorns

salt

125 g (4 oz) butter or margarine

175 g (6 oz) mixed nuts, chopped

two 227-g (8-oz) packets frozen
  chopped spinach, thawed

175 g (6 oz) fresh white
  breadcrumbs

grated rind and juice of 1 lemon

2 eggs, size 6, beaten

freshly ground pepper

150 ml (¼ pint) dry white wine

15 ml (1 tbsp) cornflour

dash of gravy browning

watercress, to garnish

1 Rinse the poussins under cold running water making sure that any blood is cleaned away, and pat the cavities dry with absorbent kitchen paper.

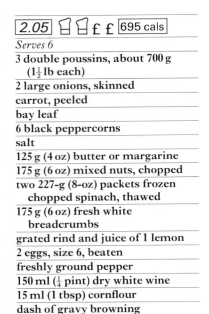

2 Place the poussins breast side down on a chopping board. Using a sharp knife, cut along the backbone.

3 With a small knife, ease flesh and skin away from bone, keeping knife close to backbone and ribcage.

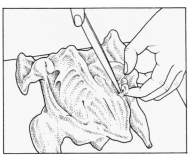

4 On reaching the joints, push the knife into them and ease them open.

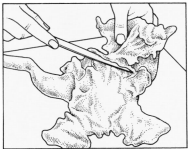

5 Continue to ease the flesh off the bone until the breast-bone is reached. Carefully separate the flesh and carcass.

6 To make the stock, place the bones, one onion, quartered, the carrot, bay leaf, peppercorns and a little salt in a pan. Add 1 litre (1¾ pints) water, bring to the boil, then simmer uncovered for about 30 minutes. Strain and reserve the stock. There should be about 568 ml (1 pint).

7 Meanwhile, make the stuffing. Chop the remaining onion finely. Heat 50 g (2 oz) butter in a pan, fry the onion and nuts for 2–3 minutes, then add the spinach and stir over a high heat. Cool slightly, then add the bread-crumbs, lemon rind and juice, egg to bind, and seasoning.

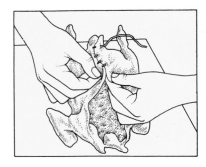

8 Lay the birds flesh side up and divide the stuffing between them. Fold skin over and sew up with cotton.

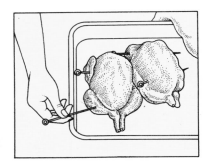

9 Push a skewer through the leg and wing joints and tie the knuckle ends together.

10 Place in a large roasting tin and spread over the remaining butter. Pour over half the stock and the wine. Roast in the oven at 200°C (400°F) mark 6 for 1 hour.

11 Put birds on a large board, remove skewers and string and cut each in half lengthwise. Place on warm serving dish.

12 Mix the cornflour with a little water; add to roasting tin with the stock. Cook for 2 minutes, stirring. Season, add browning and serve.

Menu Suggestion
Serve with Feta Cheese Soufflé (page 32) and Gooseberry Charlotte (page 262).

DEVILLED POUSSINS

| 0.55* | 🗑 | 256 cals |

* plus 1–2 hours chilling

Serves 6

| 15 ml (1 tbsp) mustard powder |
| 15 ml (1 tbsp) paprika |
| 20 ml (4 tsp) turmeric |
| 20 ml (4 tsp) ground cumin |
| 60 ml (4 tbsp) tomato ketchup |
| 15 ml (1 tbsp) lemon juice |
| 75 g (3 oz) butter, melted |
| 3 poussins, each weighing about 700 g (1½ lb) |
| 15 ml (1 tbsp) poppy seeds |

1 Measure the mustard powder, paprika, turmeric and cumin into a small bowl. Add the tomato ketchup and lemon juice. Beat well to form a thick, smooth paste. Slowly pour in the melted butter, stirring all the time.

2 Place the poussins on a chopping board, breast side down. With a small sharp knife cut right along the backbone of each bird through skin and flesh.

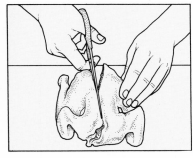

3 With scissors, cut through the backbone to open the birds up. Turn birds over, breast side up.

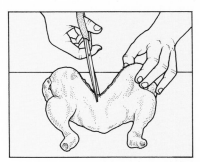

4 Continue cutting along the breast bone which will split the birds into two equal halves.

5 Lie the birds, skin side uppermost, on a large edged baking sheet. Spread the paste evenly over the surface of the birds and sprinkle with the poppy seeds. Cover loosely with cling film and leave in a cool place for at least 1–2 hours.

6 Cook the poussins (uncovered on the baking sheet) in the oven at 220°C (425°F) mark 7 for 15 minutes.

7 Remove from the oven and place under a hot grill until the skin is well browned and crisp.

8 Return to the oven, reduce temperature to 180°C (350°F) mark 4 and cook for a further 20 minutes until the poussins are tender. Serve immediately.

Menu Suggestion

Serve for an informal supper party with jacket baked potatoes topped with butter, crumbled crisp bacon, soured cream and chives. Serve ice-cold lager, beer or cider to drink, and follow with a refreshingly crisp salad of raw vegetables.

QUAIL COOKED WITH JUNIPER

| 0.35 | £ £ | 353 cals |

Serves 4

100 g (4 oz) butter

8 quail

salt

300 ml (½ pint) chicken stock

6 juniper berries, washed

30 ml (2 tbsp) gin or brandy

watercress, to garnish

1 Melt the butter in a large pan and fry the birds until brown on all sides.

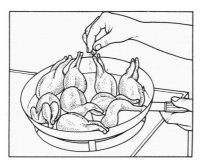

2 Sprinkle with salt. Cover the pan and cook over moderate heat for about 20 minutes. If preferred, the birds can be cooked in the oven at 180°C (350°F) mark 4.

3 When the birds are nearly cooked, add the stock, juniper berries and gin or brandy. Continue to cook for a further 10 minutes until the birds are tender.

4 To serve, put the birds on to a warmed large dish and pour the cooking liquid round them. Serve immediately, garnished with sprigs of watercress.

Menu Suggestion

Richly-flavoured quail needs contrasting plain vegetables such as creamed potatoes, broccoli or cauliflower and French beans.

PHEASANT AU PORTO

| 1.50 | £ £ ✳ | 378 cals |

Serves 6

30 ml (2 tbsp) vegetable oil

3 young pheasants, well wiped

300 ml ($\frac{1}{2}$ pint) chicken stock

120 ml (8 tbsp) port

finely grated rind and juice of
   2 oranges

50 g (2 oz) sultanas

salt and freshly ground pepper

20 ml (4 tsp) cornflour

25 g (1 oz) flaked almonds, toasted,
   to garnish

1   Heat the oil in a large flame-proof casserole. When hot, add the pheasants and brown all over.

2   Pour the stock and port over the birds. Add the orange rind and juice with the sultanas and season well. Bring to the boil. Cover tightly and cook in the oven at 170°C (325°F) mark 3 for 1–1$\frac{1}{2}$ hours.

3   Remove the birds from the casserole, then joint each pheasant into two or three pieces, depending on size, and arrange on a serving dish; keep warm.

4   Boil up juices with cornflour mixed to a smooth paste with a little water, stirring. Adjust seasoning and spoon over pheasant. Garnish with toasted flaked almonds.

GUINEA FOWL WITH GRAPES

1.00	🗋 £ £	449–545 cals

Serves 4

350 g (12 oz) seedless white grapes

30 ml (2 tbsp) brandy

1 garlic clove, skinned and finely sliced

rosemary sprigs

salt and freshly ground pepper

2 prepared guinea fowl

4 streaky bacon rashers, rinded

50 g (2 oz) butter

200 ml (7 fl oz) dry white wine

watercress, to garnish

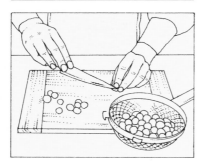

1 Blanch the grapes in boiling water for 2 minutes, then remove skins with a sharp knife.

2 Put the grapes in a bowl. Spoon over the brandy and leave to marinate, turning from time to time.

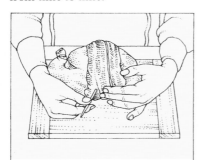

3 Put a few garlic slices, a sprig of rosemary and seasoning inside each bird. Wrap two bacon rashers round each one and secure with wooden cocktail sticks.

4 Place the guinea fowl in a casserole with the butter. Season and sprinkle with a little extra rosemary. Cover and cook in the oven at 220°C (425°F) mark 7 for 15 minutes.

5 Bring the wine to the boil in a pan. Turn the guinea fowl over and pour over the wine. Cook, uncovered, for a further 15 minutes until the birds are tender.

6 Remove the guinea fowl to a warmed serving dish and keep hot. Add the grapes to the sauce and heat through.

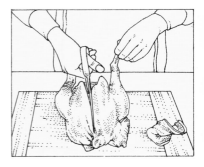

7 Remove the bacon and cut the guinea fowl in half with game scissors. Arrange the bacon over the halves, pour the sauce over and garnish with watercress.

Menu Suggestion
Serve with game chips or roast potatoes, brussels sprouts and redcurrant jelly.

NORMANDY PHEASANT

| 1.30 | 🍱 | £ £ | 588 cals |

Serves 4

1 large pheasant, jointed
salt and freshly ground pepper
25 g (1 oz) plain flour
60 ml (4 tbsp) vegetable oil
2 onions, skinned and sliced
2 celery sticks, trimmed and
    sliced
225 g (8 oz) cooking apples, peeled,
    cored and sliced
50 ml (2 tbsp) brandy or Calvados
150 ml (¼ pint) chicken stock
300 ml (½ pint) dry cider
1 bay leaf
2 eating apples, cored and sliced
    into 1 cm (½ inch) rings
15 g (½ oz) butter
2 egg yolks
150 ml (5 fl oz) single cream
fresh coriander sprigs, to garnish

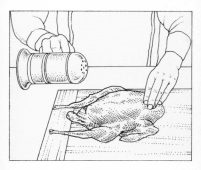

1 Coat the pheasant in seasoned flour. Heat the oil in a flame-proof casserole and fry the pheasant for 5 minutes until browned. Remove from casserole.

2 Fry the onions and celery in the casserole for 5 minutes. Add the apples and pheasant.

3 Heat, ignite and pour the brandy or Calvados over the pheasant. When flames have died add the stock, cider and bay leaf.

4 Bring to the boil, cover and cook in the oven at 180°C (350°F) mark 4 for about 1 hour. Put pheasant on a warmed platter.

5 Meanwhile, fry the apple rings in the butter until golden on both sides. Keep warm.

6 Beat the yolks into the cream and stir into the cooking juices. Warm through then pour over pheasant. Surround with the apple rings and garnish with chopped parsley.

Menu Suggestion
Serve with game chips or roast potatoes, red cabbage casserole and a seasonal green vegetable such as brussels sprouts or fresh broccoli.

MAIN COURSES
Fish and Shellfish

BAKED TROUT WITH LEMON

1.20* f 582 cals

* plus 2 hours standing time
Serves 6

6 medium rainbow trout, gutted
115 g (4½ oz) butter
90 ml (6 tbsp) lemon juice
90 ml (6 tbsp) chopped parsley
salt and freshly ground pepper
25 g (1 oz) almonds, chopped
grated rind of 1 lemon
100 g (4 oz) fresh breadcrumbs
1 egg, beaten
45 ml (3 tbsp) plain flour
300 ml (½ pint) fish stock
2 egg yolks
90 ml (6 tbsp) double cream
lemon slices and fennel tops, to
** garnish**

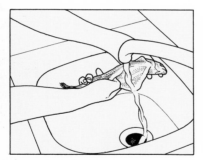

1 Wash each of the trout well under cold running water, ensuring that all blood clots under backbone are removed. Pat dry.

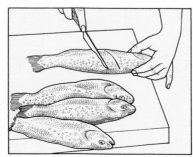

2 Make three or four diagonal slashes about 0.5 cm (¼ inch) deep on either side of each fish. Place the fish, side by side, in a shallow, ovenproof dish.

3 Melt 75 g (3 oz) butter in a small saucepan. Leave to cool, then mix in the lemon juice, 75 ml (5 tbsp) parsley and seasoning and pour over the fish. Cover with cling film and leave in a cool place (not the refrigerator) for 2 hours, turning and basting once.

4 Meanwhile, make the stuffing. Mix together the almonds, grated lemon rind, breadcrumbs, seasoning, remaining parsley and egg to bind.

5 Remove the cling film from the dish and fill the cavities of the fish with the stuffing. Cover the dish with foil and bake in the oven at 180°C (350°F) mark 4 for about 40 minutes.

6 Meanwhile, make the sauce. Melt the remaining 40 g (1½ oz) butter in a small saucepan. Add the flour and cook for 1–2 minutes, stirring. Remove from the heat and gradually stir in the stock. Bring to the boil, reduce the heat and continue to cook, stirring all the time until the sauce thickens.

7 Remove from the heat. Blend the egg yolks with the cream and stir into the sauce. Season with salt and pepper. Remove the foil from the fish and stir the cooking juices into the sauce. Reheat gently without boiling.

8 Pour some of the sauce at side of fish, garnish with lemon slices and fennel tops and serve the remaining sauce separately.

TRIGLIE AL CARTOCCIO
(RED MULLET PARCELS)

0.45	✳*	378 cals

* freeze after step 5

Serves 4

60 ml (4 tbsp) olive oil

60 ml (4 tbsp) dry white vermouth

2 garlic cloves, skinned and
   crushed

salt and freshly ground pepper

4 red mullet, each weighing about
   225 g (8 oz), cleaned

4 sprigs of rosemary

fresh rosemary sprigs and lemon
   slices, to garnish

1 Mix together the oil, vermouth and garlic. Add salt and pepper to taste.

2 Cut four rectangles of foil, each one large enough to enclose one red mullet. Brush with a little of the olive oil mixture.

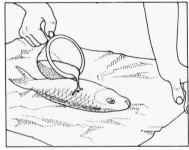

3 Place one fish in the centre of each piece of foil and pour over the remaining olive oil mixture. Place a rosemary sprig on top of each fish.

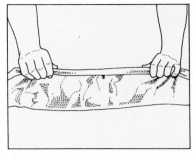

4 Bring the long sides of the foil to meet over the fish and fold over several times to close and seal completely.

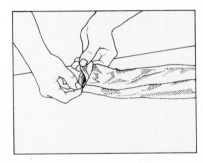

5 Fold over the ends of the foil so that the fish are completely sealed in, as if in a parcel.

6 Put the parcels in a single layer in a baking tin and bake in the oven at 180°C (350°F) mark 4 for 20 minutes or until tender.

7 To serve. Remove the fish from the parcels and place on a warmed serving dish. Pour over the juices that have collected on the foil. Garnish each fish with a fresh rosemary sprig and a slice of lemon and serve immediately.

BOUILLABAISSE

| 0.40 | £ | ✳ | 432 cals |

Serves 6

900 g (2 lb) fillets of mixed white fish and shellfish such as whiting, conger eel, monkfish and prawns

2–3 onions, skinned and sliced

1 stick of celery, washed and chopped

150 ml (¼ pint) olive oil

225 g (8 oz) tomatoes

pared rind of 1 orange

2 garlic cloves, crushed

bay leaf

2.5 ml (½ tsp) dried thyme

few parsley sprigs

salt and freshly ground pepper

pinch of saffron strands

whole prawns, to garnish

1 Wash the fish and pat it dry with absorbent kitchen paper. Remove any skin, then cut fish into fairly large, thick pieces.

2 Lightly fry the sliced onions and chopped celery in the oil in a large, heavy-based saucepan for 5 minutes or until soft. Skin and slice the tomatoes.

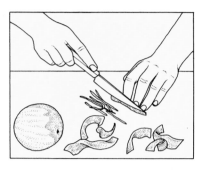

3 Finely shred the orange rind, then stir half into the onion and celery with the garlic, herbs, salt and pepper. Dissolve the saffron in a little hot water.

4 Put the fish in with the vegetables. Add the saffron water and just enough cold water to cover. Bring to the boil and simmer, uncovered, for 8 minutes.

5 Add the prawns and cook for a further 5–8 minutes. Garnish with prawns and remaining orange rind.

USING SAFFRON
Saffron strands are the dried stigma of the autumn flowering crocus. Although they are very expensive to buy (saffron is the most expensive spice in the world), always use them in recipes like this one which calls for saffron water.

HOT FISH TERRINE WITH GRUYÈRE SAUCE

2.15 £ £ 549 cals

Serves 6

75 g (3 oz) butter

1 galic clove, skinned and crushed

60 ml (4 tbsp) plain flour

750 ml (1¼ pints) milk

550 g (1¼ lb) hake fillets, skinned and chopped

150 ml (5 fl oz) double cream

10 ml (2 tsp) anchovy essence

3 eggs

1 egg yolk

salt and freshly ground pepper

30 ml (2 tbsp) chopped parsley

125 g (4 oz) shelled prawns, chopped

125 g (4 oz) Gruyère cheese, grated

watercress sprigs and 6 whole prawns, to garnish

1 Lightly butter and base line a 1.6-litre (2¾-pint) shallow loaf tin or terrine. Make sure not to use too much butter.

2 Melt 40 g (1½ oz) butter in a saucepan. Add garlic. Stir in 45 ml (3 tbsp) flour and cook for 2 minutes. Remove from the heat and gradually stir in 450 ml (¾ pint) milk. Bring to the boil, stirring. Simmer for 2 minutes.

3 In a blender or food processor, purée the sauce, raw chopped fish, cream, anchovy essence, eggs and yolk. Season lightly.

4 Spoon half the fish mixture into the tin. Sprinkle with parsley and half the prawns. Spoon in the rest of fish mixture. Cover tightly with buttered greaseproof paper.

5 Place in a roasting tin with hot water to come halfway up the sides of the terrine. Cook in the oven at 150°C (300°F) mark 2 for about 1¾ hours.

6 Just before the terrine is cooked, make the sauce. Melt 25 g (1 oz) butter in a pan. Stir in 15 ml (1 tbsp) flour and cook for 2 minutes.

7 Remove from the heat and gradually stir in the remaining milk. Bring to the boil, stirring. Simmer for 2 minutes. Off the heat, stir in the grated cheese and remaining prawns. Season to taste.

8 Invert the terrine on to a warm serving dish and tilt slightly to drain off juice. Remove cooking container. Spoon a little sauce over terrine and garnish with watercress and prawns. Serve the rest separately.

STUFFED PAUPIETTES OF SOLE

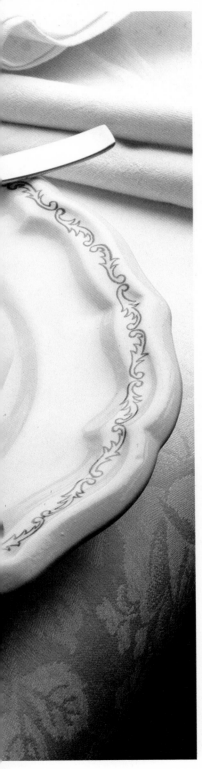

| 1.05 | £ £ | 482 cals |

Serves 6

18 lemon sole quarter-cut fillets
  (two from each side of fish)
75 g (3 oz) butter
½ onion, peeled and chopped
225 g (8 oz) button mushrooms,
  wiped and trimmed
75 g (3 oz) fresh white breadcrumbs
finely grated rind of 1 lemon
15 ml (1 tbsp) chopped fresh
  tarragon leaves
salt and freshly ground pepper
300 ml (½ pint) dry white wine
150 ml (¼ pint) water
30 ml (2 tbsp) plain flour
about 90 ml (6 tbsp) double cream,
  at room temperature
fresh tarragon sprigs, to garnish

1 Skin the fillets of sole. Hold each fillet flesh side uppermost at the tail end (dipping your fingers in a little salt helps grip the slippery skin).

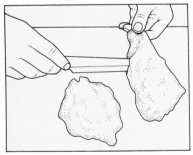

2 Using a sharp knife and a sawing action, work away from you to remove the skin. Wash fish.

3 Make the stuffing. Melt 25 g (1 oz) of the butter in a saucepan. Add the onion and fry gently until lightly coloured.

4 Meanwhile, slice half the mushrooms and chop the remainder very finely. Put the chopped mushrooms in a bowl with the breadcrumbs, lemon rind and tarragon.

5 Add the softened onion and season to taste; stir well until the mixture clings together.

6 Place a sole fillet, skinned side uppermost, on a board. Put a teaspoonful of stuffing on one end of fillet. Roll fish up around it. Secure with a cocktail stick.

7 Stand in an upright position in a well-buttered baking dish. Repeat with remaining sole fillets, placing them side by side in dish.

8 Mix together the wine and water and pour over the fish. Cover loosely with foil and bake in the oven at 190°C (375°F) mark 5 for 15 minutes.

9 Remove the fish from the cooking liquid with a slotted spoon and discard the cocktail sticks. Place the fish in a single layer in a warmed serving dish, cover and keep warm. Strain the liquid into a jug.

10 Melt 25 g (1 oz) butter in a saucepan, sprinkle in the flour and cook for 1–2 minutes, stirring. Remove from the heat then gradually stir in the strained cooking liquid. Bring to the boil, reduce the heat and simmer gently for 5 minutes, stirring until thick.

11 Meanwhile, melt the remaining butter in a frying pan, add the finely sliced mushrooms and fry gently.

12 Whisk the cream into the sauce. Pour a little sauce over each paupiette; then garnish with sliced mushrooms and tarragon sprigs. Pour any remaining sauce into a warmed sauceboat.

MALAYSIAN-STYLE PRAWNS

0.25 f f 394 cals

Serves 6

30 ml (2 tbsp) vegetable oil

1 onion, skinned and very finely chopped

2 garlic cloves, skinned and crushed

2.5-cm (1-inch) piece fresh root ginger, skinned and crushed

2 dried red chillis, finely chopped

15 ml (1 tbsp) ground coriander

10 ml (2 tsb) ground turmeric

5 ml (1 tsp) salt

700 g (1½ lb) peeled prawns

half a 200-g (7-oz) block creamed coconut, broken into pieces

about 300 ml (½ pint) boiling water

juice of 1 lime or lemon

15–25 g (½–1 oz) coconut shreds or shredded coconut (optional)

lime or lemon slices, whole prawns (optional) and fresh coriander sprigs, to garnish

1 Heat the oil in a wok or large frying pan, add the onion, garlic and ginger and fry gently for 5 minutes. Sprinkle in the chillis, spices and salt and stir-fry for 2–3 minutes more.

2 Add the prawns to the pan and stir-fry for 5 minutes until heated through and evenly coated in the spice mixture.

3 Crumble in the coconut, then gradually add the water and bring to the boil, stirring all the time (add just enough water to make a thick gravy that coats the prawns). Simmer for 5 minutes, stirring frequently. Taste and add salt, if necessary.

4 Transfer to a warmed serving dish and squeeze the juice from the lime evenly over the top. Sprinkle with the coconut shreds, if used, then garnish with lime or lemon slices, whole prawns, if used, and coriander. Serve immediately.

PRAWNS

Frozen peeled prawns can be used for this dish, but fresh prawns in their shells are usually larger, more succulent and flavoursome – even if they are fiddly and take a long time to prepare!

To cut down on cost, you can buy less prawns than specified in the recipe and make up the weight with button mushrooms. Wipe them and slice them neatly into 'T' shapes, then quickly toss them in a little butter and lemon juice. Drain them thoroughly with a slotted spoon, then add them at the end of step 2 and stir to combine with the prawns, just before you crumble in the coconut.

SMOKED HADDOCK WITH CREAM AND PERNOD

| 0.40 | £ £ | 382 cals |

Serves 4

4 smoked haddock fillets, about
    700 g (1½ lb) total weight

300 ml (½ pint) milk

few slices of onion

2 bay leaves

few black peppercorns

2.5 ml (½ tsp) crushed fennel seeds

150 ml (5 fl oz) double cream

15 g (½ oz) butter

60 ml (4 tbsp) Pernod

salt and freshly ground pepper

fennel sprigs, to garnish

1 Put the smoked haddock fillets in a large flameproof casserole. Pour in the milk and add the onion slices, bay leaves, peppercorns and fennel seeds. Pour in a little water if the liquid does not completely cover the smoked haddock.

2 Bring slowly to boiling point, then lower the heat, cover and simmer gently for 15 minutes or until the fish flakes easily when tested with a fork.

3 Remove the fish fillets from the cooking liquid and then flake into chunky pieces. Discard all skin and any bones.

4 Strain the cooking liquid and return to the rinsed-out pan. Boil to reduce slightly, then add the cream, butter and Pernod and boil again until the sauce thickens.

5 Return the fish to the liquid and heat through. Add salt and pepper to taste (taking care not to add too much salt as the fish is salty), then transfer to a warmed serving dish. Garnish with fennel sprigs and serve immediately.

Menu Suggestion

A rich and filling dinner party main course, best served with a plain accompaniment such as boiled rice or duchesse potatoes. If liked, the quantities may be halved and the dish served as a first course, with hot French bread.

SMOKED HADDOCK WITH CREAM AND PERNOD

As a starter this dish is most unusual, with its subtle flavouring of fennel and aniseed. Serve it for a special dinner party when you want to surprise your guests with something just that little bit different, but be sure to serve something quite plain as the main course.

The choice of smoked haddock at the fishmonger can sometimes be confusing. The bright yellow fish sold as 'golden cutlets' is in fact smoked cod. Thicker than smoked haddock, it is an excellent fish for dishes like this one where the fish needs to be flaked into chunky pieces.

Monkfish and Mussel Brochettes

| 0.40 | £ £ | 365 cals |

Serves 6

900 g (2 lb) monkfish, skinned and
  boned

36 mussels, cooked

18 rashers streaky bacon, rinded
  and halved

50 g (2 oz) butter, melted

60 ml (4 tbsp) chopped parsley

finely grated rind and juice of
  1 lime or lemon

4 galic cloves, skinned and crushed

salt and freshly ground pepper

shredded lettuce, bay leaves, and
  lime or lemon wedges, to
  garnish

1 Cut the fish into 42 cubes.
Using a sharp knife, shell the
mussels. Reserve the mussels and
discard the shells.

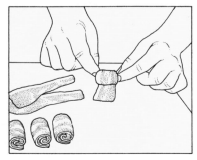

2 Roll the bacon rashers up
neatly. Thread the cubed fish,
mussels and bacon alternately on
to six oiled kebab skewers.

3 Mix together the melted butter,
parsley, lime rind and juice,
garlic and salt and pepper to taste.
(Take care when adding salt as
both the mussels and the bacon are
naturally salty.)

4 Place the brochettes on an oiled
grill or barbecue rack. Brush
with the butter mixture, then grill
under a moderate grill for 15
minutes. Turn the brochettes
frequently during cooking and
brush with the butter mixture
with each turn.

5 Arrange the hot brochettes on
a serving platter lined with
shredded lettuce. Garnish with
bay leaves and lime wedges and
serve at once with saffron rice, if
liked.

PREPARING AND COOKING FRESH MUSSELS

When buying fresh mussels from
the fishmonger, buy a good dozen
more than you need to allow for
those that are open. As soon as
you get the mussels home, put
them in a deep bowl of cold water
and leave to soak for about 1
hour, changing the water several
times. If any of the mussels are
still open after this time, throw
them away. Scrub the closed
mussels clean with a stiff brush,
scraping off any encrustations
with a knife. Put them in a large
pan with about 150 ml ($\frac{1}{4}$ pint)
dry white wine or wine and water,
garlic, herbs and seasoning to
taste. Bring to the boil, then cover
and simmer for 5–7 minutes until the shells open; discard any
that do not.

CREAMED SEAFOOD VOL-AU-VENTS

0.55* ✳* 684 cals

* plus cooling and overnight chilling
of filling; freeze filling at the end of
step 5

Serves 4

450 g (1 lb) monkfish or haddock
  fillets

1 bay leaf

few black peppercorns

few parsley sprigs

1 slice of onion

300 ml (½ pint) milk

25 g (1 oz) butter or margarine

25 g (1 oz) flour

150 ml (¼ pint) single cream

100 g (4 oz) Gruyère cheese, finely
  grated

1.25 ml (¼ tsp) ground mace or
  grated nutmeg

salt and freshly ground pepper

225 g (8 oz) prawns, defrosted and
  thoroughly dried if frozen

16 medium-sized (6.5 cm/2½ inch)
  frozen vol-au-vent cases

beaten egg, to glaze

1 Put the monkfish or haddock
in a saucepan with the bay leaf,
peppercorns, parsley and onion.
Pour over the milk, then bring to
the boil. Cover tightly, remove
from the heat and leave until cold.

2 Remove the fish from the
cooking liquid and reserve.
Flake the flesh of the fish roughly,
discarding the skin and any bones.
Set aside.

3 Melt the butter or
margarine in a heavy-based
saucepan. Sprinkle in the flour
and cook, stirring, for 1–2
minutes.

4 Remove from the heat and stir
in the strained cooking liquid a
little at a time, whisking
vigorously until smooth. Simmer
gently for 2 minutes, then add the
cream and 75 g (3 oz) of the
Gruyère cheese. Stir over very low
heat until the cheese has melted.

5 Turn the sauce into a bowl
and add the mace or nutmeg
and seasoning to taste. Gently fold
in the flaked white fish and the
prawns. Cover the surface of the
sauce closely with cling film, leave
until cold, then chill overnight.

6 Place the frozen vol-au-vent
cases on a dampened baking
sheet and brush the rims carefully
with beaten egg. Bake in the oven
at 220°C (425°F) mark 7 for about
15 minutes or according to packet
instructions.

7 Meanwhile reheat the filling
gently in a heavy-based
saucepan until hot and bubbling.
Taste and adjust seasoning.

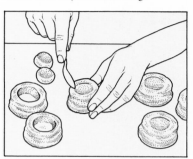

8 Remove the soft centres from
the vol-au-vent cases, spoon in
the filling, then replace the crisp
tops. Serve piping hot.

Menu Suggestion
These vol-au-vents are rather
special. Serve them as an
impressive dinner party main
course with a green vegetable such
as mange-touts, or courgettes
tossed in melted butter and the
finely grated rind and juice of a
lime.

CREAMED SEAFOOD VOL-AU-VENTS

Frozen uncooked vol-au-vent
cases, available at supermarkets
and freezer centres, are an
absolute boon to the busy cook,
because you can quite literally
take them from the packet and
pop them in the oven—and you
get perfectly shaped and
beautifully risen vol-au-vents
every time. Different manu-
facturers sell different sizes, so
you must check carefully before
buying. Cocktail vol-au-vents are
usually about a bite-sized 5 cm
(2 inches) in diameter, medium
size are 6.5 cm (2½ inches), large
are 9 cm (3½ inches), and king
size are 9.5 cm (3¾ inches). The
medium size are the ones most
widely available, and the ones to
use for most main course
dishes—allow four per serving.
Large and king size vol-au-vents,
while a good size for individual
servings, are sometimes difficult
to obtain.

CEVICHE

0.30* £ ✳* 307 cals

24 hours refrigeration; freeze after step 4. Defrost in refrigerator overnight, then continue from step 5
Serves 4

500 g (1 lb) haddock fillets
5 ml (1 tsp) coriander seeds
5 ml (1 tsp) black peppercorns
juice of 6 limes
5 ml (1 tsp) salt
30 ml (2 tbsp) olive oil
bunch of spring onions, washed, trimmed and sliced
4 tomatoes, skinned and chopped
dash of Tabasco, or to taste
30 ml (2 tbsp) chopped fresh coriander
1 avocado, to finish
lime slices and fresh coriander, to garnish

1 Skin the haddock fillets. Put the fillets skin-side down on a board and grip the tail end of the skin with fingers dipped in salt. Using a sharp knife, work away from you with a sawing action.

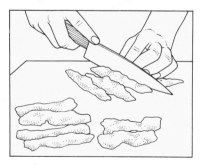

2 Wash the fillets, then pat them dry with absorbent kitchen paper. Cut the fish fillets diagonally into thin, even strips and place in a bowl.

3 Crush the coriander seeds and peppercorns to a fine powder in a mortar and pestle. Mix with the lime juice and salt, then pour over the fish. Cover and chill in the refrigerator for 24 hours, turning the fish occasionally.

4 The next day, heat the oil in a pan, add the spring onions and fry gently for 5 minutes. Add the tomatoes and Tabasco to taste and toss together over brisk heat for 1–2 minutes. Remove from the heat and leave to cool for 20–30 minutes.

5 To serve. Drain the fish from the marinade, discarding the marinade. Combine the fish with the spring onion and tomatoes and the chopped coriander. Taste and adjust seasoning, if necessary.

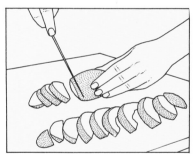

6 Halve the avocado, peel and remove the stone. Slice the flesh crossways. Arrange the slices around the inside of a serving bowl and pile the ceviche in the centre. Garnish with lime slices and coriander leaves. Serve chilled.

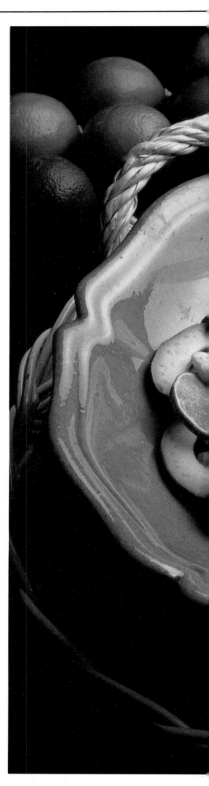

MAIN COURSES
Vegetarian

PIZZA MARGHERITA
(PIZZA WITH TOMATOES, MOZZARELLA AND BASIL)

| 1.30* | £ | ✳* | 635 cals |

* plus 1½–2 hours rising; freeze at end of step 8

Makes two 27.5 cm (11 inch) pizzas, each serving 2 people

45 ml (3 tbsp) lukewarm milk

20 g (¾ oz) fresh yeast

3.75 ml (¾ tsp) sugar

300 g (11 oz) strong white bread flour

salt and freshly ground black pepper

75 ml (5 tbsp) olive oil

1 medium onion, skinned and roughly chopped

1 garlic clove, skinned and crushed

450 g (1 lb) ripe tomatoes, skinned and roughly chopped, or 396 g (14 oz) can tomatoes

30 ml (2 tbsp) red wine or 15 ml (1 tbsp) red wine vinegar

10 ml (2 tsp) dried mixed herbs

225 g (8 oz) Mozzarella cheese, thinly sliced

20 ml (4 tsp) chopped fresh basil or 10 ml (2 tsp) dried

1 First make the pizza dough. Put the milk in a warmed jug and crumble in the yeast with your fingers. Add sugar, stir to dissolve, then stir in 60 ml (4 tbsp) flour.

2 Cover the jug with a clean tea towel; leave in a warm place for 30 minutes or until frothy.

3 Sift the remaining flour and 7.5 ml (1½ tsp) salt into a warmed large bowl. Mix in the yeast with a fork, then add 30 ml (2 tbsp) of the oil and about 90 ml (6 tbsp) warm water to draw the mixture together.

4 Turn the dough on to a floured surface and knead for 10 minutes until it is smooth and elastic. Put the dough in a large floured bowl, cover with a clean cloth and leave in a warm place for 1½–2 hours until doubled in bulk.

5 Meanwhile, prepare the tomato sauce for the topping. Heat 30 ml (2 tbsp) of the remaining oil in a heavy-based saucepan, add the onion and garlic and fry gently for about 5 minutes until soft and lightly coloured. Add the tomatoes and break up with a wooden spoon, then add the wine or wine vinegar, herbs and salt and pepper to taste. Simmer gently for about 30 minutes or until the sauce is thick and reduced.

6 Work the sauce to a purée in a blender or food processor, or alternatively, push through a sieve. Set aside.

7 Turn the risen dough on to a floured surface and roll out. Cut into two 27.5 cm (11 inch) circles, using a large plate as a guide and making the edges slightly thicker than the centres.

8 Put the pizzas on 2 oiled baking sheets. Spread the tomato sauce evenly over them, right to the edges and arrange the cheese slices on top.

9 Sprinkle the pizzas with the basil, the remaining 15 ml (1 tbsp) oil and freshly ground black pepper. Leave to prove in a warm place for about 30 minutes.

10 Bake the pizzas in the oven at 220°C (425°F) mark 7 for 25 minutes, or until the topping is melted and bubbling. Swap the baking sheets over halfway through the cooking time. Serve hot, warm or cold.

Menu Suggestion

Serve with a mixed salad. Crisp lettuce or endive, with sliced fennel, raw peppers and onion rings, are a good combination of salad ingredients. For an informal supper party, serve with a bottle of Chianti Classico.

WHOLEMEAL VEGETABLE PIE

1.00 £ ✳* 767 cals

* plus 1 hour cooling and 15 minutes chilling; * freeze at step 7 before brushing with beaten egg

Serves 4

3 medium leeks, trimmed

275 g (10 oz) swede, peeled

225 g (8 oz) turnip, peeled

4 medium carrots, peeled

100 g (4 oz) butter or margarine

225 g (8 oz) large flat mushrooms, sliced

25 g (1 oz) plain flour

300 ml ($\frac{1}{2}$ pint) vegetable stock

175 g (6 oz) Cheddar cheese, grated

30 ml (2 tbsp) chopped fresh herbs, e.g. parsley, chives, thyme, marjoram or 10 ml (2 tsp) dried

salt and freshly ground pepper

175 g (6 oz) Wholemeal Shortcrust Pastry (page 438)

beaten egg, to glaze

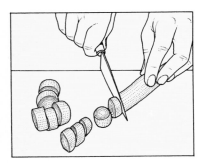

1 Cut the leeks into 2.5 cm (1 inch) lengths, then wash well under cold running water to remove any grit. Cut the swede, turnip and carrots into small bite-sized chunks.

2 Melt the butter in a large saucepan, add the prepared vegetables and fry over moderate heat for about 10 minutes until turning golden brown. Add the mushrooms and cook for a further 2–3 minutes.

3 Sprinkle in the flour and cook gently, stirring, for 1–2 minutes. Gradually blend in the vegetable stock. Bring to the boil, stirring constantly, then simmer for 5–10 minutes or until the vegetables are just tender.

4 Remove the pan from the heat and stir in the cheese, herbs and salt and pepper to taste. Pour into a 1.1 litre (2 pint) pie dish and allow to cool for about 1 hour.

5 Roll out the pastry on a floured surface. Cut out a thin strip long enough to go around the rim of the pie dish. Moisten the rim with water and place the strip of pastry on the rim.

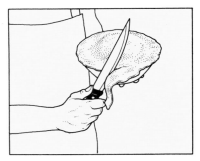

6 Roll out the remaining pastry to cover the pie. Moisten the strip of pastry on the rim of the dish, place the lid on top, trim off any excess pastry and press to seal.

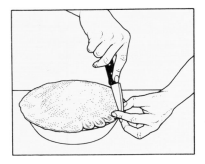

7 Knock up and flute or crimp the edge. Decorate the top with any pastry trimmings and brush with beaten egg. Chill in the refrigerator for 15 minutes.

8 Bake the pie in the oven at 190°C (375°F) mark 5 for 15–20 minutes until lightly browned. Serve hot.

Menu Suggestion

Serve this vegetarian main course with 1 or 2 green vegetables such as French beans, Brussels sprouts or stir-fried spring greens. Jacket-baked potatoes would also go well with the pie, for those who are really hungry.

WHOLEMEAL VEGETABLE PIE

Mushrooms are most nutritious, and a useful vegetable to include in a vegetarian diet because they contain more protein than any other vegetable and are also extremely rich in vitamins B1, B2 and B6, and in the minerals potassium, copper and phosphorus. The Chinese have long known that mushrooms have health-giving properties, and use dried mushrooms extensively in their cooking. For this recipe, choose the flat or 'open' mushrooms as they have a good flavour. The smaller button and cup mushrooms can be used and have the same nutritional value, but they are a little bland for a vegetable pie.

Vegetable Jalousie

`1.30*` ⬠ £ ✳* `818 cals`

* including cooling time for the filling; freeze before baking at end of step 9

Serves 4

3 medium leeks, total weight about 450 g (1 lb), trimmed

4 medium new carrots, peeled

600 g (1¼ lb) fresh broad beans, shelled, or 350 g (12 oz) frozen

salt and freshly ground pepper

25 g (1 oz) butter or margarine

50 g (2 oz) plain flour

300 ml (½ pint) milk

100 g (4 oz) Caerphilly or Wensleydale cheese, grated

45 ml (3 tbsp) grated Parmesan cheese

1.25 ml (¼ tsp) ground mace

10 ml (2 tsp) chopped fresh summer savory or 5 ml (1 tsp) dried

400 g (14 oz) frozen puff pastry, thawed

a little beaten egg, to glaze

1 Slice the leeks thickly, then wash well under cold running water to remove any grit. Scrub the carrots and slice thinly.

2 Parboil the broad beans in boiling salted water for 4 minutes. Remove with a slotted spoon and set aside. Add the carrots to the water and parboil for 2 minutes only. Remove with a slotted spoon and set aside with the carrots. Parboil the leeks for 1 minute and reserve the blanching water.

3 Melt the butter in a clean pan, add the flour and cook gently, stirring, for 1–2 minutes. Remove from the heat and gradually blend in the milk. Bring to the boil, stirring constantly, then simmer for 3 minutes until very thick and smooth. Add the cheese, mace and salt and pepper to taste.

4 Remove the cheese sauce from the heat and fold in the vegetables. Cover the surface of the sauce closely with cling film, then leave until cold.

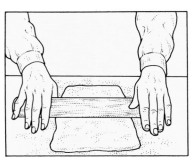

5 Meanwhile, roll out half of the pastry thinly on a lightly floured surface to a 30.5 × 23 cm (12 × 9 inch) rectangle. Place on a wetted baking sheet.

6 Stir the 30 ml (2 tbsp) of the reserved blanching water and the savory into the cold filling, then spread over the pastry on the baking sheet to within about 1 cm (½ inch) of the edges. Brush the edges with water.

7 Roll out the remaining pastry to a slightly larger rectangle than the first. Fold in half lengthways.

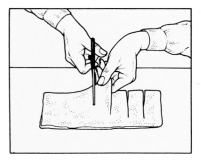

8 With kitchen scissors, cut through the double thickness of the pastry 6 times at 5 cm (2 inch) intervals.

9 Unfold the pastry and place over the top of the filling. Press the edges firmly to seal, then flute or crimp.

10 Brush the pastry with beaten egg, then bake in the oven at 220°C (425°F) mark 7 for 30 minutes until golden brown. Serve hot, cut into slices.

Menu Suggestion

Vegetable Jalousie is rich and filling. Serve with a tomato and onion salad, or a salad of crisp chicory, orange and walnut tossed in a dressing of walnut oil and cider vinegar.

VEGETABLE LASAGNE

| 1.20* | £ ✳* | 635–1008 cals |

* plus time for making tomato and cheese sauces; freeze before baking at end of step 5

Serves 4–6

75 ml (5 tbsp) olive or vegetable oil

1 large onion, skinned and roughly chopped

1–2 garlic cloves, skinned and crushed

1 large green pepper, cored, seeded and chopped

1 large red pepper, cored, seeded and chopped

450 g (1 lb) courgettes, trimmed and sliced

40 g (1½ oz) butter or margarine

450 g (1 lb) mushrooms, wiped and sliced

600 ml (1 pint) Tomato Sauce (page 440)

salt and freshly ground pepper

1.25 ml (¼ tsp) freshly grated nutmeg

600 ml (1 pint) Coating Cheese Sauce (page 440)

225 g (8 oz) lasagne (see box)

50 g (2 oz) Parmesan cheese, freshly grated

1 Heat 30 ml (2 tbsp) oil in a heavy-based frying pan. Add the onion, garlic and peppers and fry gently for about 10 minutes until they are softened.

2 Add the courgette slices in batches and fry for about 5 minutes until lightly coloured, turning them frequently and adding more oil as necessary. Remove the vegetables from the pan with a slotted spoon and set aside on a plate.

3 Melt the butter in the pan, then add the mushrooms in batches and fry over brisk heat until lightly coloured. Remove each batch with a slotted spoon and mix with the other vegetables. Pour over any pan juices, then add salt and pepper to taste.

4 Mix together the vegetables and tomato sauce. Add the nutmeg to the cheese sauce. Spoon one-third of the tomato sauce mixture over the bottom of a large baking dish. Cover with one-third of the cheese sauce, then arrange half of the pasta on top.

5 Repeat the layers of tomato, cheese sauce and pasta, then top with the remaining tomato sauce followed by the remaining cheese sauce.

6 Sprinkle the Parmesan cheese evenly over the surface of the lasagne, then bake in the oven at 180°C (350°F) mark 4 for 45 minutes until golden and bubbling. Serve hot, straight from the dish.

Menu Suggestion

Vegetable Lasagne makes a very substantial dish for vegetarians and meat eaters alike. Serve with a simple green salad tossed in a sharp vinaigrette dressing. If you are entertaining friends, a full-bodied red wine such as an Italian Valpolicella or Chianti would hold its own against the strong flavour of the lasagne.

VEGETABLE LASAGNE

Look for the boxes of Italian lasagne with the label 'no pre-cooking required', which are available at most large super-markets. This type of lasagne will save you both time and energy, because it can be layered in the dish straight from the packet. Ordinary lasagne has to be boiled, then drained before using, and it invariably sticks and tears during this process. When using lasagne straight from the packet, always be sure to use plenty of sauce between the layers, as in this recipe, or the finished dish may be dry—this is important if you intend freezing the dish before baking.

STUFFED AUBERGINES

1.30	£	524 cals

Serves 4

2 medium aubergines

salt and freshly ground pepper

75 ml (5 tbsp) olive oil

1 medium onion, skinned and finely chopped

1–2 garlic cloves, skinned and crushed

1 red or green pepper, cored, seeded and finely diced

175 g (6 oz) button mushrooms, wiped and finely chopped

4 ripe tomatoes, skinned and finely chopped

15 ml (1 tbsp) tomato purée

100 g (4 oz) long grain rice

50 g (2 oz) chopped mixed nuts

30 ml (2 tbsp) chopped fresh parsley

100 g (4 oz) Cheddar cheese, grated

75 g (3 oz) fresh wholemeal breadcrumbs

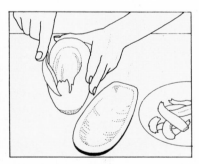

1 Slice the aubergines in half lengthways. Scoop out and reserve the flesh, leaving a narrow margin inside the skin so that the aubergines will hold their shape.

2 Sprinkle the insides of the aubergine shells with salt and stand upside down to drain for 30 minutes.

3 Dice the scooped-out aubergine flesh, then place in a colander, sprinkling each layer with salt. Cover with a plate, place heavy weights on top and leave to dégorge for 30 minutes.

4 Meanwhile, heat 60 ml (4 tbsp) of the oil in a heavy-based saucepan. Add the onion and garlic; fry gently for 5 minutes until soft. Add the diced pepper to the pan and fry gently for 5 minutes.

5 Rinse the diced aubergine under cold running water, then pat dry with absorbent kitchen paper. Add to the pan with the mushrooms, tomatoes and tomato purée. Simmer for about 5 minutes, then add the rice, nuts, parsley and salt and pepper.

6 Rinse the aubergine cases and pat dry with absorbent kitchen paper. Brush a baking dish with the remaining oil, then stand the aubergine cases in the dish. Fill with the stuffing mixture.

7 Mix the grated cheese and breadcrumbs together, then sprinkle evenly over the top of the aubergines. Bake uncovered in the oven at 180°C (350°F) mark 4 for 45 minutes. Serve hot.

Menu Suggestion
Aubergines stuffed with rice and vegetables make a most nutritious main course dish for an informal party. Serve with extra boiled rice, and Quick Tomato Sauce (page 440).

VEGETABLE KEBABS WITH TOFU SAUCE

| 0.40 | £ | 482 cals |

Serves 2

297 g (10½ oz) carton silken tofu
30 ml (2 tbsp) olive or vegetable oil
20 ml (4 tsp) soy sauce
about 30 ml (2 tbsp) lemon juice
1–2 garlic cloves, skinned and
   crushed
15 ml (1 tbsp) sesame oil (optional)
salt and freshly ground pepper
4 small courgettes
6 pieces of baby sweetcorn,
   halved crossways
16 button mushrooms, wiped
12 cherry tomatoes, or 3 medium
   tomatoes, quartered
12 bay leaves
30 ml (2 tbsp) sesame seeds

1 First prepare the tofu sauce.
Put the tofu in a blender or
food processor with half of the oil
and soy sauce, the lemon juice,
garlic and sesame oil (if using).
Work until the ingredients are
evenly combined, then add salt
and pepper to taste and more
lemon juice, if liked. Pour into a
jug and chill in the refrigerator
while making the kebabs.

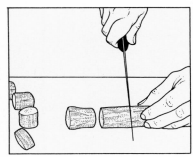

2 Trim the ends off the
courgettes, then cut each
courgette into 3 chunky pieces.
Blanch in boiling salted water for
1 minute only, then drain.

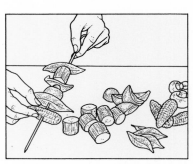

3 Thread the vegetables and bay
leaves on to 4 oiled kebab
skewers, alternating the different
ingredients as much as possible.

4 Place the kebabs on the rack
of the grill pan. Mix the
remaining oil and soy sauce with
the sesame seeds. Brush over the
kebabs. Cook under a preheated
grill for about 10 minutes, turning
frequently and brushing with
more of the oil and soy sauce
mixture.

5 Serve the vegetable kebabs
hot, with the chilled tofu sauce
handed separately in a jug or
sauceboat.

Menu Suggestion
For a nutritious main course,
arrange these tasty kebabs on a
bed of brown rice. Serve a crisp
mixed salad separately. On their
own, the kebabs also make a good
starter for a vegetarian meal, in
which case they will serve 4
people.

**VEGETABLE KEBABS
WITH TOFU SAUCE**
Silken tofu is available from
chilling cabinets in health food
shops. It is a kind of bean curd
made from soya beans, used
extensively in oriental cooking
for its nutritive value. Weight
for weight it contains as much
protein as meat, yet it is very
low in fat, and much cheaper.

CHEESE AND NUT ROAST WITH HOT TOMATO SAUCE

| 1.10 | £ | 414–621 cals |

Serves 4–6

40 g (1½ oz) butter or margarine

1 medium onion, skinned and finely chopped

125 g (4 oz) Sage Derby cheese, or Cheddar cheese plus 5 ml (1 tsp) rubbed sage (optional)

50 g (2 oz) hazelnuts, finely chopped

50 g (2 oz) Brazil nuts, finely chopped

125 g (4 oz) unsalted peanuts, finely chopped

125 g (4 oz) fresh brown breadcrumbs

2 eggs

salt and freshly ground pepper

600 ml (1 pint) Tomato Sauce (page 440)

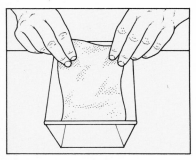

1 Using 15 g (½ oz) of the butter, grease and base-line a 900 ml (1½ pint) loaf tin.

2 Melt the remaining butter in a saucepan, add the onion and fry gently for about 5 minutes or until soft and just beginning to brown. Transfer to a bowl.

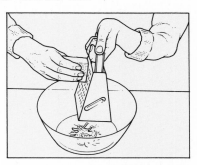

3 Grate the cheese finely into the bowl. Stir to mix with the onion, adding the sage if needed. Add the nuts, breadcrumbs and eggs and mix well again. Season to taste with salt and pepper.

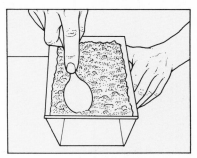

4 Press the nut mixture evenly into the prepared tin. Bake in the oven at 180°C (350°F) mark 4 for about 45 minutes, or until golden brown.

5 Leave the nut roast to cool in the tin for 2–3 minutes, then turn out on to a warmed serving dish. Cut into slices and serve hot with the tomato sauce.

Menu Suggestion
Serve this vegetarian nut roast as an alternative to roast meat or poultry.

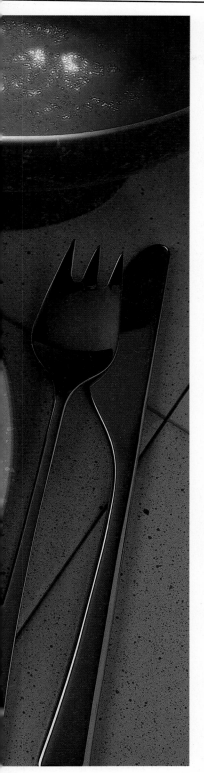

SPINACH ROULADE

| 1.00 | 🍴 | 352 cals |

Serves 3–4

900 g (2 lb) spinach, trimmed, or 450 g (1 lb) packet frozen spinach

4 eggs, size 2, separated

pinch of freshly grated nutmeg

salt and freshly ground pepper

25 g (1 oz) butter or margarine

1 medium onion, skinned and finely chopped

100 g (4 oz) curd cheese

50 g (2 oz) Gruyère cheese, grated

30 ml (2 tbsp) soured cream

Tomato Sauce, to serve (page 440)

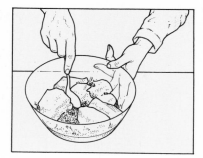

4 Whisk the egg whites until they form stiff peaks, then fold into the spinach mixture with a large metal spoon until they are evenly incorporated.

7 Turn the roulade out on to greaseproof paper, peel off the lining paper and spread the roulade immediately and quickly with the cheese mixture.

1 Grease a 35.5 × 25.5 cm (14 × 10 inch) Swiss roll tin and line with non-stick baking parchment. Set aside.

2 Wash the fresh spinach in several changes of cold water. Place in a saucepan with only the water that clings to the leaves. Cook gently, covered, for about 5 minutes until wilted or until thawed, about 7–10 minutes, if using frozen spinach.

3 Drain the spinach well and chop finely. Turn into a bowl and allow to cool slightly for about 5 minutes, then beat in the egg yolks, nutmeg and salt and pepper to taste.

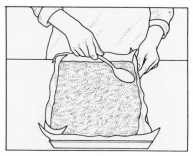

5 Spread the mixture in the prepared tin. Bake in the oven at 200°C (400°F) mark 6 for 15–20 minutes, until firm.

6 Meanwhile, prepare the filling. Melt the butter in a saucepan. Add the onion and fry gently for about 5 minutes until soft and lightly coloured. Remove from the heat and stir in the cheeses, soured cream and salt and pepper to taste.

8 Roll the roulade up by gently lifting the greaseproof paper. Serve hot, cut into thick slices, with the tomato sauce.

Menu Suggestion
Serve for a weekend lunch dish with new potatoes tossed in butter, or jacket-baked potatoes topped with soured cream and snipped chives.

SPINACH ROULADE

The curd cheese used in the filling of this roulade is a medium fat soft cheese made from semi-skimmed milk. It is naturally soured, without the addition of rennet. It has a good, firm texture, ideal for a filling such as this roulade which has to keep its shape when rolled up. Cream cheese or full fat soft cheese has a similar texture and could be used instead but it is much fattier so best avoided. Many super-markets and delicatessens now sell continental-type soft cheeses in small tubs or cartons. Called 'quark', 'fromage frais' and 'fromage blanc', these are low in fat and excellent.

Vegetables
and Salads

GRUYÈRE POTATOES

| 2.35* | £ | ✳ | 303 cals |

Serves 6

900 g (2 lb) potatoes

25 g (1 oz) butter

125 g (4 oz) Gruyére cheese, grated

freshly grated nutmeg

salt and freshly ground pepper

568 ml (1 pint) milk

1 Peel the potatoes, then slice thinly. (Do not soak them in cold water.)

2 Use a little of the butter to lightly grease a 1.4 litre (2½ pint) shallow ovenproof dish.

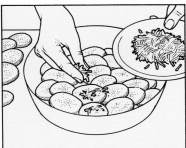

3 Layer the potatoes and most of the cheese in the dish. Add a generous grating of nutmeg, and seasoning to taste.

4 Top with cheese and then pour over the milk, which should just cover the potatoes.

5 Dot the surface with the remaining butter. Cover with foil and bake in the oven at 180°C (350°F) mark 4 for about 1½ hours or until the potatoes are quite tender and most of the milk has been absorbed. Cool, cover with clean foil and chill in the refrigerator until required.

6 Uncover and bake in the oven at 180°C (350°F) mark 4 for 45 minutes until the top is golden brown. Serve hot.

Menu Suggestion

Gruyère potatoes are a special occasion dish. Serve them for a dinner party with a main course of roast meat or a casserole, which can be cooked in the oven at the same time.

GRUYÈRE POTATOES

Gruyère potatoes are a variation of the famous French potato dish called *gratin dauphinois*, in which the potatoes are cooked in cream, rather than milk as suggested here. For a special occasion, you can use cream, or a combination of cream and milk, which will be less rich —and less expensive. Some French cooks add finely chopped onion and crushed garlic to this dish, which give it a good flavour.

Cheddar cheese can be used for an everyday occasion, but it does not give such a good melt-in-the-mouth texture as Gruyère. When preparing the potatoes for baked dishes such as this one, it is very important to slice them as thinly as possible.

GREEK-STYLE NEW POTATOES

0.45	🍳 f	280 cals

Serves 4

1 kg (2 lb) small new potatoes, preferably Cyprus
250 ml (8 fl oz) vegetable oil
125 ml (4 fl oz) white or red wine (see box)
60 ml (4 tbsp) chopped fresh coriander, mint or parsley
salt and freshly ground pepper

1 Scrub the potatoes clean, leaving them whole. Pat the potatoes thoroughly dry with a clean tea towel.

2 With a meat mallet, hit each potato once or twice so that the flesh breaks slightly. Heat the oil in a heavy-based deep frying pan, skillet or saucepan until a stale bread cube turns golden in 2–3 seconds.

3 Add the potatoes to the hot oil and fry over moderate heat, turning them frequently, until golden brown on all sides.

4 Pour off the oil, then pour the wine over the potatoes. Add half of the chopped coriander and a liberal sprinkling of salt and pepper. Shake the pan to combine the ingredients, then cover and simmer for about 15 minutes, until the potatoes are tender.

5 Turn the potatoes into a warmed serving dish and sprinkle with the remaining coriander. Serve immediately.

Menu Suggestion
These tasty potatoes are good with plain roast or grilled lamb; they are also excellent with barbecued meat, especially lamb kebabs.

GREEK-STYLE NEW POTATOES

For an authentic flavour to these potatoes, cook them in Greek retsina wine. Most retsina is white, but you can use either white or red, depending on which is easier to obtain. Retsina, or resinated wine, is something of an acquired taste. It has a strong bouquet and flavour of turpentine, which was discovered almost my mistake.

Originally, some hundreds of years ago, the wine jars or amphorae were sealed with a mixture of resin and plaster, and the flavour of the seal naturally made its way into the wine. The Greeks became so fond of the taste, that they began to add pine resin to the must during fermentation, which resulted in a heady wine with a distinctive flavour.

Tian à la Provençale
(Aubergine Gratin)

| 1.15 | 🍴 | £ | ✳* | 428 cals |

* freeze before baking at step 6

Serves 4

450 g (1 lb) aubergines

salt and freshly ground pepper

25 g (1 oz) butter or margarine

25 g (1 oz) plain flour

300 ml ($\frac{1}{2}$ pint) milk

60 ml (4 tbsp) Parmesan cheese, freshly grated

1.25 ml ($\frac{1}{4}$ tsp) freshly grated nutmeg

about 150 ml ($\frac{1}{4}$ pint) olive or vegetable oil

350 g (12 oz) tomatoes, skinned and sliced

2 garlic cloves, skinned and roughly chopped

2 eggs, beaten

1 Slice the aubergines thinly, then place in a colander, sprinkling each layer with salt. Cover with a plate, place heavy weights on top and leave to dégorge for 30 minutes.

2 Meanwhile, melt the butter in a saucepan, add the flour and cook gently, stirring, for 1–2 minutes. Remove from the heat and gradually blend in the milk. Bring to the boil, stirring constantly, then simmer for 3 minutes until thick and smooth. Add half of the cheese, the nutmeg and salt and pepper to taste, stir well to mix, then remove from the heat.

3 Rinse the aubergine slices under cold running water, then pat dry with absorbent kitchen paper.

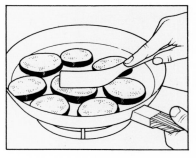

4 Pour enough oil into a heavy-based frying pan to cover the base. Heat until very hot, then add a layer of aubergine slices. Fry over moderate heat until golden brown on both sides, turning once. Remove with a slotted spoon and drain on absorbent kitchen paper. Repeat with more oil and aubergines.

5 Arrange alternate layers of aubergines and tomatoes in an oiled gratin or baking dish. Sprinkle each layer with garlic, a little salt and plenty of pepper.

6 Beat the eggs into the sauce, then pour slowly into the dish. Sprinkle the remaining cheese evenly over the top. Bake in the oven at 200°C (400°F) mark 6 for 20 minutes or until golden brown and bubbling. Serve hot.

Menu Suggestion
This substantial, creamy vegetable dish is excellent served with roast lamb or grilled chops. It also makes a tasty vegetarian dinner with potatoes and a salad.

BAKED FENNEL

1.30	£	112 cals

Serves 6

700 g (1½ lb) Florence fennel

salt and freshly ground pepper

75 g (3 oz) butter

finely grated zest of 1 large thin-skinned lemon and 30 ml (2 tbsp) fresh lemon juice

1 Trim the base and top stems of the fennel, reserving some of the feathery green tops. Quarter each head lengthwise. Blanch in boiling salted water for 5 minutes.

2 Melt the butter in a shallow flameproof casserole. Remove from the heat, and then add the lemon zest together with the lemon juice. Season.

3 Arrange fennel in the casserole in a single layer and turn in the butter. Cover tightly with lid or kitchen foil and bake in the oven at 150°C (300°F) mark 2 for about 1¼ hours. Garnish with snipped fennel tops. Serve hot.

FENNEL
Prized for its unusual aniseed flavour, fennel is called Florence fennel after the Italian city of that name – the Italians are very fond of this vegetable, which grows prolifically all over the Mediterranean. It is the bulb of the vegetable which is used in this recipe, although the leaves of the herb fennel and its seeds are also used in cooking, particularly with fish.

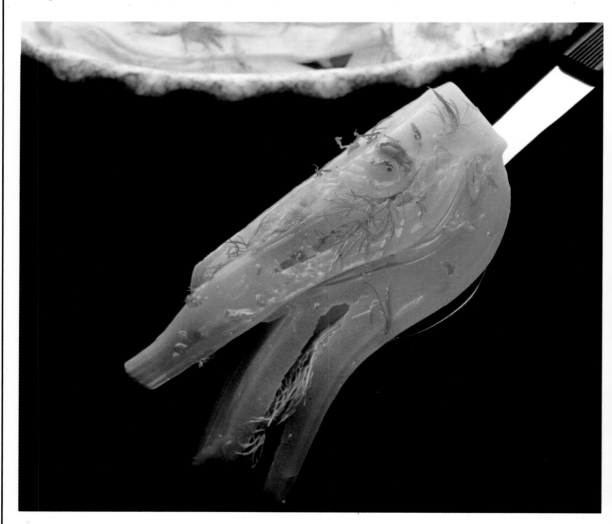

CREAMED BROCCOLI BAKE

1.30	£	220 cals

Serves 6

700 g (1½ lb) broccoli
450 ml (¾ pint) milk
salt and freshly ground pepper
50 g (2 oz) butter or margarine
60 ml (4 tbsp) plain flour
1.25 ml (¼ tsp) grated nutmeg
2 eggs separated
25 g (1 oz) fresh white breadcrumbs

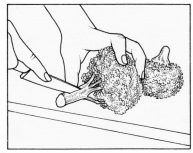

1 Trim and discard any thick broccoli stems; cut up the florets into small pieces, then wash and drain well.

2 Place the broccoli in a medium saucepan with the milk and seasoning and bring to the boil. Cover the pan tightly and simmer gently for 10–15 minutes.

3 Strain off the milk and reserve; finely chop the cooked broccoli. Rinse out and dry the saucepan, then melt the butter and stir in the flour. Cook for 1–2 minutes. Gradually stir in the reserved milk (there should be about 300 ml [½ pint]), season well and bring to the boil, bubble for 2 minutes, stirring.

4 Remove from the heat, beat in the chopped broccoli, nutmeg and egg yolks, and adjust seasoning according to taste.

5 Whisk the egg whites until stiff, and fold into the sauce. Spoon into a well greased 1.4-litre (2½-pint) shallow ovenproof dish.

6 Scatter the breadcrumbs over the top, and bake in the oven at 170°C (325°F) mark 3 for about 50 minutes or until the topping has just set. Serve immediately.

223

CHINESE STIR-FRY

0.20 £ 175 cals

Serves 6

450 g (1 lb) broccoli

350 g (12 oz) carrots

4 large courgettes

salt

30 ml (2 tbsp) sesame seed oil

1 large onion, skinned and finely
chopped

3 garlic cloves, skinned and
crushed

2.5-cm (1-inch) piece of fresh root
ginger, peeled and crushed

225 g (8 oz) beansprouts

45 ml (3 tbsp) soy sauce

30 ml (2 tbsp) clear honey

15 ml (1 tbsp) red wine vinegar

10 ml (2 tsp) tomato purée

30 ml (2 tbsp) vegetable oil

freshly ground pepper

1 Cut the broccoli into bite-sized
florets, discarding the thick
stalks. Then peel the carrots and
cut them into thin matchsticks.
Blanch the broccoli and carrots together in boiling salted water for
2 minutes only. Remove with a
slotted spoon and set aside.

2 Wash and trim the courgettes,
and cut into thin slices. Add to
the pan, bring the water back to
the boil and blanch for 1 minute
only. Drain, reserving 60 ml (4
tbsp) of the water, and set aside.

3 Heat the sesame seed oil in a
wok or large, deep frying pan.
Add the onion, garlic and ginger
and fry gently until soft and lightly
coloured. Add the beansprouts
and stir-fry for 2 minutes only.
Remove with a slotted spoon and
set aside until ready to serve.

4 In a separate jug or bowl, mix
the reserved blanching water
with the soy sauce, honey, vinegar
and tomato purée.

5 Heat the vegetable oil in the
wok, add the blanched
vegetables and stir-fry for 2
minutes or until heated through.

6 Pour in the soy sauce mixture
and add the beansprouts, then
stir-fry for 1–2 minutes until very
hot. Add salt and pepper to taste,
turn into a warmed serving dish
and serve immediately.

COURGETTES WITH MUSHROOMS

| 0.50 | £ | 166 cals |

Serves 6

1.1 kg (2½ lb) courgettes

50 g (2 oz) butter

salt and freshly ground pepper

225 g (8 oz) button mushrooms, wiped

142 ml (5 fl oz) soured cream

fresh basil sprig, to garnish

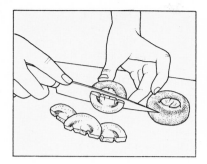

1 Wash the courgettes under cold running water. Then wipe and slice them into 0.5-cm (¼-inch) pieces, discarding the ends.

2 Melt the butter in a medium roasting tin, add the courgettes and turn over in the butter; season well with salt and pepper.

3 Bake the courgette slices in the oven at 200°C (400°F) mark 6 for about 20 minutes.

4 Meanwhile, trim and slice the mushrooms. Stir into the courgettes and return to the oven for a further 10–15 minutes.

5 Stir the soured cream and then mix through the vegetables; bubble up on top of the stove. To serve, adjust seasoning and spoon the vegetables into a serving dish. Garnish with the basil.

─── VARIATION ───

Single cream, with a squeeze of **lemon juice**, can be substituted for the **soured cream**. Stir into the vegetables and heat gently but do not boil.

French beans or **florets of young broccoli** or **cauliflower** can be used instead of the courgettes.

Make sure that the cream does not boil or it might curdle.

CAULIFLOWER AND COURGETTE TARTLETS

| 1.00* | 🥘 🥘 £ | 251 cals |

* plus 2–3 hours chilling time and 2
hours cooling time

Serves 6

75 ml (5 tbsp) dry white wine
30 ml (2 tbsp) vegetable oil
5 ml (1 tsp) chopped fresh tarragon
   or 1.25 ml ($\frac{1}{4}$ tsp) dried
1 garlic clove, skinned and crushed
salt and freshly ground pepper
225-g (8 oz) cauliflower, trimmed
   and cut into small florets
175 g (6 oz) baby courgettes
100 g (4 oz) plain flour
50 g (2 oz) wholemeal flour
75 g (3 oz) butter
15–30 ml (1–2 tbsp) water

1 To make the dressing, in a medium bowl, whisk together the wine, oil, tarragon, crushed garlic and seasoning.

2 Blanch the cauliflower florets in boiling salted water for 1 minute only. Drain well, then, while still hot, stir into the dressing.

3 Slice the courgettes into thin rings and add to the bowl, stirring gently to mix. Leave to cool, then cover with cling film and refrigerate for several hours or overnight.

4 Make pastry. Mix flours together with pinch of salt. Rub in the butter until the mixture resembles fine breadcrumbs; bind to a dough with water.

5 Knead the pastry lightly until just smooth, then roll out and use to line six 7.5-cm (3-inch) individual flan tins.

6 Bake blind (see page 438) in the oven at 200°C (400°F) mark 6 for about 15 miunutes or until just set and tinged with colour. Remove the paper and baking beans and return to the oven for a further 8–10 minutes or until well browned.

7 Cool slightly, ease cases out of tins and leave for 2 hours until completely cool. Store in an airtight container until required.

8 Just before serving, place the pastry cases on individual plates and spoon in the cauliflower and courgette salad.

GREEN BEANS WITH COCONUT

0.15*	£	165 cals

* 8 minutes if using mange-tout

Serves 6

700 g (1½ lb) fresh or frozen green beans or mange tout

salt

1 onion, skinned

50 g (2 oz) butter or margarine

50 g (2 oz) desiccated coconut

freshly ground pepper

45 ml (3 tbsp) chopped fresh parsley

1 Cook the beans in boiling salted water for 10 minutes, or 3 minutes for fresh mange tout (for frozen vegetables, follow packet instructions), until cooked but firm to the bite.

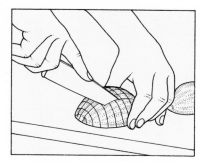

2 Meanwhile, finely chop the onion. Heat the butter in a small frying pan, add the onion and cook gently until softened, stirring occasionally.

3 Increase heat, add coconut and fry for 2–3 minutes until golden. Season and mix in parsley. Drain beans and spoon into a serving dish and sprinkle over coconut mixture.

COCONUT

Desiccated coconut is used in this recipe, but if you can buy a fresh coconut, then so much the better. Simply pierce a hole in its shell and drain off the milk, then crack the shell open with a hammer and dig out the flesh. Grate the flesh finely on a conical or box grater – you will find it far sweeter and juicier than desiccated coconut. Shredded coconut, which comes in large flakes, can also be used if your prefer: it is available at health food shops.

ZUCCHINI ALLA RICOTTA
(COURGETTES STUFFED WITH RICOTTA)

1.00	232 cals

Serves 4

8 even-sized courgettes

salt and freshly ground pepper

30 ml (2 tbsp) olive oil

1 onion, skinned and finely chopped

1 garlic clove, skinned and crushed

175 g (6 oz) Ricotta cheese

20 ml (4 tsp) chopped fresh basil or 10 ml (2 tsp) dried

300 ml (½ pint) Quick Tomato Sauce (see page 440)

45 ml (3 tbsp) dried breadcrumbs

fresh basil sprigs, to garnish

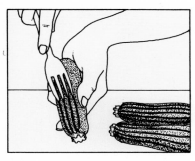

1 Score the courgettes lengthways with the prongs of a fork, then cut them in half lengthways.

2 Scoop out the flesh from the courgette halves with a sharp-edged teaspoon. Leave a thin margin of flesh next to the skin and make sure not to scoop out all the flesh from the bottoms or the skin may break.

3 Blanch the courgette shells in boiling salted water for 10 minutes. Drain, then stand skin side up on absorbent paper.

4 Heat the oil in a frying pan, add the onion, garlic and scooped-out flesh from the courgettes. Fry gently for about 5 minutes until soft and lightly coloured, then turn into a bowl and add the Ricotta, basil and salt and pepper to taste. Stir well.

5 Spoon the Ricotta filling into the drained courgette shells, dividing it equally between them.

6 Pour the tomato sauce into the bottom of a shallow ovenproof dish which is large enough to hold the courgettes in a single layer. Place the filled courgettes in the dish side by side. Sprinkle with the breadcrumbs.

7 Bake in the oven at 200°C (400°F) mark 6 for 20 minutes. Serve hot, garnished with fresh basil sprigs.

FINOCCHI GRATINATI
(FENNEL AU GRATIN)

0.40	234–351 cals

Serves 4–6

4 small bulbs of fennel, trimmed

salt and freshly ground pepper

60 ml (4 tbsp) olive oil

60 ml (4 tbsp) butter

50 g (2 oz) Fontina cheese, grated

45 ml (3 tbsp) freshly grated Parmesan cheese

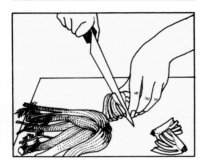

1 Using a sharp knife, carefully cut each bulb of fennel into quarters lengthways.

2 Cook the fennel quarters in a large pan of boiling salted water for 20 minutes until just tender. Drain thoroughly.

3 Heat the oil with the butter in a flameproof gratin dish. Add the fennel and toss to coat in the oil and butter.

4 Turn the fennel quarters cut side up in the dish. Sprinkle with the two cheeses and seasoning.

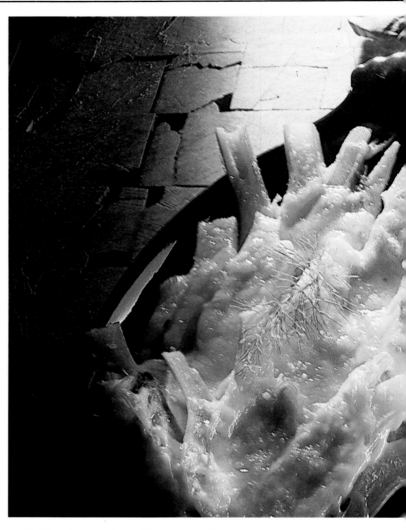

5 Grill under a preheated hot grill for 5 minutes or until the cheeses are melted and bubbling. Serve hot.

Menu Suggestion
Serve as a vegetable accompaniment; especially good with grilled or barbecued fish.

FINOCCHI GRATINATI
The Fontina cheese in this recipe is a hard, mountain cheese with a sweet, nutty flavour. If difficult to obtain, use Gruyère or Emmental instead.

SPINACI ALLA ROMANA
(SPINACH WITH SULTANAS AND PINE NUTS)

0.30	202 cals

Serves 4

25 g (1 oz) sultanas

900 g (2 lb) washed fresh spinach or 450 g (1 lb) frozen spinach

25 g (1 oz) butter

30 ml (2 tbsp) olive oil

1 garlic clove, skinned and crushed

25 g (1 oz) pine nuts

salt and freshly ground pepper

1 Put the sultanas in a bowl, pour in enough hot water to cover and leave to soak for 15 minutes until plump.

2 Place the spinach in a saucepan without any water and cook gently for 5–10 minutes, or until thawed if using frozen spinach.

3 Drain the spinach thoroughly and squeeze out as much moisture as possible. Set aside.

4 Melt the butter with the oil in a saucepan, add the garlic and cook gently for 1 minute. Add the spinach and stir until evenly coated with the butter and oil and completely heated through.

5 Drain the sultanas and stir them into the spinach with the pine nuts and salt and pepper to taste. Heat through, then serve immediately to avoid overcooking the spinach.

Menu Suggestion
Serve as a vegetable accompaniment to any meat or fish dish.

ZUCCHINI IN AGRODOLCE
(COURGETTES IN SWEET-SOUR SAUCE)

0.25	146 cals

Serves 4

450 g (1 lb) small, young courgettes
45 ml (3 tbsp) olive oil
1 small onion, skinned and finely
   chopped
1 garlic clove, skinned and crushed
salt and freshly ground pepper
30 ml (2 tbsp) white wine vinegar
10 ml (2 tsp) sugar

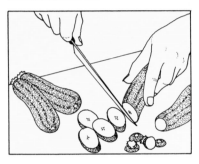

1 Trim the ends off the courgettes and discard, then cut the courgettes into thin diagonal slices.

2 Heat the oil in a large heavy-based frying pan. Add onion and garlic and fry for 5 minutes until soft but not coloured.

3 Add the courgettes and toss to coat in the oil. Sprinkle with salt and pepper to taste. Cover pan and cook gently for 5 minutes until courgettes are just tender.

4 Mix together the vinegar and sugar, then pour over the courgettes. Increase the heat and toss the courgettes in the cooking liquid for 1–2 minutes until shiny and syrupy. Taste and adjust seasoning before serving.

Menu Suggestion
Serve as a vegetable accompaniment to any meat or fish dish.

SAUTÉED CUCUMBER WITH HERBS ▶

| 0.45 | £ | 101–151 cals |

Serves 4–6

1 cucumber

salt

50 g (2 oz) butter or margarine

2 shallots or 1 small onion,
  skinned and finely chopped

15 ml (1 tbsp) fresh chopped
  rosemary or 10 ml (2 tsp) dried

2.5 ml ($\frac{1}{2}$ tsp) sugar

freshly ground pepper

60 ml (4 tbsp) soured cream

fresh rosemary sprigs, to garnish

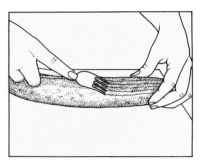

1 Using a sharp fork, run the prongs down the length of the cucumber to score. (This will give an attractive effect.)

2 Using a sharp knife, cut the cucumber into 5-cm (2-inch) lengths, then cut each piece lengthways into quarters.

3 Remove the seeds from the cucumber, then put the cucumber in a colander and sprinkle with the salt. Cover with a plate and leave to drain for 30 minutes, pressing the plate down occasionally to press out the liquid from the cucumber. Rinse and pat dry with absorbent kitchen paper.

4 Melt the butter in a large, heavy-based frying pan. Add the shallots and fry gently for 5 minutes until they are soft and lightly coloured.

5 Add the cucumber pieces to the pan, together with the rosemary, sugar and pepper to taste. Cook for 5 minutes only, stirring frequently to ensure even cooking.

6 Remove the pan from the heat and stir in the soured cream. Taste and adjust seasoning. Garnish with rosemary sprigs and serve immediately.

SAUTÉED COURGETTES WITH CHIVES

| 0.15 | £ | 105 cals |

Serves 4

450 g (1 lb) courgettes
25 g (1 oz) butter
15 ml (1 tbsp) vegetable oil
grated rind and juice of ½ lemon
salt and freshly ground pepper
15 ml (1 tbsp) fresh chives

1 Wash the courgettes and pat dry with absorbent kitchen paper. Top and tail them and thinly slice.

2 Heat the butter and oil in a pan, add the courgettes and cook over medium heat, uncovered, for 5–8 minutes. When tender but still slightly crisp, add the lemon rind and juice and seasoning to taste.

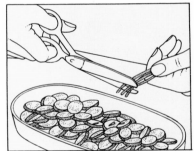

3 Turn into a heated serving dish. Snip fresh chives over the courgettes and serve immediately, while still hot.

CRISP ENDIVE WITH ORANGE AND CROÛTONS

| 0.20 | £ | 138 cals |

Serves 8

1 large head of curly endive
½ bunch of watercress
2 large oranges
2 thick slices of white bread
vegetable oil, for shallow frying
60 ml (4 tbsp) olive oil
60 ml (4 tbsp) white wine vinegar
2.5 ml (½ tsp) caster sugar
salt and freshly ground pepper

1 Remove and discard any coarse or discoloured leaves from the endive. Tear the endive into pieces, wash and dry thoroughly with a clean tea towel. Wash, trim and dry the watercress.

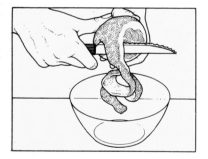

2 With a small serrated knife and working over a bowl to catch the juices, cut away all the skin and pith from the oranges. Reserve the juices.

3 Cut the orange flesh into segments, leaving the membrane behind. Remove any pips with the tip of the knife.

4 Arrange the endive, watercress and orange in a serving bowl. Cut the crusts off the bread and cut the bread into 1 cm (½ inch) cubes. Heat the vegetable oil in a frying pan, add the cubes of bread and fry until crisp and golden. Remove the croûtons with a slotted spoon and drain well on absorbent kitchen paper. Sprinkle with salt.

5 In a jug, whisk the reserved orange juice with the olive oil, vinegar, sugar and salt and pepper to taste. Pour over the salad and add the croûtons just before serving.

Menu Suggestion
This colourful winter salad is good with rich meat dishes, especially duck and game.

CRISP ENDIVE WITH ORANGE AND CROÛTONS

Although native to the Mediterranean, curly endive is now grown in other temperate countries throughout the world, and is available virtually all year round. At its best, curly endive is crisp, pale green and frondy, with a mildly bitter flavour. It does not keep well and quickly goes limp and yellow. Most heads of endive are very large, but some greengrocers will split them in halves or quarters. Take care not to confuse curly endive with the torpedo-shaped chicory. In France, chicory is called endive, whereas curly endive is called *chicorée frisée* or 'frizzy chicory'.

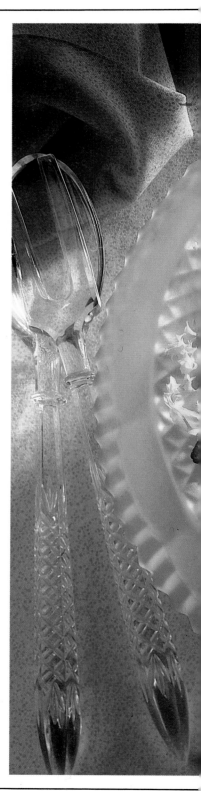

TOMATO AND OKRA VINAIGRETTE

| 0.15 | £ | 191 cals |

Serves 8

450 g (1 lb) okra
150 ml (¼ pint) vegetable oil
30 ml (2 tbsp) lemon juice
5 ml (1 tsp) tomato purée
pinch of caster sugar
salt and freshly ground pepper
450 g (1 lb) tomatoes, skinned

1 Trim off the tops and tails of the okra. Cook in boiling salted water for about 4 minutes or until just tender. Drain well and place in a bowl.

2 In a jug, whisk together the oil, lemon juice, tomato purée, sugar, and salt and pepper to taste. Pour over the warm okra and fold gently to mix.

3 Slice the tomatoes thinly. Arrange in a serving bowl with the okra and vinaigrette. Cover and chill in the refrigerator for at least 30 minutes before serving.

Menu Suggestion
Serve for an unusual and attractive first course, with hot garlic or herb bread. Or serve as a side salad —okra goes particularly well with lamb.

RADICCHIO AND ALFALFA SALAD

| 0.15 | £ | 141–212 cals |

Serves 4–6

2 heads of radicchio

50–75 g (2–3 oz) alfalfa sprouts

90 ml (6 tbsp) olive or vegetable oil

30 ml (2 tbsp) white wine vinegar

15 ml (1 tbsp) single cream (optional)

1 small garlic clove, skinned and crushed

1.25 ml ($\frac{1}{4}$ tsp) granulated sugar

salt and freshly ground pepper

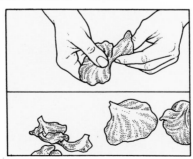

1 Tear the radicchio into bite-sized pieces. Wash, drain and pat dry on absorbent kitchen paper. Wash and dry the alfalfa sprouts.

2 Mix the alfalfa and radicchio together in a serving bowl. In a jug, whisk together the remaining ingredients, with salt and pepper to taste. Just before serving, pour over the radicchio and alfalfa and toss together.

Menu Suggestion

Serve as a side salad whenever a colourful and crunchy accompaniment is required.

TOMATO, AVOCADO AND PASTA SALAD

| 0.20 | £ | 626 cals |

Serves 4

175 g (6 oz) small wholemeal pasta
    shells
salt and freshly ground pepper
105 ml (7 tbsp) olive oil
45 ml (3 tbsp) lemon juice
5 ml (1 tsp) wholegrain mustard
30 ml (2 tbsp) chopped fresh basil
2 ripe avocados
2 red onions
16 black olives
225 g (8 oz) ripe cherry tomatoes,
    if available, or small salad
    tomatoes
fresh basil leaves, to garnish

1 Cook the pasta in plenty of boiling salted water for about 5 minutes until just tender. Drain in a colander and rinse under cold running water to stop the pasta cooking further. Cool for 20 minutes.

2 Meanwhile, whisk the oil in a bowl with the lemon juice, mustard, chopped basil and salt and pepper to taste.

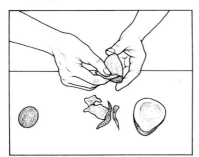

3 Halve and stone the avocados then peel off the skins. Chop the avocado flesh into large pieces and fold gently into the dressing.

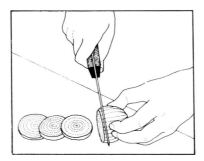

4 Slice the onions thinly into rings. Stone the olives. Halve the tomatoes and mix them with the onion rings, the olives and the cold pasta shells.

5 Spoon the pasta and tomato on to 4 individual serving plates. Spoon over the avocado and dressing and garnish with fresh basil leaves. Serve immediately.

Menu Suggestion
This pretty salad makes a delicious summer starter. Serve with chunky slices of fresh wholemeal bread and butter, with a chilled dry white wine to drink. Alternatively, serve the salad as an accompaniment to barbecued or grilled meat.

RAW SPINACH AND MUSHROOM SALAD

0.50	£	402–604 cals

Serves 2–3

225 g (8 oz) young spinach leaves
225 g (8 oz) button mushrooms
2 thick slices of white bread
90 ml (6 tbsp) olive oil
25 g (1 oz) butter or margarine
1 garlic clove, skinned and crushed
30 ml (2 tbsp) tarragon vinegar
5 ml (1 tsp) tarragon mustard
salt and freshly ground pepper

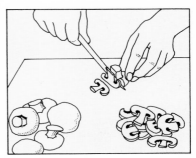

1 Wash the spinach well, discarding any damaged or yellowing leaves. Cut out and discard any thick ribs.

2 Tear the spinach leaves into a large salad bowl, discarding any thick stalks.

3 Wipe the mushrooms but do not peel them. Slice them thinly into neat 'T' shapes.

4 Add the mushrooms to the spinach. Using your hands, toss the 2 ingredients together. Set aside while making the croûtons and dressing.

5 Cut the crusts off the bread and cut the bread into 1 cm ($\frac{1}{2}$ inch) cubes. Heat the oil and butter in a frying pan, add the garlic and the cubes of bread and fry until crisp and golden. Remove the croûtons with a slotted spoon and drain well on absorbent kitchen paper.

6 Add the vinegar to the oil in the pan, with the mustard and salt and pepper to taste. Stir well to combine, then remove the pan from the heat and leave to cool for 5 minutes.

7 Add the croûtons to the salad, then the dressing. Toss well to combine and serve immediately.

CELERIAC AND BEAN SALAD

1.10* £ | 226–339 cals

* plus overnight soaking, 20 minutes cooling and 1 hour chilling

Serves 4–6

225 g (8 oz) dried flageolet beans, soaked in cold water overnight

1 large green pepper

finely grated rind and juice of 1 lemon

60 ml (4 tbsp) olive or vegetable oil

15 ml (1 tbsp) whole grain mustard

1 garlic clove, skinned and crushed

45 ml (3 tbsp) chopped fresh parsley

salt and freshly ground pepper

225 g (8 oz) celeriac

1 Drain the soaked beans and rinse well under cold running water. Put the beans in a large saucepan and cover with plenty of fresh cold water. Bring slowly to the boil, then skim off any scum with a slotted spoon. Half cover the pan with a lid and simmer gently for about 1 hour, or until the beans are just tender.

2 Meanwhile, halve the pepper and remove the core and seeds. Cut the flesh into strips and then into cubes.

3 In a bowl, whisk together the grated lemon rind, about 30 ml (2 tbsp) lemon juice, the oil, mustard, garlic, parsley and salt and pepper to taste.

4 Just before the beans are ready, peel the celeriac and chop roughly into 2.5 cm (1 inch) cubes. Blanch in boiling salted water for 5 minutes. Drain well.

5 Drain the beans well and place in a bowl. Add the celeriac and toss all the salad ingredients together while the beans and celeriac are still hot. Leave to cool for 20 minutes, then cover and chill in the refrigerator for at least 1 hour before serving. Serve chilled.

Menu Suggestion
Serve this tangy, nutritious salad with meat and poultry dishes.

WINTER CABBAGE AND CAULIFLOWER SALAD

0.25*	£	480 cals

* plus about 1 hour chilling

Serves 4

225 g (8 oz) hard white cabbage

225 g (8 oz) cauliflower florets

2 large carrots, peeled

75 g (3 oz) mixed shelled nuts, roughly chopped

50 g (2 oz) raisins

60 ml (4 tbsp) chopped fresh parsley or coriander

90 ml (6 tbsp) mayonnaise

90 ml (6 tbsp) soured cream or natural yogurt

10 ml (2 tsp) French mustard

30 ml (2 tbsp) olive or vegetable oil

juice of $\frac{1}{2}$ lemon

salt and freshly ground pepper

3 red-skinned eating apples

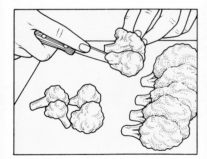

1 Shred the cabbage finely with a sharp knife and place in a large bowl. Divide the cauliflower florets into small sprigs and add to the cabbage. Mix the vegetables gently with your hands.

2 Grate the carrots into the bowl, then add the nuts, raisins and parsley. Mix the vegetables together again until evenly combined.

3 Put the remaining ingredients except the apples in a jug. Whisk well to combine, then pour over the vegetables in the bowl and toss well.

4 Core and chop the apples, but do not peel them. Add to the salad and toss again to combine with the other ingredients. Cover the bowl and chill the salad in the refrigerator for about 1 hour before serving.

Menu Suggestion

This crunchy, colourful salad can be served as an accompaniment to a selection of cold meats. With extra nuts, for vegetarians, it would make a meal in itself, served with cheese and wholemeal or granary bread.

GRAPE, WATERCRESS AND STILTON SALAD

0.20* £ £ 379 cals

* plus 1 hour chilling
Serves 4

175 g (6 oz) black grapes
1 bunch watercress
45 ml (3 tbsp) vegetable oil
15 ml (1 tbsp) lemon juice
5 ml (1 tsp) poppy seeds
pinch of caster sugar
salt and freshly ground pepper
225 g (8 oz) Stilton cheese

5 To serve, toss together the grapes, watercress, Stilton and dressing. Serve immediately.

Menu Suggestion
This special salad is excellent for buffet parties served with a selection of other salads, quiches, pâtés and cold meats.

1 Halve the grapes and remove the pips. Place in a bowl, cover and chill in the refrigerator.

2 Trim the watercress of any tough root ends. Wash thoroughly, drain and pat dry.

3 In a jug, whisk together the oil, lemon juice, poppy seeds, sugar and salt and pepper to taste.

4 Cut the rind off the Stilton and cut the cheese into 1.5 cm (¾ inch) cubes. Toss well in the prepared dressing to coat completely. Cover and chill in the refrigerator for 1 hour.

GREEK SALAD

0.20* £ 214 cals

* plus 2–3 hours or overnight chilling
Serves 4

½ large cucumber
salt and freshly ground pepper
450 g (1 lb) firm ripe tomatoes
1 medium red onion
18 black olives
125 g (4 oz) Feta cheese, cut into cubes
60 ml (4 tbsp) olive oil
15 ml (1 tbsp) lemon juice
good pinch of dried oregano

1 Peel the cucumber and slice thinly. Put into a colander or sieve, sprinkle with a little salt and leave to stand for about 15 minutes.

2 Slice the tomatoes thinly. Skin the onion and slice into thin rings. Rinse the cucumber under cold running water, drain and pat dry with absorbent kitchen paper.

3 Arrange the cucumber, tomatoes and onion in a serving dish. Scatter the olives and cubed cheese over the top.

4 In a bowl, whisk together the oil, lemon juice, oregano and salt and pepper to taste. Spoon the dressing over the salad, cover tightly with cling film and chill for 2–3 hours, or overnight. Allow to come to room temperature for 30 minutes before serving.

Menu Suggestion
In Greece, this kind of salad is usually served as a first course with hot pitta bread, or as a side dish to barbecued kebabs.

BEETROOT SALAD WITH MINT

| 0.15* | £ | 43–64 cals |

* plus 2–3 hours or overnight chilling
Serves 4–6

120 ml (8 tbsp) chopped fresh mint
700 g (1½ lb) cooked beetroot
150 ml (¼ pint) malt vinegar
5 ml (1 tsp) granulated sugar
salt and freshly ground pepper
2 medium onions, skinned and finely sliced into rings

1 Put 90 ml (6 tbsp) of the mint in a bowl and pour over 150 ml (¼ pint) boiling water. Leave to stand for 2–3 minutes.

2 Peel the beetroot and slice thinly. Place in a large shallow dish. Add the vinegar and sugar to the mint and water with salt and pepper to taste. Pour over the beetroot. Cover and chill in the refrigerator for at least 2–3 hours or overnight.

3 To serve, place alternate layers of beetroot and onion in a serving dish. Pour over the mint dressing and garnish with the remaining chopped fresh mint. Serve chilled.

Menu Suggestion
Beetroot salads go especially well with roast lamb, turkey and duck, and cold meats such as ham and salami.

BEETROOT SALAD WITH MINT
Did you know that the Victorians were extremely fond of beetroots? They not only used them as a salad vegetable, but also dried and ground them with coffee to make the coffee go further, pickled them, made them into wine, candied them as sweets—and made them into a lotion for rinsing hair!

RICE SALAD

| 0.40* | £ | 577 cals |

* plus 1 hour cooling

Serves 4

275 g (10 oz) long grain brown rice

salt and freshly ground pepper

1 head of fennel

1 red pepper

175 g (6 oz) beansprouts

75 g (3 oz) cashew nuts

90 ml (6 tbsp) corn or vegetable oil

**finely grated rind and juice of
    1 large orange**

few orange segments, to garnish

1 Cook the brown rice in plenty of boiling salted water for 30 minutes (or according to packet instructions), until tender but firm to the bite.

2 Meanwhile, prepare the remaining ingredients. Trim the fennel, reserving a few feathery tops for the garnish. Cut the top off the red pepper and remove the core and seeds. Wash the pepper and pat dry with absorbent kitchen paper.

3 Chop the fennel and red pepper finely. Wash the beansprouts and drain well. Chop the cashew nuts roughly.

4 In a jug, whisk the oil, orange rind and juice together, with salt and pepper to taste.

5 Drain the rice thoroughly, then turn into a bowl. Add the dressing while the rice is still hot and toss well to combine. Leave to stand for about 1 hour, or until the rice is cold.

6 Add the prepared vegetables and nuts to the rice and toss well to mix. Taste and adjust seasoning. Turn the salad into a serving bowl and garnish with the reserved fennel tops and the orange segments. Serve at room temperature.

Menu Suggestion

This nutty brown rice salad has a tangy orange dressing, which makes it the perfect accompaniment to rich meat dishes such as pork and duck. Alternatively, it can be served with other vegetable salads for a vegetarian meal—it goes particularly well with green salad ingredients such as chicory, endive, lettuce and watercress.

Stunning
Desserts

CRÊPES SUZETTE

0.40* 🍴 £ £ ✳*

370–554 cals

* not including making the pancake batter; freeze cooked crêpes only

Serves 4–6

105 ml (7 tbsp) orange-flavoured liqueur

pancake batter made with 300 ml (½ pint) milk (see page 439)

100 g (4 oz) unsalted butter

100 g (4 oz) caster sugar

finely grated rind and juice of 1 large orange

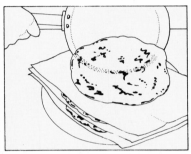

1 Stir 15 ml (1 tbsp) liqueur into the batter, then make 8–12 pancakes in the usual way (see page 151). Slide each crêpe out of the pan on to a warm plate and stack with greaseproof paper in between.

2 To serve, heat the butter and sugar together in a large, heavy-based frying pan until thick and syrupy. Add 30 ml (2 tbsp) liqueur and the orange rind and juice and heat through.

3 Fold the crêpes into triangle shapes by folding each one in half, then in half again. Place them in the frying pan and spoon over the sauce so that they become evenly coated.

4 Heat the remaining liqueur gently in a ladle or separate small pan. Transfer the crêpes and sauce to a warmed serving dish, pour over the warmed liqueur and set alight. Carry the crêpes to the table immediately, while they are still flaming.

CRÊPES SUZETTE

A classic French dessert; with its spectacular flambéed finish, crêpes Suzette is just perfect for a special dinner party. Traditionally flambéed at the table in a copper chafing dish in restaurants specialising in *haute cuisine*, the crêpes can look just as good at home carried flaming to the table on a silver or fine china plate.

This recipe uses orange juice and orange-flavoured liqueur, although the original classic recipe contained mandarin juice and orange liqueur, both in the crêpe batter and in the filling. If you wish to make this classic version rather than our more modern variation, try the following: Add 5 ml (1 tsp) each mandarin juice and orange-flavoured liqueur to the pancake batter before frying. Make a filling by creaming together 50 g (2 oz) each of unsalted butter and caster sugar. Work in the finely grated rind and juice of 1 mandarin orange and 15 ml (1 tbsp) orange-flavoured liqueur. When the crêpes are cooked, spread them with filling, fold into triangles, place in the serving dish and flambé with more liqueur.

FRUDITÉS

| 0.20 | f f | 245 cals |

Serves 6

150 ml (5 fl oz) double cream

142 ml (5 fl oz) soured cream

30 ml (2 tbsp) icing sugar, sifted

225 g (8 oz) apricots

225 g (8 oz) strawberries

175 g (6 oz) black or green grapes

2 crisp eating apples

2 bananas

juice of 1 lemon

1 First prepare the dip. Whip the two creams together with the icing sugar until standing in soft peaks. Pipe or spoon into six individual dishes.

2 Prepare the fruit. Halve and stone the apricots. Wash the strawberries under cold running water, but do not hull them.

3 Halve the grapes if they are not the seedless variety and flick out the seeds.

4 Quarter and core the apples, but do not peel them. Peel the bananas and cut into 4-cm (1½-inch) chunks.

5 Arrange the fruit on individual serving plates and sprinkle immediately with lemon juice to prevent discoloration.

6 Place the dishes of cream dip next to the fruit and serve immediately. Use fingers or small fondue forks to dunk the fruit into the cream dip.

FRUDITÉS

This is a sweet version of the French starter *crudités* which consists of fresh raw vegetables served with a vinaigrette dressing or mayonnaise-type dip. Instead of vegetables, frudités uses raw fresh fruit served with a sweet creamy dip! And it's as much fun for your guests as a fondue party if you provide forks for dipping the fruit into the dressing. Frudités can be made at any time of year, with whatever fruit happens to be in season. As long as the fruit is in peak condition and the combination of different types interesting, the dish is bound to be a success.

In the winter, when fruit is scarce and more expensive, you can cut up squares of plain home-made cake (such as Genoese sponge or Madeira) to help bulk up the quantity of fruit. And if you are entertaining children amongst your guests, they would appreciate a chocolate sauce to dip their fruit into—either make a hot chocolate sauce as you would for ice cream, or use a commercial variety if time is short.

POIRES BELLE HÉLÈNE

2.00 | £ £ | 357 cals

Serves 6

100 g (4 oz) sugar

900 ml (1½ pints) water

thinly pared rind and juice of 2 oranges

6 cooking pears (preferably Conference)

225 g (8 oz) plain chocolate, broken into pieces

60 ml (4 tbsp) orange-flavoured liqueur

orange slices, to decorate

1 Put the sugar, water and half the orange rind in a large heavy-based saucepan and heat gently, without stirring, until the sugar has dissolved.

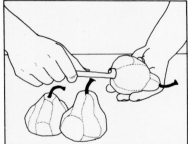

2 Meanwhile, peel the pears quickly (to prevent discoloration), leaving the stalks on. Cut out the cores from the bottom and level them so that the pears will stand upright.

3 Stand the pears in the syrup, cover the pan and simmer gently for 20 minutes or until tender. Remove from the heat and leave to cool, covered tightly. Spoon the syrup over the pears occasionally during cooling.

4 Meanwhile, make the decoration. Cut the remaining orange rind into thin matchstick (julienne) strips. Blanch in boiling water for 2 minutes, then drain and immediately refresh under cold running water. Leave to drain on absorbent kitchen paper.

5 Make the chocolate sauce. Put the chocolate and liqueur in a heatproof bowl standing over a pan of gently simmering water. Heat gently until chocolate melts.

6 Remove the pears from the syrup, stand on a large serving dish, or 6 individual dishes and chill for 2 hours. Discard the orange rind from the syrup. Stir the melted chocolate into 150 ml (¼ pint) of the syrup with the orange juice, then slowly bring to the boil, stirring constantly. Simmer, stirring, until the sauce is thick and syrupy.

7 To serve, pour the hot chocolate sauce over the cold pears and sprinkle with the orange julienne. Decorate with orange slices and serve immediately.

POMMES BRISTOL

| 0.45* | 🥄 | £ | 303 cals |

* plus cooling and overnight chilling

Serves 4

225 g (8 oz) sugar

450 ml (¾ pint) water

1 vanilla pod

4 crisp dessert apples (e.g. Granny Smiths or Cox's Orange Pippin)

2 small oranges

30 ml (2 tbsp) orange-flavoured liqueur (optional)

1 Put half the sugar in a heavy-based saucepan with 300 ml (½ pint) of the water and the vanilla pod. Heat gently until the sugar has dissolved, then simmer, without stirring, for 2–3 minutes.

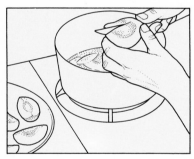

2 Meanwhile, peel, quarter and core the apples. Slice them into the pan of syrup, remove from the heat and cover with a lid.

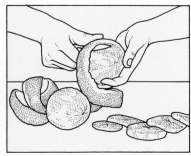

3 Cut the rind and pith off the oranges with a serrated knife, working from top to bottom in a spiral motion. Slice into thin rounds or sections.

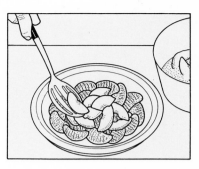

4 When the apples are cold, remove them carefully from the syrup with a slotted spoon. Arrange them on a shallow serving dish with the orange. Discard the vanilla pod from the syrup and stir in the liqueur, if using. Pour over the apples and oranges, cover with cling film and chill in the refrigerator overnight.

5 Put the remaining sugar and water in the saucepan and heat gently until the sugar has dissolved. Boil rapidly until the syrup turns a rich caramel in colour, then pour immediately into a greased shallow baking tin or tray. Leave in a cold place overnight.

6 Crush the caramel into small pieces by hitting it with the end of a rolling pin or a mallet. Sprinkle over the apples and oranges and serve immediately (the caramel will soften if left on the fruit and syrup for many minutes).

Menu Suggestion

Serve this fruity dessert after a rich main course.

PINEAPPLE AND BANANA FLAMBÉ

| 0.50 | £ £ | 235–313 cals |

Serves 6–8

| 1 medium pineapple |
| 900 g (2 lb) firm bananas |
| 125 g (4 oz) dried figs |
| 50 g (2 oz) butter or margarine |
| 125 g (4 oz) demerara sugar |
| 45 ml (3 tbsp) lemon juice |
| 2.5 ml (½ tsp) ground mixed spice |
| 60 ml (4 tbsp) dark rum |

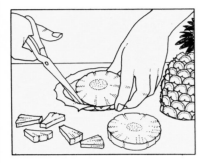

1 Slice the pineapple into 1-cm (½-inch) pieces. Snip off the skin and cut the flesh into chunks, discarding the core.

2 Peel and thickly slice the bananas into the bottom of a shallow ovenproof dish; spoon the pineapple on top.

3 Cut the figs into coarse shreds and scatter over the fruit. Then put the butter, sugar, strained lemon juice and spice together in a saucepan and heat until well blended; pour over the prepared fruit.

4 Cover tightly and bake in the oven at 200°C (400°F) mark 6 for 25 minutes until the fruit is tender.

5 Heat the rum gently in a small saucepan, remove from the heat and ignite with a match. Pour immediately over the fruit and bring the dish to the table while still flaming.

SERVING IDEA

For a special occasion such as a dinner party, you can serve this dessert in the pineapple shells. It will look really spectacular if carried flaming to the table, and any mixture which will not fit into the pineapple shells can be served separately in a fruit bowl.

To make two pineapple shells from one pineapple: with a large, sharp knife, slice the pineapple in half lengthways, cutting right through the crown and base. Insert the blade of a long, ser- rated knife into the flesh of one pineapple half, about 5 mm (¼ inch) in from the edge of the shell, and cut all around the inside. Cut through the flesh in parallel lines, first lengthways and then crossways to produce squares of flesh (take care not to cut through the skin at the base). Scoop out the flesh with a sharp-edged teaspoon. Repeat with the second pineapple half, then turn both shells upside-down and leave to drain before filling.

MERINGUE SURPRISE CASSIS

0.45* £ £ ✳

370–493 cals

* plus 1 hour cooling and at least 4 hours freezing

Serves 6–8

15 ml (1 tbsp) arrowroot

6 egg yolks and 2 egg whites

50 g (2 oz) vanilla sugar

300 ml (½ pint) milk

300 ml (10 fl oz) double cream

16 baby meringues

350 g (12 oz) frozen blackcurrants

juice of 1 lemon

50 g (2 oz) icing sugar, or to taste

45 ml (3 tbsp) blackcurrant liqueur

1 Put the arrowroot in a heat-proof bowl and blend to a paste with the egg yolks and vanilla sugar.

2 Scald the milk by bringing it up to boiling point, then stir slowly into the egg yolk mixture.

3 Stand the bowl over a pan of gently simmering water and stir until the custard is thick enough to coat the back of a wooden spoon.

4 Remove from the heat, cover the surface of the custard closely with cling film to prevent a skin forming and leave for 1 hour.

5 Whip the cream until it just holds its shape, then fold into the cold custard. Whisk the egg whites until stiff, then fold in until evenly incorporated.

6 Crush 10 of the meringues roughly and fold into the custard mixture until evenly distributed.

7 Base-line an 18-cm (6-inch) Charlotte mould, soufflé dish or cake tin with non-stick parchment paper. Pour in the custard mixture, cover the mould, then freeze for at least 4 hours or overnight until solid.

8 Meanwhile, make the blackcurrant sauce. Reserve a few whole frozen blackcurrants for decoration.

9 Put the remaining frozen blackcurrants and the lemon juice in a heavy-based saucepan and heat gently until defrosted, shaking the pan constantly.

10 Cook gently for 10 minutes, then tip into a sieve and press with the back of a spoon to extract as much juice as possible.

11 Sift the icing sugar into the blackcurrant juice, then stir in the liqueur. Leave until cold, taste and add more sugar if liked.

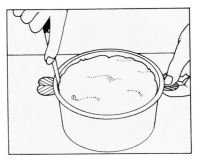

12 To serve, run a knife around the dessert in the mould, then carefully turn out on to a serving plate. Remove paper.

13 Pour a little of the sauce over the dessert, then decorate with the reserved blackcurrants and the remaining meringues. Serve at once, with the remaining sauce handed separately.

—— VARIATION ——

Although frozen blackcurrants are available at most large supermarkets and freezer centres, raspberries are more readily available, and can equally well be used for this recipe. Replace the blackcurrant liqueur with *framboise*, a French raspberry liqueur sold in good off-licences. Alternatively, kirsch (a liqueur made from cherries which is available in miniature bottles), goes well with the flavour of raspberries—and blackcurrants too.

CHARLOTTE RUSSE

| 1.35* | 🍴 🍴 £ | 447 cals |

* plus 50 minutes cooling and 4 hours setting

Serves 6

135-g (4¾-oz) packet lemon jelly, broken into squares

about 450 ml (¾ pint) boiling water

45 ml (3 tbsp) lemon juice

2 glacé cherries, quartered

piece of angelica, cut into triangles

300 ml (½ pint) milk

1 vanilla pod

45 ml (3 tbsp) water

15 ml (3 tsp) gelatine

3 egg yolks

45 ml (3 tbsp) caster sugar

about 18 sponge fingers

300 ml (10 fl oz) whipping cream

1 Dissolve the jelly in a measuring jug, according to the packet instructions, using the lemon juice and enough boiling water to make 600 ml (1 pint). Cool for 20 minutes. Spoon a thin covering of cool jelly into the base of a 1.1-litre (2-pint) charlotte tin; refrigerate for about 20 minutes or until set.

2 When set, arrange the cherry quarters and angelica triangles on top. Carefully spoon over cool liquid jelly to a depth of about 2.5 cm (1 inch). Refrigerate for about 30 minutes to set, together with the remaining jelly.

3 Bring the milk slowly to the boil with the vanilla pod; take off the heat, cover and leave to infuse for at least 10 minutes. Put the water in a small bowl and sprinkle in the gelatine. Stand the bowl over a saucepan of hot water and heat gently until dissolved. Remove the bowl from the water and set aside to cool slightly.

4 Using a wooden spoon, beat together the egg yolks and sugar until well mixed, then stir in the strained milk. Return to the pan and cook gently, stirring all the time until the custard is thick enough to just coat the back of the spoon—do *not* boil. Pour into a large bowl, stir in the gelatine and allow to cool for 30 minutes.

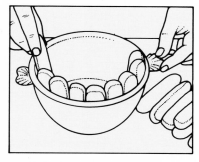

5 Trim the sponge fingers so that they just fit the tin; reserve the trimmings. Stand the fingers closely together, sugar side out, around the edge of the tin.

6 Lightly whip the cream and stir into the cool custard. Place the bowl in a roasting tin. Pour in enough iced water to come halfway up its sides. Stir occasionally for about 10 minutes until the custard is on the point of setting and has a *thick* pouring consistency. Pour gently into the lined mould without disturbing the sponge fingers.

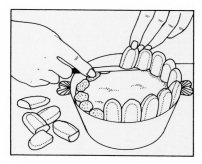

7 Trim the sponge fingers level with the custard. Lay the trimmings together with the reserved trimmings on top of the custard. Cover with cling film and refrigerate for at least 3 hours to set.

8 To turn out, using fingertips, ease the sponge fingers away from the tin, then tilt it slightly to allow an airlock to form between the two. Dip the base of the tin in hot water for about 5 seconds only— to loosen the jelly. Invert the pudding on to a damp plate, shake tin gently, then ease it carefully off the finished charlotte.

9 Loosen the remaining set jelly by dipping the jug in hot water for a few seconds only. Turn out on to a board lined with damp greaseproof paper. Moisten a large knife and chop the jelly into small pieces. Spoon the jelly around the charlotte russe.

CHARLOTTE RUSSE

A classic French dessert, this charlotte Russe (Russian charlotte) is made with a filling of *crème bavarois*—a rich vanilla-flavoured egg custard. Sometimes the custard is flavoured with chocolate, almond-flavoured liqueur or kirsch. Fresh raspberries can also be added when they are in season.

GOOSEBERRY CHARLOTTE

0.50* ⊟ ⊟ £ £ ✳* 457 cals

* plus 45 minutes cooling time and
2 hours setting time; freeze at the end
of step 7

Serves 6

450 g (1 lb) gooseberries, topped
  and tailed

90 ml (6 tbsp) water

75 g (3 oz) caster sugar

10 ml (2 tsp) gelatine

2 egg yolks

300 ml (½ pint) milk

300 ml (10 fl oz) double cream

20 langue de chat biscuits,
  trimmed to size

angelica, to decorate

1 Wash the gooseberries and
drain well. Place in a small
saucepan with 60 ml (4 tbsp)
water. Cover the pan and simmer
for about 10 minutes until the fruit
softens to a pulpy consistency.

2 Purée in a blender or food
processor, then sieve to
remove the pips. Stir in 50 g (2 oz)
of the sugar. Place 30 ml (2 tbsp)
water into a bowl and sprinkle in
the gelatine. Allow the gelatine to
soak until it has become spongy.

3 Meanwhile, make the custard.
Beat the egg yolks with
remaining sugar until light in
colour. In a small saucepan, warm
the milk, and pour over the eggs
and sugar, stirring until blended.

4 Return to the pan and cook
over a low heat, stirring all the
time, until the custard thickens
sufficiently to lightly coat the back
of the spoon – do not boil.

5 Take off the heat and immediately add the soaked gelatine;
stir until dissolved. Pour the
custard out into a large bowl and
mix in the gooseberry purée, leave
for 45 minutes to cool.

6 Lightly whip the cream and
when the gooseberry mixture
is cold, but not set, stir in half the
cream until evenly blended.

7 Oil and base line a 15-cm
(6-inch) soufflé type non-metal
straight sided dish and pour in the
gooseberry mixture. Refrigerate
for 1–2 hours to set. When firm,
turn out on to a flat serving plate.

8 Spread a thin covering of the
remaining cream around the
edge of the charlotte.

9 Spoon the rest of the cream
into a piping bag fitted with a
1-cm (½-inch) large star nozzle,
and pipe the cream around the top
edge. Decorate with angelica. Just
before serving arrange the biscuits
carefully around the outside.

GOOSEBERRIES
There are many varieties, round
or long, hairy or smooth, cooking
or dessert. Their pale green
colour and unique flavour make
them unbeatable for fruit fools.

Cooking gooseberries, used in
pies and puddings and for jam,
etc, are usually green, very sour,
with firm flesh and a fairly large
number of seeds. Dessert gooseberries can be green, yellow-
white or a russet colour, often
with a hairy skin, and they
usually have soft, pulpy, sweet
flesh and large seeds.

PETITS POTS AU CHOCOLAT

1.45*	£	410 cals

* plus 1 hour cooling

Serves 6

15 ml (1 tbsp) coffee beans

3 egg yolks

1 egg

75 g (3 oz) caster sugar

700 ml (1¼ pints) milk and single cream mixed

75 g (3 oz) plain chocolate

150 ml (5 fl oz) whipping cream and coffee dragées, to decorate

1 Toast the coffee beans under a moderate grill for a few minutes, then set aside.

2 Beat together the egg yolks, whole egg and sugar until the mixture is very pale.

3 Place the milk, cream and coffee beans in a saucepan and bring to the boil.

4 Strain the hot milk on to the egg mixture, stirring all the time. Discard the coffee beans.

5 Return the mixture to the saucepan, break up the chocolate and add to the pan. Stir over gentle heat (do not boil) for about 5 minutes until the chocolate has almost melted and mixture is *slightly* thickened. Whisk lightly until evenly blended.

6 Stand six individual 150-ml (¼-pint) ramekin dishes or custard pots in a roasting tin, then pour in enough hot water to come halfway up the sides of the dishes. Pour the custard mixture slowly into the dishes, dividing it equally between them. Cover, then bake in the oven at 150°C (300°F) mark 2 for 1–1¼ hours or until the custard is lightly set.

7 Leave to cool. To serve, whip the cream and spoon into a piping bag fitted with a large star nozzle. Pipe a whirl on top and decorate with coffee dragées.

CHOCOLATE

These little chocolate pots rely heavily on the flavour of the chocolate used in their making. So it is essential to use a good-quality chocolate. Plain chocolate is specified because it has better melting qualities than milk chocolate, and it also contains rather less sugar. For best results, look for French and Belgian plain cooking chocolates in delicatessens and specialist supermarkets.

HOT CHOCOLATE SOUFFLÉ

1.00 £ £ 629 cals

Serves 4

50 g (2 oz) caster sugar, plus extra
    to coat

50 g (2 oz) plain chocolate, broken
    into pieces

45 ml (3 tbsp) brandy

25 g (1 oz) butter or margarine

15 g ($\frac{1}{2}$ oz) plain flour

150 ml ($\frac{1}{4}$ pint) milk

3 egg yolks and 4 egg whites

icing sugar, to dredge

hot chocolate sauce (see page 441),
    to serve

5 Whisk the egg whites until
stiff, then fold into the chocolate mixture. Turn into the prepared soufflé dish and bake
immediately in the oven at 200°C
(400°F) mark 6 for 35 minutes
until well risen. Dredge with icing
sugar and serve the soufflé
immediately, with hot chocolate
sauce handed separately.

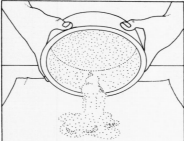

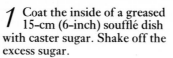

1 Coat the inside of a greased
15-cm (6-inch) soufflé dish
with caster sugar. Shake off the
excess sugar.

2 Put the chocolate and brandy
in a heatproof bowl standing
over a pan of simmering water.
Heat gently until melted. Remove
bowl from the pan.

3 Melt the fat in a separate
saucepan, add the flour and
cook for 2 minutes, stirring all the
time. Remove from the heat and
gradually add the milk, then return to the heat and bring to the
boil, stirring. Simmer for 2
minutes until thick and smooth.

4 Remove the pan from the heat
and stir in the caster sugar,
melted chocolate and egg yolks,
one at a time.

TIPS ON MAKING A HOT SOUFFLÉ

Making a hot soufflé is easier
than you think. Here are a few
helpful hints for success every
time:

● Preheat the oven to the required temperature before starting the recipe, and preheat a
baking sheet on the centre shelf
at the same time. This ensures
that the soufflé starts cooking
immediately it is put into the
oven. Remove any shelves above
the centre shelf before baking to
allow room for rising.

● Make sure the egg whites are
whisked stiffly before folding
them into the sauce mixture. To
test if they are stiff enough,
turn the bowl upside down —
they should not drop.

● To lighten the sauce mixture,
fold a tablespoon of the stiffly
whisked egg whites into the
sauce before folding in the rest.

MARBLED APRICOT SOUFFLÉ

2.00* ☐ £ £ ✳

439–585 cals

* plus overnight soaking, 1½ hours cooling and 4 hours setting

Serves 6–8

225 g (8 oz) dried apricots, soaked overnight in cold water

180 ml (12 tbsp) water

175 g (6 oz) caster sugar

30 ml (2 tbsp) almond-flavoured liqueur

15 ml (3 tsp) gelatine

4 eggs, separated

300 ml (10 fl oz) double cream

few drops of orange food colouring

ratafia biscuits and whipped cream, to decorate

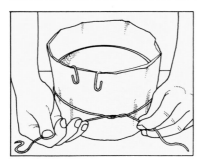

1 Prepare a 15-cm (6-inch) soufflé dish: cut a double thickness of greaseproof paper long enough to go around the outside of the dish and 5–7.5 cm (2–3 inches) deeper. Secure the dish around the outside with paper clips and string.

2 Drain the soaked dried apricots, then put them in a saucepan with 120 ml (8 tbsp) of the water and 50 g (2 oz) of the sugar. Heat gently until the sugar has dissolved, then cover and simmer for about 30 minutes until tender. Leave to cool slightly, then rub through a sieve or purée in a blender. Stir in the liqueur and leave to cool for about 30 minutes.

3 Meanwhile, place the remaining water in a small heatproof bowl and sprinkle in the gelatine. Stand the bowl over a saucepan of hot water and heat gently until dissolved. Remove the bowl from the water and cool slightly.

4 Put the egg yolks and remaining sugar in a large heatproof bowl and stand over the pan of gently simmering water. Whisk until the mixture is thick and holds a ribbon trail, then remove from the heat and leave for about 1 hour until cold, whisking occasionally.

5 Whip the cream until it will stand in soft peaks. Whisk the egg whites until stiff.

6 Stir the gelatine liquid into the apricot purée, then fold this into the egg yolk mixture until evenly blended. Next fold in the whipped cream, then egg whites.

7 Transfer half the mixture to a separate bowl and tint with the food colouring.

8 Put alternate spoonfuls of the two mixtures into the prepared soufflé dish. Level the surface, then chill in the refrigerator for at least 4 hours until set.

9 Carefully remove the paper from the edge of the soufflé. Press the crushed ratafias around the exposed edge. Decorate top with apricots and whipped cream.

MANGO MOUSSE

1.00* ☐ £ £ 375 cals

* plus 15 minutes freezing or 1 hour chilling, and overnight refrigeration

Serves 6

2 ripe mangoes

3 eggs

1 egg yolk

40 g (1½ oz) caster sugar

finely grated rind of 1 orange

60 ml (4 tbsp) orange-flavoured liqueur or orange juice

300 ml (½ pint) double cream

15 ml (1 tbsp) powdered gelatine

30 ml (2 tbsp) lemon juice

30 ml (2 tbsp) water

shreds of blanched orange rind, to decorate

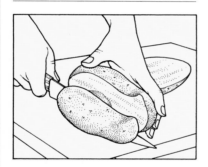

1 Cut a thick slice from either side of each central mango stone, keeping the knife close to the stone.

2 Scrape the mango flesh out of the skin and from around the stone. Place in a blender or food processor and work to a smooth purée, then rub through a nylon sieve into a bowl. Set aside.

3 With an electric mixer, beat the eggs, egg yolk and sugar in a separate bowl until thick and light in colour. The beaters should leave a ribbon trail on the surface.

4 Add the mango purée. Whisk in the orange rind and the liqueur or orange juice to the egg mixture a little at a time, whisking well after each addition.

5 Whip half the cream until it is the same consistency as the mango mousse, then fold in.

6 Sprinkle the gelatine over the lemon juice and water in a small heatproof bowl. Leave for 5 minutes until spongy, then stand the bowl in a pan of gently simmering water to dissolve.

7 Pour the liquid gelatine into the mango mousse, stirring gently to distribute it evenly. Pour slowly into a chilled large serving dish. Freeze for 15 minutes or chill for 1 hour. Cover with cling film and chill overnight.

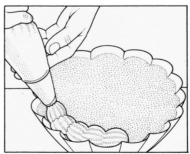

8 Whip the remaining cream until stiff, then use to pipe a shell border around the edge of the mousse. Sprinkle with orange shreds. Serve chilled.

ZUPPA INGLESE
(MARSALA AND CREAM TRIFLE)

1.45* £ £ 414–552 cals

* plus at least 4 hours chilling

Serves 6–8

568 ml (1 pint) milk

1 vanilla pod

4 eggs

50 g (2 oz) caster sugar

225 ml (8 fl oz) Marsala

150 ml (¼ pint) water

16 trifle sponge cakes

300 ml (10 fl oz) double cream

glacé cherries and angelica, to decorate

1 Make the custard. Scald the milk with the vanilla pod and immediately remove from the heat. Leave to infuse for 20 minutes, then strain.

2 Put the eggs and sugar in a heatproof bowl and lightly whisk together. Slowly pour in the milk, whisking all the time.

3 Stand the bowl over a pan of gently simmering water and stir until thick enough to coat the back of a spoon. (Be patient — this can take as long as twenty minutes.)

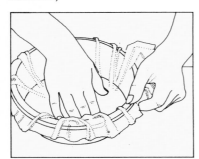

4 Remove the bowl from the heat, cover the surface of the custard closely with cling film and leave until cold.

5 Mix the Marsala and water together in a shallow dish. Dip a few of the trifle sponges in the liquid, then use them to line the bottom of a glass serving bowl.

6 Pour one-third of the cold custard over the sponges. Dip a few more trifle sponges in the liquid and place on top of the custard. Cover with another third of the custard.

7 In a separate bowl, whip the cream until thick, then spread half over the custard.

8 Finish with a layer each of the remaining sponges and liquid, the custard and cream. Chill in the refrigerator for at least 4 hours, preferably overnight. Decorate with glacé cherries and angelica just before serving.

Menu Suggestion
Serve this boozy trifle for a dinner party dessert or special teatime treat — as you would any other trifle.

272

NÈGRE EN CHEMISE

| 0.30* | 🏠 £ £ ✳ | 854 cals |

* plus 2–3 hours setting

Serves 8

350 g (12 oz) plain chocolate,
   broken into pieces

100 ml (4 fl oz) water

75 g (3 oz) butter or margarine

100 g (4 oz) praline, crushed (see
   page 142)

15 ml (1 tbsp) brandy

450 ml (15 fl oz) double cream

chocolate buttons, to decorate

1 Put the chocolate and water in
a heatproof bowl standing over
a pan of simmering water. Heat
gently until melted. Remove bowl
from the pan and cool slightly.

2 Meanwhile, cream the fat in a
bowl until pale. Add the
melted chocolate and gradually
beat in praline. Stir in brandy.

3 Lightly whip the cream and
fold half into the chocolate
mixture. Turn the mixture into a
lightly oiled 900-ml (1½-pint)
basin and refrigerate for 2–3 hours
until set.

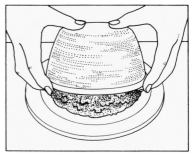

4 To serve. Quickly dip the
basin into hot water, place a
serving plate on top and invert.
Lift off the basin.

5 Fill a piping bag, fitted with a
large star nozzle, with the
remaining cream and pipe around
the base of the dessert. Decorate
with chocolate buttons.
Refrigerate until serving time.

ICED ZABAGLIONE

0.25*	⊟	£	366 cals

* plus 30 minutes cooling and 2 hours freezing

Serves 6

4 egg yolks

65 g (2½ oz) caster sugar

100 ml (4 fl oz) marsala

200 ml (7 fl oz) double cream

30 ml (2 tbsp) iced water

30 ml (2 tbsp) icing sugar

orange shreds, to decorate

sponge fingers, to serve

1 Put the egg yolks and sugar in a large bowl. Beat together, add the marsala and beat again.

2 Place the bowl over a saucepan of simmering water and heat gently, whisking the mixture until it is very thick and creamy and forms soft peaks. Remove the bowl from the heat and leave to cool for about 30 minutes.

3 Place the cream and water in a bowl and sift in the icing sugar. Whisk until stiff then fold into the cooled egg mixture. Chill in the refrigerator for about 2 hours until firm.

4 Spoon the iced zabaglione into six individual glasses, decorate with orange shreds and serve with sponge fingers handed separately.

SNOWCAP ICED PUDDING

| 1.15* | 🗇 £ £ ✳ | 303–405 cals |

* plus 2 hours setting and overnight freezing

Serves 6–8

150 ml ($\frac{1}{4}$ pint) kirsch

60 ml (4 tbsp) water

about 15 sponge fingers

450 ml ($\frac{3}{4}$ pint) chocolate chip ice cream

225 g (8 oz) ripe cherries, pitted and roughly chopped

450 ml ($\frac{3}{4}$ pint) vanilla ice cream

150 ml (5 fl oz) double cream

1 Cut out a circle of greaseproof paper and use it to line the base of a 1.1-litre (2$\frac{1}{2}$-pint) pudding basin.

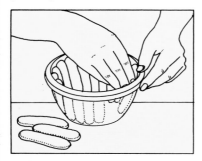

2 Mix the kirsch with the water and dip the sponge fingers one at a time into the mixture. Use to line the sides of the pudding basin, trimming them to fit so that there are no gaps in between. Fill the base of the basin with leftover pieces of sponge. Refrigerate for 15 minutes.

3 Stir any remaining kirsch liquid into the chocolate ice cream and mash the ice cream well with a fork to soften it slightly and make it smooth.

4 Spoon the chocolate ice cream into the basin and work it up the sides of the sponge fingers to the top of the basin so that it forms an even layer. Freeze for about 2 hours until firm.

5 Mix the cherries into the vanilla ice cream and mash well with a fork as in step 3.

6 Spoon the vanilla ice cream into the centre of the basin and smooth it over the top so that it covers the chocolate ice cream and the sponge fingers. Cover with foil and freeze overnight.

7 To serve, whip the cream until it will just hold its shape. Run a knife around the inside of the basin, then turn the ice cream out on to a serving plate.

8 Spoon the cream over the top and let it just start to run down the sides, then freeze immediately for about 15 minutes or until the cream has frozen solid. Serve straight from the freezer.

CASSATA
(ICE CREAM AND FRUIT BOMBE)

2.00*	🍳 £ £ ✳	332 cals

* plus 18–21 hours freezing, 2 hours macerating and 1 hour 30 minutes–1 hour 40 minutes to soften

Serves 8

3 egg yolks

75 g (3 oz) caster sugar

300 ml (½ pint) milk, plus 15 ml (1 tbsp)

50 g (2 oz) plain chocolate

225 g (8 oz) ripe strawberries, sliced

1.25 ml (¼ tsp) vanilla flavouring

300 ml (10 fl oz) double cream

red food colouring

15 g (½ oz) pistachio nuts

4 glacé cherries

30 ml (2 tbsp) chopped mixed peel

30 ml (2 tbsp) orange-flavoured liqueur

1 Using a wooden spoon or rotary whisk, beat the egg yolks and caster sugar together until thick and pale in colour.

2 Make the custard. In a medium saucepan, scald 300 ml (½ pint) milk. Pour on to the egg mixture, stirring well. Return to the pan and cook over a low heat, *without boiling*, until the custard thickens slightly. Strain into a bowl and cool for 30 minutes.

3 Break up the chocolate and place with 15 ml (1 tbsp) milk in a bowl standing in a pan of hot water. Leave until chocolate melts. Add two-thirds of the cool custard to the chocolate, stirring to blend.

4 Purée the strawberries in a blender or food processor; sieve into the remaining custard and stir in the vanilla flavouring.

5 In a separate bowl, lightly whip 150 ml (5 fl oz) of the cream. Stir two-thirds of this through the cold chocolate mixture and the remainder into the strawberry, adding red colouring to the latter if necessary.

6 Pour the mixtures into separate shallow polythene containers and freeze for about 4 hours until mushy in texture.

7 When the mixtures are mushy, take them out of the freezer and turn them into separate bowls.

8 Beat vigorously with a whisk or wooden spoon to break down the ice crystals. Spoon back into the plastic containers, cover and freeze for a further 4–6 hours until quite firm.

9 Put a disc of non-stick paper in the base of a 1.1-litre (2-pint) pudding basin. Put empty basin into freezer. Leave chocolate ice cream at room temperature for about 20 minutes to soften slightly.

10 Line the basin evenly with chocolate ice cream, using a round-bowled spoon. Freeze for about 1 hour until firm.

11 Take the strawberry ice cream out of the freezer and leave at room temperature for 20–30 minutes to soften slightly.

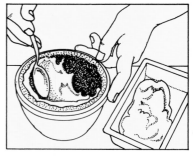

12 Work the strawberry ice cream with a spoon to make it more pliable (it will be firmer than the chocolate ice cream), then use to make a second lining of ice cream in the basin. Freeze, covered, for 1–2 hours until firm.

13 Pour boiling water over the pistachio nuts, leave to stand for 10 minutes, skin and chop roughly. Cut cherries into small pieces and macerate with the nuts, peel and liqueur for 2 hours, covered.

14 In a separate bowl, stiffly whisk the remaining cream and fold in the cherry mixture. Spoon into the centre of the cassata. Freeze, covered, for 4 hours.

15 Stand the pudding basin in a bowl of hot water for a few seconds to loosen the cassata. Slip a knife around the top edge to ensure it is loose and invert on to a serving platter; remove the paper. Leave in the refrigerator for about 40 minutes to 'come to'. Serve the cassata in wedges.

Menu Suggestion
A rich fruit and ice cream bombe for a special occasion dessert. Serve only after a plain or light main course dish.

CASSATA

Recipes for Cassata are confusing, because there are two different types. The recipe given here is for Cassata Gelata, which is an ice cream bombe. The other type is known as Cassata Siciliana and is a chilled dessert made from layers of Ricotta cheese and sponge cake. It is a Sicilian speciality which is traditionally served at Easter and other festivities such as weddings.

RASPBERRY PARFAIT

0.30* 🍴 £ £ ✳ 351 cals

* plus 2–3 hours freezing and 30 minutes softening

Serves 6

450 g (1 lb) fresh raspberries, hulled

75 g (3 oz) icing sugar, sifted

75 g (3 oz) granulated sugar

100 ml (4 fl oz) water

2 egg whites

15 ml (1 tbsp) kirsch or raspberry-flavoured liqueur (optional)

squeeze of lemon juice

300 ml (10 fl oz) double cream

fresh mint leaves, to decorate

1 Purée the raspberries in a blender or food processor, then push through a sieve to remove the pips. Stir icing sugar into purée.

2 Put the granulated sugar and water into a heavy-based saucepan and dissolve over gentle heat.

3 When dissolved, bring to the boil and boil until slightly tacky. Remove from the heat.

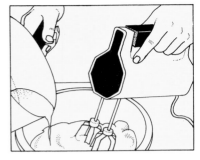

4 Whisk the egg whites until very stiff, then pour the hot sugar syrup on to them, whisking until thick, shiny and mousse-like. Leave for 10 minutes until cool.

5 Flavour the raspberry purée with the liqueur, if using, and the lemon juice. Fold into the meringue mixture.

6 Lightly whip the cream and fold into the raspberry mixture. Taste for sweetness and add more sugar if necessary. Pour into a chilled shallow freezer container and freeze for 3–4 hours until the mixture is firm.

7 Allow the raspberry parfait to soften for 30 minutes in the refrigerator before serving. Decorate with the mint leaves.

PARFAIT

The term *parfait* can be confusing. Originally it was used to describe an iced coffee cream, but nowadays the term is often used in restaurants to describe any fancy ice cream—usually the type that has been set in a bombe mould. Strictly speaking, a parfait should be made from a mousse-like mixture such as this one in which a hot sugar syrup is mixed with beaten egg whites, then enriched with cream.

KIWI FRUIT SORBET

$\boxed{0.30*}$ 🍴 £ ❄ $\boxed{103 \text{ cals}}$

* plus 30 minutes cooling and 6 hours freezing

Serves 6

50 g (2 oz) sugar

150 ml (¼ pint) water

6 kiwi fruit

2 egg whites

slices of kiwi fruit, to decorate

orange-flavoured liqueur and wafers, to serve

1 Place the sugar in saucepan with the water. Heat gently until the sugar dissolves, then simmer for 2 minutes. Cool for 30 minutes.

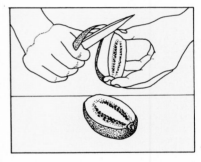

2 Halve the kiwi fruit and peel thinly or pull away the skins without damaging the flesh.

3 Place the fruit in a blender or food processor with the cool syrup. Work to a smooth purée, then pass through a nylon sieve to remove the pips. Pour into a chilled shallow freezer container. Freeze for 2 hours until mushy.

4 Beat the mixture with a fork to break down any ice crystals.

5 Whisk the egg whites until stiff, then fold through the fruit mixture until evenly blended. Return to freezer for 4 hours.

6 Scoop into individual glass dishes, decorate and spoon over some liqueur. Serve with wafers.

GRANITA ALL' ARANCIA
(ORANGE WATER ICE)

0.25*	£	✳	161 cals

* plus 8 hours freezing

Serves 6

175 g (6 oz) sugar

450 ml (¾ pint) water

10 large oranges

1½ lemons

1 Make the sugar syrup. Place the sugar and water in a medium saucepan. Heat gently until the sugar dissolves, then boil gently for 10 minutes without stirring.

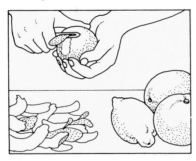

2 Meanwhile, using a potato peeler, thinly pare off the rind from four of the oranges and the lemons.

3 Add the orange and lemon rind to the sugar syrup and leave to go quite cold.

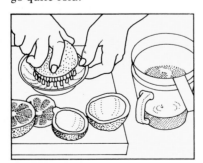

4 Squeeze the juice from the four oranges and the lemons. Strain into a measuring jug — there should be 450 ml (¾ pint).

5 Strain the cold syrup into a shallow freezer container and stir in the fruit juices. Mix well, cover and freeze for about 4 hours until mushy in texture.

6 Remove from the freezer and turn the frozen mixture into a bowl. Beat well with a fork to break down the ice crystals. Return to the freezer container and freeze for at least 4 hours until the mixture is firm.

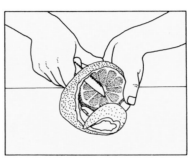

7 Meanwhile, using a serrated knife, cut away the peel and pith from the remaining oranges.

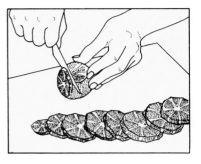

8 Slice the oranges down into thin rings, ease out and discard any pips. Place the oranges in a serving bowl; cover tightly with cling film and refrigerate until serving time.

9 Place the water ice in the refrigerator for 45 minutes to soften before serving. Serve with the fresh orange slices.

Menu Suggestion
Serve this tangy water ice for a dinner party dessert after a rich or substantial main course.

VARIATIONS

Granita al Limone
(Lemon Water Ice)
With 6–8 lemons as a basis, follow the recipe using the pared rind of four lemons and enough juice to give 450 ml (¾ pint).

Granita di Fragole
(Strawberry Water Ice)
With 700 g (1½ lb) strawberries, puréed and sieved, and the pared rind and juice of 1 orange as a basis, follow the recipe, using the strawberry purée and orange juice instead of the orange and lemon juices in step 4.

Granita di Caffé
(Coffee Water Ice)
Put 30 ml (2 tbsp) sugar and 50 g (2 oz) finely ground Italian coffee in a jug, pour over 600 ml (1 pint) boiling water and leave to stand for 1 hour. Strain the coffee through a filter paper or muslin, then follow the recipe after the straining in step 5.

WALNUT MERINGUE CAKE

3.00* £ ✳ 528 cals

* plus 1 hour cooling and 2 hours chilling

Serves 6

4 egg whites
175 g (6 oz) caster sugar
2.5 ml (½ tsp) white wine vinegar
75 g (3 oz) walnut pieces, chopped
300 ml (10 fl oz) double cream
200 ml (7 fl oz) lemon curd
chocolate curls, to decorate

1 Line two baking sheets with non-stick paper. Whisk the egg whites to stiff peaks.

2 Beat in 30 ml (2 tbsp) sugar with the vinegar. Fold in the walnuts with the remaining sugar.

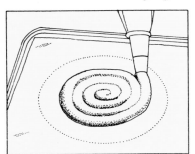

3 Spoon the meringue mixture into a piping bag fitted with a 1-cm (½-inch) plain nozzle. Pipe out two 20-cm (8-inch) rounds on the prepared baking sheets.

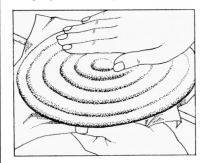

4 Bake in the oven at 110°C (225°F) mark ¼ for about 2 hours. Ease off the paper and place on wire racks for 1 hour to cool.

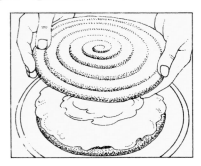

5 Whip cream until it holds its shape. Place one meringue on a dish; top with half cream.

6 Spoon the lemon curd into the centre of the cream and top with the second meringue round. Pipe the remaining cream around the edge. Refrigerate for 2 hours, then decorate with chocolate curls.

—— VARIATION ——

For a change, you can always use chopped hazel nuts or chopped almonds. Instead of chocolate curls, finely chopped nuts or praline are good alternatives.

FROZEN RASPBERRY MERINGUE

0.30*	£ £ ✳*	454 cals

* plus at least 3 hours cooling and 6
hours freezing; freeze after stage 4

Serves 6

700 g (1½ lb) fresh raspberries,
   hulled

60 ml (4 tbsp) icing sugar

60 ml (4 tbsp) orange-flavoured
   liqueur

300 ml (10 fl oz) double cream

150 ml (5 fl oz) single cream

18 meringue shells (made from 3
   egg whites, see page 441)

1 Put half the raspberries into a
large bowl. Sift over the icing
sugar, add the liqueur and mix
gently. Cover and leave in a cool
place for 3–4 hours or overnight
until the raspberry juices run.

2 Purée the raspberry mixture in
a blender or food processor
until smooth and press through a
nylon sieve to remove the pips.

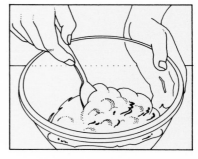

3 Whip the creams together until
they just hold their shape.
Break up the meringues into 3–4
pieces each and stir through the
cream with the raspberry purée
until just mixed but still marbled
in appearance.

4 Oil a 1.7-litre (3-pint) ring
mould. Spoon the mixture into
the prepared mould, overwrap and
freeze at least 6 hours.

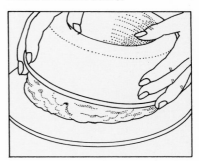

5 To serve: take straight from
the freezer. Ease out of the
mould and pile the remaining
raspberries in the centre.

MERINGUE BASKET

| 6.00* ☐ ☐ £ | 317–423 cals |

* plus 20 minutes cooling

Serves 6–8

4 egg whites

225 g (8 oz) icing sugar

1 small pineapple

3 bananas

300 ml (10 fl oz) whipping cream

30 ml (2 tbsp) kirsch

coarsely grated chocolate,
   to decorate

1 Line three baking sheets with non-stick baking parchment (turn rimmed baking sheets upside down and use the bases), and draw a 19-cm (7½-inch) circle on each. Turn the paper over so that the pencilled circle is visible but does not come into contact with the meringues and mark them.

2 Place 3 egg whites in a clean, dry heatproof bowl, and place the bowl over a pan of simmering water. Sift in 175 g (6 oz) of the icing sugar.

3 Whisk the egg whites and sugar vigorously over the simmering water until the mixture stands in very stiff peaks. Do not allow the bowl to get too hot or the meringue will crust around edges.

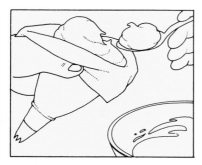

4 Fit a piping bag with a large star nozzle. Spoon in one third of the meringue mixture. Secure the paper to the baking sheets with a little meringue.

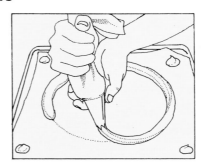

5 Pipe rings of meringue about 1 cm (½ inch) thick inside two of the circles on the paper.

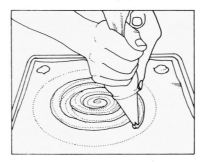

6 Fill the bag with the remaining meringue and, starting from centre, pipe a continuous coil of meringue on the third sheet of paper. Place all in the oven at 100°C (200°F) gas mark Low for 2½–3 hours to dry out.

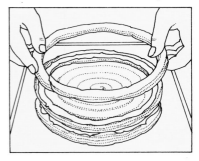

7 Use the remaining egg white and sugar to make meringue as before and put into the piping bag. Remove the cooked meringue rings from the paper and layer up on the base, piping a ring of fresh meringue between each. Return to oven for a further 1½–2 hours. Slide on to a wire rack and peel off base paper when cool.

8 Cut the pineapple across into 1-cm (½-inch) slices and snip off skin. Cut out core and divide flesh into bite-size chunks. Peel bananas and cut into 1-cm (½-inch) slices. Mix the fruits together, reserving a little pineapple and banana for decoration.

9 Just before serving, stand the meringue shell on a flat serving plate. Lightly whip the cream and fold in the kirsch; spoon half into the base of the basket and top with the fruit. Whirl the remaining cream over the top and decorate with the reserved pineapple, banana and the grated chocolate.

MAKING MERINGUES

There are three basic types of meringue. *Meringue suisse* is the most common and the most simple—egg whites are stiffly whisked, then caster sugar is folded in. *Meringue cuite* is the type of meringue used for this basket. It is firmer than *meringue suisse* and therefore better able to hold up when filled with fruit and cream as here. Although its name suggests that it is cooked, it is in fact only whisked over hot water before being baked in the same way as *meringue suisse*. *Meringue italienne* is made by combining sugar syrup with egg whites; it is difficult to make, and mostly used by professionals.

DOBOS TORTE

| 2.10 | 🍲 🍲 £ | 655 cals |

Serves 8

4 eggs

275 g (10 oz) caster sugar

150 g (5 oz) plain flour

100 g (4 oz) plain chocolate

3 egg whites

175 g (6 oz) icing sugar

225 g (8 oz) butter

50 g (2 oz) crushed biscuits or
chopped nuts, to decorate

1 Line two baking sheets with
non-stick paper. Put the whole
eggs into a heatproof bowl with
175 g (6 oz) caster sugar and place
over simmering water, whisking
until the mixture is thick enough
to leave a trail on the surface when
the whisk is lifted, then remove
from the heat.

2 Sift half the flour over the
mixture and fold in lightly with
a metal spoon. Add the remaining
flour in the same way.

3 Carefully spread some of the
mixture out on the baking
sheets in large rounds measuring
about 20 cm (8 inches) in diameter.
Bake in the oven at 190°C (375°F)
mark 5 for 7–10 minutes until
golden brown.

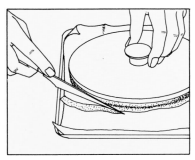

4 Loosen from the baking sheets
and trim each round to a neat
shape with a sharp knife, using a
saucepan lid as a guide. Transfer
them on to wire racks and leave
for about 15 minutes to cool.

5 Re-line the baking sheets,
spread on more mixture. Bake,
trim and cool as before. There will
be enough mixture to make six or
seven rounds.

6 Select the round with the best
surface and lay it on an oiled
baking sheet.

7 Put the remaining caster sugar
in a small, heavy based saucepan. Over a gentle heat, dissolve
the sugar, without stirring, and
boil it steadily to a rich brown.

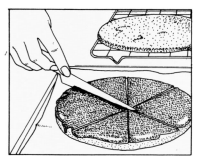

8 Pour it over the round on the
baking sheet, spreading it with
a knife brushed with oil. Mark
into eight sections and trim round
the edge.

9 Break the chocolate into a
heatproof bowl and place over
simmering water. Stir until the
chocolate is melted, then remove
from the heat.

10 Put the egg whites and icing
sugar into a heatproof bowl
and place over simmering water
Whisk until very thick, then remove from the heat.

11 Put the butter into a bowl
and beat until pale and soft.
Beat the egg and sugar mixture
into it gradually, then stir in the
melted chocolate.

12 Sandwich the remaining
biscuit rounds together with
some of the filling and put the
caramel-covered one on top.

13 Spread the sides of the torte
with more filling and press
the crushed biscuit crumbs or
chopped nuts round the sides.

14 Spoon the remaining filling
into a piping bag fitted with
a star nozzle and pipe a decorative
border round the top edge.

——————— VARIATION ———————

For a simpler filling, melt 50 g
(2 oz) plain chocolate as above and
leave to cool slightly. Cream 150 g
(5 oz) butter and gradually beat in
225 g (8 oz) sifted icing sugar.
Beat in the melted chocolate while
it is still soft.

DOBOS TORTE
The old Austro–Hungarian em-
pire is the home of this elaborate
'drum cake'. Versions of the traditional sponge rounds, layered
with chocolate cream and glazed
with caramel, are still to be found
in the best cafés and pastry shops
from Vienna to Budapest.

Be sure to mark the caramel
into portions before it hardens or
it will be extremely difficult to
cut.

PINEAPPLE GRIESTORTE

2.00* 🍴 £ 280–373 cals

* includes 30 minutes standing time

Serves 6–8

3 eggs, separated

125 g (4 oz) caster sugar

376-g (13¼-oz) can pineapple pieces, drained and juice reserved

75 g (3 oz) semolina

300 ml (10 fl oz) whipping cream

100 g (4 oz) chopped mixed nuts, toasted

1 Grease a 20-cm (8-inch) round cake tin. Base-line with greaseproof paper and grease the paper.

2 Whisk the egg yolks and sugar in a bowl until pale and really thick. Stir in 30 ml (2 tbsp) of the reserved pineapple juice together with the semolina.

3 Whisk the egg whites until stiff, then gently fold into the yolks and sugar mixture.

4 Turn into the prepared tin. Bake in the oven at 180°C (350°F) mark 4 for about 40 minutes or until the sponge springs back when pressed lightly with a finger and has shrunk away a little from the tin. Turn out on to a wire rack and leave 30 minutes to cool.

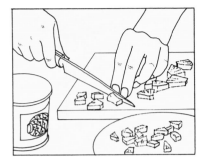

5 Roughly chop the pineapple pieces. Lightly whip the cream. Split the cake in half and fill with half the cream and half the pineapple. Spread a little of the cream around the sides and top of the cake and press the nuts on the side. Pipe the remaining cream in whirls and decorate with pineapple.

APPLE HAZEL NUT GENOESE

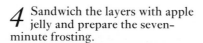

| 1.15* | £ ✳* | 450 cals |

*plus 1–2 hours cooling and 2–3 hours standing time; freeze after stage 3

Serves 6

3 eggs

100 g (4 oz) caster sugar

50 g (2 oz) plain flour

15 ml (1 tbsp) cornflour

25 g (1 oz) ground hazel nuts

75 g (3 oz) butter, melted and cooled

90 ml (6 tbsp) apple jelly

seven-minute frosting (see page 441) using 30 ml (2 tbsp) thick unsweetened apple purée instead of water

1 Grease two 18-cm (7-inch) straight-sided sandwich tins. Base-line with greaseproof paper and grease the paper.

2 Whisk the eggs and caster sugar in a bowl until very thick. Sift in the flour and cornflour and add hazel nuts, then fold in butter.

3 Turn into the prepared tins and bake in the oven at 180°C (350°F) mark 4 for about 25 minutes or until the sponge springs back when pressed lightly with a finger and has shrunk away a little from the tin. Turn out on to a wire rack and leave 1–2 hours to cool.

4 Sandwich the layers with apple jelly and prepare the seven-minute frosting.

5 Cover the cake with the frosting, peaking up the surface. Leave for 2–3 hours before serving to allow the frosting to firm up.

LEMON AND PASSION-FRUIT GÂTEAU

1.30* £ £ ✳* 278–347 cals

* plus 1–2 hours cooling and 2–3
hours macerating; freeze after stage 5

Serves 8–10

50 g (2 oz) butter

4 eggs

125 g (4 oz) caster sugar

finely grated rind and juice of 1
    lemon

125 g (4 oz) plain flour

225 g (8 oz) strawberries, hulled and
    thinly sliced

50 g (2 oz) icing sugar

3 passion-fruit

150 ml (5 fl oz) whipping cream

142 ml (5 fl oz) soured cream

1 Grease a deep 20-cm (8-inch)
round cake tin. Base-line with
greaseproof paper. Grease paper,
then dust with sugar and flour.

2 Melt the butter in a small
saucepan; do not boil. Remove
from the heat and cool for 10
minutes.

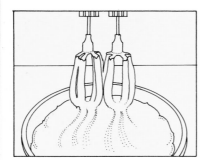

3 In another bowl, whisk together the eggs, caster sugar
and lemon rind until very pale and
thick enough to leave a trail. Sift
the flour over the egg mixture.

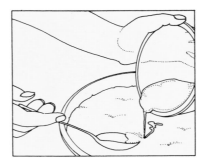

4 Drizzle over the butter. Fold
in thoroughly. Turn the mixture into the prepared tin.

5 Bake in the oven at 190°C
(375°F) mark 5 for 35–40
minutes or until a fine warmed
skewer inserted in the centre comes
out clean. Turn out on to a wire
rack and cool for 1–2 hours.

6 Meanwhile, put the strawberries into a bowl with the
lemon juice and 25 g (1 oz) icing
sugar and leave to macerate for
2–3 hours. When the cake is cold,
split in half and drizzle both halves
with the juices from the fruit.

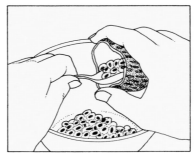

7 Using a sharp knife, cut the
passion-fruit in half and scoop
out the pulp. Discard the skin.
Lightly whip the cream, fold in
the soured cream and passion-fruit
seeds.

8 Sandwich the cakes together
with the strawberries and
cream mixture and dust with the
remaining icing sugar to serve.

GÂTEAU ST HONORÉ

| 2.00 | 🍳🍳🍳 £ £ ✳* | 709 cals |

* after stage 5

Serves 6

1 quantity pâte sucrée (page 439)

beaten egg, to glaze

1 quantity choux pastry (page 439)

300 ml (10 fl oz) double cream

45 ml (3 tbsp) sugar

45 ml (3 tbsp) water

1 quantity crème pâtissière (page 441)

angelica and glacé cherries

1 Roll out the pâte sucrée on a lightly floured working surface to an 18-cm (7-inch) round. Place on a baking sheet and prick all over with a fork. Brush a 1 cm (½ inch) band round the edge with beaten egg.

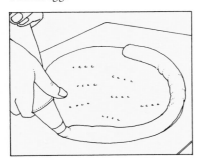

2 Put the choux pastry into a piping bag fitted with a medium plain nozzle and pipe a circle round the edge. Brush with beaten egg.

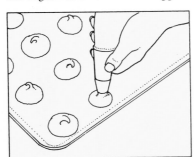

3 Dampen a baking sheet and pipe about twenty walnut-sized choux balls on to it. Brush with beaten egg.

4 Bake both the flan and the choux balls in the oven at 190°C (375°F) mark 5 for about 15 minutes or until well risen and golden brown.

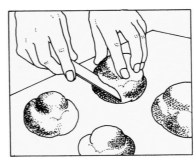

5 Make a slit in the side of each bun to release the steam, then transfer with the flan on to a wire rack and leave for 15–20 minutes to cool.

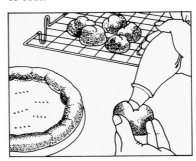

6 Whip the cream until stiff. Reserving a little cream for the top of the gateau, put the rest into a piping bag fitted with a medium plain nozzle and pipe some into each of the cold choux buns.

7 Put the sugar with the water into a heavy based saucepan and boil until the edge just begins to turn straw-coloured. Dip the tops of the choux buns in this syrup, using a skewer or tongs to hold them.

8 Use the remainder of the syrup to stick the buns on to the choux pastry border to form a wall. Fill the centre of the gateau with the crème pâtissière mixture.

9 Pipe the reserved cream around the edge, in between the choux balls. Decorate with angelica and cherries.

ST HONORÉ

This Parisian speciality is named in honour of an early French bishop, honoured as the patron saint of bakers and *pâtissièrs*. Gâteau St Honoré is a classic, always made with two types of pastry and two types of cream, assembled with the rich golden glaze of caramel. Pâte sucrée is used for the base, an ideal lining pastry to hold the crème pâtissière filling. The piped choux pastry that forms the walls of the gâteau is crisp and golden outside, hollow inside to take generous quantities of whipped double cream. Complete the decoration if you wish with spun sugar (see page 84).

PALMIERS

| 1.00 | £ ✳* | 323 cals |

* after stage 6

Makes 12

**368-g (13-oz) packet frozen puff
  pastry, thawed, or ½ quantity
  puff pastry (see page 439)**
caster sugar, for dredging
150 ml (5 fl oz) double cream
75 ml (3 fl oz) single cream

1 Roll out the pastry on a lightly
  floured working surface to a
rectangle measuring 30 × 25 cm
(12 × 10 inches).

2 Dredge with caster sugar. Fold
  the long sides of the puff pastry
halfway towards the centre.

3 Dredge with more caster sugar
  and fold again, taking the sides
right to the centre.

4 Dredge with sugar again and
  fold in half lengthways, hiding
the first folds and pressing lightly.

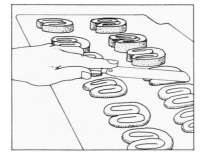

5 Cut across the pastry length
  into 24 equal-sized slices.
Dampen a baking sheet and place
the palmiers on it, cut-side down.
Flatten them slightly with a palette
knife or the palm of your hand.

6 Bake in the oven at 220°C
  (425°F) mark 7 for 8 minutes
until golden brown. Turn each
over and bake for a further 4
minutes. Transfer to a wire rack
and leave for about 20 minutes to
cool.

7 Whip the creams together with
  a little caster sugar, until lightly
peaked. Sandwich the palmiers
together with the cream before
serving. Sprinkle with caster sugar.

CREAM HORNS

| 1.45 | £ ✳* | 247 cals |

*after stage 4

Makes 8

212-g (7½-oz) packet frozen puff
   pastry, thawed, or ¼ quantity
   puff pastry (see page 439)

beaten egg, to glaze

raspberry jam

150 ml (5 fl oz) double cream

75 ml (3 fl oz) single cream

icing sugar, to decorate

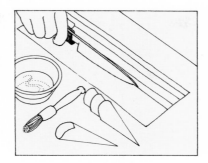

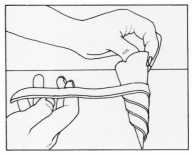

1 Roll out the pastry on a lightly
floured working surface to a
strip measuring 66 × 10 cm (26 × 4
inches). Cut the pastry lengthways
with a sharp knife into eight 1-cm
(½-inch) ribbons.

2 Grease eight cream horn tins.
Moisten one edge of each
pastry strip and wind each round a
horn tin starting at the tip, overlapping 3 mm (⅛ inch) and finishing neatly on underside. The
pastry should not overlap the
metal rim. Brush with beaten egg.

3 Dampen a baking sheet and
arrange the cream horns on it,
join-side down. Bake in the oven
at 220°C (425°F) mark 7 for 10
minutes until golden brown.

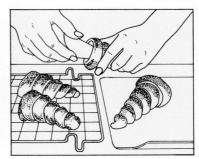

4 Cool for a few minutes then
carefully twist each tin, holding the pastry lightly in the other
hand, to ease it out of the pastry
horn. Leave the horns for about 30
minutes to cool completely.

5 When cold, fill the tip of each
horn with a little jam. Whip
the two creams together until stiff
and fill the horns down to the jam.
Sift the icing sugar and use to
dredge the horns.

FRESH PEAR SHORTCAKE

| 1.45 | f | ✱ | 444 cals |

Serves 6

150 g (5 oz) self-raising flour
25 g (1 oz) ground rice
grated rind of 1 lemon
50 g (2 oz) soft dark brown sugar
150 g (5 oz) butter
3 ripe large, even-sized pears, about 450 g (1 lb) in weight
125 g (4 oz) full fat soft cheese
1 egg
few drops almond flavouring
flaked almonds

1 Lightly grease a 20.5-cm (8-inch) loose-based fluted flan tin and set aside. In a mixing bowl, stir together the self-raising flour, ground rice and the grated lemon rind and mix them well.

2 Sieve the soft dark brown sugar into the bowl. Rub in the butter and continue lightly kneading the mixture until it forms a dough.

3 Press the dough into the prepared tin with floured fingertips. Mark into six portions and prick well with a fork.

4 Bake in the oven at 190°C (375°F) mark 5 for 30–35 minutes until light brown and cooked through. Leave in the tin to cool slightly.

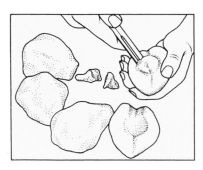

5 Using a sharp knife, peel and halve the pears. Then scoop out the cores using a teaspoon or corer. Discard the cores.

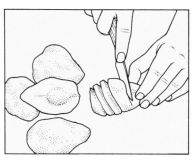

6 Slice each pear half crosswise, into pieces 3-mm ($\frac{1}{8}$-inch) thick, keeping the slices together. Then place a sliced pear half on each portion of shortcake, fanning out the slices a little.

7 Beat together the soft cheese, egg and almond flavouring until smooth, then spoon over the pears, completely covering both fruit and shortcake.

8 Bake in the oven at 180°C (350°F) mark 4 for 40 minutes until golden. Ease out of the tin and serve warm or cold.

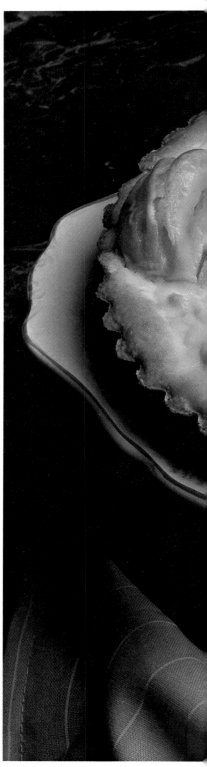

RASPBERRY WALNUT TORTE

| 1.45* | 🔲 £ £ | 539 cals |

* plus 30 minutes chilling

Serves 8

100 g (4 oz) walnuts

100 g (4 oz) unsalted butter

75 g (3 oz) caster sugar

175 g (6 oz) plain flour

450 g (1 lb) fresh raspberries

50 g (2 oz) icing sugar

30 ml (2 tbsp) raspberry-flavoured liqueur or kirsch (optional)

300 ml (10 fl oz) double cream

150 ml (5 fl oz) single cream

1 Grind the walnuts finely in a mouli grater, electric blender or food processor.

2 Cream the butter and sugar together until light and fluffy, then beat in the walnuts and flour. Divide the dough into three.

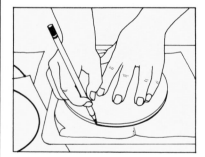

3 Draw three 20.5-cm (8-inch) circles on non-stick baking parchment. Place these on baking sheets.

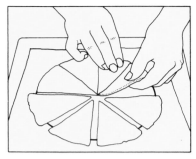

4 Put a piece of dough in the centre of each circle and press with the heel of your hand until dough is same size as circle.

5 Cut one of the circles into eight triangles with a sharp knife and ease them slightly apart. Refrigerate the pastries for 30 minutes. Bake in the oven at

190°C (375°F) mark 5 for 15–20 minutes, swapping over the sheets to ensure the pastries brown evenly. Leave to cool and harden for 10 minutes on the paper, then transfer to wire racks to cool completely.

6 Meanwhile, reserve one third of the whole raspberries for decoration. Put the rest in a bowl with the icing sugar and liqueur, if using. Crush the fruit with a fork, then leave to macerate while the pastry is cooling.

7 Assemble the torte just before serving. Whip the creams together until thick, then fold in the crushed raspberries and juice. Stand one round of pastry on a flat serving plate and spread with half of the cream mixture. Top with the remaining round of pastry and the remaining cream mixture.

8 Arrange the triangles of pastry on top of the cream, wedging them in at an angle. Scatter the reserved whole raspberries in between. Serve as soon as possible.

NON-STICK BAKING PARCHMENT

The pastry for this torte is made with ground walnuts, which make it oily and therefore more prone to sticking than ordinary pastries. Whereas greaseproof paper and foil can be used for most baking, non-stick baking parchment is recommended here because it is silicone treated and by far the best paper to use for sticky or oily mixtures. Buy it by the roll at large supermarkets, hardware stores and specialist kitchen shops.

PINEAPPLE CHEESECAKE

| 2.15* | £ £ ✳* | 720 cals |

* plus 2 hours standing time in oven and 2 hours cooling time; freeze without topping

Serves 6

50 g (2 oz) digestive biscuits

15 g ($\frac{1}{2}$ oz) butter

4 eggs, size 2, separated

225 g (8 oz) caster sugar

450 g (1 lb) full fat soft cheese

40 g (1$\frac{1}{2}$ oz) plain flour, sifted

30 ml (2 tbsp) lemon juice

284 ml (10 fl oz) soured cream

432-g (14$\frac{1}{2}$ oz) can pineapple slices

20 ml (4 tsp) arrowroot

300 ml (10 fl oz) double cream

90 g (3$\frac{1}{2}$ oz) walnut halves

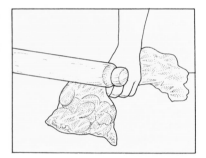

1 Put the biscuits in a strong polythene bag and crush them with a rolling pin. Lightly grease a 19-cm (7$\frac{1}{2}$-inch) round loose-bottomed cake tin and set aside.

2 Melt the butter and stir in the biscuit crumbs. Press this mixture over the base of the tin. Chill for 30 minutes to set.

3 Whisk the egg yolks with the sugar until thick and creamy. In a separate bowl, beat the cheese lightly. Add the whisked mixture to the cheese and mix until smooth. Stir in the flour, lemon juice and soured cream.

4 Whisk the egg whites until stiff and fold into the cheese and lemon mixture. Pour into the cake tin and level the surface.

5 Bake in the oven at 130°C (250°F) mark $\frac{1}{2}$ for 1$\frac{1}{2}$ hours. Turn off the heat and leave in the oven for 2 hours without opening the door. Remove from the oven and leave for 2 hours to cool in the tin. When cool, carefully remove cheesecake from the tin.

6 Drain the pineapple, reserving 150 ml ($\frac{1}{4}$ pint) syrup, and arrange over the top of the cheesecake. Blend the arrowroot with a little of the syrup. Bring the remaining syrup to the boil.

7 Add the arrowroot and, stirring all the time, cook for a few minutes until thickened. Leave to cool slightly, then spoon the syrup over the pineapple on top of the cheesecake.

8 Finely chop the walnuts, reserving twelve halves. Whip the cream until stiff and spread a little over the sides of the cheesecake, reserving a little for decoration.

9 Press the chopped walnuts around the sides. Pipe the remaining cream on top and decorate with walnut halves.

Menu Suggestion
Serve with Italian Squid Salad (page 34) and Pork Loin with Cider (page 113).

—— ALTERNATIVE TOPPINGS ——

142 ml (5 fl oz) soured cream and 25 g (1 oz) toasted flaked almonds sprinkled on top.

225 g (8 oz) fresh strawberries, hulled, and 150 ml (5 fl oz) whipping cream, piped in rosettes.

STRAWBERRY SAVARIN

| 2.00* | 🍽 £ £ ✳* | 257 cals |

*plus 1 hour chilling if served cold; freeze after baking in stage 5

Serves 6

15 g (½ oz) fresh yeast or 7.5 ml (1½ tsp) dried yeast plus a pinch of sugar

45 ml (3 tbsp) tepid milk

2 eggs, lightly beaten

50 g (2 oz) butter, melted and cooled

100 g (4 oz) plain flour

15 ml (1 tbsp) caster sugar

25 g (1 oz) desiccated coconut

90 ml (6 tbsp) redcurrant jelly or sieved strawberry jam

75 ml (5 tbsp) lemon juice

225 g (8 oz) strawberries, hulled and thinly sliced

1 Lightly oil a 1.3-litre (2¼-pint) savarin tin or ring mould and turn it upside down on absorbent kitchen paper to drain off the excess oil.

2 Crumble the fresh yeast into a bowl and cream with the tepid milk until smooth. If using the dried yeast and sugar, sprinkle the mixture into the tepid milk and leave in a warm place for 15 minutes until frothy. Gradually beat the eggs and butter into the yeast liquid.

3 Mix the flour in a bowl with the sugar and coconut. With a wooden spoon, gradually stir in the yeast mixture to form a thick smooth batter.

4 Turn into the prepared tin, cover and leave to rise for about 30 minutes or until the savarin is nearly doubled in size.

5 Bake in the oven at 190°C (375°F) mark 5 for 35–40 minutes until golden. Turn out on to a wire rack placed over a large plate. Put the jelly and lemon juice into a small pan over low heat.

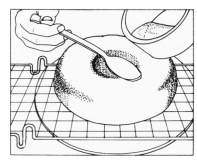

6 When the jelly is melted spoon over the warm savarin until well glazed, allowing any excess to collect on the plate under the wire rack. Transfer the savarin to a serving plate.

7 Return the excess jelly mixture to the pan and add the strawberries; stir to coat. Remove from heat and cool for 15–20 minutes or until almost set, then spoon over the savarin. Serve warm or cold with soured cream.

—— VARIATION ——

To make Strawberry babas, divide the yeast batter between six 9-cm (3½-inch) ring tins. Leave to rise until the moulds are nearly two-thirds full then bake for 15–20 minutes. Replace the lemon juice with brandy or kirsch, soak each baba well and place on individual serving plates. Finish with strawberries and soured cream as above.

APFEL STRUDEL

2.45* 🗇 🗇 £	321–401 cals

*plus 1 hour standing time

Serves 8–10

225 g (8 oz) plain flour
2.5 ml (½ tsp) salt
1 egg, slightly beaten
30 ml (2 tbsp) vegetable oil
60 ml (4 tbsp) lukewarm water
45 ml (3 tbsp) seedless raisins
45 ml (3 tbsp) currants
75 g (3 oz) caster sugar
2.5 ml (½ tsp) ground cinnamon
1 kg (2¼ lb) cooking apples, peeled, cored and grated
45 ml (3 tbsp) melted butter
100 g (4 oz) ground almonds
icing sugar, to decorate

1 Lightly oil a baking sheet. Put the flour and salt into a large bowl, make a well in the centre and pour in the egg and oil.

2 Add the water gradually, stirring with a fork to make a soft, sticky dough. Work the dough in the bowl until it leaves the sides, then turn it out on to a lightly floured surface and knead for about 15 minutes.

3 Form into a ball, place on a cloth and cover with a warmed bowl. Leave to 'rest' in a warm place for 1 hour. Put the raisins, currants, sugar, cinnamon and apples into a bowl and mix together thoroughly.

4 Warm the rolling pin. Spread a clean cotton cloth on the table and sprinkle lightly with 15–30 ml (1–2 tbsp) flour.

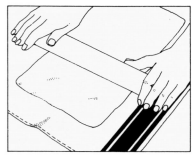

5 Place the dough on the cloth and roll out into a rectangle about 3 mm (⅛ inch) thick, lifting and turning it to prevent sticking.

6 Gently stretch the dough, working from the centre to the outside, until it is paper-thin.

7 Trim the edges to form a rectangle about 68.5 × 61 cm (27 × 24 inches). Leave the strudel dough on the cloth to dry and 'rest' for 15 minutes.

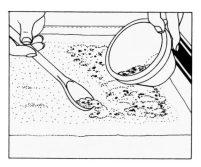

8 Position the dough with one of the long sides towards you, brush with melted butter and sprinkle with ground almonds.

9 Spread the apple mixture over the dough, leaving a 5-cm (2-inch) border uncovered all round the edge. Fold these pastry edges over the apple mixture, towards the centre.

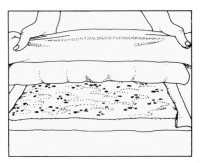

10 Lift the corners of the cloth nearest to you over the pastry, and roll up the strudel. Stop after each turn to pat into shape and to keep the roll even.

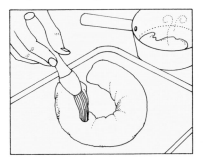

11 Form the roll into a horseshoe shape, slide it on to the prepared baking sheet and brush it with melted butter.

12 Bake in the oven at 190°C (375°F) mark 5 for about 40 minutes or until golden brown. Dredge the strudel with icing sugar. Serve hot or cold, in slices, with cream.

Drinks Party

The quickest and easiest way to entertain a crowd is to throw a drinks party, keeping the mood informal and the food simple. To serve 15–20 people, make all 3 dips suggested here, or choose 1 or 2 and increase the quantities accordingly. Serve with sticks of raw vegetables, small crackers and Italian grissini. Make double the quantity of Asparagus Tranches and Smoked Salmon and Cheese Tartlets, but only a single quantity of the Golden Fish Nuggets. The Hot Party Punch should be sufficient to serve 15–20, but make extra if you are unsure of your guests' drinking habits!

AVOCADO AND BLUE CHEESE DIP

0.20	1842 cals

175 g (6 oz) blue cheese (eg Stilton, Gorgonzola or Dolcelatte, to taste)

300 ml (½ pint) soured cream

2 ripe avocados

juice of ½ lemon

salt and freshly ground pepper

a few slices of avocado, to garnish (optional)

1 Crumble the cheese into a bowl and mash with a fork until smooth and creamy.

2 Work the soured cream gradually into the cheese until it is evenly incorporated.

3 Cut the avocados in half and remove the stones. With a teaspoon, scoop the flesh out of the skins into a separate bowl.

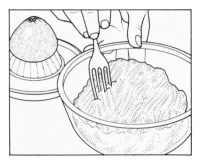

4 Add the lemon juice and mash the flesh quickly with a fork. Stir the mashed avocado flesh into the cheese and cream mixture, then add seasoning to taste and stir again.

5 Cover tightly with cling film and chill in the refrigerator until serving time. (Do not prepare more than 2 hours in advance or the avocado flesh will discolour and spoil the appearance of the dip.)

6 Spoon the dip into serving bowls. Garnish with avocado slices, if liked, and serve immediately.

CREAMY FISH DIP

| 0.20 | £ £ ✳* | 4123 cals |

* freeze at the end of step 2

two 198 g (7 oz) cans crab meat

two 198 g (7 oz) cans shrimps

450 g (1 lb) full-fat soft cheese

60 ml (4 tbsp) creamed horseradish

finely grated rind and juice of 1 lemon

5 ml (1 tsp) paprika

freshly ground pepper

lemon slices, to garnish

1 Drain the crab meat and shrimps and put the flesh in an electric blender or food processor. Work until the flesh is broken down to a pulp.

2 Add the cheese in batches and work until evenly combined with the fish. When all the cheese is incorporated, work in the creamed horseradish, lemon rind and juice, paprika and pepper.

3 Turn the mixture into serving bowls and grind black pepper liberally over the surface. Garnish with lemon slices and chill in the refrigerator until serving time.

HOT PARTY PUNCH

| 0.35 | 131–175 cals |

Makes 4.8 litres (8 pints)

12 cloves,

2 oranges

4.8 litres (8 pints) dry cider

100 g (4 oz) sugar

175 ml (6 fl oz) brandy

pinch of ground cinnamon

pinch of ground ginger

2 red-skinned dessert apples

1 Press the cloves into the whole oranges and place in a large saucepan. Pour in the cider and sugar and heat gently until simmering, stirring occasionally.

2 Stir in the brandy and spices, then simmer for 20 minutes.

3 To serve, core and slice the apples (but do not peel them). Pour the punch into a warmed bowl and float the apple slices on the top. Ladle into individual glasses as required.

HOT TOMATO DIP

| 0.30* | 3231 cals |

* plus cooling time

45 ml (3 tbsp) vegetable oil

1 large onion, skinned and finely chopped

2 garlic cloves, skinned and crushed

2.5 ml (½ tsp) chilli powder

450 g (1 lb) ripe tomatoes, skinned and chopped

300 ml (½ pint) thick homemade mayonnaise (see page 151)

dash of Tabasco sauce, to taste

salt and freshly ground pepper

1 Heat the oil in a heavy-based saucepan, add the onion and garlic and fry gently for about 5 minutes until almost soft.

2 Add the chilli powder and fry for 1–2 minutes, stirring constantly, to prevent it from burning. Add the tomatoes and stir well with a wooden spoon to break them up. Add seasoning to taste and bring to the boil, then lower the heat and simmer, uncovered, for 20 minutes until thick. Remove from the heat and leave until completely cold.

3 Turn the tomato sauce into a bowl and stir in the mayonnaise. Add Tabasco to taste. Stir well to mix, then taste and adjust the seasoning. Spoon the mixture into serving bowls, cover with cling film and chill in the refrigerator until serving time.

ASPARAGUS TRANCHES

0.40*	72 cals

* plus 30 minutes cooling

Makes 24

12 spears fresh asparagus, trimmed, or 283 g (10 oz) can asparagus tips, drained

salt and freshly ground pepper

212 g (7½ oz) packet frozen puff pastry, thawed

60 ml (4 tbsp) thick mayonnaise

2.5 ml (½ tsp) lemon juice

25 g (1 oz) walnuts, finely chopped

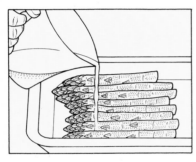

1 Place the asparagus in a large roasting tin. Cover with water and add a good pinch of salt.

2 Bring the water to the boil, then simmer until the asparagus is just tender. Remove and drain.

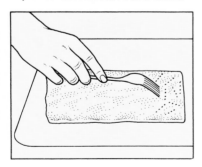

3 Roll the pastry out on a lightly floured surface to a 40.5 × 15 cm (16 × 6 inch) rectangle. Cut this in two to make 2 smaller rectangles, each measuring 20.5 × 15 cm (8 × 6 inches). Place on a wetted baking sheet. Prick all over.

4 Bake the tranches in the oven at 200°C (400°F) mark 6 for 10–15 minutes or until puffed up and golden. Transfer very carefully to a wire rack and leave to cool (about 30 minutes).

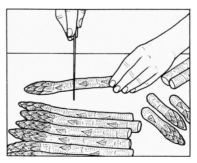

5 Cut the asparagus into 5 cm (2 inch) lengths, measuring from the tip. If using thick fresh asparagus, halve each tip lengthwise. Put the off-cuts in a blender or food processor with the mayonnaise, lemon juice and seasoning and work together until evenly combined.

6 Not more than 30 minutes before serving, trim the pastry rectangles neatly with a sharp knife to 15 × 10 cm (6 × 4 inches).

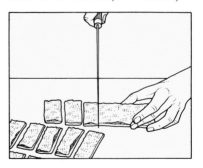

7 Spread the asparagus mayonnaise evenly over the surface of the pastry. Cut into 24 fingers, each 5 cm × 2.5 cm (2 × 1 inch). Arrange an asparagus tip on each finger, and sprinkle with the chopped walnuts.

SMOKED SALMON AND CHEESE TARTLETS

0.40*	£	101 cals

* plus 30 minutes cooling

Makes 30 tartlets

368 g (13 oz) packet frozen
   shortcrust pastry, thawed

175 g (6 oz) packet soft cheese with
   chopped chives

1 egg, beaten

150 ml ($\frac{1}{4}$ pint) single cream

100 g (4 oz) smoked salmon
   trimmings

freshly ground pepper

about 50 g (2 oz) grated Parmesan

slices of radish and strips of
   canned pimento and anchovy
   fillets, to garnish

1 Roll out the pastry on a
floured surface and cut 30
rounds each 6.5 cm (2$\frac{1}{2}$ inch). Put
these in greased patty tins. Bake
blind for about 10 minutes.

2 Put the cheese in a bowl and
gradually beat in the egg and
cream until the mixture is smooth.

3 Snip the smoked salmon in
small pieces into the cheese
mixture. Add pepper to taste.

4 Divide the filling equally
between the tartlet cases and
sprinkle with Parmesan cheese.
Bake in the oven at 180°C (350°F)
mark 4 for about 15 minutes or
until the custard mixture is set.

5 Transfer the tartlet cases to a
wire rack and leave to cool for
30 minutes. Garnish with radish
slices and strips of pimento and
anchovy before serving.

GOLDEN FISH NUGGETS
WITH GARLIC DIP

0.45	1967 cals

Makes about 30

450 g (1 lb) monkfish

120 ml (8 tbsp) dried breadcrumbs

60 ml (4 tbsp) sesame seeds

30 ml (2 tbsp) flour

salt and freshly ground pepper

15 ml (1 tbsp) paprika

1 egg, size 2, beaten

45 ml (3 tbsp) snipped fresh chives
   or 15 ml (3 tsp) dried

1 garlic clove, skinned and crushed

300 ml ($\frac{1}{2}$ pint) soured cream

vegetable oil, for deep-frying

snipped fresh chives, to garnish

1 Skin the monkfish and cut into
2.5 cm (1 inch) pieces.
Combine the breadcrumbs and
sesame seeds.

——— VARIATION ———

Use **sliced chicken breasts**
instead of the fish, crumbed and
fried in the same way. Instead of
the garlic dip, serve them with a
raita sauce made from **chopped
fresh mint, coriander, natural
yogurt, cucumber** and **garlic**.

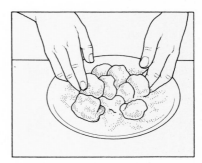

2 Toss the fish in the flour
seasoned with salt and pepper
to taste and the paprika. Dip in
the beaten egg and finely coat in
the breadcrumb and sesame seed
mixture. Chill in the refrigerator
for at least 30 minutes to set the
breadcrumb and sesame coating.

3 Combine the chives with
crushed garlic and soured
cream. Chill until serving time.

4 Heat the oil in a deep-fat frier
to 180°C (350°F) and deep-fry
the nuggets of fish for 3–4
minutes until golden. Drain well
on absorbent kitchen paper. Serve
hot, with the garlic dip.

311

SNACKS AND FINGER FOODS

SPICED MINI MEATBALLS WITH PEANUT DIP

| 0.35 | £ ✳* | 80 cals |

* meatballs will freeze; dip will not

75 g (3 oz) block creamed coconut, broken into pieces

120 ml (8 tbsp) boiling water

60 ml (4 tbsp) crunchy peanut butter

30 ml (2 tbsp) soft brown sugar

5 ml (1 tsp) chilli sauce

salt and freshly ground pepper

450 g (1 lb) fine or ground minced beef

30 ml (2 tbsp) natural yogurt

30 ml (2 tbsp) soy sauce

5 ml (1 tsp) ground coriander

5 ml (1 tsp) ground turmeric

5 ml (1 tsp) olive or vegetable oil

vegetable oil, for deep frying

1 Make the dip. Put the coconut in a saucepan, add the boiling water and stir until the coconut has dissolved. Add the next three ingredients and season to taste; stir over gentle heat until thick and well combined. Remove from the heat and set aside.

2 Make the meatballs. Put the remaining ingredients in a bowl and season to taste. Mix with your hands until well combined, squeezing the mixture so that it clings together.

3 Form the mixture into about fifty bite-sized balls by rolling heaped teaspoonfuls in the palms of your hands.

4 Heat the oil in a deep-fat frier to 190°C (375°F). Add the meatballs about 10 at a time and deep-fry for 1–2 minutes only until lightly coloured. Remove with a slotted spoon and drain on absorbent kitchen paper while frying the remainder.

5 Spear each meatball with a cocktail stick. Reheat the dip, stirring constantly to keep smooth. Pour the dip into a small bowl and place in the centre of a large, circular platter. Arrange the meatballs around the bowl of dip. Serve both meatballs and dip hot.

ANCHOVY CRESCENTS

| 0.45 | £ | ✳* | 337 cals |

* freeze before frying

175 g (6 oz) full fat soft cheese

two 50-g (2-oz) cans anchovies, drained and soaked in milk for 20 minutes

finely grated rind of 2 lemons

30 ml (2 tbsp) finely chopped fresh parsley

1.25–2.5 ml ($\frac{1}{4}$–$\frac{1}{2}$ tsp) paprika, according to taste

freshly ground pepper

368-g (13-oz) packet frozen puff pastry, thawed or 225 g (8 oz) homemade (see page 438)

vegetable oil, for deep-frying

grated Parmesan cheese, to finish (optional)

1 Put the cheese in a bowl and beat until creamy. Drain the anchovies, rinse and pat dry with absorbent kitchen paper. Mash them roughly, then add them to the cheese with the lemon rind and parsley. Add paprika and pepper to taste and beat well to mix.

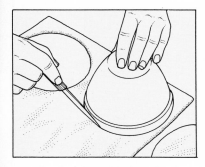

2 Roll out half the pastry on a lightly floured surface and cut out seven to eight 12-cm (5-inch) circles using a basin or small plate as a guide. Halve each circle.

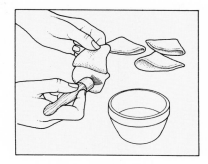

3 Brush the edges of one semi-circle with water, then fold in half and seal the straight edge to make a cone shape.

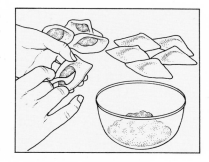

4 Fill each cone with about 5 ml (1 tsp) of the cheese mixture, then press and crimp the top edge to seal. Repeat with the remaining semi-circles, then roll out and repeat with the remaining half of the dough, to make about thirty crescents in all.

5 Heat the oil in a deep-fat frier to 190°C (375°F). Lower the crescents into the oil a few at a time and deep-fry for 1–2 minutes until puffed up and golden brown.

6 Remove with a slotted spoon and drain on absorbent paper while frying the remainder. Sprinkle with Parmesan and paprika while still hot, if liked. Serve warm.

MUSHROOM SAVOURIES

| 0.15* | £ | 33 cals |

* plus 2–3 hours chilling

450 g (1 lb) button mushrooms, wiped

25 g (1 oz) butter

50 g (2 oz) fresh brown breadcrumbs

20 ml (4 tsp) mango chutney

salt and pepper

seasoned flour

2 eggs, size 2, beaten

grated Parmesan cheese

mayonnaise, to serve

1 Chop the mushroom stalks finely. Melt the butter in a pan, stir in the stalks and half the crumbs. Sauté for 2–3 minutes. Off the heat, stir in the chutney; season.

2 Sandwich two mushroom caps together with a little of the mixture. Roll the mushrooms in seasoned flour, dip in egg and coat with the remaining breadcrumbs mixed with 50 g (2 oz) grated Parmesan. Chill for 2–3 hours.

3 Deep-fry for 3–4 minutes until golden brown. Drain well and roll in Parmesan. Leave to cool completely. Serve on cocktail sticks with mayonnaise.

Christmastime Parties

Christmas is the time for large gatherings. A wonderful time for socialising, but sometimes a worrying and exhausting time for the one who's providing the eats. In this chapter there are lots of ideas which should make the catering plain sailing. They're all dishes that can be made well ahead of time, and which can feed large numbers, so that when it comes to party time, you can relax and enjoy yourself too.

GLAZED GAMMON

| 3.15* | 465 cals |

* plus at least 3 hours or overnight
soaking, and cooling

Serves 12

2.3 kg (5 lb) joint of gammon
1 onion, skinned
whole cloves
1 carrot, peeled
1 teaspoon ground mixed spice
6 black peppercorns
2 bay leaves
60 ml (4 tbsp) red wine or red wine
  vinegar
60 ml (4 tbsp) brandy
juice of 1 large lemon
30 ml (2 tbsp) redcurrant jelly
watercress and spiced peaches,
  to garnish (optional)

1 Soak the gammon joint in
several changes of water for at
least 3 hours, preferably overnight. Drain, then weigh and
calculate the cooking time, allowing 25 minutes per 450 g (1 lb),
plus 25 minutes.

2 Put the gammon into a very
large saucepan. Add the onion
stuck with a few cloves, the carrot,
mixed spice, peppercorns, bay
leaves and wine or wine vinegar.

3 Pour in enough cold water to
cover the gammon and bring
to the boil. Lower the heat, cover
and simmer for half of the calculated cooking time. Remove from
the pan and discard the liquid.

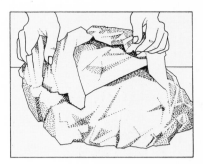

4 With a sharp knife, strip the
skin off the gammon while still
hot. Wrap the joint in foil and
bake in the oven at 180°C (350°F)
mark 4 for all but 30 minutes of
the remaining cooking time.
Unwrap the joint.

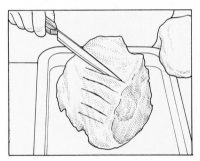

5 With the point of a sharp
knife, score a diamond pattern
in the fat. Insert cloves into the
intersections of the diamonds.

6 Put the brandy, lemon juice
and redcurrant jelly in a small
heavy-based saucepan and heat
gently until the jelly has melted.
Boil until reduced to a glaze, then
quickly brush over the exposed
fat. Return to the oven, increase
the temperature to 220°C (425°F)
mark 7 and cook for a further 30
minutes. Serve cold, garnished
with spiced peaches.

Menu Suggestion
Glazed Gammon makes an
impressive table centrepiece for a
buffet party. Cut a few slices of
gammon, then leave the rest for
guests to help themselves.

PARTY PÂTÉ

2.45* £ £ ✳ 305–381 cals

* plus cooling and chilling for 1–3 days

Serves 8–10

225 g (8 oz) belly pork, rind and bone removed

225 g (8 oz) chicken livers

100 g (4 oz) fresh white crustless bread

225 g (8 oz) pork sausagemeat

30 ml (2 tbsp) juniper berries, crushed

30 ml (2 tbsp) cranberry sauce

2.5 ml (½ tsp) grated nutmeg

120 ml (8 tbsp) brandy

2 oranges

salt and freshly ground pepper

1 egg, beaten

450 g (1 lb) boneless game (eg breast of pheasant or rabbit)

orange slices and whole juniper berries, to garnish

1 Mince the belly pork with the chicken livers and bread, or work in a food processor. Turn into a bowl, add the sausagemeat, juniper berries, cranberry sauce, nutmeg and half of the brandy.

2 Mix well together. Grate the rind and squeeze the juice of 1 of the oranges. Add to the pâté mixture with salt and pepper to taste, then bind with beaten egg.

3 Put half of the pâté mixture into a greased and base-lined 1 kg (2 lb) loaf tin, pressing it down with the back of the spoon.

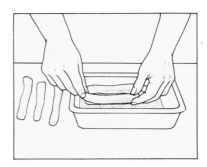

4 Cut the game into thin, even slices and arrange over the pâté mixture. Cover with the remaining pâté and press down.

5 Cover the tin with lightly oiled foil. Stand it in a roasting tin half filled with hot water. Bake at 170°C (325°F) mark 3 for 2 hours.

6 Lift the dish out of the water and place heavy weights on top of the foil covering. Leave until cold, then refrigerate for 1–3 days before serving.

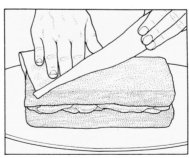

7 To serve, unmould onto a serving plate and wipe away excess fat with absorbent kitchen paper. Squeeze the juice of the remaining orange and pour into a small heavy-based pan. Add the remaining brandy and boil rapidly until reduced. Brush all over the pâté and garnish with orange slices and juniper berries.

Menu Suggestion

Serve this strongly-flavoured pâté with granary French bread and a full-bodied red wine.

TURKEY TERRINE

| 2.00* | £ | ✳ | 311–415 cals |

* plus 2 hours cooling and overnight chilling

Serves 6–8

225 g (8 oz) cooked turkey meat

225 g (8 oz) turkey or pig's liver

175 g (6 oz) thinly sliced streaky bacon rashers, rinded

1 medium onion

225 g (8 oz) sausagemeat

1 garlic clove, skinned and crushed

15 ml (1 tbsp) chopped fresh sage or 5 ml (1 tsp) dried

45 ml (3 tbsp) double cream

30 ml (2 tbsp) brandy

1 egg

salt and freshly ground pepper

bay leaf

1 Mince the turkey, liver, 50 g (2 oz) of the bacon and the onion. (Alternatively, work in a food processor.)

2 Put the minced mixture in a bowl. Add the sausagemeat, garlic, sage, cream, brandy, egg and salt and pepper to taste. Mix with a spoon until all the ingredients are evenly combined.

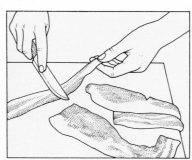

3 Stretch the remaining bacon rashers with the flat side of a blade of a large cook's knife.

4 Use the bacon rashers to line a 1.1 litre (2 pint) terrine or loaf tin, making sure there are no gaps.

5 Spoon the meat mixture into the container and place a bay leaf on top. Cover tightly with foil or a lid, then stand the container in a roasting tin.

6 Pour 3.5 cm (1½ inches) hot water into the roasting tin, then bake in the oven at 170°C (325°F) mark 3 for about 1½ hours. Remove from the water bath and leave to cool for 2 hours. Place heavy weights on top of the terrine and chill in the refrigerator overnight.

7 To serve, turn the terrine out of the container onto a plate and cut into slices.

Menu Suggestion

Turkey Terrine is a good dish for a buffet party because it is so easy to serve. A selection of salads would be the best accompaniments, especially the Red Cabbage on page 327.

TURKEY TERRINE

The method of baking a terrine in a roasting tin with hot water, called a *bain marie* or water bath, is essential if the mixture is to cook properly—the hot water distributes the oven heat evenly through the mixture and gives a moist result. Special water baths can be bought at kitchen equipment shops, but an ordinary roasting tin does the job just as well, and can be used in the oven or on top of the cooker according to individual recipe instructions. Always cover the mixture tightly with foil when cooking in a water bath, or the top of the terrine will form an unpleasant hard crust.

GALANTINE OF DUCKLING

3.00* 🥘 🥘 £ £ ✳ | 405 cals |

* plus 2 hours cooling and 8 hours chilling

Serves 8

2 kg (4½ lb) oven-ready duckling

225 g (8 oz) minced pork

225 g (8 oz) minced veal

125 g (4 oz) fresh breadcrumbs

125 g (4 oz) sliced cooked ham, roughly chopped

8 stuffed green olives, roughly chopped

finely grated rind of 1 orange

10 ml (2 tsp) chopped fresh sage or 2.5 ml (½ tsp) dried

salt and freshly ground pepper

1 egg, beaten

fresh sage sprigs, to garnish

1 Remove the giblets and place the duckling breast side down on a board. Using a small, sharp knife, cut straight along the back bone through the skin and flesh.

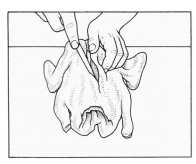

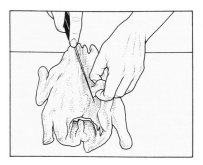

2 Start the boning from 1 side of the duckling. Carefully fillet and scrape the flesh and skin away from the rib cage (see above). Ease out the 'oyster' (the small pad of flesh at either side of the back bone. See above right).

3 As the leg joint is reached, locate and loosen the ball and socket joint with the point of the knife. Sever the ligaments to free the leg from the carcass. Loosen the ball and socket wing joint in the same way. Cut out the narrow bone protruding above the wing joint, scraping clear of the flesh.

4 Ease the skin and flesh away from the carcass and detach the leg and wing joints from the other side of the bird.

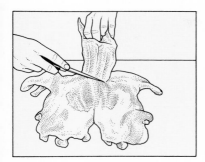

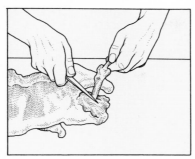

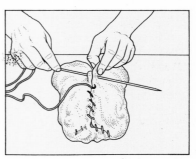

9 Spoon a little stuffing into the leg cavities, pressing it in firmly. Mound the remaining stuffing in the centre of the body section.

5 Scrape the flesh away from the breast bone, cutting closely against the ridge of the breast bone to free the carcass. Be very careful not to puncture the skin around the breast bone or the stuffing will ooze out.

6 With the duckling skin side down, loosen the exposed tips of the leg bones. Gradually scrape and push the flesh off the bones. Work around the hinge joint and then pull the leg completely inside out, detaching the bone from the flesh as far down as possible. Snip away sinews and then push the flesh back into the leg skin.

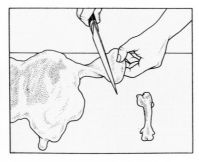

7 Snap the wing joints open. Push and scrape the flesh off the first joint. Ease out this bone and chop off wings at elbows. Trim any excess skin and fat from both ends of the duckling. Retain sufficient skin to sew around the stuffing.

8 Make the stuffing. Put the minced pork and veal in to a large bowl with the breadcrumbs. Add the ham, olives, orange rind, sage and plenty of salt and pepper. Mix well, then bind with the beaten egg.

10 Using a needle and fine string or cotton, sew up the body and wing cavities with neat, overlapping stitches. Turn the bird over, breast side up, push back into shape and secure with skewers.

11 Weigh the duckling and calculate the cooking time, allowing 25 minutes per 450 g (1 lb). Place on a rack placed over a roasting tin. Sprinkle with salt. Roast in the oven for the calculated cooking time at 180°C (350°F) mark 4, basting occasionally.

12 When the duckling is cooked, the juices should run clear when the bird is pierced with a fine skewer. Cool for at least 2 hours, then chill in the refrigerator for 8 hours or over-night. To serve, ease out string and slice. Garnish with sprigs of sage.

Menu Suggestion
Galantine of Duckling is a splendid dish for a cold table.

GAME PÂTÉ EN CROÛTE

| 2.30* | 🍴 | £ £ | ✳ | 773–1030 cals |

* plus 8 hours marinating, 6 hours
cooling and 30 minutes to come to
room temperature

Serves 6–8

**2 pheasants or mixture of game
to give 450 g (1 lb) meat**

150 ml ($\frac{1}{4}$ pint) port

4 juniper berries, crushed

350 g (12 oz) plain flour

7.5 ml (1$\frac{1}{2}$ tsp) salt

**150 ml ($\frac{1}{4}$ pint) milk or milk and
water mixed**

50 g (2 oz) lard

50 g (2 oz) butter

350 g (12 oz) lean pork

350 g (12 oz) pork fat

**100 g (4 oz) lean veal or chicken
breast**

5 ml (1 tsp) ground allspice

1 garlic clove, skinned and crushed

salt and freshly ground pepper

1 egg, beaten, to glaze

15 g ($\frac{1}{2}$ oz) gelatine

**600 ml (1 pint) cold game stock or
28.35 g (1 oz) packet aspic
powder**

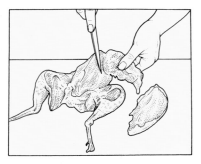

1 Remove all the flesh from the
pheasant, keeping breast meat
as whole as possible; discard skin.
Place all this meat in a shallow
dish, pour over the port, add
crushed juniper berries, cover and
marinate in the refrigerator for 8
hours or overnight.

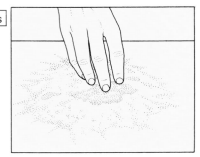

2 To make the pastry: mix the
flour and salt together on a
board or work surface. Pour the
milk or milk and water into a
saucepan, add the lard and butter
and bring to the boil. Pour on to
the dry ingredients. Working
quickly, beat to make a soft dough.
Lightly pinch together with one
hand; knead until smooth.

3 Cover the dough with cling
film and leave to rest in the
refrigerator for 20–30 minutes.
Cut off three-quarters of the
pastry and roll out to a thickness
of 0.5 cm ($\frac{1}{4}$ inch). Make it large
enough to fit an 21.5 cm (8$\frac{1}{2}$ inch)
hinged pie mould.

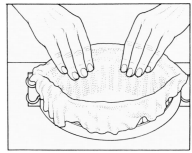

4 Place the pie mould on a
baking sheet and lift the rolled
pastry into it. Press carefully into
the mould and trim to stand
0.5 cm ($\frac{1}{4}$ inch) above the rim.

5 Mince all the marinated
pheasant flesh, except for the
breast, with the pork, pork fat,
and veal or chicken. Add the
allspice, garlic, salt and pepper.

6 Take the pheasant breasts out
of the marinade and bat them
out thinly between sheets of strong
cling film or heavy-duty foil.
Strain the marinade, discard the
juniper berries and add the
marinade to the minced meats.

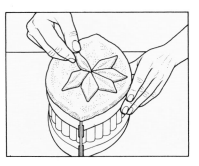

7 Layer the minced mixture and
pheasant breasts in the pie.
Roll out the remaining pastry and
place on top of the filling.
Dampen the edges, pinch them
together and flute. Cut a hole in
the centre of the pastry lid,
decorate with pastry leaves.

8 Brush the pastry with beaten
egg, then bake the pâté in the
oven at 220°C (425°F) mark 7 for
15–20 minutes. Reduce the temperature to 180°C (350°F) mark 4
and bake for 1 hour until the pâté
is tender when tested through the
hole with skewer.

9 Remove the sides of the tin and brush the pie with beaten egg. Bake for another 30 minutes. Cool completely for at least 4 hours.

10 Heat the stock in a saucepan and sprinkle in the gelatine. Stir briskly until dissolved. Leave to cool slightly. (If using packet aspic powder, make up 600 ml (1 pint) liquid aspic jelly according to manufacturer's instructions and leave until cool but not set.)

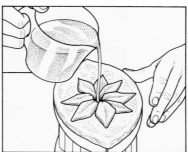

11 Pour the liquid through the hole in the pastry lid, leave to cool completely, for at least 2 hours then chill in the refrigerator. Leave at cool room temperature for 30 minutes before serving.

Menu Suggestion
Serve for a very special dinner party starter with a good French Côte du Rhône. No accompaniment is necessary. Alternatively, serve for a buffet party with a selection of salads.

SMOKED SALMON QUICHE

1.00* £ £ ✳* 336–420 cals

* plus 30 minutes chilling; freeze
for 1 month only

Serves 8–10

225 g (8 oz) plain flour

salt and freshly ground pepper

115 g (4 oz) butter or margarine

1 egg yolk

10 ml (2 tsp) lemon juice

about 30 ml (2 tbsp) cold water

175 g (6 oz) full-fat soft cheese

300 ml (½ pint) single or double
   cream

3 eggs

175 g (6 oz) smoked salmon pieces

finely grated rind of 1 lemon

5 ml (1 tsp) paprika

1 Sift the flour and a pinch of
salt together into a bowl. Cut
the butter into small pieces and
add to the flour.

2 Lightly rub in the butter with
your fingertips until the
mixture resembles fine
breadcrumbs.

3 Add the egg yolk and half of
the lemon juice, then add
enough water to bind the mixture
together in large lumps.

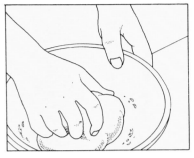

4 With 1 hand, collect the
mixture together to form a
ball. Knead lightly for a few
seconds to give a firm, smooth
dough. Do not overhandle.

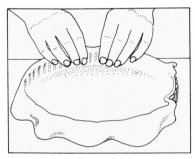

5 Roll out the dough on a
floured surface and use to line
a 25.5 cm (10 inch) loose-bottomed
metal flan tin. Chill in the
refrigerator for 30 minutes.

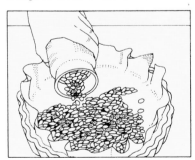

6 Prick the pastry base and then
line with foil and fill with
baking beans. Bake blind on a
preheated baking sheet in the oven
at 200°C (400°F) mark 6 for 10
minutes. Remove the foil and
beans and return to the oven for a
further 5 minutes.

7 Prepare the filling. Put the
cheese in a bowl and gradually
whisk in the cream. When well
mixed and smooth, add the eggs
and beat well to mix.

8 Add the salmon, grated lemon
rind and remaining lemon
juice. Season with a little salt and
plenty of pepper, then add half of
the paprika and beat well to mix.

9 Pour the filling into the baked
flan case and bake in the oven
at 190°C (375°F) mark 5 for 25–30
minutes until set. Sprinkle with
the remaining paprika while very
hot. Serve warm or cold.

Menu Suggestion
Serve for a buffet, with
champagne and salads.

WATERCRESS AND RICOTTA QUICHE

1.00*	✳	402–536 cals

* plus 30 minutes chilling

Serves 6–8

pastry made with 225 g (8 oz) flour (see left)

50 g (2 oz) butter or margarine

1 bunch of spring onions, trimmed and finely chopped

2 bunches of watercress

100 g (4 oz) Ricotta or curd cheese

300 ml ($\frac{1}{2}$ pint) single or double cream (or whipping)

3 eggs, beaten

2.5 ml ($\frac{1}{2}$ tsp) grated nutmeg

salt and freshly ground pepper

1 Line a 25.5 cm (10 inch) loose-bottomed metal flan tin with the pastry. Bake blind on a pre-heated baking sheet (see left).

2 Prepare the filling. Melt the butter in a saucepan, add the spring onions and fry gently for about 5 minutes until softened. Add the watercress and fry for a few minutes more, stirring frequently.

3 Transfer the contents of the pan to a blender or food processor. Add the next 4 ingredients with salt and pepper to taste and work until smooth and evenly blended.

4 Pour the filling into the baked flan case and bake in the oven at 190°C (375°F) mark 5 for 25–30 minutes until set. Serve warm or leave until cold.

Menu Suggestion

Watercress and Ricotta Quiche has quite a hot and spicy 'kick' to it. Serve as part of a buffet party spread with mayonnaise- or cream-based salads.

PRAWN AND MUSHROOM BOUCHÉES

| 1.30* | ⧉ | £ £ | 174 cals |

* plus cooling time

Makes 64

100 ml (4 fl oz) dry white wine

75 g (3 oz) butter or margarine

450 g (1 lb) peeled prawns, thawed

225 g (8 oz) button mushrooms, wiped and thinly sliced

75 g (3 oz) plain flour

568 ml (1 pint) milk

300 ml (½ pint) double cream

225 g (8 oz) Gruyère or Emmental

60 ml (4 tbsp) grated Parmesan

salt and freshly ground pepper

four 397 g (14 oz) packets frozen puff pastry, thawed

beaten egg, to glaze

chopped fresh parsley, unshelled prawns and lemon twists, to garnish

1 First make the filling. Pour the wine into a small, heavy-based saucepan and bring to the boil. Boil rapidly until reduced to 15 ml (1 tbsp). Remove from heat.

2 Melt the butter in a clean large saucepan, add the mushrooms and prawns and fry over moderate heat, stirring constantly, for about 5 minutes. Remove with a slotted spoon and drain on absorbent kitchen paper.

3 Add the flour to the juices in the pan and cook gently, stirring, for 1–2 minutes. Remove from the heat and gradually blend in the milk. Bring to the boil, stirring constantly, then simmer for 3 minutes until thick and smooth.

4 Add the cream and reduced white wine, then the Gruyère and Parmesan. Simmer, stirring, until the cheese melts, then remove from the heat and fold in the drained prawns and mushrooms. Season with plenty of salt and pepper, cover with cling film and leave to go cold.

5 Meanwhile, make the bouchée cases. Roll out each packet of pastry to an oblong 24.5 × 23 cm (9½ × 9 inches).

6 Using a plain 5 cm (2 inch) round or oval cutter, cut out 16 rounds from each oblong. Place the rounds on dampened baking sheets and brush with beaten egg.

7 Using a plain 2.5 cm (1 inch) round cutter, cut partway through the centre of each round.

8 Bake in the oven at 220°C (425°F) mark 7 for about 10 minutes. Remove the soft centres from each bouchée and cool.

9 To serve, fill the cooled cases with cold filling and reheat in the oven at 180°C (350°F) mark 4 for about 5 minutes. Serve hot, garnished with prawns and lemon.

Menu Suggestion
Bouchées (or 'little mouthfuls') can be eaten with the fingers; just right for a cocktail party.

RED CABBAGE SALAD

| 0.30 | £ | 272 cals |

Serves 8

900 g (2 lb) red cabbage
150 ml (¼ pint) olive oil
150 ml (¼ pint) white wine vinegar
15 ml (1 tbsp) sugar
5 ml (1 tsp) paprika
60 ml (4 tbsp) redcurrant jelly
50 g (2 oz) Danish Blue
salt and freshly ground pepper
4 crisp dessert apples (eg Granny Smith's)

1 Shred the cabbage finely with a sharp knife, discarding any damaged outer leaves and thick, woody stalks.

2 Put the olive oil in a large bowl with the wine vinegar, sugar and paprika. Whisk vigorously with a fork until well combined. Heat the redcurrant jelly gently in a small saucepan until runny, then whisk into the dressing.

3 Crumble the cheese into the dressing, add salt and pepper to taste and whisk again.

4 Core the apples (but do not peel them). Slice them thinly, then place in a large salad bowl with the shredded cabbage. Pour over the dressing and toss well.

5 Cover the bowl tightly with cling film and chill in the refrigerator until serving time (up to 24 hours).

Menu Suggestion
Red Cabbage Salad is excellent served with any cold roast meat for buffet parties, and is also particularly good with hot roast pork and game—the sharpness of the dressing offsets the richness of the meat.

RED CABBAGE SALAD
The method used here of marinating red cabbage in oil and wine vinegar is a Danish one. The marinade has a softening as well as a flavouring effect on hard cabbage, so that the end result is almost as if the cabbage has been cooked. Called *rødkål* in Danish, red cabbage is traditionally served with cold pork, and with the Danish pork and beef meatballs called *frikadeller*.

CHEESE D'ARTOIS

0.45*	£	✳	60–80 cals

* plus 30 minutes chilling

Makes 30–40

150 g (5 oz) Gruyère, grated

25 g (1 oz) walnut pieces, coarsely chopped

freshly ground pepper

1 egg, beaten

370 g (13 oz) packet frozen puff pastry, thawed

1 In a bowl, mix together the cheese, nuts and pepper to taste. Bind with the egg, reserving a little egg to glaze the pastry.

2 Roll out the pastry to a rectangle 40.5 × 38 cm (16 × 15 inches).

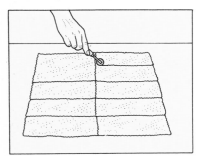

3 Cut the pastry into 10 strips, each measuring 20.5 × 7.5 cm (8 × 3 inches), using a pastry wheel for an attractive edge.

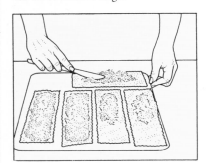

4 Lay 5 strips on an ungreased baking sheet, divide the filling equally between them and spread it out evenly, almost to the edges.

5 Cover with the remaining 5 strips and lightly press the edges to seal. Cover with cling film and chill in the refrigerator for 30 minutes.

6 Mark each strip into 6–8 fingers and brush with the reserved egg. Bake in the oven at 200°C (400°F) mark 6 for about 15 minutes until risen and golden brown. Cut the pastry through into fingers and serve immediately.

Menu Suggestion

Serve these nutty cheese fingers for cocktail 'nibbles' during the festive season, or at a Christmas party.

CHEESE D'ARTOIS

D'Artois or *Dartois* is a French pastry dish, made with either puff pastry as here, or with flaky pastry. Cheese is a popular filling, but there are also many French recipes for sweet *dartois*. French pastry cream (*crème pâtissière*) is used for the filling, sometimes flavoured with vanilla, ground almonds or rum. The method of making a pastry 'sandwich' then marking it into fingers, is always the same, for both the sweet and the savoury versions of *D'Artois*.

HAM PINWHEELS

0.15* £ 15 cals

* plus 2 hours chilling

Makes about 30 pinwheels

75 g (3 oz) full-fat soft cheese

10 ml (2 tsp) creamed horseradish

5 ml (1 tsp) finely chopped gherkins

salt and freshly ground pepper

113 g (4 oz) packet (5 thin slices)
    lean ham

cucumber slices, to garnish

1 Mix the cheese, creamed horseradish and gherkins together and beat until soft. Add salt and pepper to taste.

2 On a flat surface, lay out the slices of ham. Spread the cheese mixture over the slices.

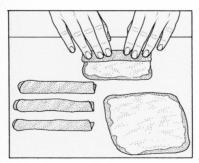

3 Roll up the slices like Swiss rolls. Put on a plate, seam side downwards, then cover with cling film. Chill in the refrigerator for at least 2 hours.

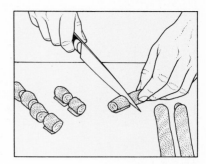

4 To serve, cut each roll into 2 cm ($\frac{3}{4}$ inch) thick slices with a sharp knife. Garnish with cucumber slices.

Menu Suggestion
Ham Pinwheels are just the thing to pass round at a Christmas drinks party. They look attractive on a large serving platter, and are easy to eat with the fingers.

HAM PINWHEELS

Just a teaspoon or two of horseradish can make all the difference to a filling, sauce or salad dressing. Horseradish is a perennial plant related to mustard; it has a powerfully hot bite to it, and should always be used in very small quantities. It is extremely easy to grow in the garden, and also easy to deal with at the harvesting stage. Simply lift the roots in the autumn, scrub them, then grate them into a jar and cover with wine vinegar. The creamed horseradish specified in this recipe is a commercially bottled condiment of grated horseradish mixed with vinegar, sugar, oil and cream. It is milder than grated horseradish.

HOT CHEESE

| 0.15* | £ ✳ | 53 cals |

* plus 1 hour chilling

Makes 24

3 rashers streaky bacon, rinded

100 g (4 oz) Cheddar, finely grated

50 g (2 oz) plain flour

50 g (2 oz) butter, softened

salt and freshly ground pepper

pinch of cayenne

15 ml (1 tbsp) caraway or sesame seeds

watercresss sprigs, to garnish (optional)

1 Grill the bacon until crisp, then chop finely. Place in a bowl with the other ingredients and work together until they form a ball.

2 Roll the mixture into 24 balls and arrange on a large un-greased baking sheet. Cover with cling film and chill in the refrigerator for at least 1 hour until firm.

3 To serve, uncover and bake in the oven at 190°C (375°F) mark 5 for about 10 minutes until golden. Serve hot, garnished with watercress sprigs if liked

Menu Suggestion
These tiny cheese and bacon flavour balls make perfect finger food for a drinks party when guests are standing up. For even easier eating, spear each ball on a cocktail stick before arranging them on a large platter.

333

CHEESE TWISTS

| 0.35* | £ | ✳ | 21 cals |

* plus 30 minutes chilling
Makes about 70

65 g (2½ oz) butter, softened

40 g (1½ oz) full-fat soft cheese

1 egg yolk

175 g (6 oz) plain flour

salt

cayenne

30 ml (2 tbsp) freshly grated
  Parmesan

1 In a bowl, beat the butter with the soft cheese and egg yolk. Sift in the flour with a pinch each of salt and cayenne, then stir until evenly mixed. Stir in 10 ml (2 tsp) water to form a dough.

2 Knead the dough lightly until smooth; wrap in cling film and chill for 30 minutes.

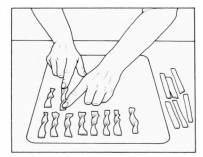

3 Roll out the pastry thinly and cut into narrow strips measuring about 7.5 cm × 5 mm (3 × ¼ inch). Twist the strips and place on ungreased baking sheets, pressing the ends down well to prevent the strips unwinding. Sprinkle with the Parmesan.

4 Bake in the oven at 180°C (350°F) mark 4 for about 15 minutes. Transfer to wire racks and leave to cool for about 15 minutes. Store in an airtight container for up to 2 weeks.

Menu Suggestion
Serve for a Christmas drinks party, on platters or in bowls.

— VARIATIONS —

MEDALLIONS
Prepare pastry, roll out and cut into 2.5 cm (1 inch) rounds. Sprinkle with Parmesan and bake. Cool. Either sandwich together or top the rounds with softened pâté, fish paste or cream cheese; garnish with slices of olives, radish or gherkin.

BLUE CHEESE STRAWS
Rub the butter into the flour with the seasonings. Grate 75 g (3 oz) blue cheese into the mixture, add the egg yolk and 2.5 ml (½ tsp) Dijon mustard. Mix to form a soft dough. Wrap and chill for 30 minutes and proceed from step 3.

SALTED ALMONDS OR HAZELNUTS

| 0.40* | £ £ | 2139 cals |

* plus 30 minutes cooling
Makes 350 g (12 oz)

350 g (12 oz) shelled almonds or
  hazelnuts

25 g (1 oz) butter or margarine

10 ml (2 tsp) salt

1 If the almonds are not blanched, put them in a bowl, cover with boiling water and leave for 3–4 minutes.

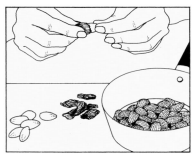

2 Drain the almonds, then plunge into cold water for 1 minute. Slide off the skins between your fingers.

3 To skin hazelnuts, put under a grill for 2–3 minutes, shaking the pan occasionally. Turn into a clean tea towel and rub off the skins.

4 Melt the butter in a roasting tin and add the almonds or hazelnuts, tossing them until they are evenly coated.

5 Roast in the oven at 150°C (300°F) mark 2 for 30 minutes, stirring occasionally. Add the salt and toss well. Cool for 30 minutes. Store in an airtight container for up to 2 weeks.

Menu Suggestion
Serve in bowls for a Christmas drinks party (see page 429 for Christmas drinks recipes).

— VARIATIONS —

CURRIED ALMONDS
Follow the recipe up to the beginning of step 4. Add 15 ml (1 tbsp) curry powder to the butter and continue to the end of the recipe. Use 5 ml (1 tsp) salt only.

SPICY PAPRIKA ALMONDS OR CASHEWS
Follow the recipe up to the beginning of step 4. Add 15 ml (1 tbsp) paprika and 2.5 ml (½ tsp) Chilli Seasoning to the butter and continue to the end of the recipe. Use 5 ml (1 tsp) salt only.

DANISH MUSHROOMS

| 0.15 | f | 24 cals |

Makes about 20

225 g (8 oz) even-sized button mushrooms

150 ml (¼ pint) soured cream

50 g (2 oz) jar black Danish-style caviar

parsley or dill sprigs, to garnish (optional)

1 Remove the stalks from the mushrooms and discard. Wipe the mushroom caps with a clean, damp cloth.

2 Divide the soured cream between the mushroom caps and spoon a little Danish caviar over each one. Garnish with tiny parsley or dill sprigs, if liked. Serve within 30 minutes.

Menu Suggestion
Arrange Danish Mushrooms on a serving platter to hand round at a cocktail party. Served on individual plates, they also make a most unusual starter for a dinner party.

CRANBERRY CHEESECAKE

0.35*	£	477 cals

* plus 5 hours chilling and 30 minutes cooling

Serves 10

225 g (8 oz) full-fat soft cheese
2 eggs, separated
finely grated rind and juice of 2 lemons
225 g (8 oz) caster sugar
300 ml ($\frac{1}{2}$ pint) natural yogurt
300 ml ($\frac{1}{2}$ pint) double cream
15 ml (1 tbsp) gelatine
175 g (6 oz) wheatmeal (digestive) biscuits
75 g (3 oz) butter
225 g (8 oz) cranberries
10 ml (2 tsp) arrowroot

1 In a bowl, beat together cheese, egg yolks, lemon rind, 50 g (2 oz) of the sugar and the yogurt. Whip the cream lightly and fold into the cheese mixture.

2 In a small saucepan, heat 75 ml (5 tbsp) of lemon juice with 30 ml (2 tbsp) water. Sprinkle in the gelatine, stir briskly until dissolved. Stir into the cheese mixture and leave to cool.

3 Whisk the egg whites until standing in soft peaks, then fold into the cheese mixture until evenly incorporated.

4 Pour the mixture into a lightly oiled 25.5 cm (10 inch) fluted savarin spring form tin. Chill in the refrigerator for 3–4 hours until completely set.

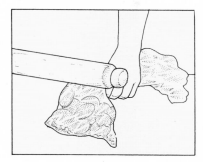

5 Put the biscuits in a polythene bag and crush with a rolling pin. Turn into a bowl.

6 Melt the butter in a small saucepan, then stir into the crushed biscuits.

7 Spoon the butter and biscuit mixture over the set cheese-cake and pat down firmly. Chill again for 1 hour until set.

8 Cook the cranberries, remaining sugar and 150 ml ($\frac{1}{4}$ pint) water for about 10 minutes until soft but still whole. Blend a little water with the arrowroot, stir into the cranberry mixture and slowly bring to boiling point. Cook for 2–3 minutes then leave to cool for 30 minutes.

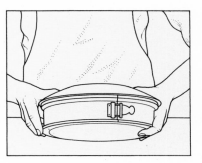

9 Invert the cheesecake on to a flat serving plate. Spoon the cranberry mixture into the centre before serving.

Menu Suggestion
Cranberry Cheesecake looks good as part of a buffet party spread. Serve with a jug of fresh pouring cream or soured cream, for those who like it.

CRANBERRY CHEESECAKE

The majority of the world's cranberries are harvested in North America. The name cranberry was given to the fruit by the Pilgrims in the 17th century, who thought the pink blossom of the cranberry looked like the heads of cranes. The nickname "crane berry" soon became shortened to cranberry, and in the early 19th century the Americans started cultivating the wild fruit on a large scale.

The North American Indians believed that this crimson red, tangy fruit had medicinal qualities, and the juice was used to draw poison out of arrow wounds. They also used the juice as a meat preservative, and as a natural dye for cloth.

PARTY PASSION PAVLOVA

| 1.30 | 🍴 | 299–374 cals |

Serves 8–10

4 egg whites

pinch of salt

275 g (10 oz) caster sugar

5 ml (1 tsp) vanilla flavouring

6.25 ml (1¼ tsp) cornflour

6.25 ml (1¼ tsp) vinegar

4 kiwi fruit

4 satsumas or mandarin oranges

few thin slices of preserved or stem ginger

60 ml (4 tbsp) whisky

30 ml (2 tbsp) ginger wine or syrup from the stem ginger

300 ml (½ pint) double or whipping cream

150 ml (¼ pint) thick, set yogurt or Quark

4 fresh passion fruit

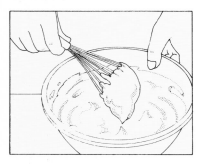

1 Put the egg whites in a large bowl and whisk until stiff and standing in peaks. Whisk in the salt and 125 g (4 oz) of the sugar until the meringue is glossy.

2 With a metal spoon, fold in another 125 g (4 oz) of the sugar with the vanilla flavouring, cornflour and vinegar.

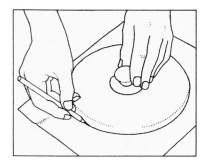

3 Draw a 25.5 cm (10 inch) circle on a large sheet of non-stick baking parchment. Place the paper, marked side down, on a baking sheet.

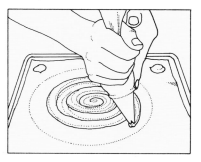

4 Spoon the meringue into a large piping bag fitted with a large plain nozzle. Pipe the meringue in a spiral, starting at the centre of the marked circle and working outwards towards the edge.

5 Pipe a second layer of meringue on top of the outer edge of the circle, to make a raised lip to prevent the topping spilling over the edge when serving.

6 Bake in the oven at 150°C (300°F) mark 2 for 1 hour until crisp and dry. With 2 fish slices or wide metal spatulas, lift the pavlova off the baking parchment and onto a wire rack. Leave to cool.

7 Meanwhile, prepare the topping. Peel the kiwi fruit and slice thinly. Peel the satsumas and divide into segments. Put the preserved or stem ginger in a bowl with the remaining sugar, the whisky and ginger wine or syrup. Add the prepared fruit and stir gently to mix. Whip the cream and yogurt together until thick.

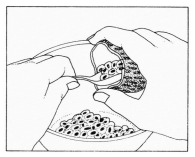

8 Just before serving, transfer the cold pavlova to a large serving platter. Spread the cream mixture in the centre, then arrange the fruit decoratively on top. Pour over any juices. Slice the passion fruit in half, scoop out the flesh with a teaspoon, then sprinkle over the top of the pavlova. Serve within 1 hour or the topping will make the pavlova too soft.

Menu Suggestion

Pavlova is an impressive dessert for a Christmas party. It needs no accompaniment other than a chilled dessert wine.

INDIVIDUAL APRICOT AND ORANGE SOUFFLÉS

| 1.30* | 🥄 | £ £ | ✳ | 334 cals |

* plus at least 4 hours chilling

Makes 6

a little vegetable oil, for brushing

3 eggs, separated

75 g (3 oz) caster sugar

15 ml (3 tsp) gelatine

finely grated rind and juice of 1 large orange

411 g (14½ oz) can apricot halves in syrup

60 ml (4 tbsp) orange-flavoured liqueur

150 ml (¼ pint) double cream

45 ml (3 tbsp) crushed ratafias or finely chopped almonds, and blanched orange shreds, to decorate

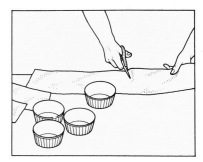

1 Cut strips of double grease-proof paper long enough to go round the outside of 6 individual soufflé dishes and 5 cm (2 inches) higher.

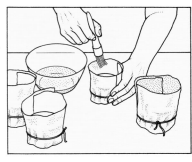

2 Tie the strips on the dishes securely with string and brush the inside of the paper lightly with a little vegetable oil.

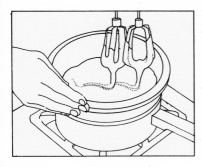

3 Put the egg yolks and sugar in a heatproof bowl standing over a pan of gently simmering water. Whisk until very thick and light and the beaters leave a ribbon trail when lifted.

4 Remove the bowl from the heat and continue whisking until cool.

5 In a saucepan, heat the orange juice. Take off the heat and sprinkle in the gelatine. Stir briskly until dissolved. Cool.

6 Meanwhile, work the apricots and their syrup in a blender or food processor (reserving 4 apricot halves for the decoration). Whisk the purée into the egg mixture with the orange rind and liqueur.

7 Whip the cream until it just holds its shape. In a separate bowl, whisk the egg whites until stiff and standing in peaks.

8 Stir the gelatine liquid into the egg yolk and sugar mixture, then fold in the cream followed by the egg whites. Pour slowly into the prepared dishes. Chill in the refrigerator for at least 4 hours, overnight if possible.

9 To serve, carefully remove the paper collars and brush a little oil around the exposed edge of the soufflé mixture.

10 Press the ratafias or nuts around the edge. Slice the reserved apricots and arrange decoratively on top of the soufflés with the orange shreds.

Menu Suggestion
Individual soufflés are a good idea for a buffet party because they make portion control and serving so easy. The apricot and orange flavour is very rich and creamy, so no accompaniment is necessary.

Anniversary Buffet for 15 to 20 People

MENU

CRISPY CHICKEN NIBBLES

CREAMY WATERCRESS QUICHE
(Make 2)

HOT CRAB AND RICOTTA QUICHE
(Make 2)

SALATA PIZZAIOLA
(Make 3)

THREE-CHEESE LASAGNE
(Make 2)

FRESH CHERRY AND LEMON
CHEESECAKE
(Make 2)

BOODLE'S ORANGE FOOL
(Make 2)

FRUIT PUNCH (p. 429)

CRISPY CHICKEN NIBBLES

0.50* £ ✳*	30 cals

* plus 1 hour standing time and
2 hours refrigeration; freeze
before frying

Makes about 100

**6 boneless chicken breasts, total
  weight about 900 g (2 lb), skinned**
75 ml (5 tbsp) soy sauce
10 ml (2 tsp) ground ginger
5 ml (1 tsp) English mustard
90 ml (6 tbsp) plain flour
3 eggs, beaten
350 g (12 oz) white breadcrumbs
75 g (3 oz) sesame seeds
vegetable oil, for deep-frying

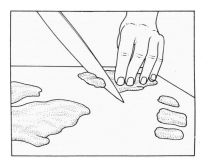

1 Cut the chicken into about 100
thin, bite-sized strips. Put the
strips in a large, shallow dish.
Mix together the soy, ginger and
mustard, then add to the chicken
and stir; cover. Leave for 1 hour.

2 Coat chicken strips in flour.
Dip in beaten egg, then coat in
breadcrumbs mixed with sesame
seeds. Squeeze into torpedos.

3 Chill, spaced apart, for 1–2
hours to firm. Heat the oil in a
deep-fat frier to 190°C (375°F).
Deep-fry about 12 strips at a time
for 5 minutes, turning them frequently to ensure they turn an
even golden brown.

4 Drain on absorbent kitchen
paper and keep hot in a low
oven while frying the remainder.
Serve hot.

CREAMY WATERCRESS QUICHE

| 0.55 | £ | ✳ | 404 cals |

Serves 6

shortcrust pastry made with 175 g
  (6 oz) flour (see recipe opposite)

50 g (2 oz) butter

1 large onion, skinned and chopped

1 bunch watercress, chopped

2 eggs

150 ml ($\frac{1}{4}$ pint) milk

150 ml (5 fl oz) single cream

salt and freshly ground pepper

1 Line a 20.5-cm (8-inch) flan dish with the pastry. Place the dish on a baking sheet. Bake blind (see page 153).

2 Melt the butter in a saucepan, add the onion and cook, stirring occasionally, for 3 minutes until soft. Add the watercress, reserving a sprig to garnish, and cook for a further 3–4 minutes. Remove the pan from the heat and set aside.

3 Whisk together the eggs, milk, cream and seasoning. Stir in the cooked watercress mixture and pour into the flan case.

4 Bake in the oven at 190°C (375°F) mark 5 for 35 minutes or until set. Serve hot or warm. Garnish with a sprig of watercress.

HOT CRAB AND RICOTTA QUICHE

| 1.00 | £ £ | 421 cals |

Serves 6

175 g (6 oz) plain flour

salt and freshly ground pepper

40 g (1$\frac{1}{2}$ oz) butter or block
  margarine

40 g (1$\frac{1}{2}$ oz) lard

30 ml (2 tbsp) water

2 eggs

150 ml (5 fl oz) single cream

150 ml ($\frac{1}{4}$ pint) milk

225 g (8 oz) crab meat

175 g (6 oz) Ricotta cheese

30 ml (2 tbsp) grated Parmesan

1 Make the pastry. Mix the flour and a pinch of salt together in a bowl. Rub in the fats until the mixture resembles fine breadcrumbs.

2 Bind to a firm dough with the cold water. Roll out on a lightly floured surface and use to line six 8.5-cm (3$\frac{1}{2}$-inch) fluted loose-bottomed flan tins or a 20.5-cm (8-inch) flan dish placed on a baking sheet. Bake blind (see page 438) in the oven at 200°C (400°F) mark 6 for 10–15 minutes.

3 Whisk the eggs, milk and cream together in a bowl. Flake the crabmeat, crumble the Ricotta and add to the egg mixture with the Parmesan and plenty of seasoning. Pour into flan cases and bake in the oven at 190°C (375°F) mark 5 for 35 minutes until golden.

SALATA PIZZAIOLA

0.15*	£	380 cals

* plus 1 hour refrigeration

Serves 6

450 g (1 lb) tomatoes, skinned and thinly sliced

150 ml (¼ pint) olive oil

45–60 ml (3–4 tbsp) red wine vinegar

30 ml (2 tbsp) chopped fresh basil

salt and freshly ground pepper

1.25 ml (¼ tsp) sugar

175 g (6 oz) sliced Italian salami

175 g (6 oz) Fontina or Mozzarella cheese

two 50-g (2-oz) cans anchovies in oil, drained and soaked in milk 20 minutes

115-g (4-oz) can mussels, drained

1 Arrange the tomato slices, over-lapping, on a flat, circular serving platter. Whisk together the oil, 45 ml (3 tbsp) vinegar, half the basil and salt and pepper to taste. Add more vinegar if liked. Sprinkle the tomatoes evenly with the sugar, then pour over half the dressing.

2 Cut the salami into thin strips, removing the skin. Arrange a section of salami on top of the tomatoes, forming a pie-shaped edge radiating out from centre.

3 Cut the cheese into strips and arrange in the same way next to the salami. Place the mussels next to the cheese.

4 Repeat these sections of salami, cheese and mussels until they meet the first section of salami. Drain the anchovies and pat dry. Use lines of anchovies to separate the different toppings.

5 Drizzle over the remaining dressing, then refrigerate for 2–3 hours. Sprinkle with the remaining basil just before serving.

THREE-CHEESE LASAGNE

| 1.30 | £ ✳ | 520 cals |

Serves 10

397-g (14-oz) can tomatoes
small onion, skinned and chopped
celery stick, trimmed and chopped
garlic clove, skinned and crushed
bay leaf
salt and freshly ground pepper
450 g (1 lb) minced beef
1 egg
50 g (2 oz) Parmesan cheese, grated
75 g (3 oz) plain flour
60 ml (4 tbsp) olive or vegetable oil
75 g (3 oz) butter or margarine
750 ml (1¼ pints) milk
100 g (4 oz) mild cured ham,
   chopped
100 g (4 oz) Mozzarella cheese,
   thinly sliced
100 g (4 oz) Bel Paese cheese, cut
   into strips
150 ml (5 fl oz) single cream
400 g (14 oz) lasagne

1 Prepare the tomato sauce by placing the tomatoes, onion, celery, garlic and bay leaf in a small pan, bring to the boil and simmer, uncovered, for 30 minutes. Stir occasionally to prevent sticking.

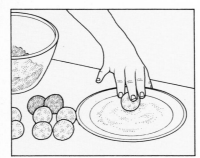

2 Discard the bay leaf and rub mixture through a sieve or purée in a blender. Season. Combine beef, egg, half the Parmesan and seasoning. Shape the mixture into twenty-four meatballs. Roll lightly in a little seasoned flour.

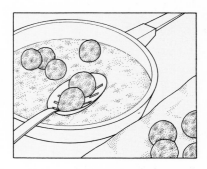

3 Heat the oil in a pan and cook the meatballs for about 5 minutes until brown. Remove with slotted spoon and drain.

4 Melt the butter in a pan, add in 65 g (2½ oz) flour and stirring, cook gently for 1 minute. Remove from the heat and gradually stir in the milk.

5 Bring to the boil and cook, stirring all the time, until the sauce thickens. Stir in the ham, Mozzarella, Bel Paese, cream and seasoning.

6 Prepare the lasagne as directed on the packet. In a large, greased, oval or rectangular ovenproof dish, layer up the lasagne, meatballs, tomato and white sauces, finishing with a layer of lasagne topped with white sauce.

7 Sprinkle over the remaining Parmesan cheese, then bake in the oven at 200°C (400°F) mark 6 for 20–25 minutes until golden brown.

FRESH CHERRY AND LEMON CHEESECAKE

0.30*	🍴 £	492 cals

* plus 2–3 hours refrigeration

Serves 10

75 g (3 oz) butter

125 g (4 oz) caster sugar

150 g (5 oz) plain flour

egg yolk

225 g (8 oz) full fat soft cheese

225 g (8 oz) cottage cheese, sieved

2 eggs, separated

2 juicy lemons

142 ml (5 fl oz) soured cream

300 ml (10 fl oz) double cream

15 ml (1 tbsp) gelatine

45 ml (3 tbsp) water

225 g (8 oz) fresh red cherries, halved and stoned, or 213-g (7½-oz) can cherries, drained

angelica, to decorate

1 Cream butter with 75 g (3 oz) sugar. Mix to a firm dough with the flour and egg yolk. Roll out half to fit the base of a 20.5-cm (8-inch) spring release cake tin, and the other half to fit a 20.5-cm (8-inch) plain flan ring.

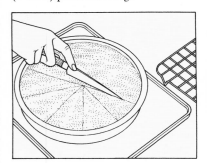

2 Bake both in the oven at 180°C (350°F) mark 4 for about 15 minutes. Cut the flan ring round into ten wedges and cool on a wire rack. Leave other round in tin.

3 With an electric mixer beat together the cheeses, 2 egg yolks, finely grated rind of the lemons, 75 ml (5 tbsp) lemon juice, remaining sugar and soured cream. Stir in half the double cream.

4 Soak the gelatine in water and dissolve, stir into cheese mixture. Refrigerate for 2–3 hours until beginning to set.

5 Whisk the egg whites until stiff. Fold cherries and egg whites into cheese mixture, turn into tin, refrigerate. Cover when firm.

6 Unmould. Place pastry wedges on top and decorate the cheesecake with angelica and the remaining double cream.

FULL FAT SOFT CHEESE AND COTTAGE CHEESE

Full fat soft cheese and cottage cheese are the two main ingredients of this cheesecake recipe, and you may wonder if it is necessary to use both. Full fat cream cheese contains 47.4 grammes of fat per 100 grammes of cheese, whereas cottage cheese contains only 4 grammes per 100 grammes. The recipe *can* be made with all full fat soft cheese if you like, but this will give a heavier result.

BOODLE'S ORANGE FOOL

2.10* £ 332 cals

* includes 2 hours refrigeration

Serves 6

4–6 trifle sponge cakes, cut into
   1-cm (½-inch) thick slices
grated rind and juice of 2 oranges
grated rind and juice of 1 lemon
25–50 g (1–2 oz) sugar
300 ml (10 fl oz) double cream
orange slices or segments, to
   decorate

1 Use the sponge cake slices to line the bottom and halfway up the sides of a deep dish or bowl.

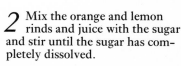

2 Mix the orange and lemon rinds and juice with the sugar and stir until the sugar has completely dissolved.

3 In another bowl whip the cream until it just starts to thicken, then slowly add the sweetened fruit juice, continuing to whip the cream as you do so. Whip until the cream is light and thickened and the juice all absorbed.

4 Pour the mixture over the sponge cakes and refrigerate for at least 2 hours, longer if possible, so that the juice can permeate the sponge cakes and the cream thicken. Decorate with segments or slices of fresh orange.

BOODLE'S CLUB
This delicious orange fool has been a speciality for years at Boodle's Club in St James's Street, London, which was founded in 1764. It is so popular with the members of the club that the chef dares not take it off the menu! And many of the members are so fond of it that they've taken the recipe home with them – for their wives to make. This is our version.

Wedding Buffet for 50 People

AVOCADO MOUSSES

| 0.15* | £ £ | 535 cals |

* plus 2–3 hours refrigeration
Makes 12 as a starter

4 ripe avocados, about 900 g (2 lb)
  total weight, peeled and stoned
2 onions, skinned and grated
1 egg, hard-boiled and chopped
2 garlic cloves, crushed
60 ml (4 tbsp) lemon juice
300 ml (10 fl oz) soured cream
600 ml (1 pint) mayonnaise
salt and freshly ground pepper
30 ml (2 tbsp) gelatine
60 ml (4 tbsp) water
3 egg whites
halved stuffed olives and endive,
  to garnish

1 Peel and stone the avocados. Press through a nylon sieve. Stir onion and egg into avocado with the garlic. Mix lemon juice, soured cream and mayonnaise and beat into avocado mixture. Season.

2 In a small bowl, sprinkle the gelatine over 60 ml (4 tbsp) water. Leave for 2–3 minutes. Heat gently over a pan of hot water until completely dissolved. Pour into the avocado mixture in a thin steady stream, beating all the time.

3 Whisk egg whites until stiff; fold into avocado mixture. Adjust seasoning. Spoon into individual serving dishes (about 175 ml [6 fl oz] each).

4 Cover with cling film, chill for 2–3 hours, then serve garnished with stuffed olives and endive.

Vegetable and Ham Terrine

2.00*	🍴 £	397 cals

* plus overnight refrigeration

Serves 10 as a starter

about 30 young spinach leaves
3 large carrots
2 red peppers
350 g (12 oz) French beans
450 g (1 lb) full fat soft cheese
450 g (1 lb) boiled ham
1.25 ml ($\frac{1}{4}$ tsp) Tabasco sauce
freshly ground pepper to taste
2 egg whites

1 Remove large stalks from spinach. Blanch leaves in boiling water for 10 seconds. Drain and dry; reserve water.

2 Line the base and sides of a 1-kg (2-lb) loaf tin with the spinach leaves, making sure there are no gaps. Reserve five leaves.

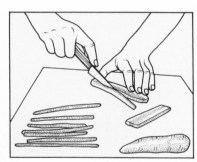

3 Using a vegetable peeler, peel the carrots, then cut them lengthways into matchsticks.

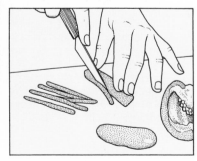

4 Cut the peppers in half, then remove the core and seeds and slice the flesh into thin strips. Top and tail the beans.

5 Blanch the prepared vegetables in the spinach water. Allow 2 minutes blanching time for each type of vegetable.

6 Put the cheese in a food processor. Tear the ham into shreds, add to the cheese with the Tabasco, pepper and egg whites. Work to a smooth mixture.

7 Divide the cheese and ham mixture into five even-sized pieces so that terrine looks even.

8 Put a portion of the cheese and ham mixture in the bottom of the tin, spreading it out evenly. Top with half the beans, placing them lengthways and close together.

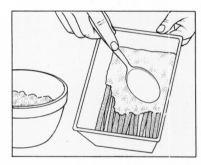

9 Cover the beans with another portion of cheese and ham, then with the carrots, placing them lengthways as the beans. Top with another layer of cheese and ham, then a layer of red pepper strips.

10 Repeat cheese and ham layer, then beans and another cheese layer. Finish with layer of reserved spinach. Cover with foil.

11 Bake the terrine in a hot bain marie in the oven at 180°C (350°F) mark 4 for 1$\frac{1}{2}$ hours. Remove and leave to cool. When completely cold, refrigerate overnight. To serve, turn the terrine out on to an oblong plate or board. Serve sliced.

CHICKEN GALANTINE

2.00* ▯ ▯ £ £ ✳* 244 cals

* plus 2–3 hours cooling time and 1
   hour setting time; freeze before
   adding aspic jelly.

Makes 15 small buffet portions

1.4 kg (3 lb) chicken, with giblets
2 onions, skinned
50 g (2 oz) mushrooms
50 g (2 oz) butter
finely grated rind and juice of 1 lemon
10 ml (2 tsp) ground coriander
1 garlic clove, skinned and crushed
450 g (1 lb) pork sausagemeat
1 egg, beaten
salt and freshly ground pepper
50 g (2 oz) sliced tongue
50 g (2 oz) sliced ham
about 300 ml (½ pint) liquid aspic jelly
cucumber, olives, tarragon and hard-boiled egg, to garnish

1 Bone the chicken (see page 158). (Alternatively, you can ask your butcher to do this for you.) Reserve the liver.

2 Prepare the stuffing. Finely chop the onions, mushrooms and liver. Sauté in the butter with the lemon rind, coriander and garlic, until softened. Stir in 30 ml (2 tbsp) lemon juice. Cool. Mix with sausagemeat and egg. Season.

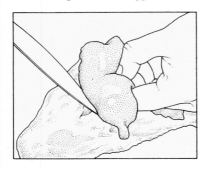

3 Lay the chicken out, with its flesh side uppermost. Remove breast fillets with a knife.

4 Place half the stuffing over the centre of the bird. Cover with the tongue. Add the fillets, cover with the ham and then finish with the remaining stuffing.

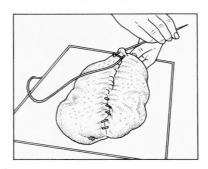

5 Sew up the chicken into a neat shape. Wrap tightly in a double layer of muslin. Secure well, sewing up the join. Place in a large pan with just enough boiling water to cover.

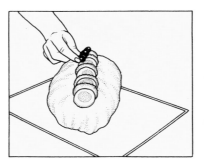

6 Bring to the boil, cover and simmer for 1½ hours. Lift from the pan. Cool for 2–3 hours. When cold, remove cloth and string. Make the aspic jelly and use to coat the chicken. Garnish. Cover with more aspic. Leave to set for about 2 hours, and serve sliced.

POACHED SALMON

| 0.35* | £ £ | 190 cals |

* plus 3 hours cooling and 1½ hours setting time

Makes 15 small buffet portions

1 small salmon, about 1.8 kg (4 lb)
150 ml (¼ pint) dry white wine
slices of onion
bay leaf
salt and freshly ground pepper
300 ml (½ pint) liquid aspic jelly
lemon slices, cucumber, black olives, whole prawns and endive, to garnish
mayonnaise, to serve

1 Rinse the fish, remove eyes and trim tail and fins. Place in a fish kettle. Pour over wine and enough water to just cover fish. Add onion, bay leaf, salt and pepper. Bring slowly to the boil, cover and simmer for 25 minutes.

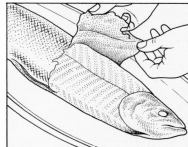

2 Lift out of liquor; cool for 2–3 hours. Ease off skin. Place fish on serving platter.

3 As the aspic begins to set, brush some over the fish. Leave to set for 1–1½ hours. Coat with several layers of aspic.

4 Garnish with slices of lemon, cucumber skin and olives. Brush more aspic on top. Arrange endive, whole prawns and sliced cucumber and lemon on side of dish and serve with mayonnaise.

EXOTIC FRUIT SALAD

0.15* £ £ ✳	75 cals

* plus 2–3 hours chilling time

Serves 10

| 1 medium pineapple |
| 1 mango |
| 1 papaya (optional) |
| 3 nectarines |
| 100 g (4 oz) black or green grapes |
| 1 ogen melon, halved and seeded |
| juice of 3 large oranges |
| juice of 1 lemon |
| 45 ml (3 tbsp) orange liqueur |
| fresh mint sprigs, to decorate |

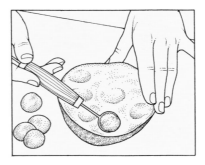

1 Cut the pineapple into 1 cm (½ inch) slices. Remove skin and cut flesh into cubes. Place in dish.

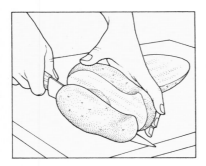

2 Cut a chunk off each side of the mango lengthways to expose the stone. Ease off the flesh. Remove outer skin and slice flesh thinly. Add to dish. Repeat with papaya and add to dish.

3 Wash nectarines and slice flesh away from stone. Add to dish with halved and seeded grapes.

4 With a melon baller scoop out melon flesh into dish. Scrape out remaining flesh, chop and add to the serving dish.

5 Mix together the orange juice, lemon juice and liqueur. Pour over the fruit and chill for 2–3 hours. Decorate with mint.

STRAWBERRY AND KIWI FRUIT FLAN

0.35*	£ £	303 cals

* plus 1 hour cooling time

Serves 10

454 g (1 lb) packet frozen puff
 pastry, thawed, or 225 g (8 oz)
 homemade (page 439)

beaten egg

340-g (12-oz) jar apricot jam

30 ml (2 tbsp) lemon juice

450 g (1 lb) fresh strawberries

3 medium kiwi fruit

1 Roll out three-quarters of the pastry to a 30.5-cm (12-inch) round. Place the dough on a baking sheet and prick well all over. Make sure you do not puncture the base of the pastry round.

2 Using a 7.5-cm (3-inch) fluted cutter, stamp out eight to ten crescents from the pastry dough which remains.

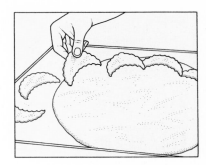

3 Brush the pastry round with beaten egg and arrange the crescents around the edge; brush these with egg, too.

4 Bake the pastry case in the oven at 220°C (425°F) mark 7 for 12 minutes. Prick the base again, then lower the heat to 170°C (325°F) mark 3 for a further 10 minutes; remove from oven and leave to cool for 1 hour.

5 Warm the apricot jam and lemon juice, sieve and return to the pan. Brush a little over the base of the pastry case.

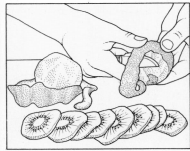

6 Hull the strawberries, peel and slice the kiwi fruit. Arrange the fruit in wedge shapes in the pastry case, radiating outwards from the centre to the pastry crescents.

7 Using the pastry brush, glaze the fruit and pastry edge with remaining jam.

Barbecue Party for 10 People

MENU

ICED TZAZIKI SOUP

MUSTARD CHICKEN DRUMSTICKS

HONEY-GLAZED KEBABS

PINE NUT PILAFF
((Make 2)

PIPERANA

RASPBERRY PAVLOVA
(Make 2)

BLACKCURRANT RIPPLE ICE CREAM

KIR (page 429)
(Make 10)

ICED TZAZIKI SOUP

| 0.10* | £ | 51 cals |

* plus 2–3 hours chilling time

Serves 10

2 medium cucumbers, peeled
900 ml (1½ pints) natural yogurt
2 small garlic cloves, crushed
45 ml (3 tbsp) chopped fresh mint
750 ml (1¼ pints) chicken stock
salt and freshly ground pepper
mint leaves, to garnish

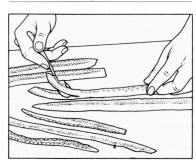

1 Wash the cucumber and pat dry with absorbent kitchen paper. Quarter the cucumber lengthways and discard the seeds, using a teaspoon.

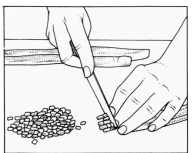

2 Dice the cucumber finely, cutting up three or four strips at a time. Then place yogurt in a bowl and stir in cucumber, garlic and chopped mint.

3 Stir in the chicken stock and season. Place in the refrigerator for 2–3 hours to chill. Then serve, garnished with mint.

MUSTARD CHICKEN DRUMSTICKS

| 0.35 | £ | 125 cals |

Serves 10

50 g (2 oz) butter
45 ml (3 tbsp) coarse grain mustard
1 lemon
5 ml (1 tsp) chopped fresh tarragon or rosemary
salt and freshly ground pepper
10 chicken drumsticks
rosemary sprigs, to garnish

1 In a bowl, cream the butter until soft. Work in the mustard a little at a time using a wooden spoon. Grate in the lemon rind; gradually beat in 15 ml (1 tbsp) lemon juice and the herbs and seasoning.

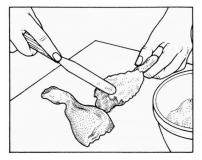

2 Spread the mustard butter over the chicken pieces, coating evenly. Chill in the refrigerator, if not cooking immediately.

3 Barbecue for 10–15 minutes on each side until the skin is crisp, golden and the chicken is tender. Keep back some of the mustard butter and spread on the chicken pieces as they cook.

HONEY-GLAZED KEBABS

| 0.30* | 350 cals* |

* plus 4 hours marinating; calories
   include pitta bread

Serves 10

1.1 kg (2½ lb) boned lean shoulder
   or leg of lamb

432-g (15¼-oz) can pineapple slices

75 ml (5 tbsp) clear honey

75 ml (5 tbsp) soy sauce

45 ml (3 tbsp) tomato ketchup

12.5 ml (2½ tsp) malt vinegar

2 large garlic cloves, crushed

5 small sprigs fresh rosemary

salt and freshly ground pepper

2 medium green peppers

275 g (10 oz) button mushrooms

pitta bread or large baps, to serve

1 Using a sharp knife, trim any
excess fat from the meat and
cut into 2.5-cm (1-inch) cubes.
Place in a bowl and set aside.

2 Drain the pineapple juice into
a small saucepan, adding the
honey, soy sauce, tomato ketchup,
vinegar, garlic, rosemary and
seasoning. Heat until the honey
melts; cool. Pour over meat, cover
and leave for at least 4 hours (in as
cool a place as possible).

3 Halve and seed the peppers
and cut into bite-sized pieces.
Cut the pineapple slices into
similar-sized pieces.

4 Drain the lamb, reserve the
marinade and thread on to 20
skewers with the pineapple, pepper
and mushrooms.

5 Brush with the marinade and
barbecue for 15–20 minutes,
turning and basting frequently.
Serve pocketed in warmed pitta
bread or baps.

HONEY
Honey was the first sweetener
known to man – the ancient
Greeks and Romans were ad-
dicted to it, long before sugar
was ever heard of. Honey is made
up of several different types
of sugar – fructose and glucose
being the major two – and it is
known to be very nutritious. It is
rich in vitamins B_1 and C, ribo-
flavin and niacin, and minerals.

PINE NUT PILAFF

0.40 ✳ 252 cals

Serves 6

350 g (12 oz) Basmati rice
75 g (3 oz) butter
1 onion, skinned and chopped
2 large garlic cloves, skinned and
 finely chopped
8 cardamom pods, crushed
1.1 litres (2 pints) hot chicken stock
salt and freshly ground pepper
15 ml (1 tbsp) olive oil
100 g (4 oz) pine nuts
orange or yellow food colouring
50 g (2 oz) seedless raisins
fresh coriander, to garnish

1 Rinse the rice under cold running water. Drain well. Then melt 50 g (2 oz) of the butter in a large flameproof casserole. Add the onion and garlic and fry gently until soft and golden.

2 Add the rice and fry, stirring until the grains begin to burst. Add the cardamoms, then pour in the hot stock and bring to the boil. Add salt and pepper to taste and stir once. Lower the heat, cover and simmer gently for 15 minutes.

3 Meanwhile melt 15 g (½ oz) butter with the oil in a separate pan. Add the pine nuts and fry until golden brown, shaking the pan constantly. Drain on absorbent kitchen paper, turning occasionally.

4 Sprinkle a few drops of food colouring over the rice, cover again and simmer for a further 10 minutes until rice is tender.

5 Fork two-thirds of the pine nuts into the rice with the raisins and the remaining butter. Taste and adjust seasoning. Cover, turn off the heat and leave to stand for 5 minutes. Serve garnished with the remaining pine nuts and the coriander.

PIPERANA

| 0.30* | £ | 82 cals |

* plus overnight standing time

Serves 10

10 peppers (red, green and yellow)

4 large garlic cloves, skinned and crushed

5–10 ml (1–2 tsp) grated onion

150 ml (¼ pint) olive oil

60 ml (4 tbsp) lemon juice

45 ml (3 tbsp) chopped fresh herbs (marjoram, thyme, parsley, etc.)

pinch of sugar, or to taste

salt and freshly ground pepper

1 Cook the peppers whole on the barbecue (or under the grill), turning them constantly until their skins are charred all over.

2 Remove from the heat, place in a bowl and immediately cover tightly with a damp, clean tea-towel. Leave until the peppers are cold, overnight if possible.

3 Hold the peppers over a bowl and rub the skins off with your fingers. Let the juices collect in the bowl. Discard skins. Tear the pepper flesh into long, thin shreds with your fingers, discarding stems, cores and seeds.

4 Put the garlic in a screw-top jar with the grated onion, oil, the lemon juice and reserved pepper juices. Add the herbs, with sugar and salt and pepper to taste. Shake well to mix.

5 Arrange the peppers decoratively on a plate. Pour over the dressing, then leave to stand for at least 10 minutes before serving.

RASPBERRY PAVLOVA

| 1.10* £ £ ✳* | 348 cals |

* plus 2 hours cooling time; freeze
without topping

Serves 6

3 egg whites

175 g (6 oz) caster sugar

2.5 ml ($\frac{1}{2}$ tsp) vanilla flavouring

2.5 ml ($\frac{1}{2}$ tsp) distilled white wine
   vinegar

5 ml (1 tsp) cornflour

300 ml (10 fl oz) double cream

350 g (12 oz) fresh raspberries,
   washed and hulled

1 Draw an 18-cm (7-inch) circle
on a sheet of non-stick paper
and place the paper on a baking
sheet.

2 Whisk the egg whites until very
stiff. Whisk in half the sugar
then carefully fold in the remaining sugar, the vanilla flavouring,
white wine vinegar and cornflour
with a metal spoon.

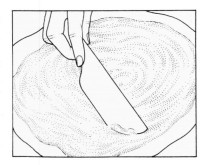

3 Spread the meringue mixture
over the circle and bake in the
oven at 150°C (300°F) mark 2 for
about 1 hour until crisp and dry.
Leave to cool on the baking sheet
for 2 hours then carefully peel off
the non-stick paper.

4 Whisk the cream until stiff.
Slide the meringue on to a flat
plate, pile the cream on it and
arrange the raspberries on top.

BLACKCURRANT RIPPLE ICE CREAM

| 0.30* | £ | ✳ | 350 cals |

* plus 6–7 hours freezing time and
  30 minutes refrigeration

Serves 8

568 ml (1 pint) milk
1 vanilla pod
6 egg yolks
350 g (12 oz) sugar
600 ml (20 fl oz) whipping cream
450 g (1 lb) blackcurrants
120 ml (8 tbsp) water

1 Bring the milk and vanilla pod almost to the boil. Take off the heat, cover and leave to cool for at least 15 minutes.

2 Beat egg yolks and half the sugar together, stir in the milk and strain back into the pan. Cook the custard gently over a low heat. Do not boil.

3 Pour into a chilled, shallow container and leave to cool. Freeze for about 2 hours until mushy in texture around edges.

4 Turn into a large, chilled basin and mash with a flat whisk or fork. Whisk the cream until stiff and fold into the frozen mixture. Freeze for 2 hours until mushy.

5 Stalk and rinse the currants. Cook with the sugar and water until soft. Purée in blender and sieve to remove seeds. Cool.

6 Take the ice cream out of the freezer and whisk to a spreading consistency. Spoon a layer into freezer container. Pour over some of the blackcurrant purée. Continue to layer. Cover; return to freezer for 2 hours. To serve, allow to soften in the refrigerator for about 30 minutes.

Portable Picnic

If you're planning a picnic, you want to be able to get up and go, especially if the weather promises to be good. All the recipes in this picnic menu keep and travel well, so you can make them and pack them ready the night before.

FRIED SALAMI CHICKEN

0.45* **593 cals**

* plus 1 hour cooling time
Serves 6

12 chicken drumsticks, skinned
24 slices of salami, skinned
 (about 100 g [4 oz])
3 eggs, size 2, beaten
450 g (1 lb) fresh breadcrumbs
vegetable oil for deep frying

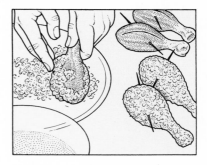

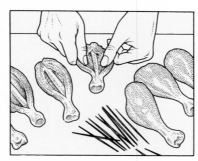

1 *To prepare* (45 minutes):
Make an incision to the bone along 1 side of each chicken drumstick and loosen the flesh around the bone.

2 Place 2 slices of salami around the bone, pull the chicken flesh together and secure with cocktail sticks.

3 Dip the salami-filled chicken first into beaten egg, then breadcrumbs and pat the crumbs in well. Repeat the egg and bread-crumb process to give a good coating.

4 Heat the oil in a deep-fat fryer to 180°C (350°F) and fry the chicken for 7–10 minutes, until golden brown and cooked through. Drain on absorbent kitchen paper and leave to cool for about 1 hour.

5 *To serve* (5 minutes): Carefully remove the cocktail sticks from the drumsticks before packing.

FRIED SALAMI CHICKEN

Virtually any salami can be used for this recipe, but it is best to avoid the fatty Danish salami, which is easily recognisable by its bright pink appearance. Instead, choose a good Italian salami such as Genova or Napoli. Hungarian salamis are also good, as is Cervelat, which is a partially dried sausage rather than a true salami.

ASPARAGUS AND BACON QUICHE

1.15* 619 cals

* plus 1 hour cooling, and chilling

Serves 6

700 g (1½ lb) fresh asparagus spears (about 24), or 225 g (8 oz) frozen

225 g (8 oz) plain flour

125 g (4 oz) butter or margarine

about 60 ml (4 tbsp) ice-cold water

125 g (4 oz) thinly sliced streaky bacon, rinded

4 egg yolks

450 ml (¾ pint) single cream

100 g (4 oz) Gruyère cheese, grated

salt and freshly ground pepper

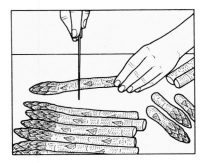

1 To prepare (1 hour 10 minutes): Trim the heads off fresh asparagus to the length of about 4 cm (1½ inches). (Use the stalks for soup.) Blanch the heads in boiling salted water for 5 minutes; drain. If using frozen asparagus, cook in boiling water for 5 minutes then drain and trim as above.

2 Put the flour in a bowl, add the butter and rub in with the fingertips until the mixture re-sembles fine breadcrumbs. Add enough ice-cold water to bind to a firm dough.

3 Turn the dough out on to a floured surface and roll out to fit a 25 cm (10 inch) fluted flan dish. Bake blind in the oven at 190°C (375°F) mark 5 for 15 minutes until set but not browned.

4 Meanwhile, with a knife, stretch the bacon rashers on a flat surface. Wrap a small piece around each asparagus head.

5 In a bowl, mix the egg yolks with the cream, grated cheese and seasoning to taste. Spoon into the flan case.

6 Arrange the asparagus and bacon rolls in the custard. Reduce the oven temperature to 180°C (350°F) mark 4 and bake for 30–35 minutes or until set and golden brown. Cool for 1 hour, then wrap in cling film and store in the refrigerator until required (but not longer than 2 days).

7 To serve (5 minutes): Cut into wedges.

ASPARAGUS AND BACON QUICHE

To make a quick asparagus soup with the stalks not used in this recipe: chop the stalks and cook them in butter with a little finely chopped onion. Add 1.1 litres (2 pints) chicken stock, the finely grated rind and juice of ½ a lemon and salt and pepper to taste. Simmer for about 20 minutes until the asparagus is tender, then purée in a blender or food processor. Reheat with 150 ml (¼ pint) single cream before serving.

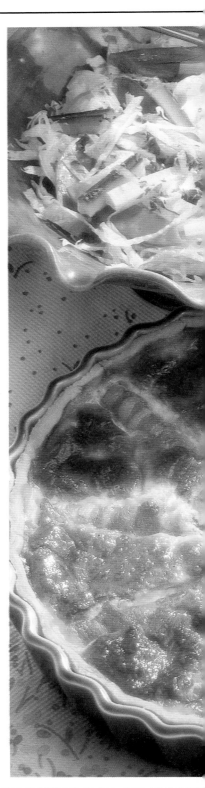

MANGE-TOUT SALAD

0.20* £ 155 cals

* plus 30 minutes cooling

Serves 6

225 g (8 oz) mange-touts, trimmed
salt and freshly ground pepper
30 ml (2 tbsp) vegetable oil
1 cucumber
30 ml (2 tbsp) single cream
45 ml (3 tbsp) French dressing (see page 155)
chopped fresh parsley and mint

1 *To prepare* (15 minutes): Cook the mange-touts in boiling salted water for about 4 minutes; drain and return to the pan. While still hot, add the oil and toss until well coated. Leave to cool for at least 30 minutes, then cover and chill in the refrigerator until required.

2 Cut the cucumber into 5 cm (2 inch) sticks, add to the mange-touts, cover with cling film and chill in the refrigerator until required.

3 Whisk the cream and French dressing together with the parsley and mint, pour into a screw-topped jar and chill in the refrigerator until required.

4 *To serve* (5 minutes): Place the mange-touts and cucumber in a salad bowl. Shake the dressing once more, pour over the vegetables and serve immediately.

363

POTTED CHEESE WITH MINT

| 0.20* | £ | ✳ | 409 cals |

* plus at least 2 hours chilling

Serves 6

75 g (3 oz) butter, at room
    temperature

225 g (8 oz) Red Leicester or
    Cheddar cheese

15 ml (1 tbsp) chopped fresh mint

60 ml (4 tbsp) soured cream

freshly ground pepper

mint leaves, to garnish

brown bread or crispbreads,
    to serve

1 *To prepare* (15 minutes): Put
the butter in a bowl and beat
until really soft. Grate in the
cheese, then beat it gradually into
the butter.

2 Stir in the chopped mint and
soured cream, adding freshly
ground pepper to taste. (Salt
should not be required as the
cheese contains sufficient.)

3 Spoon into 4–6 individual
serving dishes and garnish
with mint leaves. Cover with cling
film and chill in the refrigerator
for at least 2 hours.

4 *To serve* (5 minutes): Spread
on slices of brown bread or
crispbreads.

POTTED CHEESE WITH MINT

The English semi-hard Red
Leicester is excellent for making
potted cheese because of its
interesting orange-red colour.
It also has the right kind of flaky
texture which blends smoothly
and makes it easy to spread. Red
Leicester is also a good melting
cheese, so try it in cooking
instead of Cheddar.

SPICED APPLE TORTE

| 1.20* | £ | ✳ | 627 cals |

* plus 1 hour cooling

Serves 6

175 g (6 oz) butter or margarine
175 g (6 oz) light soft brown sugar
75 g (3 oz) oat flakes
5 ml (1 tsp) ground cinnamon
450 g (1 lb) cooking apples
finely grated rind of 1 lemon
45 ml (3 tbsp) lemon juice
2 eggs, beaten
125 g (4 oz) self-raising flour
5 ml (1 tsp) ground mixed spice
300 ml ($\frac{1}{2}$ pint) single cream,
   to serve

1 *To prepare* (75 minutes): Melt 50 g (2 oz) of the butter or margarine in a saucepan. Add 50 g (2 oz) of the sugar and the oats and cinnamon and fry gently, stirring, until golden.

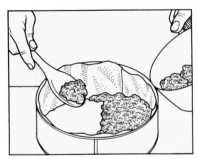

2 Spoon the mixture into a greased and lined 19 cm (7$\frac{1}{2}$ inch) round cake tin.

3 Peel and core the apples, then slice them thinly into a bowl. Stir in the lemon rind and juice. Set aside.

4 Put the remaining butter or margarine in a separate bowl, add the remaining sugar and beat together until light and fluffy. Beat in the eggs gradually. Sift in the flour with the spice and stir in, followed by the apple mixture.

5 Spoon the mixture into the cake tin and level the surface. Bake in the oven at 180°C (350°F) mark 4 for about 50 minutes. Turn out on to a baking sheet lined with non-stick paper. Cool completely: about 1 hour. Cover and chill until required or for up to 2 days.

6 *To serve* (5 minutes): Unwrap, cut into wedges and serve with single cream.

SPICED APPLE TORTE

This cake tastes equally delicious with orange flavouring, so you can ring the changes each time you make it—which is bound to be often! Substitute the finely grated rind of 1 medium orange for the lemon rind, and the same quantity of freshly squeezed orange juice as specified for lemon in the recipe.

At the end of the summer when there are plenty of fresh pears about, you can use cooking pears such as Conference, instead of the apples. Pears taste best with lemon, but you may prefer to use ground ginger rather than cinnamon, since ginger and pears have a special affinity for one another.

Afternoon Tea Party for 20 People

MENU

SACHERTORTE

(Make 2)

———— · ————

PARTY PINWHEELS

———— · ————

CHEESY PÂTÉ CHEQUERBOARDS

———— · ————

SALMON AND PARMA ROLLUPS

———— · ————

GLAZED FRUIT BOATS

SACHERTORTE

| 1.10 | £ £ | 456 cals |

Serves 10

200 g (7 oz) plain chocolate
175 g (6 oz) unsalted butter
100 g (4 oz) caster sugar
100 g (4 oz) ground almonds
4 eggs, separated
50 g (2 oz) fresh brown breadcrumbs
30 ml (2 tbsp) apricot jam, melted and sieved
50 g (2 oz) icing sugar
10 ml (2 tsp) hot water
chocolate curls, to decorate

1 Line the base of a 23-cm (9-inch) spring release cake tin and brush with melted butter. Break half the chocolate into a bowl. Place the bowl over a pan of simmering water and stir until melted. Remove from the heat.

2 Cream 125 g (4 oz) butter and the sugar together until light and fluffy. Add the almonds. Stir in the egg yolks, breadcrumbs and the melted chocolate. Beat the ingredients well together.

3 Whisk the egg whites until stiff and fold half into the chocolate mixture, then fold in the remaining egg whites. Pour into the prepared tin and level the surface.

4 Bake the cake in the oven at 180°C (350°F) mark 4 for 40–45 minutes until it is firm to the touch.

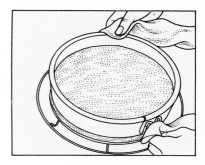

5 Cover with a damp tea-towel, leave for 5 minutes to cool slightly then unclip the sides and invert on to a wire rack. Remove the base. Turn the cake uppermost and cover again. Leave the cake until cold. Brush the top with the melted apricot jam.

6 Melt the remaining chocolate with the remaining butter in a bowl over simmering water. Remove the bowl from the heat. Sift in the icing sugar and mix well. Stir in the water and leave to stand for 5 minutes.

7 Spread the icing on top of the cake, easing it gently to the edge to cover the sides. Leave to set then sprinkle with chocolate curls to decorate.

GLAZED FRUIT BOATS

| 0.45* | 🍴 🍴 | 164 cals |

* plus 1 hour chilling

Makes 24

250 g (9 oz) plain flour

pinch of salt

125 g (4½ oz) unsalted butter

15 g (½ oz) caster sugar

egg, beaten

3 egg yolks

75 g (3 oz) caster sugar

25 ml (1½ tbsp) plain flour

25 ml (1½ tbsp) cornflour

450 ml (¾ pint) milk

25 ml (1½ tbsp) Strega liqueur

about 100 g (4 oz) green grapes, halved and seeded

about 100 g (4 oz) black grapes, halved and seeded

30 ml (2 tbsp) sieved lime marmalade

30 ml (2 tbsp) water

30 ml (2 tbsp) redcurrant jelly

1 Make the pastry. Sift the flour and salt into a bowl. Add the butter in small pieces, then rub in until the mixture resembles fine breadcrumbs. Stir in the sugar, then the beaten egg. Mix to a smooth dough. Wrap and refrigerate for about 30 minutes.

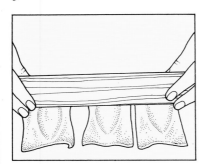

2 Roll out the dough on a lightly floured surface and use to line 24 large barquette moulds. Prick bases with a fork, then stand on baking sheets and chill again in the refrigerator for 30 minutes.

3 Bake in the oven at 180°C (350°F) mark 4 for 15–20 minutes until pastry is crisp and lightly coloured. Leave until cold.

4 Make the *crème patissière*. Mix the egg yolks, sugar and flours together with a little milk. Scald remaining milk, pour in a thin, steady stream on to egg yolk mixture, then return to pan and simmer until thick and smooth.

5 Cover with cling film and leave until cold. Stir in the liqueur, then spoon a little into each boat. Top half the boats with green grapes and the other half with black, making sure the *crème patissière* is covered.

6 Heat the marmalade with 15 ml (1 tbsp) water, stirring, then brush over green grapes. Repeat with redcurrant jelly and remaining water and brush over black grapes. Leave to cool and set, then refrigerate until serving time. Serve chilled.

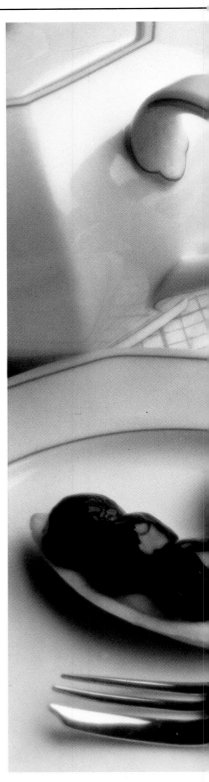

PARTY PINWHEELS

| 0.15* | £ | ✳ | 84 cals |

* plus 1 hour chilling
Makes about 100

350 g (12 oz) full fat soft cheese at
    room temperature
200-g (7-oz) can shrimps, drained
juice of ½ lemon
1.25 ml (¼ tsp) cayenne pepper
about 5 ml (1 tsp) tomato purée
salt and freshly ground pepper
1 bunch watercress, finely chopped
finely grated rind of 1 orange
30 ml (2 tbsp) fresh orange juice
large fresh white sandwich loaf
softened butter, for spreading
large wholemeal sandwich loaf

1 Divide the cheese in half and
put into separate bowls. Mash
the shrimps, then beat into one
bowl of cheese with lemon juice
and cayenne. Add enough tomato
purée to colour pink. Season.

2 Beat the watercress into the
other bowl of cheese. Add the
orange rind and juice, to make
a spreading consistency. Add salt
and pepper to taste.

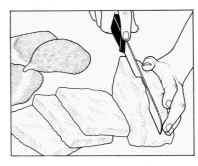

3 Cut the crusts off the white
loaf, then cut into seven slices
lengthways. Spread each slice liberally with butter, right to the
edges, then spread each with the
shrimp filling.

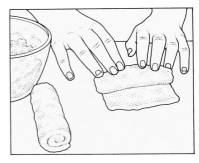

4 Roll up each slice from one
short end, then wrap each one
individually in cling film. Refrigerate for 1 hour. Repeat step 3 with
the wholemeal loaf, butter and
watercress filling. Roll up, wrap
and refrigerate as with the shrimp
filling.

5 Unwrap the rolls and cut each
one across into about eight
slices. Arrange on a sandwich
plate, alternating colours.

CHEESY PÂTÉ CHEQUERBOARDS

| 0.15* | £ | 49 cals |

* plus 1 hour chilling
Makes 60

15 slices white bread
10 large slices dark rye bread
4 eggs, hard-boiled, finely mashed
175 g (6 oz) Red Leicester cheese,
    finely grated
about 60 ml (4 tbsp) mayonnaise
English mustard powder, to taste
salt and freshly ground pepper
softened butter, for spreading
175 g (6 oz) fine liver pâté

1 Cut the crusts off the bread.
Place a slice of rye bread on
top of a slice of white bread and
trim them to the same size. Repeat
with remaining slices. Mix eggs
and cheese, add enough mayonnaise for a spreading consistency.
Add mustard, salt and pepper.

2 Spread one slice of white bread
with butter right to the edges.
Spread generously with filling, top
with a slice of rye. Butter the rye
right to the edges, then spread
with pâté. Repeat layers once more.

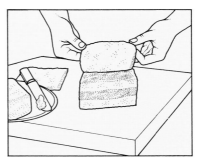

3 Spread one slice of white
bread with butter, then place
buttered side down on top of pâté
filling. Wrap closely in cling film
and refrigerate for at least 1 hour.

4 Make four more layered sandwiches in this way, wrapping
them in cling film and putting
them in the refrigerator as you
make them.

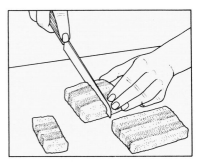

5 Just before serving, unwrap
each sandwich and cut into four
lengthways. Cut each piece across
into three, to make twelve chequerboards from each sandwich. Arrange on a plate and serve.

SALMON AND PARMA ROLLUPS

| 0.15 | £ £ | 34 cals |

Makes about 40

100 g (4 oz) unsalted butter
45 ml (3 tbsp) chopped fresh herbs
10 ml (2 tsp) French mustard
freshly ground black pepper
10 slices smoked salmon
20 slices Parma ham
two 425-g (15-oz) cans asparagus,
    drained and trimmed
lemon wedges, to garnish

1 Beat the butter to a spreading
consistency with the herbs,
mustard and pepper to taste. Cut
the salmon slices in half lengthways. Spread a little of mixture
over salmon.

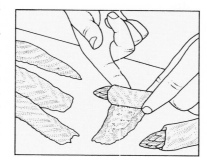

2 Place an asparagus spear at one
end. Roll the salmon up around
the asparagus to enclose it completely, letting the tip of the
asparagus protrude slightly at the
end of the roll. Try to make them
an even size.

3 Repeat with the remaining
salmon and asparagus, then
with the ham. Place rolls on a serving platter, arranging them in
a circle radiating out from the
centre. Garnish with lemon and
refrigerate before serving.

Parma Ham
Parma ham or *prosciutto* is world
famous and needs little introduc-
tion. The *prosciutto* from Parma
is reputed to be the best. It
should be pale red in colour,
sweet and tender, and it should
be thinly cut. In Italy *prosciutto*
is eaten with melon, the scented
deep yellow kind, or with fresh
figs, green or black.

Children's Birthday Party for 10 six year-olds

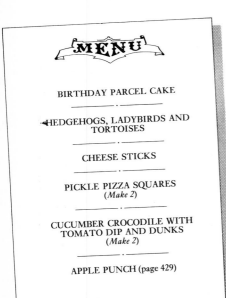

·＝MENU＝·

BIRTHDAY PARCEL CAKE

HEDGEHOGS, LADYBIRDS AND TORTOISES

CHEESE STICKS

PICKLE PIZZA SQUARES
(Make 2)

CUCUMBER CROCODILE WITH TOMATO DIP AND DUNKS
(Make 2)

APPLE PUNCH (page 429)

BIRTHDAY PARCEL CAKE

| 1.00* | ⊟ ⊟ £ ✳* | 368 cals |

* plus overnight setting; freeze basic cake before adding decoration

Serves 10

175 g (6 oz) plain flour
7.5 ml (1½ tsp) baking powder
175 g (6 oz) soft tub margarine
175 g (6 oz) caster sugar
3 eggs
5 ml (1 tsp) vanilla flavouring
100 g (4 oz) butter, softened
225 g (8 oz) icing sugar, sifted
10 ml (2 tsp) lemon juice
225 g (8 oz) marzipan
1 egg white, lightly beaten
600 g (1¼ lb) white fondant icing
food colouring

1 Sift the flour and baking powder into a bowl. Add margarine, caster sugar, eggs and vanilla flavouring, then beat for 1–2 minutes until light and fluffy. Divide evenly between two greased and lined 18-cm (7½-inch) square cake tins.

2 Bake in the oven at 190°C (375°F) gas 5 for 20 minutes or until the centres of the cakes spring back when lightly pressed with the fingertips. Leave to cool in the tins for 2 minutes, then turn both cakes out on to a wire rack and cool.

3 Make the buttercream. Beat the butter in a bowl until light and fluffy, then gradually beat in the icing sugar until well blended. Stir in the lemon juice.

4 Sandwich the cakes together with all but 30 ml (2 tbsp) of the buttercream. Put the cake on a cake board and spread the reserved buttercream smoothly over the top and sides. Set aside.

5 For the decoration, knead the marzipan until pliable, then knead in a few drops of food colouring until evenly coloured.

6 Roll out on a surface lightly sprinkled with icing sugar to the following shapes: two strips measuring 30 × 2.5 cm (12 × 1 inch), three strips measuring 15 × 2.5 cm (6 × 1 inch); one strip measuring 7.5 × 2.5 cm (3 × 1 inch); one strip measuring 5 × 2.5 cm (2 × 1 inch). Set aside.

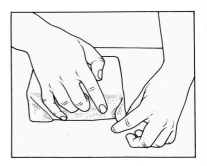

7 Knead the fondant icing until smooth and pliable. Put a small amount aside for the gift tag and thread, then roll out the remainder to a 30-cm (12-inch) square. Place over cake and mitre the corners like a parcel.

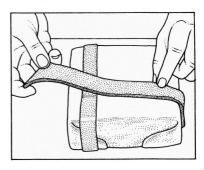

8 Brush one side of the 30-cm (12-inch)-long strips with a little of the beaten egg white, then place them this side down on top of the cake to look like ribbon on a parcel.

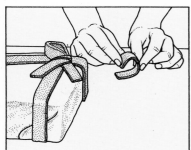

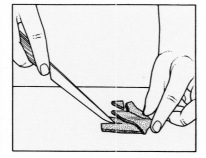

FINISHING THE DECORATION

If you are feeling artistic, finish off the cake by drawing a design on the fondant to make it look like wrapping paper. The simplest way to do this is to use edible food colouring pens. Available from specialist kitchen shops, they look just like felt tips. Don't forget to finish off tag.

9 Loop the three 15-cm (6-inch) strips to look like a bow and fix on top of cake with egg white. Use 7.5-cm (3-inch) strip to form the centre of the bow.

10 Cut 5-cm (2-inch) strip in a V-shape to form end of ribbon. Fix into place with egg white. Use reserved fondant to make tag and thread, then fix on cake. Leave overnight.

CHEESE STICKS

| 0.30 | £ | ✳ | 84 cals |

Makes about 100 sticks

100 g (4 oz) plain flour

pinch of salt

50 g (2 oz) butter or margarine

50 g (2 oz) mature Cheddar cheese

1 egg, beaten

Parmesan cheese, grated

1 Mix the flour and salt in a bowl. Rub in fat until mixture resembles fine breadcrumbs.

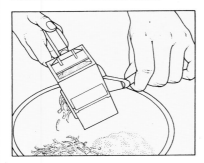

2 Grate in the cheddar, using a Mouli or other fine grater. Bind together with a little beaten egg and knead lightly.

3 Roll out on a floured surface to an oblong 25.5 × 15 cm (10 × 6 inch). Brush with beaten egg; sprinkle liberally with Parmesan. Press cheese lightly into egg.

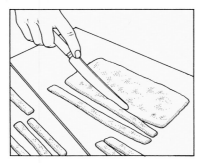

4 Cut into sticks 6 cm × 0.5 cm (2½ × ¼ inch) and place on ungreased baking sheets. Bake in the oven at 200°C (400°F) mark 6 for 10 minutes until golden. Cool.

PICKLE PIZZA SQUARES

| 0.50 | £ ✳ | 304 cals |

Makes 10 slices

75 g (3 oz) margarine
275 g (10 oz) plain wholemeal flour
salt and freshly ground pepper
7.5 ml (1½ tsp) baking powder
45 ml (3 tbsp) tomato relish
30 ml (2 tbsp) water
1 onion, skinned
175 g (6 oz) luncheon meat or ham
100 g (4 oz) Cheddar cheese, grated
1 egg, size 2, beaten
2 rashers of streaky bacon

1 In a large bowl rub margarine into the flour, salt and baking powder. Stir in tomato relish and the water.

2 Bind to a smooth manageable dough. Roll out into a 33 × 23 cm (13 × 9 inch) rectangle. Trim the edges with a knife.

3 Finely chop the onion and meat. Combine with the cheese and stir in the egg. Season. Cut bacon in thin strips.

4 Spread the mixture evenly over the surface to cover the dough. Garnish with the bacon strips, arranged in a pattern.

5 Bake in the oven at 190°C (375°F) mark 5 for about 30 minutes until the cheese bubbles up and is golden and the dough is cooked. Serve hot cut into squares.

CUCUMBER CROCODILE WITH TOMATO DIP AND DUNKS

| 0.45 | 🍴 🍴 | 348 cals |

Serves 10

450 g (1 lb) chipolata sausages
225 g (8 oz) Cheddar cheese
1 large, slightly curved cucumber
150 ml (¼ pint) mayonnaise
30 ml (2 tbsp) tomato ketchup
salt and freshly ground pepper
celery, carrots and cucumber
    sticks, to serve

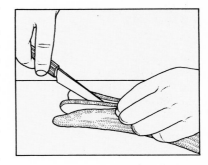

1 Twist each chipolata into two and snip apart. Cook in the oven at 190°C (375°F) mark 5 for about 20 minutes until golden. Place on cocktail sticks. Cut the cheese into 1-cm (½-inch) cubes. Place on cocktail sticks. Mix together the mayonnaise, tomato ketchup and seasoning. Spoon into a small bowl, cover and chill well.

2 To make the crocodile, cut out a 7.5 cm (3 inch) wedge of cucumber to form the mouth. Then cut out the teeth. Cut out a small hole for the eyes and press in a small piece of tomato. Arrange sausage and cheese cubes in crocodile.

3 Serve the dip with the crocodile and the sausages and cheese sticks of celery, crisps, carrot, and cheese sticks (left).

HEDGEHOGS, LADYBIRDS AND TORTOISES

| 1.00 | 🗆 🗆 £ ✳* | 212 cals |

* freeze buns only

Makes 15

50 g (2 oz) butter
50 g (2 oz) caster sugar
1 egg beaten
50 g (2 oz) self-raising flour
15 ml (1 tbsp) milk

For the hedgehogs:
chocolate butter icing, chocolate buttons, silver or gold balls, dolly mixture jellies

For the ladybirds:
75 g (3 oz) marzipan, red edible food colouring, stiff white glacé icing, polka dots

For the tortoises:
175 g (6 oz) marzipan, apricot jam, brown and green edible food colouring, silver balls

1 Cream the butter and sugar together thoroughly then gradually beat in the egg. Lastly fold in the flour and milk.

2 Divide the mixture between fifteen well-greased patty tins with rounded bases. Bake in the oven at 180°C (350°F) mark 4 for about 15 minutes, then leave to cool on wire racks.

3 Make the hedgehogs. Cover five of the cold buns with chocolate butter icing, shaping to form a snout. Decorate with halved chocolate buttons, silver or gold balls for eyes and dolly mixture jellies for snout.

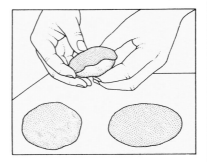

4 Make the ladybirds. Colour the marzipan a deep pink with red colouring, roll out thinly and use to cover a further five buns. Using white glacé icing, pipe lines and spots on to the backs of the ladybirds and use chocolate polka dots for eyes.

5 Make the tortoises. Colour two-thirds of the marzipan a deep green with green colouring, and the remaining third a deep brown with brown colouring. Cover the remaining five buns with a layer of the green marzipan.

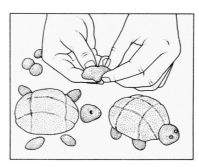

6 With a skewer mark on the 'shell' markings. Use the brown marzipan to form heads, legs and tails and attach to the tortoise body with a little jam. Make eyes with silver balls.

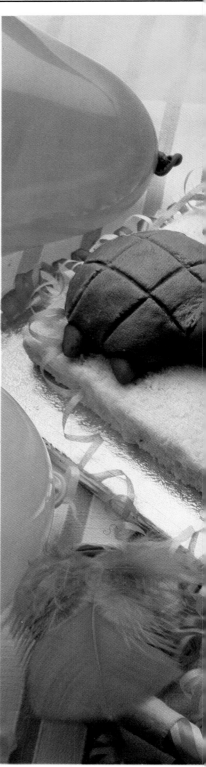

Brunch Party

A brunch party for 8 people is a wonderful idea for weekend entertaining, and far more relaxing than a dinner party, for both guests and hosts alike.

The brunch idea is popular in America, especially in big cities where it is often served in restaurants and bars on Sundays. Simply offer each guest a glass of Champagne Cocktail as soon as they arrive, then let them help themselves to the food.

CHAMPAGNE COCKTAIL

0.05	£ £	151 cals

Makes 8

8 sugar lumps

120 ml (8 tbsp) peach or apricot brandy

1 bottle champagne, well chilled

8 strips of thinly pared orange rind or 8 orange slices (optional)

1 Put a sugar lump in the bottom of each of 8 champagne glasses. Pour 15 ml (1 tbsp) of brandy into each glass and leave to soak for a few minutes.

2 Open the champagne and pour into the glasses straightaway. Serve immediately, each glass garnished with an orange twist or orange slice, if liked.

——————— VARIATION ———————

If liked, a few drops of **Angostura bitters** may be sprinkled over the sugar lumps before the brandy.

BAGELS WITH SMOKED SALMON AND CREAM CHEESE

0.30	£ £	1458 cals

Serves 8

225 g (8 oz) packet unsalted butter, chilled

12 bagels

700 g (1½ lb) cream cheese

24 thin slices smoked salmon

freshly ground black pepper

lemon wedges, to serve

1 Make butter curls. Draw a butter curler towards you along the length of the block of butter. Pile the curls up as you make them in a chilled serving bowl. Chill in the refrigerator until serving time.

2 Warm the bagels through in the oven at 170°C (325°F) mark 3 for 10 minutes.

3 Meanwhile, put the cream cheese in 1 or 2 serving bowls. Arrange the smoked salmon slices attractively on a wooden board, grind a little black pepper on top. Garnish with lemon wedges.

4 Split each bagel in half cross-ways and place in a napkin-lined basket. Serve immediately, while still warm. Guests help themselves —spreading bagels with butter and cream cheese, topping each one with a slice of salmon and a squeeze of lemon.

ENTERTAINING
FRIENDS
AT THE WEEKEND

Saturday Lunch

Friends or relations
arriving Saturday
lunchtime and staying
over until Sunday lunch?
Make it a relaxed
weekend with these
suggested menus, all of
which can be prepared in
the days leading up to the
Saturday, thus leaving
you free to enjoy the
company of your guests.
Start with an elegant
seafood and French bean
salad for Saturday lunch,
followed by homemade
bread rolls and cheese.
First impressions count!

SEAFOOD IN SAFFRON MAYONNAISE

| 0.55 | 🍴 £ £ | 493 cals |

Serves 6

450 g (1 lb) white fish fillets (haddock, cod or monkfish)

1 bay leaf

1 slice lemon

125 g (4 oz) peeled prawns

125 g (4 oz) cooked, shelled mussels

few saffron threads

1 egg yolk

150 ml (¼ pint) vegetable oil

10 ml (2 tsp) white wine vinegar

salt and freshly ground pepper

450 g (1 lb) French beans, topped, tailed and cooked

chopped fresh parsley, to garnish

1 *To prepare* (45 minutes): Place the fish in a large frying pan, cover with water and add the bay leaf and lemon slice. Bring to the boil, then immediately lower the heat and poach gently for 10–15 minutes until cooked. Strain off the poaching liquid, reserving 60 ml (4 tbsp). Cool the fish for at least 20 minutes.

2 Skin the fish and roughly flake the flesh. Place in a bowl with the prawns and mussels, cover and chill for up to 2 days.

3 Meanwhile put the reserved fish liquor in a small saucepan, add the saffron threads and heat gently. Remove from the heat and leave to infuse until cold and golden yellow in colour.

4 Put the egg yolk in a bowl and beat well. Beat in the oil a drop at a time, then continue adding in a thin, steady stream until the mixture is very thick. Stir in half the vinegar and continue beating in the oil until all is incorporated. Stir in the remaining vinegar.

5 Strain the saffron liquid into the mayonnaise and whisk to the consistency of single cream. Add seasoning to taste, cover and chill in the refrigerator for up to 2 days.

6 *To serve* (10 minutes): Arrange the French beans on a long serving dish. Pile the fish mixture down the centre of the beans and spoon over the mayonnaise. Serve immediately, garnished with parsley.

SEAFOOD IN SAFFRON MAYONNAISE

Most good fishmongers sell monkfish, and if you can get it for this recipe, then you will find it better for a special occasion than cod or haddock. Although more expensive, its flavour is rather like that of lobster, and its flesh is very thick, firm and white—again like lobster, or scampi. Monkfish hasn't always been such a highly prized fish. Because of its unattractive appearance when whole, it used to be unpopular, but once the head is removed and the fish cut into fillets by the fishmonger, you need never know how ugly it was! In some areas it is known as angler fish or frog fish, and if you have eaten it in Mediterranean countries you will probably know it by either its Spanish name of *rape*, or by the French name *lotte* or *ange de mer*, or the Italian *rospo* (which means frog).

QUICK WHOLEMEAL ROLLS

| 0.35* | £ | ✳ | 149 cals |

* plus 1 hour rising

Makes 12

15 g ($\frac{1}{2}$ oz) fresh yeast or 7.5 ml ($1\frac{1}{2}$ tsp) dried

10 ml (2 tsp) sugar

300 ml ($\frac{1}{2}$ pint) tepid water

225 g (8 oz) strong white flour

225 g (8 oz) strong wholewheat flour

10 ml (2 tsp) salt

15 g ($\frac{1}{2}$ oz) lard

cracked wheat, to decorate

1 *To prepare* (35 minutes):
Grease a baking sheet. Blend the fresh yeast, 5 ml (1 tsp) sugar and the water. If using dried yeast, dissolve 5 ml (1 tsp) sugar in the water, sprinkle in the yeast and leave to froth for 15 minutes.

2 Sift the flours into a bowl with the salt and 5 ml (1 tsp) sugar. Rub in the fat. Add the yeast mixture and mix to a soft dough. Turn on to a lightly floured surface and knead for about 2 minutes until smooth.

3 Divide the dough into 12 equal pieces and shape into rounds. Place on the greased baking sheet, brush with water and sprinkle the tops with cracked wheat. Cover with a clean damp tea cloth and leave to rise in a warm place for about 1 hour until doubled in size.

4 Bake at 230°C (450°F) mark 8 for 15–20 minutes or until golden brown. Cool for at least 15 minutes on a wire rack.

GARLIC AND BLACK PEPPERCORN CHEESE

| 0.45* | £ | ✳ | 113 cals |

* plus 2½–4 days draining and chilling
Makes 450 g (1 lb)

600 ml (1 pint) single cream
568 ml (1 pint) milk
30 ml (2 tbsp) buttermilk
1 garlic clove, skinned
5 ml (1 tsp) salt
15 ml (1 tbsp) chopped fresh mixed
   herbs (parsley, chervil, chives,
   thyme)
30 ml (2 tbsp) black peppercorns,
   coarsely crushed
cucumber slices, to garnish

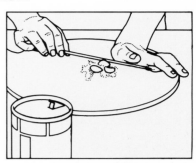

1 *To prepare* (35 minutes): Put the cream and milk in a saucepan and heat gently to blood heat or 32–38°C (90–100°F); stir in the buttermilk. Pour the mixture into a bowl.

2 Cover the bowl with cling film and leave in a warm place for 24–48 hours until the cream mixture turns to soft curds.

3 Line a colander with muslin or all-purpose kitchen cloth and place it in the sink. Pour the curds into the colander and drain for 10 minutes.

4 Place the colander on a rack in a saucepan, cover with cling film and chill in the refrigerator for 18–24 hours.

5 On a board, crush the garlic to a smooth purée with the flat of a round-bladed knife and the salt. Spoon the curds from the colander into a bowl and stir in the mixed herbs, garlic and peppercorns.

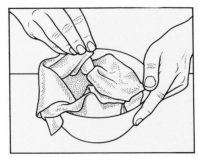

6 Line a small plastic punnet or earthenware cheese mould with a double layer of damp cheesecloth or all-purpose kitchen cloth, leaving a 5 cm (2 inch) overhang. Spoon in the curds and fold the cheesecloth over the top.

7 Invert the punnet or mould on to a wire rack placed over a shallow dish, cover tightly with cling film and chill for 18–24 hours.

8 *To serve* (10 minutes): Unmould the cheese on to a plate, remove the cheesecloth and garnish with cucumber slices. Serve chilled.

Saturday Dinner

This should be the high spot of the weekend. If you've planned not to eat out, then your menu at home should match that of the best restaurant in town! Start with a refreshingly tangy Avocado and Orange Salad with Citrus Dressing. Follow with a rich veal dish with wine, mushrooms and cream, which both looks and tastes very special, and yet is incredibly simple to prepare. Then finish the meal with Iced Strawberry Soufflé — a spectacular finale to any meal.

Avocado and Orange Salad with Citrus Dressing

0.40*	462 cals

* plus 1 hour or overnight chilling

Serves 6

150 ml ($\frac{1}{4}$ pint) vegetable oil

105 ml (7 tbsp) freshly squeezed grapefruit juice

15 ml (1 tbsp) snipped chives

2.5 ml ($\frac{1}{2}$ tsp) sugar

salt and freshly ground pepper

3 medium oranges

3 ripe avocados

1 *To prepare* (25 minutes): Put the oil in a screw-top jar with the grapefruit juice, chives, sugar and seasoning to taste. Shake well to mix.

2 Working in a spiral motion, remove the rind and white pith from the oranges with a serrated knife.

3 Cut the oranges into segments and place in a shallow dish. Shake the dressing again, then pour over the oranges. Cover the dish with cling film and chill in the refrigerator for at least 1 hour, or for up to 24 hours if more convenient.

4 *To serve* (15 minutes): Cut the avocados in half and twist to remove the stones. Peel off the skin, then slice the flesh neatly.

5 Remove the orange segments from the marinade and arrange on individual plates, alternating with avocado slices. Pour over the marinade and serve immediately.

VEAL ESCALOPES WITH CREAM AND MUSHROOM SAUCE

0.55* | 445 cals

* plus cooling and chilling

Serves 6

6 veal escalopes, about 100 g (4 oz) each

30 ml (2 tbsp) plain flour

salt and freshly ground pepper

50 g (2 oz) butter

30 ml (2 tbsp) olive oil

350 g (12 oz) button mushrooms, sliced

350 ml (12 fl oz) dry white wine

10 ml (2 tsp) chopped fresh tarragon or 5 ml (1 tsp) dried

200 ml (7 fl oz) double cream

tarragon sprigs, to garnish

1 *To prepare* (35 minutes): Trim each veal escalope to remove any skin, then cut each one in half.

2 Place the escalopes well apart between sheets of non-stick paper or heavy-duty cling film. Bat out well, using a meat mallet or rolling pin, until the escalopes are very thin. Remove paper or film, then coat the escalopes in the flour seasoned with salt and pepper.

3 Melt the butter with the oil in a heavy-based frying pan. Add the escalopes a few at a time and fry over moderate heat until lightly coloured on both sides. Remove with a spatula and set aside on a plate.

4 Add the mushrooms to the pan and fry until the juices run. Add the wine and bring slowly to the boil, stirring, then return the escalopes to the pan, pile the mushrooms on top and sprinkle with the tarragon and seasoning to taste. Turn into a shallow dish. Leave to cool, then cover and refrigerate until ready to serve (overnight, if convenient).

5 *To serve* (20 minutes): Cook over moderate heat and bring slowly to the boil. Lower the heat, cover and simmer for 5–10 minutes until heated through. Remove the veal from the cooking liquid with a slotted spoon, arrange in a warmed serving dish and keep hot. Stir the cream into the pan and simmer until the sauce thickens. Taste and adjust seasoning, then pour over the veal. Serve immediately, garnished with sprigs of tarragon.

VEAL ESCALOPES WITH CREAM AND MUSHROOM SAUCE

Although veal is an expensive meat to buy, escalopes work out less so because they are beaten very thin and therefore weigh very little.

Escalopes come from the leg of the calf. The topside is the choicest cut, from which come the most tender escalopes. Slightly less expensive but still good are the escalopes from the thick flank. Some butchers sell escalopes cut from the 'skirt' of the animal. These have a good flavour, but they do have a coarse grain which makes it necessary to cook them longer. Check with your butcher when buying so you can be sure of the cooking time.

ICED STRAWBERRY SOUFFLÉ

3.05* ☐ £ £ ✳ 569 cals

* plus 1–2 hours setting, 3 hours freezing, 2 hours softening

Serves 6

225 g (8 oz) strawberries

60 ml (4 tbsp) almond-flavoured liqueur

30 ml (2 tbsp) lemon juice

15 ml (1 tbsp) icing sugar

300 ml ($\frac{1}{2}$ pint) double cream

45 ml (3 tbsp) water

15 ml (1 tbsp) powdered gelatine

4 eggs, separated

175 g (6 oz) caster sugar

225 g (8 oz) strawberries

25 g (1 oz) small ratafias or macaroons

150 ml ($\frac{1}{4}$ pint) double cream

1 To prepare (1 hour): Put the strawberries in a bowl and stir in the liqueur, lemon juice and icing sugar. Cover and leave to marinate for 30 minutes.

2 Put the strawberries in a blender or food processor and work to a purée. Sieve to remove the seeds.

3 Tie a double band of grease-proof paper around the edge of a 1.1 litre (2 pint) soufflé dish to form a 5 cm (2 inch) collar. Stand a straight-sided 450 g (1 lb) jam jar in the centre.

4 Lightly whip the 300 ml ($\frac{1}{2}$ pint) of cream until it just holds its shape.

5 Put the water into a small saucepan, sprinkle over the gelatine and leave to soak for about 5 minutes until spongy. Dissolve slowly over gentle heat.

6 Put the egg yolks and caster sugar in a bowl and whisk with an electric whisk until very light and creamy. Fold in the strawberry purée, whipped cream and dissolved gelatine.

7 Whisk the egg whites until stiff but not dry and fold into the strawberry mixture.

8 Pour the mixture into the prepared dish, keeping the jam jar in the centre. Chill in the refrigerator for 1–2 hours until set, then transfer to the freezer for at least 3 hours, until firm.

9 To serve (2 hours 5 minutes): Remove the soufflé from the freezer and fill the jam jar with hot water. Twist gently to remove it. Fill the centre with the strawberries. Finely crush the ratafias or macaroons. Ease off the paper collar and coat the sides of the soufflé with crushed ratafias. Decorate with the cream, whipped.

10 Transfer to the main body of the refrigerator for about 2 hours to soften before serving.

Sunday Lunch

Entertaining on Sunday should be a relaxed affair, whether for family or friends, and this lunch menu for 6 people has been devised to be just that. The Watercress and Orange Soup can be prepared up to the reheating stage the day before, and the accompanying rolls can be made in less than an hour while the pork is roasting. Potatoes can be roasted with the pork, and the Crunchy Cabbage accompaniment takes only 15 minutes to prepare and cook. And for dessert, there's a good old-fashioned crumble, which can be prepared the night before, then popped into the oven when the main course is served.

WATERCRESS AND ORANGE SOUP

| 0.45 | ✳ | 140 cals |

Serves 6

2 large bunches watercress, trimmed and washed

50 g (2 oz) butter or margarine

2 medium onions, roughly chopped

45 ml (3 tbsp) flour

1.1 litres (2 pints) chicken stock

salt and freshly ground pepper

finely grated rind and juice of 1 orange

150 ml ($\frac{1}{4}$ pint) single cream (optional)

few slices of orange, to garnish

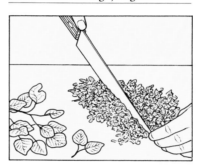

1 Reserve a few sprigs of watercress for the garnish, then chop the rest.

2 Melt the fat in a large saucepan. Add the chopped watercress and onions, cover and cook gently for 10–15 minutes.

3 Remove the pan from the heat and stir in the flour, stock and seasoning. Bring slowly to the boil, stirring all the time. Cover and simmer gently for 30 minutes. Stir in the orange rind and juice.

4 Leave to cool a little, then purée in an electric blender or food processor.

5 Return the soup to the rinsed-out pan and reheat. Stir in the single cream (if using) and heat through. (Do not boil or the soup will curdle.) Adjust the seasoning. Serve garnished with orange slices and watercress sprigs.

VARIATION

If preferred, this soup can be served chilled. Do not reheat as in step 5, simply stir in half of the single cream after the soup has gone cold. Chill in the refrigerator for at least 2 hours before serving, then swirl in the remaining cream just before serving.

POPPYSEED ROLLS

0.55*	£	✳	88 cals

* plus 20 minutes cooling

Makes 12 rolls

280 g (10 oz) white bread mix

450 ml (3 tbsp) poppyseeds

200 ml (7 fl oz) warm milk

beaten egg and milk, mixed, to glaze

1 Empty the bread mix into a bowl, add 30 ml (2 tbsp) of the poppyseeds and stir well to mix.

2 Add the warm milk and mix well with a wooden spoon to form a firm dough.

3 Turn the dough onto a floured surface and knead according to packet instructions until smooth.

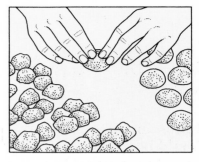

4 Cut the dough into 36 equal pieces. Shape each piece into a ball with your hands.

5 Sprinkle 2 baking sheets with flour, then place the dough balls on the sheets, in triangular groups of three. Leave to rise in a warm place for 10 minutes.

6 Brush the rolls with the beaten egg and milk mixture and then sprinkle with the remaining poppyseeds.

7 Bake in the oven at 200°C (400°F) mark 6 for about 20 minutes until golden. Cool the rolls for about 20 minutes on a wire rack before serving.

FRENCH PORK IN WINE

| 3.30 | £ £ | 982 cals |

Serves 6

2 kg (4½ lb) loin of pork, boned
salt and freshly ground pepper
3 garlic cloves, skinned
few fresh or dried sage sprigs
30 ml (2 tbsp) olive oil
25 g (1 oz) butter
300 ml (½ pint) dry white wine
30 ml (2 tbsp) redcurrant jelly
fresh sage leaves, to garnish

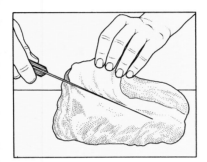

1 Lay the joint of pork out flat on a board and cut off the skin and fat with a sharp knife.

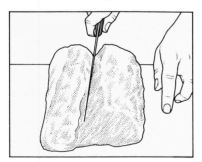

2 With a sharp, pointed knife, make a shallow cut along the length of the inside of the meat (this will make it easier to roll). Sprinkle the meat liberally with salt and pepper.

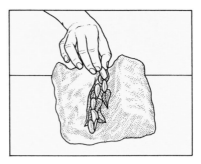

3 Cut each garlic clove into 3–4 slivers, then place at regular intervals along the length of the meat with the sprigs of sage.

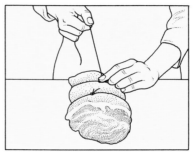

4 Roll the meat up lengthways and tie at regular intervals with string. Heat the oil and butter in a large flameproof casserole into which the pork just fits. Put the pork in the casserole and lightly brown on all sides.

5 Pour in the wine and bring slowly to the boil, then cover and cook in the oven at 170°C (325°F) mark 3 for 3 hours until tender, basting occasionally.

6 To serve, remove the pork from the casserole and set aside in a warm place to settle for 15 minutes before carving. Stir the redcurrant jelly into the cooking liquid and boil rapidly to reduce.

7 Remove the string from the pork and place the joint on a warmed serving platter. Drizzle a little sauce over the pork and garnish with fresh sage leaves.

CRUNCHY CABBAGE

| 0.15 | £ | ✳ | 95 cals |

Serves 6

350 g (12 oz) red cabbage

225 g (8 oz) cooked beetroot, skinned

1 medium onion, skinned and thinly sliced

about 30 ml (2 tbsp) peanut or vegetable oil

30 ml (2 tbsp) creamed horseradish

salt and freshly ground pepper

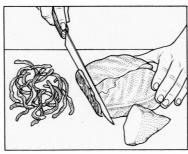

1 Finely shred the red cabbage, discarding the core and any thick, woody stalks.

2 Grate the beetroot on the coarse side of a conical or box grater or, if preferred, chop finely.

3 Heat 30 ml (2 tbsp) oil in a wok or large frying pan until smoking. Stir in the cabbage and onion. Cook over high heat for 3–4 minutes, stirring all the time, until the cabbage has softened a little but still retains its crispness. Add a little more oil if necessary.

4 Stir in the beetroot, horse-radish and seasoning to taste. Cook, stirring, for a further few minutes to heat through. Serve immediately.

SHERRIED PLUM CRUMBLE

| 0.45 | 282 cals |

Serves 6

397 g (14 oz) can red plums

30 ml (2 tbsp) sherry

100 g (4 oz) flour

50 g (2 oz) butter or margarine

25 g (1 oz) chopped almonds

50 g (2 oz) demerara sugar

fresh pouring cream, natural yogurt or soured cream, to serve

1 Strain the plums and remove the stones. Divide the plums equally between four small soufflé dishes and sprinkle a little sherry over each.

2 Make the crumble topping. Sift the flour into a bowl, then rub in the fat until the mixture resembles fine breadcrumbs. Stir in the almonds and sugar. Sprinkle evenly over the plums.

3 Bake in the oven at 190°C (375°F) mark 5 for about 30 minutes until golden brown on top. Serve hot, with cream, yogurt or soured cream.

Cold Lunch Party

For summer entertaining in the garden, nothing could be more relaxing than a cold lunch party — especially when all the preparations can be done beforehand. Salmon in Puff Pastry makes a spectacular table centre-piece, and the two salad accompaniments complement each other perfectly. All you need to serve with them is plenty of crusty French bread and butter, and a selection of cheeses. Finish with the Open Pear Flan, and your guests will be amazed how perfect the food is, with no sign of cooking!

SALMON IN PUFF PASTRY

1.45*	£ £ ✳*	583–640 cals

* plus 30 minutes chilling, 1 hour cooling and 30 minutes at room temperature

Serves 6

1 bunch watercress

45 ml (3 tbsp) soured cream

finely grated rind of $\frac{1}{2}$ lemon

salt and freshly ground pepper

1.1–1.4 kg (2$\frac{1}{2}$–3 lb salmon or sea trout, cleaned and filleted (see box)

1 quantity puff pastry (see page 439) or two 368 g (13 oz) packets frozen puff pastry, thawed

beaten egg, to glaze

1 *To prepare* (1 hour 10 minutes): Wash the watercress and trim off the root ends. Chop roughly, then place in a bowl with the soured cream. Add the lemon rind and seasoning to taste, then stir until the ingredients are well mixed.

2 Using a sharp knife and holding the tail end of 1 salmon fillet, scrape the flesh away from the skin. Repeat with the other fillets.

3 Place two fillets skinned side down on a board and spoon on the prepared watercress filling. Top with the remaining fillets.

4 If using frozen pastry, stack one piece on top of the other. Roll out the home-made or frozen pastry to a rectangle about 30 × 23 cm (12 × 9 inches).

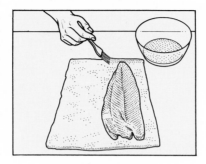

5 Carefully place the fish on the pastry, leaving a 5 mm ($\frac{1}{4}$ inch) border. Brush the edges of the pastry with beaten egg.

6 Fold the pastry over the fish to enclose it completely. Seal and trim, then knock up the edges. Lift on to a baking sheet and chill in the refrigerator for at least 30 minutes.

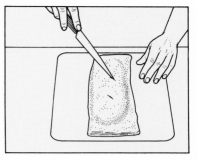

7 Use the remaining egg to glaze the pastry. Make 2 small holes in the pastry to allow the steam to escape. Place the baking sheet in the oven and bake at 200°C (400°F) mark 6 for about 45 minutes until the pastry is well risen and golden brown. To test, make a small slit through the thickest part of the fish — the flesh should begin to flake. Cool for at least 1 hour then wrap in cling film or foil and refrigerate for up to one day.

8 *To serve* (35 minutes): Remove the salmon from the refrigerator and unwrap. Leave at room temperature for 30 minutes before serving.

SALMON IN PUFF PASTRY

Your fishmonger will clean the salmon for you, but to get four neat fillets, you may prefer to fillet it yourself. Cut off the head and tail and snip off the fins. Rinse the fish and pat dry. Place on a board, head end towards you, and snip along the belly from head to tail. Starting with the flesh nearest to the belly, ease the flesh away from the bones, using a filleting knife and short sharp strokes. Open out the fish and slide the knife tip under the end of the exposed bone. Using a similar action as before, work along the length of the fish to remove the bone completely. Pluck out any small bones in the flesh. Snip the skin between the halves to give two fillets, then neaten the edges. Repeat the process with the other fillet.

FENNEL WITH GREEN PEPPERCORN DRESSING

| 1.00* | £ | 103 cals |

* plus 20 minutes cooling

Serves 6

3 heads of fennel
salt and freshly ground pepper
15–30 ml (1–2 tbsp) lemon juice
150 ml ($\frac{1}{4}$ pint) whipping cream
15 ml (1 tbsp) green peppercorns
**10 ml (2 tsp) white wine or
    tarragon vinegar**

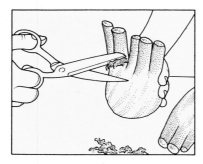

1 To prepare (50 minutes): Trim any green leafy tops from the fennel and reserve. Cook the fennel in plenty of boiling salted water to which the lemon juice has been added, for 30–35 minutes or until just tender.

2 Drain well, then rinse immediately under cold running water. Cool completely; about 20 minutes. Cover and chill.

3 Lightly whip the cream. Roughly crush or chop the peppercorns, then fold them into the cream with the vinegar and seasoning to taste. Cover and chill.

4 To serve (10 minutes): Split the fennel heads in half and place on a flat serving dish. Spoon over the peppercorn dressing and garnish with the reserved snipped fennel tops.

PASTA AND ANCHOVY SALAD WITH GARLIC DRESSING

0.55*	406 cals

* plus at least 2 hours or overnight standing

Serves 6

two 50 g (2 oz) cans anchovies in oil
45 ml (3 tbsp) milk
350 g (12 oz) small pasta shapes (see box)
salt and freshly ground pepper
1 garlic clove, skinned and roughly chopped
75 ml (3 fl oz) vegetable oil
juice of ½ lemon
185 g (6½ oz) can pimientos, drained
60 ml (4 tbsp) mayonnaise

1 *To prepare* (45 minutes): Drain the anchovies, place in a bowl and add the milk. Leave to soak for 30 minutes (this helps remove excess salt).

2 Meanwhile, cook the pasta in plenty of boiling salted water according to the packet instructions until *al dente* (tender but firm to the bite).

3 Drain the anchovies and rinse under cold running water. Pat dry with absorbent kitchen paper.

4 Reserve a few of the anchovies whole for garnishing and crush the remainder to a paste with the garlic. Add the oil and lemon juice gradually, whisking with a fork until thick. Add pepper to taste.

5 Drain the pasta and turn into a large bowl. Pour in the dressing immediately and toss well to mix. Leave to cool, then cover and chill in the refrigerator for at least 2 hours, or overnight if more convenient.

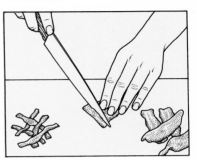

6 *To serve* (10 minutes): Cut the pimiento into thin strips. Add to the pasta salad, reserving a few for garnish. Add the mayonnaise and toss gently to mix. Taste and adjust seasoning. Pile the salad into a serving bowl and arrange the remaining whole anchovies and pimiento strips in a lattice pattern over the top. Serve at room temperature.

PASTA AND ANCHOVY SALAD WITH GARLIC DRESSING

Supermarkets and delicatessens now stock a huge variety of different pasta shapes, which make interesting salads as well as the more usual hot pasta dishes which are served with a sauce. For salads, don't buy the very tiny pasta shapes—these are only for use in soups. Choose small shapes such as *conchiglie* (seashells), which are excellent for trapping salad dressings and preventing ingredients sinking to the bottom of the salad bowl. *Fusilli* (spirals) and *farfalle* (bow ties) can also be used.

OPEN PEAR FLAN

| 1.20* | ⊟ £ £ ✳* | 464 cals |

*plus 1 hour cooling; freeze at the end of step 6

Serves 6

1½ quantities pâte sucrée (see page 439)

50 g (2 oz) butter

50 g (2 oz) caster sugar

1 egg, size 6, beaten

50 g (2 oz) ground almonds

20 ml (4 tsp) plain flour

10 ml (2 tsp) pear- or almond-flavoured liqueur

3 ripe pears (Conference, William or Packham)

100 g (4 oz) apricot jam

30 ml (2 tbsp) water

1 *To prepare* (1 hour 10 minutes): Roll out the pâte sucrée on a lightly floured work surface and use to line a 25 cm (10 inch) loose–bottomed fluted flan ring. Prick the bottom with a fork and chill in the refrigerator for at least 15 minutes.

2 Meanwhile, put the butter and sugar in a bowl and beat together until light and fluffy. Beat in the egg and stir in the ground almonds, flour and liqueur. Pour into the pastry case and level the surface.

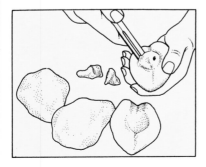

3 Carefully peel the pears, cut them in half lengthways, and remove the core with a melon baller or teaspoon.

4 Lay each pear half cut side down, and cut them crossways into thin slices. Keeping each pear half intact, place on the almond mixture to form the spokes of a wheel, then press each half slightly to fan out the pear slices.

5 Bake in the oven at 200°C (400°F) mark 6 for 10–15 minutes until the pastry just begins to brown. Turn the oven temperature down to 180°C (350°F) mark 4 and bake for a further 20–25 minutes.

6 Remove from the oven and cool for 1 hour. Store in an airtight container for not longer than 1 day.

7 *To serve* (10 minutes): Place the jam in a saucepan and add the water. Heat gently, stirring until the jam softens. Bring to the boil and simmer for 1 minute. Sieve and brush over the flan while still warm.

Fork Supper

A simple fork supper is perfect for informal entertaining—say after the theatre or a concert. This menu serves 8, but it can be easily adjusted for more or less. The Lamb and Mushroom au Gratin, a pasta dish like cannelloni, with a lamb, mushroom and tomato filling, can be made up to 1–2 days in advance, as can the Fresh Pineapple Compote. Simply pop the gratin dish in the oven and put the final decorations on the pineapple while your guests are having pre-supper drinks.

LAMB AND MUSHROOM AU GRATIN

2.00* 🍴 £ ✳* 566 cals

* plus 10 minutes cooling; freeze at the end of step 5

Serves 8

65 g (2½ oz) butter

700 g (1½ lb) mushrooms, finely chopped

15 ml (1 tbsp) vegetable oil

700 g (1½ lb) lean minced lamb

1 garlic clove, skinned and crushed

227 g (8 oz) can tomatoes, drained

75 g (3 oz) plain flour

15 ml (1 tbsp) chopped fresh oregano or 5 ml (1 tsp) dried

15 ml (1 tbsp) chopped fresh rosemary or 5 ml (1 tsp) dried

150 ml (¼ pint) dry white wine

salt and freshly ground pepper

16 sheets cooked lasagne, about 275 g (10 oz) raw weight

900 ml (1½ pints) milk

100 g (4 oz) Cheddar cheese, grated

100 g (4 oz) Mozzarella cheese, grated or finely chopped

1 *To prepare* (1 hour 15 minutes): Melt 25 g (1 oz) of the butter in a large saucepan, add the mushrooms and cook over moderate heat for about 10 minutes until soft and reduced in volume.

2 Heat the oil in a large frying pan, add the lamb and brown well; drain off all the fat. Stir in the garlic, mushrooms, tomatoes, 30 ml (2 tbsp) of the flour and the herbs. Cook for 1–2 minutes, then add the wine and seasoning to taste. Bring to the boil, then simmer for about 30 minutes, uncovered. Cool for 10 minutes.

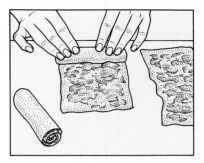

3 Spread the mixture over the sheets of lasagne and roll up each sheet from one short side.

4 Cut the rolls into three. Pack tightly together, standing upright, in one large or two small 5 cm (2 inch) deep straight-sided ovenproof dishes.

5 Melt the remaining butter in a saucepan, add the remaining flour and cook over low heat, stirring with a wooden spoon, for 2 minutes. Gradually blend in the milk, stirring after each addition to prevent lumps forming. Bring to the boil slowly, then simmer for 2–3 minutes, stirring. Add plenty of seasoning then pour over the pasta. Leave to cool, then cover and chill in the refrigerator until required.

6 *To serve* (45 minutes): Bake in the oven at 200°C (400°F) mark 6 for about 40 minutes. Uncover, sprinkle with the cheeses and grill until golden. Serve hot.

FRESH PINEAPPLE COMPOTE

0.50* ⬚ £ £ 114 cals

* plus overnight chilling

Serves 8

2 small ripe pineapples

60 ml (4 tbsp) orange-flavoured liqueur

567 g (1 lb 4 oz) can lychees in syrup

shelled pistachio nuts, to decorate

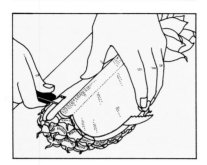

1 To prepare (35 minutes): Cut each pineapple lengthways into quarters, slicing through the 'crown' at the top. Cut out the hard central cores and discard.

2 Using a serrated knife, carefully cut all around the edge of each pineapple 'boat' between the flesh and the skin.

3 Carefully work the knife underneath the pineapple flesh, to release it completely from the skin. Cut the flesh into bite-sized cubes. Wrap the pineapple shells in cling film and set aside.

4 Put the pineapple cubes in a bowl and sprinkle over the liqueur. Drain the lychees, pouring the syrup into a saucepan. Add three-quarters of the lychees to the pineapple.

5 Boil the lychee syrup until reduced by half, then leave to cool. Add to the pineapple and lychees and fold gently to mix. Cover the bowl with cling film and chill overnight, with the pineapple shells and reserved lychees.

6 To serve (15 minutes): Cut the reserved lychees into flower shapes. Divide the pineapple and lychees equally between the 8 shells and pour over the syrup. Decorate with the lychee 'flowers' and pistachios. Serve chilled.

FRESH PINEAPPLE COMPOTE

Canned lychees are available at most good supermarkets. They have a deliciously sweet flavour and unusual texture, and can be used in fruit salads of all kinds to add a touch of exotic interest. Lychees (also called lichees and litchis) are native to China, but they also grow in India and South Africa. The fresh fruit are available at some specialist markets and greengrocers in late summer, but they are not easy to recognise if you are only familiar with the canned fruit. The skin of fresh lychees is rough and brittle, almost like a bark.

Christmas Eve Menu

Plan to get present wrapping and preparations for the Christmas day meal out of the way early on Christmas Eve, so that you can relax at home with a few friends. Offer them a Champagne Cocktail when they arrive, then serve this beautifully decorated Salmon and Asparagus Mousse as the evening wears on. It will get the Christmas festivities off to a glamorous start.

SALMON AND ASPARAGUS MOUSSE

| 0.45* | 🍴 🍴 £ £ | 265 cals |

* plus $1\frac{3}{4}$ hours setting time

Serves 8

25 g (1 oz) aspic powder

25 g (1 oz) butter

25 g (1 oz) plain flour

300 ml ($\frac{1}{2}$ pint) milk

1.25 ml ($\frac{1}{4}$ tsp) mustard powder

pinch of cayenne

salt and freshly ground pepper

15 ml (1 tbsp) cider vinegar

3 eggs, separated

two 220 g ($7\frac{1}{2}$ oz) cans salmon, drained and flaked

22.5 ml ($1\frac{1}{2}$ tbsp) gelatine

150 ml ($\frac{1}{4}$ pint) double cream, lightly whipped

225 g (8 oz) packet frozen asparagus, cooked and cooled

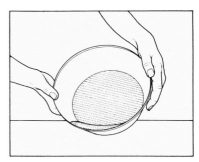

1 Make up the aspic jelly with 600 ml (1 pint) water according to packet instructions. Leave until just on the point of setting, then pour a little into a 20.5 cm (8 inch) spring-release cake tin fitted with a plain base, or into a 1.7-litre (3-pint) fluted mould. Use the jelly to coat the sides of the tin, then chill in the refrigerator for about 20 minutes until set.

2 When set, pour more aspic jelly into the tin until it is 0.5 cm ($\frac{1}{4}$ inch) deep. Chill again for about 20 minutes until set.

7 Pour half of the mixture into a blender or food processor and work until smooth. Turn out and repeat with remainder. Leave for about 30 minutes until just beginning to set.

8 Lightly whip the cream and fold into the mixture. Whisk the egg whites until just holding soft peaks, then fold in carefully until evenly incorporated. Spoon into the tin. Cover and chill in the refrigerator for at least 1 hour until set.

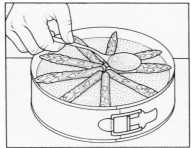

9 When set, arrange the asparagus spears on top. Spoon the remaining aspic jelly over and leave in a cold place for 30 minutes until set.

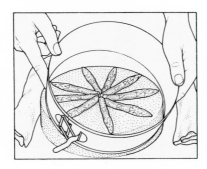

10 To unmould, hold a warm cloth round the sides of the tin, release the clip and remove the ring. Warm the base and slide the mousse on to a serving plate.

Menu Suggestion
Serve with Melba toast and butter curls, and a selection of salads. A potato salad would go well, and a contrasting crunchy celery, apple and walnut salad.

3 Meanwhile, put the butter in a blender or food processor with the flour, milk, mustard, cayenne and salt and pepper to taste. Work until smooth.

4 Pour into a saucepan, bring to the boil and cook for 3 minutes, stirring constantly. Remove from the heat, beat in the vinegar and then the egg yolks.

5 Return the mixture to the heat and cook gently without boiling for a further 2–3 minutes. Remove from the heat, stir in the drained salmon and check the seasoning.

6 Put 90 ml (6 tbsp) liquid aspic in a small heatproof bowl. Sprinkle in the gelatine and leave to stand for 5 minutes until spongy. Stand the bowl in a saucepan of gently simmering water until the gelatine is dissolved. Add to the salmon mixture.

CHAMPAGNE COCKTAIL

| 0.05 | f f | 116–154 cals |

Serves 6–8

6–8 small sugar lumps
Angostura bitters
juice of 1½–2 lemons, strained
90–120 ml (6–8 tbsp) brandy
1 bottle of champagne, chilled
**wafer-thin lemon slices,
    to decorate (optional)**

1 Put 1 sugar lump in the bottom of 6–8 tall champagne flutes and pour 4 dashes of Angostura bitters over each.

2 Add the strained lemon juice and brandy to each and top up with champagne. Float a thin slice of lemon on top of each glass, if liked. Serve immediately.

Alternative Christmas

It's not every year that you want the same traditional fare at Christmastime. Maybe there are less of you than usual, or maybe you simply feel like a change. This menu will fit the bill whatever the reason, and can easily be adapted to serve different numbers, from as few as two, to as many as six.

PRAWNS WITH AVOCADO DRESSING

0.45*	£ £	444–666 cals

* plus up to 2 hours chilling

Serves 4–6

30 ml (2 tbsp) olive oil

1 small onion, skinned and finely
  chopped

2 celery sticks, trimmed and finely
  chopped

5 ml (1 tsp) paprika

2 ripe avocados

75 ml (3 fl oz) thick homemade
  mayonnaise (page 441)

75 ml (3 fl oz) double or whipping
  cream

350 g (12 oz) peeled prawns,
  defrosted and thoroughly dried
  if frozen

finely grated rind and juice of 1
  lime or lemon

few drops of Tabasco sauce, to
  taste

salt and freshly ground pepper

lettuce leaves, to serve

unpeeled prawns and lime twists,
  to garnish (optional)

1 Heat the oil in a small saucepan, add the onion and fry
gently until soft but not coloured.
Add the celery and paprika and
fry, stirring, for 1–2 minutes.
Transfer to a bowl and cool.

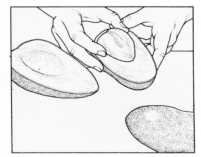

2 Meanwhile, halve, stone and
peel 1 of the avocados and
mash the flesh in a bowl.
Gradually work in the mayonnaise
until evenly combined, then stir in
the onion and celery mixture.

3 Whip the cream until it holds
its shape. Fold the prawns into
the avocado mixture, then the
cream. Add the lime rind, with
Tabasco and salt and pepper to
taste. Cover the bowl with cling
film and chill in the refrigerator
for up to 2 hours before serving.
(Do not leave for longer or the
avocado may discolour the
dressing.)

4 To serve, line one large dish,
or 4–6 glasses with shredded
lettuce leaves and sprinkle with
salt and pepper. Pile the prawn
salad in the centre.

5 Halve, stone and peel the
remaining avocado and slice
neatly. Arrange on top of the salad
in a decorative pattern and
sprinkle with the lime juice. Serve
immediately, garnished with
unpeeled prawns and lime twists,
if liked.

Menu Suggestion
Serve this rich starter with thinly
sliced wholemeal bread and
butter. Champagne or a sparkling
dry white wine would be the most
appropriate drink.

ROAST PHEASANT

| 1.05 | 🍳 £ £ | 308–461 cals |

Serves 4–6

1 brace of pheasants, plucked and drawn

50 g (2 oz) butter

salt and freshly ground pepper

6 rashers of streaky bacon

25 ml (5 tsp) plain flour

450 ml (¾ pint) chicken stock

gravy browning

15–30 ml (1–2 tbsp) medium dry sherry

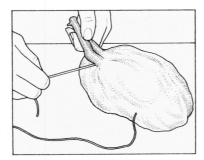

1 Wipe the pheasants and pat dry with absorbent kitchen paper. Place a good knob of butter inside each bird with plenty of salt and pepper. Truss the birds.

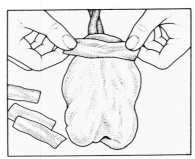

2 Remove the rind from the bacon. Cut each rasher in half, then lay over the breasts of the birds to protect them.

3 Melt the remaining butter in a small roasting tin. Put the birds in the tin and roast in the oven at 200°C (400°F) mark 6 for about 35 minutes depending on size, basting frequently.

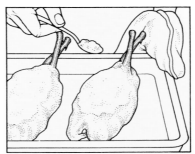

4 Remove the bacon and keep it warm. Brush the breasts with some of the cooking juices and sprinkle 5 ml (1 tsp) flour over each bird. Return to the oven for another 10 minutes.

5 Remove the trussing strings and place the pheasants on a warmed serving dish. Keep warm, uncovered.

6 Pour off all but 30 ml (2 tbsp) fat from the roasting tin and place the tin on top of the cooker. Sprinkle the remaining flour into the residual fat, stir until blended and smooth, then fry gently until russet-coloured, stirring frequently.

7 Stir in the stock gradually, add salt and pepper to taste and bring to the boil. Cook for 3–4 minutes, add a drop of gravy browning if necessary, then stir in the sherry.

8 Garnish the pheasants with the bacon pieces and serve the gravy separately.

MINCEMEAT TART

1.30*	☐	✳*	662–993 cals

* plus chilling and cooling; freeze before baking at step 7

Serves 4–6

225 g (8 oz) plain flour

pinch of salt

100 g (4 oz) ground almonds

100 g (4 oz) caster sugar

100 g (4 oz) butter

1 egg, beaten

225 g (8 oz) mincemeat

50 g (2 oz) slivered or flaked almonds, chopped

30 ml (2 tbsp) almond-flavoured liqueur, rum or brandy

1 medium cooking apple

45–60 ml (3–4 tbsp) apricot jam, to glaze

single cream or vanilla ice cream, to serve

1 Make the almond pastry. Sift the flour and salt onto a marble slab or other cold surface and stir in the almonds and sugar. Make a well in the centre.

2 Cut the butter into small dice and place in the centre of the flour. Work with the fingertips, gradually drawing the flour mixture into the centre and rubbing it into the butter. Stir in the beaten egg.

3 Gather the dough together and form into a rough ball. (The dough is rich and quite sticky, so work as quickly and lightly as possible, with cold hands.) Wrap the ball of dough in foil and chill in the refrigerator for 30 minutes.

4 Reserve a little dough for the lattice. With your fingertips, press the remaining dough into a 20.5 cm (8 inch) loose-bottomed flan tin standing on a baking sheet. Chill in the refrigerator for a further 15 minutes.

5 Meanwhile, prepare the filling. Put the mincemeat in a bowl with the chopped almonds and liqueur. Peel and core the apple, then grate into the bowl. Stir well to mix, then spoon into the chilled flan case. Level the surface.

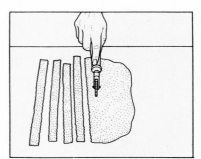

6 Roll out the reserved dough and cut into strips for the lattice, using a pastry wheel to give a pretty edge.

7 Place the strips over the filling in a lattice pattern, then seal the edges with water. Bake in the oven at 190°C (375°F) mark 5 for 35 minutes until the pastry is a light golden brown.

8 Leave the filling to settle for 10–15 minutes. Heat the apricot jam gently in a saucepan, then sieve and brush over the top of the tart to glaze. Leave for a further 10–15 minutes and serve warm or cold, with single cream or scoops of vanilla ice cream.

Menu Suggestion

Mincemeat Tart makes the most delicious dessert with cream or ice cream, but it is just as good served plain as a teatime cake.

MINCEMEAT TART

As its name suggests, mincemeat was originally made with minced meat. The combination of fruit, spices and a large amount of alcohol had a preservative effect on the meat, which was stored in stone crocks, and always left to mature from at least the beginning of December. Beef, tongue and venison were the usual meats included in mincemeat, but nowadays only fruit is used, and shredded beef suet is added to make up for the lack of meat. If you can spare the time, it is much better to make your own mincemeat for Christmas, to be sure of knowing exactly what goes into it. Many commercial brands have far too much suet and a watery flavour and texture, although some of the more expensive varieties do contain plump fruit and a fair amount of alcohol. Read the label carefully before buying, and inspect the contents through the glass jar if possible.

Christmas Lunch for 8 People

MENU

AVOCADO AND KIWI FRUIT
VINAIGRETTE

FESTIVE TURKEY SURPRISE

SPECIAL FRIED SPROUTS

ONIONS À LA GRECQUE

ICED CHRISTMAS PUDDING

MULLED WINE (page 429)

AVOCADO AND KIWI FRUIT VINAIGRETTE

| 0.15* | £ £ | 295 cals |

* plus 2 hours refrigeration

Serves 8

1 egg

150 ml (¼ pint) olive oil

60 ml (4 tbsp) white wine vinegar

45 ml (3 tbsp) chopped parsley

salt and freshly ground pepper

4 kiwi fruit

3 small ripe avocados

watercress sprigs, to garnish

French bread, to serve

1 Boil the egg for 6 minutes only. Meanwhile, whisk together the oil, vinegar, parsley and seasonings in a medium bowl.

2 Run cold water over the boiled egg to cool. Shell the egg. Scoop out the yolk into the dressing. Chop the egg white finely and add to the dressing, whisking well to ensure it is evenly mixed.

3 Peel the kiwi fruit and slice it into rings, discarding the ends. Stir into the dressing, cover and refrigerate for at least 2 hours.

4 Halve, peel and slice the avocados and arrange on individual serving plates together with the drained kiwi fruit slices.

5 Spoon the dressing over the avocados and kiwi fruit and garnish with watercress sprigs. Serve with crusty French bread.

AVOCADOS

Avocados are available all year round in supermarkets and greengrocers, and different types are sold according to the time of year and country of origin. They are rich in vitamin C and unsaturated fats. The commonest variety of avocado has a smooth, green, shiny skin, but others with rough skins which darken when ripe, are becoming increasingly widely available. Both types have soft, pale green flesh, and are suitable for use in this recipe.

Only use ripe avocados in salads. To test for ripeness, press fruit gently at the pointed end with your fingers – it should give slightly. When buying avocados, if you are not eating them on the day of purchase, it is best to buy them under-ripe rather than just ripe. Wrap them in newspaper and leave them in a warm place to ripen.

FESTIVE TURKEY SURPRISE

| 4.35 | 🍲 🍲 £ £ | 402 cals |

Serves about 20

3.9 kg (8½ lb) oven-ready turkey

1 onion, skinned and chopped

100 g (4 oz) celery, finely chopped

450 g (1 lb) cooking apples, peeled, cored and roughly chopped

100 g (4 oz) butter

700 g (1½ lb) pork sausagemeat

50 g (2 oz) fresh white breadcrumbs

grated rind and juice of an orange

50 g (2 oz) chopped walnuts

2.5 ml (½ tsp) dried thyme

salt and freshly ground pepper

2 eggs, size 6, beaten

1.4 kg (2½ lb) boneless bacon joint, boiled and skinned

1 Bone the turkey (see page 158), or ask the butcher to do this for you. Sauté the onion, celery and apples together in half the melted butter for 5 minutes; cool.

2 Work into the sausagemeat and breadcrumbs, adding the grated orange rind, walnuts, thyme and seasoning. Bind with the eggs.

3 Lay out the boned bird, flesh side up. Spread the stuffing over the bird, more generously in the thigh positions. Place the cooked bacon joint lengthwise down the centre of the bird.

4 Tuck the neck end in towards the filling, draw the long sides of the bird over the stuffing and sew it neatly together with fine string to completely encase the stuffing. Use overlapping stitches and do not roll too tightly or the bird will burst during cooking. Secure the string loosely for easy removal. Weigh the bird.

5 Place it, breast side up, on foil in a roasting tin. Spread with remaining butter and add the orange juice. Wrap in foil. Weigh.

6 Roast in the oven at 180°C (350°F) mark 4 for 15 minutes per 450 g (1 lb) plus 15 minutes. Unwrap for last 30 minutes, to brown. Serve the turkey hot with bacon rolls and gravy made from the juices, or chill and serve cold. As with traditional roast turkey, this is ideal for eating cold on Boxing Day; quantities have been calculated accordingly.

SPECIAL FRIED SPROUTS

| 0.30 | £ | 140 cals |

Serves 8

900 g (2 lb) Brussels sprouts

salt and freshly ground pepper

75 g (3 oz) butter

450 g (1 lb) button mushrooms, sliced

2.5 ml (½ tsp) grated nutmeg

120 ml (8 tbsp) soured cream

1 Trim the stalks from the sprouts and discard any discoloured or damaged outer leaves. Cut a cross in the base of each sprout with a small, sharp knife.

2 Plunge the sprouts into a large pan of boiling salted water, bring back to the boil and simmer for 15 minutes. Drain thoroughly.

3 Melt the butter in a large, heavy-based pan (a wok or deep frying-pan is ideal). Add the sprouts and mushrooms with the nutmeg, then stir-fry for about 5 minutes until the vegetables are well mixed and heated through.

4 Add salt and pepper to taste, then turn into a warmed serving dish. To serve, stir the soured cream then drizzle over sprouts.

Onions à la Grecque

1.00	£	172 cals

Serves 8

900 g (2 lb) small pickling onions

75 ml (5 tbsp) olive oil

15 ml (1 tbsp) clear honey

300 ml ($\frac{1}{2}$ pint) water

150 ml ($\frac{1}{4}$ pint) dry white wine

10 ml (2 tsp) tomato purée

salt and freshly ground pepper

100 g (4 oz) seedless raisins

30 ml (2 tbsp) chopped fresh
   coriander or parsley

1 Peel the onions. Blanch in boiling water for 1 minute only, then drain and rinse under cold running water. Remove the onion skins carefully with your fingers and a small, sharp knife.

2 Put the onions in a large, heavy-based pan with the remaining ingredients except the raisins and chopped coriander.

3 Add salt and pepper to taste. Bring to the boil, then lower the heat, cover and simmer gently for 30 minutes.

4 Add the raisins to the pan and continue cooking, uncovered, for a further 15 minutes or until onions are tender but still whole. Taste and adjust seasoning, then stir in the chopped coriander. Turn into a warmed serving dish and serve hot.

À LA GRECQUE
The French term *à la grecque*, used here to describe a dish of onions, is more commonly used to describe a cold mushroom dish. There are no hard-and-fast rules about the exact ingredients an *à la grecque* dish should contain, but it is usually white wine, tomato purée and raisins, with plenty of chopped parsley.

ICED CHRISTMAS PUDDING

0.25* £ £ ✳ 429 cals

* plus 2–3 hours soaking fruit, 30 minutes cooling, 4–5 hours freezing and 20 minutes softening

Serves 8

225 g (8 oz) mixed dried fruit
50 g (2 oz) glacé cherries, halved
75 ml (5 tbsp) brandy
450 ml (¾ pint) milk
3 eggs
140 g (4½ oz) caster sugar
300 ml (10 fl oz) double cream
150 ml (5 fl oz) single cream

1 Place the mixed dried fruit and glacé cherries in a bowl, spoon over the brandy, cover and leave to soak for 2–3 hours. Bring the milk nearly to boil, beat the eggs with the sugar until well mixed.

2 Pour on the milk, return to the pan and cook over a gentle heat, without boiling, until the custard coats the back of the spoon. Strain and cool for 30 minutes.

3 Whip the creams together, and mix into the custard with the fruit and brandy mixture.

4 Turn into a large bowl and freeze for 2 hours until mushy. Mix well and pack into a 1.7-litre (3-pint) pudding basin base-lined with non-stick paper. Freeze for 2–3 hours until firm.

5 Take out of the freezer approximately 20 minutes before serving. Turn out and decorate with holly. Serve immediately.

USEFUL INFORMATION
AND
BASIC RECIPES

Entertaining at Home

Whether you're planning a buffet party for a hundred, or simply thinking of inviting a few friends in for dinner, this section of the book is designed to help you.

Tips and hints on all kinds of parties are here, from cocktail gatherings to dinner parties, even a wedding reception.

INFORMAL PARTIES

BRUNCHES, LUNCHEONS AND AFTERNOON TEAS

This type of party can be a purely social occasion for a sizeable number of friends, neighbors and members of the family, such as a christening, or it may arise because there is a committee meeting or some other activity taking place in your home. Whatever the reason, it's a good way of entertaining a large number of people without going to all the expense and effort of a dinner party.

Serve the food on trays lined with paper napkins (enlist a friend to help with the serving), and provide napkins for your guests to use. Serve dainty sandwiches for tea, with crusts cut off and unusual fillings. Different shapes will add interest too, as will small cakes and/or sweet pastries.

In winter, a few hot savory hors d'oeuvre will be welcome; or some hot soup served in mugs.

For an after-dinner dessert party, homemade pastries and small cakes are lovely, with perhaps a large cake for the table centerpiece. A tray or two of bite-sized open sandwiches will also be welcome, bearing in mind that food shouldn't be too substantial. Always make fresh coffee for this type of party and offer both cream and milk with coffee sugar.

SANDWICHES AND FILLINGS

If you buy uncut sandwich loaves, you can control the thickness of the slices – and slicing will be considerably simplified – if you use an electric carving knife. Use the following to guide you.

A large loaf, about 2 pounds, gives 20 slices.

A small loaf, about 1 pound, gives 10 slices.

About 8 oz butter or margarine spreads 10–12 sandwiches.

About 4 oz butter or margarine spreads 10–12 bread rolls.

APPROXIMATE COFFEE QUANTITIES

	1 Serving	24–26 Servings	50 Servings
Coffee (ground for coffee maker)	1 cup	$\frac{1}{2}$ pound coffee $1\frac{1}{4}$ gallons water If you make the coffee in advance, reheat it without boiling.	1 pound coffee $2\frac{1}{2}$ gallons water

COCKTAIL PARTIES

A cocktail party offers a fairly in-expensive way of entertaining large numbers of people without having to get involved in serious cooking. The term "cocktail party" is a slight misnomer, however, since often very few proper cocktails are

served. It's perfectly acceptable, for example, to offer a choice of only two cocktails, with sherry and/or white wine as a third choice, whiskey as a possible fourth, and plenty of fruit juices and soft drinks. If you *are* only serving two cocktails, however, they should be contrasting.

Guests should be well informed about what to expect, in terms of drink, food and time. Cocktail parties should ideally leave people free to go off and enjoy the rest of the evening elsewhere, so the maximum length of time should be about 2 hours. Food should not be so substantial that guests are unable to enjoy their evening meal, nor so paltry that they have to suffer the consequences of drinking on an empty stomach.

Since most people will be drinking and eating standing up, the food must be bite-sized and easy to eat. Canapés are the obvious choice and these and other cocktail nibbles such as nuts, chips, olives, gherkins, cocktail sausages on sticks, and savory dips with raw vegetables and bread sticks for dunking can be put out around the room. Try to serve something hot and savory about halfway through.

CHILDREN'S BIRTHDAY PARTIES

Preparing food for children's parties is a chance to be creative, but there's no need to make *all* the food fancy. Always popular with every age group are chips, sausages on sticks and other savory nibbles. Also, sandwiches with plain, everyday fillings go down better than cakes and breads.

Don't be surprised either if homemade strawberry tarts are left and bought cookies disappear. Children often prefer food that looks familiar. The one exception to this rule is the birthday cake. Never miss it. Keep the food easy to eat, especially for the very young. All children enjoy fizzy drinks, though sometimes younger children might prefer milk shakes.

Try and keep the number of guests manageable. Organize the program beforehand. Allow for 1 hour or more of boisterous play before serving and have an entertainment or organized games afterwards. Children over eight can stand more activity, but no party should last longer than 3 hours for small children, or 4 for older ones.

Before the day remember to stock up the first-aid box; keep a box of matches at hand – but out

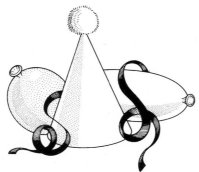

of reach of the children – to light the cake candles when the time comes; and have ready masses of small prizes for the winners of the various games. Finally, have a small present and a balloon ready for everyone to take home – it needn't be anything elaborate, but make sure no one is left out.

BARBECUES

Barbecue parties, whether at lunch time or in the evening, are a good idea for entertaining large numbers – people can spread themselves out, so space and eating arrangements are rarely a problem.

Barbecues range from do-it-yourself brick-built affairs to sophisticated (and expensive) equipment. Essential items, however, are equipment such as strong grills, long-handled forks, tongs and slices for turning food, pastry brushes for basting and thick oven gloves to protect the hands. Good-quality briquettes, fire-lighters and matches are other essentials – so too is adequate area lighting for evening barbecues.

Self-service is essential: arrange stacks of plates (paper ones will do) on a long table together with glasses, cutlery and napkins and the non-barbecued food. Everyone can then help themselves to these and line up at the barbecue for hot food. It's not even essential for the host or hostess to do the barbecuing – some guests might like to do it themselves.

If it rains before all the food is cooked, don't ever attempt to barbecue indoors or in the garage because fumes can be dangerous. You will either have to resort to using the broiler or cooking under an umbrella. Many of the new barbecues on the market have lids – otherwise you can improvise with a metal trash can.

LARGE BUFFET PARTIES

If you are entertaining a very large number of people and want to provide a full meal, a buffet party is the ideal choice. The maximum number you should try to cater for is 100, however – anything over this is best left to the professionals.

First and foremost, it's virtually impossible to cater for this large a number with the average family's quota of china, cutlery and chairs, so you will have to organize where all this is coming from well in advance. Don't be afraid to ask your friends to help out with plates, serving dishes and so on. A few recruited helpers are essential for the preparation and serving anyway – it would be almost impossible to manage completely on your own for a very large buffet party.

Depending on the formality of the occasion, paper plates and plastic cutlery *can* be considered, although these are not very successful. Good-quality paper napkins and cloths are a better buy, because they come in so many different attractive colors.

Glasses are available from rentals but you might prefer buying inexpensive plastic ones. Don't forget to buy wines and spirits *well* ahead (especially if your party is around Christmas time).

Decide on the menu really well in advance, because it will take you a long time to finalize quantities (consult our chart for guidance) and the logistics of the whole exercise. The best thing is to have a meeting with your helpers at least a month in advance of the party's date and for you all to make detailed lists of exactly who is doing what, when.

Try to choose food that can be eaten easily without a table: a full set of cutlery should be available, but guests will feel far more comfortable if they are able to eat with a fork alone. For a very large number of people, the majority of food is bound to be cold, but one or two hot dishes will always be welcome.

Offer a good balance of sweet and savory dishes and concentrate on setting the buffet table beautifully, so that it will be the center of attraction. Choose dishes that can be frozen ahead of time (most things store well in the freezer for at least three months)

like quiches, pâtés, tarts, pastries, sandwich fillings, cakes and pies. This should leave you ample time nearer the date to deal with the perishable items like salads.

Having the right equipment is half the battle when it comes to party preparation. A freezer is obviously essential for large-scale entertaining; so too is a food processor for chopping, grinding and slicing in large quantities. An electric grinder or processor cuts pâté preparation time down to minutes rather than hours, and mixers and blenders are a boon for taking all the hard work out of beating, whipping and puréeing, etc. Electric carving knives and slicing machines are wonderful for accurate portion control — incredibly important when catering for many.

Equipment for making tea and coffee mustn't be overlooked on this sort of occasion, as your own family percolator or teapot simply won't be able to cope when everyone wants refreshing hot drinks before they go home. Work out quantities (see p. 420) and how you will organise the provision of this number of drinks.

SETTING THE TABLE

Arranging a buffet table correctly is all-important when catering for large numbers. It should not only look attractive, but should be laid out in such a way as to cause minimum inconvenience to your guests. Arrange the table so that guests can move easily around it, progressing naturally from plates and cutlery to the main dishes and the side dishes (see right). If desserts are included on the same table, put them where they can be reached after other dishes are cleared away.

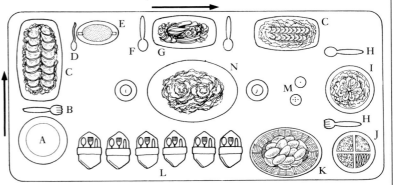

A	Plates	H	Salad servers
B	Serving fork	I	Salad bowl
C	Main dish	J	Pickles and relishes
D	Sauce ladle	K	Roll basket
E	Sauce boat	L	Napkins and cutlery
F	Serving spoon	M	Salt and pepper
G	Vegetable dish	N	Centerpiece and candles

APPROXIMATE QUANTITIES FOR BUFFET PARTIES

	1 portion	24–26 portions	Notes
Cheese (for biscuits)	1–1½ oz	1½–2 lb cheese plus 1 lb butter 2 lb biscuits	Allow the larger amounts for an assorted cheeseboard.
Cheese (for wine-and-cheese party)	3 oz	4½–5 lb of at least 4 types	Buy more than this if serving a cheese dip.
Cooked meat	3–4 oz	5–6½ lb	
Fish cocktail: shrimp, tuna or crab	1 oz	1½ lb fish 2–3 lettuces 4 cups sauce	In stemmed glasses, garnished with a shrimp.
Meat with bone boneless	5 oz 3–4 oz	7–8 lb 5–6½ lb	Cold roasts or barbecue chops. Casseroles, meatballs, sausages.
Pâté (for wine-and-pâté party)	3–4 oz	5–6½ lb	Halve if for appetizer.
Poultry: turkey chicken	3–4 oz (boneless) 5–8 oz	16 lb (dressed) Six 2½–3 lb birds (dressed)	Serve hot or cold.
Rice or pasta	1½ oz (uncooked)	2 lb	Cook a day ahead, reheat in boiling water.
Salad vegetables lettuce cucumber tomatoes boiled potatoes	 $\frac{1}{6}$ 1 inch 1–2 2 oz	 3–4 2 cucumbers 3 lb 3 lb	 Dress at last minute. For potato salads.
Sauces: French dressing	 1¼ cups for 12 portions	 2–2½ cups for 20 portions	Make in a lidded container and shake together just before serving.
Mayonnaise	2½ cups for 12 portions	1 quart for 20 portions	
Soups: cream, clear or iced	1 cup	1 gallon	Serve garnished in mugs or cups.

GIVING A DINNER PARTY

Giving a dinner party should be a pleasure, not a chore. If you go about it in the right way, your guests will feel at ease from the moment they walk through the front door, and you, too, will enjoy their company unflustered and completely calm.

Having carefully chosen your guests, and telephoned them or issued invitations well ahead (see right), the next step is to choose the menu and plan both the shopping and which dishes can be cooked in advance. Make lists of everything that has to be done and of the food and wine that has to be bought. Take account of the time you will have available for shopping and of any ingredients that will need to be ordered well ahead. Remember that many ingredients will store well in the freezer if necessary.

Table settings should be planned in accordance with your menu (see page 426). However simple, make the table setting both eye-catching and practical—however beautiful it is before everyone sits down, it must also work well, in an un-cluttered way, while your guests are eating. On the day of the party, the table can be laid, in the morning, or whenever you have time to spare. When the table is ready, close the door to keep out any children and pets.

As your guests arrive, put them at their ease by offering them an aperitif. Make sure that everyone is relaxed (with a full glass) before you return to the kitchen to check on any last-minute cooking. If two of you are giving the dinner party, organize your duties well in advance—one of you should be in charge of the drinks (including serving wine with the meal), while the other sees to the food. If you are giving a dinner party on your own, ask one of your guests to help you with the drinks.

INVITATIONS

Impromptu entertaining, while fun, can also be nerve-racking. Things will be much easier all round if parties are planned ahead. Two weeks is probably ample as far as your own pre-parations are concerned, but more time will be required if you are to find the right people free on the right date: three to four weeks for an average-sized party, at least four weeks for a larger party, and six weeks for events such as wedding receptions.

Invitations to informal dinner parties are normally made by telephone, but for large formal par-ties, most people find it easier to send out invitations – either on hand-written notes or cards, or the printed kind on which the details are filled in by hand (see right). Specially printed cards must be sent out for formal occasions, and will have to be ordered well in advance. Keep a list of the people you have invited and check them off as they reply.

Make things easier for your guests by including the following points on your invitations.

- A note at the bottom that says RSVP, and your telephone number.
- A mention not only of the time and place, but also the type of party it will be, such as Buffet Supper or Lunch. (An invitation to "Sherry" or "Cocktails" automatically assumes that only small cocktail snacks will be served.)

You're invited to a dinner party
at 8 Woodstock Terrace
on December 21st
time 8.30 p.m.
telephone 450-6782

RSVP

MENU PLANNING

When planning a dinner party menu, it is important to be aware of your guests' likes and dislikes, to be realistic about your abilities as a cook and your kitchen's capa-bilities, and to have plenty of time to spend with your guests.

Whatever your menu, it should contain three or more well-balanced courses. The "wet and dry" rule is a good one to follow when planning actual dishes; that is, a "wet" course such as a soup or casserole should precede a "dry" one such as a grilled steak or an apple tart. Aim, too, for balance in "weight" of the courses. A thick soup with

dumplings, followed by chicken fricassée and a cheesecake for dessert is far too filling for all but the heartiest of appetites.

Flavor balance is the next part of the equation to consider. This is easily achieved by serving fish for one of the first two courses and meat or a meat-based dish (such as pâté) as the other. Similarly, one course based on a vegetable or fruit (such as avocado pear or melon), and one based on meat or fish makes a well-balanced combina-tion. Fruit puddings go well with most menus, but avoid creamy desserts if either of the preceding courses has been served with a cream sauce. If fruit was served in either of the first courses, it is best to choose an alternative such as a chocolate-based recipe for the dessert.

Color is important in menu planning, too. Unless you are specifically aiming for an effect of all one color, aim for a pretty but complementary mix of colors in the food you serve. This can be achieved both through the recipes and their ingredients and with the help of garnishes and decorations.

Last but not least, plan the menu so that you leave plenty of time to be with your guests. A dish that needs very careful timing, such as a steak or Chicken Kiev, for example, will not allow for the fact that guests may not be punctual, or that people linger over their food longer than you had originally anticipated.

TIPS FOR A SUCCESSFUL DINNER PARTY

- Plan well ahead, down to the last detail.

- Prepare everything as much in advance as possible. Even fresh vegetables and salads can be prepared and put into plastic bags in the refrigerator.

- Leave time to relax and entertain your guests properly.

- Keep place settings pretty but not over-elaborate.

- Make sure guests have all the necessary plates and cutlery.

- Keep the lighting soft and subtle.

- Make sure you have enough ice for drinks.

- Eat away – but not too far away – from the kitchen.

- Make full use of sideboards and side-tables to save clutter and legwork.

- Don't panic if things go wrong – keep smiling and improvise – your guests will never know!

THE CHEESEBOARD

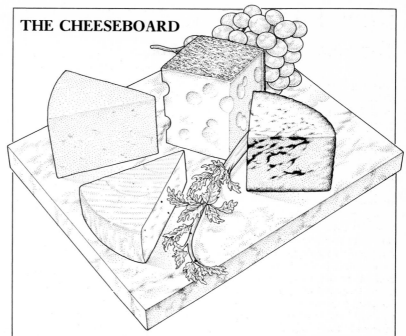

At an informal dinner party, a cheeseboard and fresh fruit can be served in place of a dessert. At a more formal dinner party, however, cheese should be served as an extra course *in addition* to the dessert. Though often served before the meal as an appetizer, cheese is also acceptable to serve like the French do, before the dessert.

If buying cheese for a party several days in advance, take account of the degree to which it will mature before it is served, particularly if you are choosing cheeses such as Brie or Camembert which are only at their best for a short period. Store cheese wrapped in plastic wrap in the refrigerator, unless you want it to ripen at room temperature, but always remove it from the refrigerator and unwrap it at least 1 hour before serving. As well as bringing out the flavor, this will prevent the cheese from sweating unattractively when it is served.

A really good cheeseboard will contain a generous selection of different cheeses both for visual appeal and in order to cater for a wide range of tastes. Include mild cheeses such as mild cheddar, Wensleydale or Gruyère, blue-veined cheeses such as Stilton or Gorgonzola; soft and pungent cheeses such as Brie or Camembert; a robust Cheddar or Leicester and perhaps a soft cheese such as Bel paese or a soft French Boursin. Goat's or sheep's milk cheese also adds interest.

To accompany the cheese, serve a selection of crackers and biscuits, plus some rolls or French bread, since many people prefer these as an accompaniment to strongly flavored cheeses. Butter should also be offered. Sticks of crisp celery and fresh fruit such as grapes can either be arranged on the cheeseboard itself or served separately.

If you wish, provide guests with a fork as well as a knife so that they can eat their cheese on its own. On the cheeseboard itself, provide at least one cheese knife for serving, and more if the board contains cheeses with very well-defined flavors.

PREPARING THE TABLE

SEATING YOUR GUESTS

Seat guests at a dinner party so that, as far as possible, men and women are placed alternately round the table. Husbands and wives should be near, but not directly opposite, each other. Host and hostess should always sit at opposite ends of a rectangular table or opposite each other at a round table, even if this upsets the alternate man/woman arrangement. The chief female guest should sit to the right of the host, the chief male guest to the right of the hostess. The diagram below shows an ideal seating arrangement for few people.

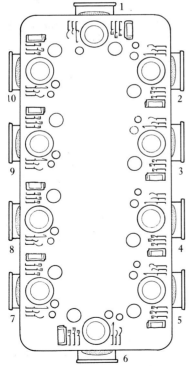

1 Host; 2 Second woman; 3 Man; 4 Woman; 5 Chief male guest; 6 Hostess; 7 Second man; 8 Woman; 9 Man; 10 Chief female guest.

SETTING THE TABLE

When laying each place setting at the table (see below), arrange the knives and forks so that they are used from the outside inwards.

Knife blades should always face inwards. The dessert spoon and fork should be placed above, so that the handle of the dessert spoon points toward the knife blades. For a formal dinner party, arrange the napkin on the side plate to the left of the setting, or in a napkin ring to the right. For an informal setting, the napkin can be simply placed on the center plate if wished. Arrange glasses for water and wine above the knives. Finish your table decorations with a central flower arrangement. Candles should be placed equidistant from the table ends or placed in a pretty group at the table center.

NAPKINS

A dinner table is set off to perfection by a fine tablecloth and decoratively folded napkins. Ideally, the napkins should be of starched linen or other good-quality material, in a color that matches or contrasts with that of the tablecloth, but you can use good-quality, thick paper napkins as a reasonable substitute.

Napkins can be simply folded into triangles or rectangles, and look wonderful housed in decorative napkin rings of either traditional or modern design.

Another way of adding a decorative and impressive touch to the dinner table is by folding napkins into shapes such as the ones shown on these pages.

WATERLILY

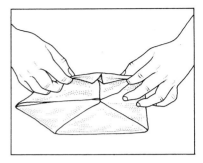

1 Lay starched napkin out flat, fold all four points into the center. Then repeat this same procedure twice more.

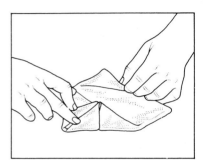

2 When this has been done, turn the napkin over, then fold the four points into the center again.

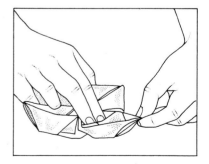

3 Holding the center of the napkin very firmly with the fingers of one hand, use your other hand to unfold a "petal" from beneath each of the four corners of the napkin as shown.

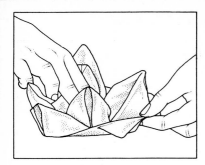

4 Carefully pull out four more petals between the original ones in the same way.

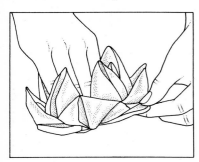

5 The waterlily should now have eight points. Then pull out four petals from beneath the original four as in steps 3 and 4.

6 The completed waterlily now has twelve points, as shown in the illustration above.

BISHOP'S HAT

For this type of fold, the napkin need not be stiffly starched.

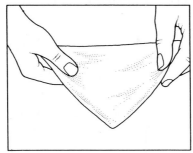

1 Fold the napkin into four to make a square shape. Take the point where the two folded sides meet to a point just above the center of the square.

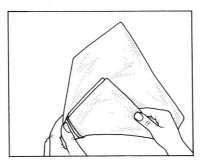

2 Turn the napkin over, then fold back the two sides of the napkin so that they overlap.

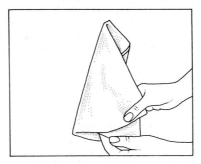

3 Tuck the point of one side into the pocket on the other side. Stand the completed "bishop's hat" napkin on its base.

BUTTERFLY

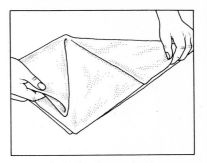

1 Lay starched napkin out flat, fold in half diagonally to make a triangle with point facing upwards. Fold point at bottom right-hand corner up to tip of triangle; fold bottom left-hand corner up to apex.

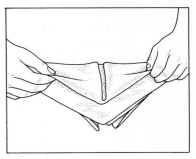

2 Turn this diamond shape over, keeping a firm hold on the loose points, then fold opposite points of the diamond upward to create a triangle.

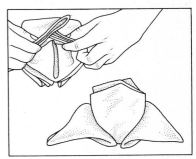

3 Tuck the left-hand corner firmly inside the right hand one. Stand the napkin up on its end, then turn down free pieces at the sides to form the "wings."

Drinks

When entertaining friends and relatives, whether it's a roomful at a wedding reception or just a couple at a dinner party, the choosing and serving of drinks is just as important as the food. Here are all the drinks you should ever have to serve – from aperitifs, wine and Champagne, right through to cups and punches, after-dinner port and liqueurs, and even coffee.

APERITIFS

Before dinner, it is customary to serve an aperitif or cocktail, with hors d'oeuvre or canapés. The aperitif may be a traditional drink such as sherry—dry, sweet or amontillado as you prefer—or a standard spirit-based drink such as gin or vodka and tonic, or whiskey with soda or dry ginger.

Other possibilities are drinks flavored with aromatic herbs such as Campari (with ice, soda and a slice of orange), and the many types of vermouth. Vermouth may be served on its own with ice and lemon or orange, made into a long drink with tonic or mineral water or used to spark up gin or vodka.

You can also make a huge variety of cocktails. For a professional touch, try frosting cocktail glasses with sugar or salt: first dip the rims in very lightly beaten egg white, then dip them in sugar or salt and leave them for several hours to dry.

Other aperitifs include Champagne and drinks more often served after dinner, such as port or Madeira, usually served chilled in this case.

WINE

Good wine is the perfect complement to good food, but there is a great deal of mystique surrounding the subject of which wines should be served with particular foods.

The cardinal rule used to be that white wine should accompany the first course or fish or chicken, and that red wines were for serving with red meat and game. A sweet wine, it was decreed, should accompany the dessert course. Nowadays, however, it is much more important to consider the taste and "weight" of the food you are serving and to choose your wines accordingly. A light food such as fish needs an equally light wine, while heavier dishes such as casseroles need richer, more full-bodied wines. While white wines certainly go well with light starters and have an acidity which offsets the flavor of fish perfectly, a young, light-bodied red wine will often do just as well; similarly, a full-bodied white wine, such as a white Burgundy can be as good with a beef casserole or game pie as a rich red. A sweet wine is, of course, still best for desserts. See our chart below.

WINE WITH FOOD

First courses (not soups), salads, cold meats: Any dry to medium white wine, but particularly Muscadet, Chablis, Pouilly Fumé

Soups: Sherry, Madeira, any dry white wine or light dry red wine but particularly dry Sauternes, Graves

Fish: Any light dry or medium white wine or a light red, particularly Muscadet, Mosel, Meursault, Chablis, Hermitage Blanc

Red meat, game: Any sturdy, full-bodied red, particularly Bordeaux, Chianti, Barolo, Côtes du Rhône, Valpolicella, Médoc, St Emilion

White meat (not stuffed or served with heavy sauce): Any full-bodied white or a medium-bodied red, particularly Chianti Classico, Alsatian Riesling

Cheese: Port, or a young red wine such as Beaujolais Nouveau

Dessert: Any sweet white wine, particularly Asti Spumante, sweet Sauternes, Vouvray, Marsala, Sweet Muscatel, Champagne

* These are, of course, only guidelines. Do not be afraid to experiment and take advantage of special offers and bin ends when out wine shopping, or if you order wine by mail order. Equally, make use of friends' recommendations.

CUPS AND PUNCHES

Fruit cups and punches make a refreshing change from wine in hot weather and are also a good way of catering for large numbers. Try some of the following recipes.

MULLED WINE

Serves about 8

2½ cups water
1 cup sugar
8 cloves
1 stick of cinnamon
4 lemons, thinly sliced
2 bottles burgundy or bordeaux
2 oranges or lemons, thinly sliced, to decorate

1 Bring the water, sugar, cloves and cinnamon to the boil. Add the lemons, stir and leave to stand for 10 minutes.

2 Pour back into the saucepan and add the wine. Heat but do not boil.

3 Strain the wine into a bowl and serve hot, decorated with the orange or lemon slices.

CHAMPAGNE CUP

Serves about 8

large piece of ice
1½ Tbsp apricot brandy
1½ Tbsp orange-flavored liqueur
¼ cup brandy
1 bottle Champagne, chilled
1 cup soda water
fruit, to decorate

Put the ice in a large jug and add the ingredients in the order given. Stir well and decorate with slices of fruit in season. Serve at once.

FRUIT PUNCH

Serves about 20

2 bottles of dry white wine
2 bottles of red wine
6 Tbsp orange-flavored liqueur
2 eating apples, cored and sliced
pieces of melon
orange slices, quartered
few strawberries
crushed ice
2 quarts lemon soda

Pour the wines and liqueur over the fruit and ice in a bowl. Chill, then add the lemonade. Serve at once, while ice-cold.

APPLE PUNCH

Serves 8–10

2 red-skinned eating apples
2 large oranges
1 cup apple juice
5 cups soda water
5 cups dry ginger ale

1 Rub the apples with a clean dry towel; quarter, core and slice. Slice the oranges into small pieces, discarding the seeds.

2 Place the apple juice and prepared fruits into a large bowl, cover and chill for about 2 hours. Chill the bottles of soda water and ginger ale.

3 Just before serving, measure out the soda water and ginger ale and combine with the apple juice. Ladle into glasses for serving.

KIR

Makes 1 serving

4 parts dry white wine
1 part black currant liqueur

Thoroughly chill the wine before combining it with the liqueur; serve in a tall red wine glass.

OPENING A CHAMPAGNE BOTTLE

1 Hold the Champagne bottle in one hand, and remove the wire muzzle around the top of the bottle with the other.

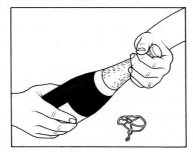

2 Slightly tilt the bottle and hold the cork firmly, rotating the bottle at the same time.

3 Pull the bottle down gently and slowly to reduce internal pressure. The cork will come out with a soft "pop." Wipe rim.

AFTER-DINNER DRINKS

After dinner, when your guests are relaxed and ready for their coffee, is the time when you should offer brandy, liqueurs or port. These are by no means obligatory, but they do make a wonderful end to a dinner party.

If you only have the resources to choose one after-dinner drink, then brandy or port are always safe options. Some brandies are given a star rating (5-star being the best), but this is not standard. VSOP (Very Special Old Pale) means that a brandy has matured for at least 5 years. The names Cognac and Armagnac mean that the wines from which the brandy was made come from these specific wine-growing regions.

BRANDY AND LIQUEUR GLASSES
Serve brandy in a large, balloon-shaped glass. The drinker can then swirl the brandy around as it warms with the heat of the hands, thus allowing the aroma to develop.

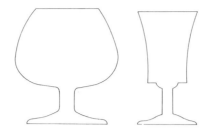

Liqueurs should be served in small glasses – either wide-rimmed or taller, with parallel sides and a shape like a sherry glass.

PORT
Port is a drink surrounded with traditions and customs. Vintage port, which takes 15–20 years to mature, should always be decanted through a muslin filter before it is drunk, as should crusted port which is port treated as a vintage but not actually made in a vintage year. Other ports do not need this treatment. Ports which are ready to drink without decanting can be ruby, tawny or white. Ruby port is rich and red, but does not have the subtle maturity of a tawny port. White port is made from white grapes.

COFFEE
Coffee makes a perfect finale to a dinner party, and it is customary for guests to retire to comfortable chairs, away from the table, to drink it (with brandy or liqueurs if liked), but if the conversation is flowing freely it may seem best for guests to have a first serving of coffee at the table rather than to break up the flow of "chat."

Fresh coffee can be bought as beans or ready-ground. If you do not have your own coffee grinder it is best to buy the beans, then have them ground to the coarseness you prefer in the shop. Whatever the type of coffee you choose (see below) you should ensure it is as fresh as possible; that is, it is purchased from a reputable coffee merchant or other reliable outlet which has a fast turnover. Whole beans will keep their freshly roasted flavor for up to two weeks in an airtight tin, but ground coffee will only keep for 7–10 days, even in an airtight tin in the refrigerator. Beans will keep for 4–5 months and ground coffee for 4–5 weeks in the freezer.

TYPES OF LIQUEUR
There are so many flavors of liqueurs to choose from that the selection must, in the last analysis, be a personal one. The following are some of the most popular, described with their predominant flavors:

Advocaat: eggs (or alcoholic egg custard!)
Amaretto: apricots and almonds
Anisette: aniseed
Aquavit: schnapps (potato or grain spirit) flavored with caraway or dill
Bénédictine: herby liqueur in a brandy base
Calvados: apple brandy
Cassis: black currant
Chartreuse: herbs – the yellow is less strong than the green
Cointreau: bitter orange peel
Crème de menthe: mint

Curaçao: bitter orange
Drambuie: whisky, herbs and (perhaps) heather honey
Galliano: yellow Italian herb liqueur
Grand Marnier: orange-flavored, based on Cognac
Kahlua: strong Mexican coffee-flavored liqueur
Kummel: caraway
Maraschino: cherries
Ouzo: Greek aniseed liqueur
Royal Mint Chocolate: peppermint and chocolate
Southern Comfort: American whiskey-based liqueur with oranges, other fruits and herbs
Strega: combination of over 70 herbs and barks in a sweetish liqueur
Tia Maria: Blue mountain coffee, spices and rum

TYPES OF COFFEE

These are the types of coffee blends suitable for a dinner party:

American roast: light and mild; very popular generally.
New Orleans roast: a darker coffee, mixed with chicory.
French roast: very dark, rich flavor especially good after dinner.
Italian roast: the strongest, with an espresso flavor.

MAKING COFFEE

The best coffee is made with freshly roasted and ground beans and with freshly boiled water. As a rule, allow 1 Tbsp coffee per cup water. This is also about the amount you should allow per guest.

You should also offer your guests a choice of regular and decaffinated coffee. Brewed water-process decaffinated coffee can be as good as regular coffee.

However you make coffee, it should *never* be allowed to boil, since this ruins the flavor. The following are the most successful methods:

Infusion method: medium-ground coffee beans are placed in a warmed pot and boiling water poured over them. After 4–5 minutes' infusion, the coffee is strained straight into the cups or into a clean, warm jug. There is a more sophisticated version of the infusion method marketed as *La Cafetière* (above). The coffee jug contains strainer which is plunged through the coffee before serving.

ESPRESSO

Served in tiny cups, espresso is highly concentrated coffee made by forcing steam through dark roast coffee beans. Serve only with sugar.

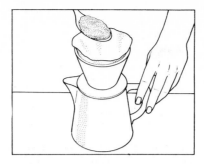

Filter methods (above and below): in these methods, hot water passes through a filter paper containing finely ground coffee beans. There are many versions of this method, many incorporating electrical devices to keep the made coffee warm.

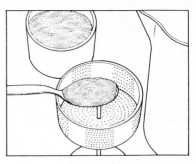

Percolator method: water is brought to the boil in the percolator and forced over coffee grounds in a basket in its top. Although electric percolators have a timing device, there is a risk of the coffee becoming "stewed."

Cona or syphon method: a special coffee maker in which boiling water is forced from a lower container into an upper container in which medium-ground coffee is placed. When the coffee maker is removed from the heat the prepared coffee flows down into the lower container again, from which it is served.

SERVING COFFEE

Serve after-dinner coffee in small cups. If guests prefer coffee with milk or cream, use cold milk or light cream, *never* boiled milk. Offer granulated sugar or special coffee sugar crystals as a sweetener.

IRISH COFFEE

1 Warm as many goblets as needed, then put 1 measure of whiskey and 1 teaspoon light brown sugar in each.

2 Pour in piping hot coffee to come about 1 inch from the top.

3 Pour heavy cream over the back of a teaspoon into the glass. The cream will float on top.

Use other liqueurs to make the following coffees:
Rum (Caribbean coffee)
Kirsch (German coffee)
Calvados (Normandy coffee)
Tia Maria (Calypso coffee)
Strega (Witch's coffee)
Cointreau and Curaçao can also be used, if wished.

Eating Outdoors

Relaxed and informal, eating outdoors in hot sunny weather is one of the high spots of summer. Barbecues and picnics suit every large group and members of the family, so everyone can join in. If you are the host or hostess, make sure you give yourself time to enjoy yourself, too—the information in this chapter is designed with this in mind.

Eating outdoors can be an enjoyable experience as long as the weather is fine and the food is well planned for the occasion.

If eating outdoors on a terrace or patio, for example, choose 'fork foods' which do not need cutting or which can be easily managed on a lap, and organize the food and drink so that you are not continually rushing back and forth to the house.

PICNICS

Picnics will need even more careful planning. As well as planning eating and drinking utensils, you must remember rugs, groundsheets or picnic chairs to sit on, and also the food **must** be as tasty and interesting as possible within your limitations. Even the most informal picnic need not, for example, be based on sandwiches. Equally good picnic fare includes pies and patties, croquettes and rissoles, cubes of meat or firm fish, chicken portions and so on. Slices of a fairly firm cake, sweet biscuits and buns, plus fresh fruit are ideal desserts for eating with the fingers.

When packing food for a picnic, use small polythene bags for items such as cheese, cooked meats and solid salad ingredients. For more delicate foods such as quiches, pizzas, hard-boiled eggs and open flans, use cake tins or rigid polythene boxes and make sure that the foods are kept upright.

To transport food for picnics, the best choices are zip-up insulated (padded) bags or, even better, rigid polystyrene insulated boxes. To keep these bags and boxes cool, pack pre-frozen ice sachets or ice blocks in with the food.

For taking liquids on picnics, the vacuum flask is absolutely invaluable. The exceptions to the rule are Champagne, wines and fizzy drinks, which are best taken to picnics in the container in which they are purchased. When using a vacuum flask, always fill it as much as possible—any air trapped on the top will reduce the flask's insulating qualities. Do not, however, plan to keep food or liquids in a vacuum flask for more than 8 hours.

BARBECUES

When buying a new barbecue, concentrate on size. As a rough guide, it takes a barbecue grid diameter of at least half a metre (18 inches) to cook enough food for eight people at a time.

Make sure the unit is sturdy and stable, and that it offers some control over the positioning of the grid. A rotisserie spit is a handy optional extra for cooking whole chickens and joints of meat; aim for one that is battery- or electrically operated. A meat thermometer is another essential item for cooking large pieces of meat and poultry.

Long-handled barbecue tools are also essential: tongs, forks, slices and spatulas are the most useful for safe handling of food to and from the barbecue grid, and well-insulated oven gloves will provide added protection. A basting brush for brushing foods with oil or marinades, foil for wrapping certain foods, and absorbent kitchen paper for mopping up spills and wiping hands are also needed. A pair of bellows is a good idea for fanning reluctant flames and a bulb syringe for damping down those that get out of hand.

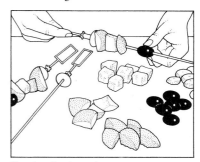

Putting food on skewers

Metal or wooden skewers are worth buying if you like kebabs, so, too, is a metal barbecue cage for cooking delicate items such as fish, which might disintegrate after over-handling.

Getting the fire ready Plan to start the barbecue fire 30–45 minutes before you want to begin cooking—the coals should be glowing red at night, lightly covered in white-grey ash in daylight. There must never be any flame while you are cooking. Charcoal or charcoal briquettes are the ideal fuel. Use proprietary charcoal lighters for lighting the barbecue; never use petrol, paraffin, methylated spirits or any other volatile fuel. To keep the charcoal at the right heat throughout the cooking time, always feed fresh charcoal on gradually from the outer edge, pushing a ring of fuel from the edge of the fire into the centre.

Lighting the fire

1 Arrange some firelighters in the bottom of the barbecue.

2 Pile the charcoal in a pyramid about 5–7.5 cm (2–3 inches) high over the top. (For a large joint, spread the charcoal in a single 2.5-cm [1-inch] layer.)

3 When the coals are burning strongly, spread them out in an even layer, then, just before you are ready to cook, put the grid in the position required so that it can heat up. To keep the charcoal at the right heat throughout the cooking time, always feed fresh charcoal on gradually from the outer edge, pushing a ring of fuel from the edge of the fire into the centre. Never throw charcoal directly on top of the fire—flames will leap up or you will have masses of unwanted smoke. Gentle heat is suitable for most foods, so feed the fire regularly and in small amounts —large quantities will reduce the heat too much and cause uneven cooking.

Any kind of food that can be fried or grilled is suitable for barbecuing. And barbecue cooking times can be calculated as the same as conventional grilling and frying times.

SANDWICHES

As soon as you have made sandwiches for a picnic, pack them in rigid polythene containers and seal them, or wrap them in cling film, foil or polythene bags, to keep them as fresh and moist as possible. The chart opposite gives some good ideas for fillings, but there are also many different types of bread and styles of sandwich to choose from.

For sandwiches made from conventional slices of bread, there are many ways in which you can ring the changes. Use one slice of brown bread and one of white in each sandwich for an interesting effect, or make double or triple deckers with 3 or 4 slices of bread and 2 or 3 different fillings (see right). Make rolled sandwiches by rolling up asparagus spears, ham slices or smoked salmon Swiss roll style in slices of bread from which the crusts have been removed. For pinwheels, spread slices of bread with a colourful filling, roll them up and refrigerate them. Just before serving cut each roll into thin slices. Toasted sandwiches if freshly made just before the picnic party departs, wrapped in foil and packed in an insulated box, are food for picnics on more chilly days. French bread sandwiches are hearty picnic fare. Omelette and salad is a traditional filling, or you could make a *pan bagna* (see page 56).

Pitta bread, when cut in half, reveals 'pockets' which are ideal for stuffing with the usual sort of sandwich ingredients, and with more substantial fillings such as spiced potato, lentils or vegetables.

Meat fillings
Cooked beef—sliced or minced with horseradish cream, mustard or soured cream
Corned beef with chopped watercress or celery
Minced lamb with soured cream and mint
Minced chicken with cottage cheese and pineapple
Minced pork and ham with cranberry sauce
Turkey with redcurrant jelly
Salami, tomato and cress
Pâté with walnuts and orange slices
Tongue with cream cheese and green peppers

Fish fillings
Salmon with chopped or sliced radishes
Smoked salmon with lettuce and lemon juice
Tuna with Russian salad
Shrimps with minced mussels
Crab (flaked) with avocado
Prawns, cottage cheese and green peppercorns
Herrings with sliced beetroot and soured cream
Rollmop herrings, mashed, with onion and tomato slices
Sardines with chopped watercress
Pilchards (mashed) with cottage cheese
Kippers with tomato and celery

Egg fillings
Egg mayonnaise with capers
Omelette (cold) cut into strips
Egg mayonnaise with avocado
Sliced egg with cream cheese and chives
Scrambled egg with bacon
Scrambled egg with watercress

Cheese fillings
Cheddar (grated) with chopped nuts and grated apple
Mashed Stilton with shredded spinach
Curd cheese with beansprouts
Danish blue with sliced grapes
Lymeswold or Blue Brie with orange slices
Cream cheese with chopped walnuts and olives
Cheddar cheese with fruit pickle
Cream cheese with grated carrots
Mozzarella and avocado
Brie and tomato
Camembert and cucumber
Feta, sliced onions and tomatoes
Caerphilly and mustard pickle
Edam with celery and chutney

Presenting the Food

One of the secrets of successful entertaining is knowing how to present the food you have so carefully cooked in the most attractive way. And this doesn't mean that you have to be an expert at piping, or a whizz with aspic! Here are ideas for garnishing and decorating, all of which are stunningly effective, yet amazingly simple to do.

GARNISHES

Add a professional touch to your cooking by using some of the savory garnishes suggested on these pages. The garnishes can simply be placed on the dish or, if the dish in question is already covered with a layer of aspic, can themselves be fixed in position with aspic. To do this, simply dip the prepared garnishes in aspic and set them in position, then, when they are well set, cover the entire dish with another aspic layer.

Garnishes and decorations should, as a rule, be edible; they should also look fresh and shiny, not stale and dull. This fresh effect can be enhanced by the use of aspic or a sweet jelly, both on the dish itself, or as part of the garnish. Here are a few ideas for attractive garnishes and decorations.

SPRING ONION TASSELS

1 Remove the base and most of the green part from each of the spring onions.

2 Make several parallel slits from the top of each onion to within about 1 inch of the base.

3 Allow the onions to stand in a bowl of iced water for about 1 hour to curl, then drain well before using.

LEMON TWISTS

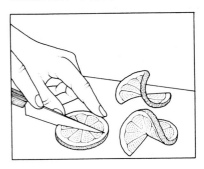

Cut thin slices of lemon. Make a cut to the center of each slice then twist into an S-shape. A sprig of parsley or another herb may be placed at the center of the twist for extra color. This method can also be used with orange, lime or cucumber slices.

CELERY FRILLS

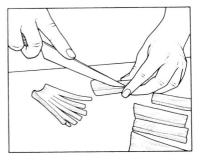

1 Cut sticks of celery into pieces about 3 inches long. Make parallel cuts in each end of the celery about 1 inch deep, then flatten out the celery.

2 At each end, make a careful cut into the "teeth," so that the teeth are cut in half lengthways.

3 Leave the prepared sticks of celery in iced water for about 1 hour so that the frill can curl up.

TOMATO ROSES

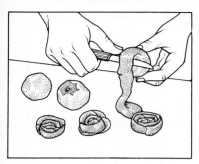

1 Using a small sharp knife, cut the skin and a very thin layer of flesh from a tomato, starting at the top and working round in the way that you would peel an orange.

2 Trim the ends of the peel neatly, then curl it up so that it forms a flower shape. Secure with a toothpick until ready to use.

RADISH ROSES

1 Trim each radish. Starting at the top of the radish, make rows of small cuts into the radish flesh to make petals. The number of rows will depend on the size of the radish.

2 Place the prepared radishes in a bowl of iced water for about 1 hour so that the "petals" open out to form a rose.

WATERLILY ORANGES

1 Using a small, thin-bladed knife, make a slantwise cut in the equator of an orange to the center.

2 Without removing the knife, make a series of zig-zag cuts all round the equator of the fruit. Gently twist the two halves apart.

This can also be used on tomatoes, grapefruit, lemons or similar savory garnishes.

FLUTED MUSHROOMS

1 Choose firm, white button mushrooms. Hold a small sharp knife with the blade parallel to the mushroom stalk.

2 Keeping your thumb and fingers well away from the blade, turn the mushroom against the knife so that thin, curved strips of the mushroom skin are removed evenly all round.

MIMOSA EGGS

Separate the egg yolks from the whites of hard-boiled eggs. Chop the whites finely then sieve the yolks. The sieved yolk can also be formed into small balls to look like mimosa flowers.

GHERKIN FANS

Make parallel cuts in gherkins to within about $\frac{1}{2}$ inch of the base. Open out into a fan shape.

CUCUMBER WHEELS

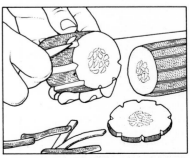

Using a sharp knife, remove thin strips of skin evenly from all round a cucumber. Then cut into slices.

DECORATIONS

Effective decorations for sweet dishes range from the stunningly simple to the sophistication of piped cream or icing. Even if you are not an experienced cook, you can try some of the suggestions shown here.

PASTRY TASSELS

Cut out a strip of pastry about 4 inches long and 1 inch wide. Make parallel cuts along the strip to end about $\frac{1}{4}$ inch from the edge. Roll up the pastry, stand it on its end and fan out the cut edge. Insert into center hole in pastry-topped pies.

PRALINE

Slowly dissolve 75 g (3 oz) sugar in 60 ml (4 tbsp) water over gentle heat, then increase the heat and boil until the liquid has turned to a rich caramel colour. Add 25 g (1 oz) blanched almonds, chopped and toasted. Pour the mixture immediately onto an oiled baking sheet. Leave to set for about 10 minutes. Crush caramel with a rolling pin or in a food processor or blender.

MARZIPAN FRUITS

Color batches of marzipan with orange and green food coloring. With your fingers, shape small amounts of the orange marzipan into balls. Stick a trimmed whole clove in the end for the bud of the fruit. Roll on the fine side of a conical or box grater to give the texture of orange skin, then roll in sugar. Attach "leaves" made from the green-colored marzipan. Use on cakes, or as petits fours or in a candy box.

CHOCOLATE CURLS

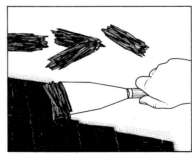

Melt chocolate in a double boiler or a bowl over a pan of hot water, then pour and spread on to a cold surface (ideally a marble slab) and leave until just on the point of setting. Push the blade of a large knife away from you at an angle to make curls. Use to decorate cakes, mousses and soufflés.

For less dramatic, though simpler, chocolate curls, shave a bar of chilled chocolate with a vegetable peeler.

CANDIED FLOWERS

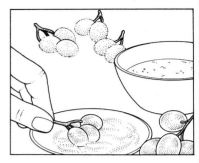

Whisk together the white of 1 egg with 2 teaspoonfuls of cold water to give a frothy mixture. Brush the mixture onto fruits or flowers, then dip these in sugar. Shake off any excess, then spread out on waxed paper and leave in the air to dry for at least 24 hours. Use to decorate cakes, mousses and soufflés.

CITRUS JULIENNE

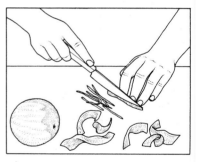

Remove very thin strips of rind from citrus fruit with a paring knife or vegetable peeler, making sure that the strips contain no traces of pith. Blanch the strips in boiling water for about 3 minutes, then drain and rinse under cold running water. Dry thoroughly and cut into julienne strips about $\frac{1}{4}$ inch thick and about 2 inches long. Use to sprinkle over desserts; looks especially good on rosettes of whipped cream or butter cream icing.

CHOCOLATE LEAVES

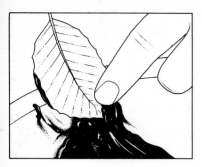

1 Melt the chocolate in a double boiler or a bowl over a pan of hot water.

2 Using rose leaves which have been thoroughly washed and dried, drag the upper surface of each leaf through the chocolate, making sure that the underside of the leaf does not become chocolate-coated too. Or use a pastry brush to brush chocolate on leaves.

3 Turn the leaves chocolate-side up and place on waxed paper to set. When the chocolate has set, carefully peel off the leaf.

JELLY FLOWERS

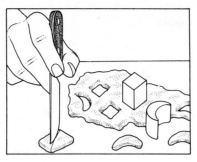

1 Make up some very firm fruit gelatine of the color you wish and use aspic cutters or a sharp knife to make petal shapes.

2 Construct flowers—using the gelatine petals, angelica strips for stems and silver dragees for the centers. Whole blanched almonds can be alternated with the gelatine in the flowers.

Arrange the shapes on the top or around the edges just before serving. The gelatine flowers will keep in the refrigerator 2–3 days. Store in an airtight container.

PIPED ROSETTES

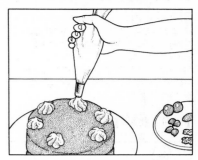

Whip heavy cream until stiff but not buttery in texture, then, using a piping bag and a star nozzle, pipe rosettes of cream around a dessert or cake and top each one with a nut, cherry or some other kind of fruit. Or sprinkle with grated chocolate, toasted chopped nuts or toasted shredded coconut.

ICING SUGAR PATTERNS

1 Place a patterned paper doily, or a template you have cut yourself, on a cake (or get someone to help by holding it just above the surface of a delicate cake or dessert).

2 Sift over confectioners sugar—the pattern of holes will be reproduced on the surface of the cake or dessert.

Chocolate powder can be used in a similar way on a lightly colored cake.

COLOR MATCHES

Here are some ideas for using color matches in food and their decorations: they should set you thinking to try some color combinations of your own.

Red, white and green as in tomatoes, Mozzarella and avocado

Black, white and yellow as in hard-boiled eggs topped with lumpfish roe

Pink, black and green as in ham cornets stuffed with cream cheese and spinach and garnished with black olives

Beige, green and yellow as in veal, fish or chicken with cucumber and lemon twists

Strong colors with pale ones such as a salad of grated raw beets, carrot and celeriac

Shades of orange as in orange mousse with pale orange cream rosettes topped with julienne orange strips

Brown and purple as in chocolate cake with frosted African violets

Orange and green as in carrots with chopped fresh tarragon leaves

Pale yellow and dark red as in lemon soufflé decorated with blackberries

Light brownish yellow and **deep purple** as in rolled-up filled dessert crêpes with black currant sauce

Basic Recipes

This chapter is packed with all the basic recipes you need to make up the dishes in this book. From simple things with basic methods like stocks, sauces and dressings, to pastry recipes and how to prepare and cook vegetable accompaniments (there's even a whole page devoted to cooking potatoes).

SHORTCRUST PASTRY

175 g (6 oz) plain white or wholemeal flour

pinch of salt

75 g (3 oz) butter or block margarine and lard

about 30 ml (2 tbsp) cold water

1 Mix the flour and salt together in a bowel. Cut the fat into small pieces and add it to the flour.

2 Using both hands, rub the fat into the flour between finger and thumb tips until the mixture resembles fine breadcrumbs.

3 Add the water, sprinkling it evenly over the surface. Stir it in with a round-bladed knife until the mixture begins to stick together in large lumps.

4 With one hand, collect the mixture together and knead lightly for a few seconds to give a firm, smooth dough. The pastry can be used straight away, but is better allowed to 'rest' for about 30 minutes. It can also be wrapped in cling film and kept in the refrigerator for a day or two.

5 *To roll out:* sprinkle a very little flour on a working surface and the rolling pin, not on the pastry, and roll out the dough evenly in one direction only, turning it occasionally. The ideal thickness is usually about 0.3 cm ($\frac{1}{8}$ inch). Do not pull or stretch the pastry. When cooking shortcrust pastry, the usual oven temperature is 200–220°C (400–425°F) mark 6–7.

BAKING BLIND

Baking blind is the process of baking a pastry case without the filling—essential if the filling is to be uncooked or if it only requires a short cooking time. First shape the pastry into the baking tin. Prick the pastry base with a fork. For large cases, cut a round of greaseproof paper rather larger

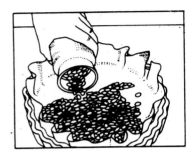

than the tin. Use this to line the pastry and weight it down with some dried beans, pasta or rice. Alternatively, screw up a piece of foil and use that to line the base of the pastry case. Bake the pastry at the temperature given in the recipe for 10–15 minutes, then remove the baking beans and paper or foil lining and return the tin to the oven for a further 5 minutes to crisp the pastry. Leave the baked case to cool and shrink slightly before removing it from the tin. (The baking beans can be kept for use again.)

For small cases, it is usually sufficient to prick the pastry well with a fork before baking.

Baked unfilled pastry cases can be kept for a few days in an airtight container.

PUFF PASTRY

450 g (1 lb) strong plain flour
pinch of salt
450 g (1 lb) butter
about 300 ml (½ pint) cold water
15 ml (1 tbsp) lemon juice
beaten egg, to glaze

1 Mix the strong plain flour and pinch of salt together in a large bowl.

2 Cut 50 g (2 oz) off the butter and pat the remainder with a rolling pin into a slab 2 cm (¾ inch) thick.

3 Rub the 50 g (2 oz) butter into the flour with the finger and thumb tips. Stir in enough water and lemon juice to make a soft, elastic dough.

4 Turn the dough on to a lightly floured surface, then knead until smooth. Shape into a round and cut through half the depth in a cross shape.

5 Open out the flaps to form a star. Roll out, keeping the centre four times as thick as the flaps.

6 Place the slab of butter in the centre of the dough and fold over the flaps, envelope-style. Press gently with the rolling pin.

7 Roll out into a rectangle measuring about 40 × 20 cm (16 × 8 inches). Fold the bottom third up and the top third down, keeping the edges straight. Seal the edges by pressing with the rolling pin.

8 Wrap the pastry loosely in greaseproof paper and leave it to rest in the refrigerator or a cool place for about 30 minutes.

9 Put the pastry on a lightly floured surface with the folded edges to the sides and repeat the rolling, folding and resting sequence five times.

10 After the final resting, roll out the pastry on a lightly floured surface and shape as required. Brush with beaten egg before baking. The usual oven temperature for puff pastry is 230°C (450°F) mark 8.

PÂTE SUCRÉE

100 g (4 oz) plain flour
pinch of salt
50 g (2 oz) caster sugar
50 g (2 oz) butter, at room temperature
2 egg yolks

1 Sift the flour and salt together on to a working surface or, preferably, a marble slab.

2 Make a well in the centre of the mixture and add the sugar, butter and egg yolks.

3 Using the fingertips of one hand, pinch and work the sugar, butter and egg yolks together until well blended. Gradually work in all the flour, adding a little water if necessary to bind it together.

4 Knead lightly until smooth, then wrap the pastry in foil or cling film and leave to 'rest' in the refrigerator or a cool place for about 1 hour.

5 Roll out the pastry on a lightly floured surface and use as required. *Pâte sucrée* is usually cooked at 190°C (375°F) mark 5.

CHOUX PASTRY

50 g (2 oz) butter or block margarine
150 ml (¼ pint) water
65 g (2½ oz) plain flour, sifted
2 eggs, lightly beaten

1 Put the fat and water together in a pan, heat gently until the fat has melted, then bring to the boil. Remove pan from heat.

2 Tip all the flour at once into the hot liquid. Beat thoroughly with a wooden spoon, then return the pan to the heat.

3 Continue beating the mixture until it is smooth and forms a ball in the centre of the pan. (Take care not to over-beat or the mixture will become fatty.) Remove from the heat and leave the mixture to cool for a minute or two.

4 Beat in the egg, a little at a time, adding only just enough to give a piping consistency. Beat the mixture vigorously at this stage to trap as much air as possible. Continue beating until the mixture develops an obvious sheen, then use as required. When cooking choux pastry the usual oven temperature is 200–220°C (400–425°F) mark 6–7.

PANCAKES

Makes 8 pancakes
125 g (4 oz) plain flour
pinch of salt
1 egg
300 ml (½ pint) milk
lard or vegetable oil

1 Mix the flour and salt together in a bowl. Make a well in the centre and break in the egg. Add half the liquid, then gradually work in the flour from the sides of the bowl. Beat until smooth.

2 Add the remaining liquid gradually. Beat until the ingredients are well mixed.

3 Heat a little lard or oil in a small frying pan, running it around the pan to coat the sides. Pour in a little batter, tilting the pan to form an even coating.

4 Place over moderate heat and cook until golden underneath, then turn with a palette knife and cook the other side. Slide the pancake on to a plate lined with greaseproof paper. Repeat.

STOCKS, SAUCES AND DRESSINGS

BASIC BONE STOCK

Makes about 1.1 litres (2 pints)

900 g (2 lb) meat bones, fresh or from cooked meat

cold water

2 onions

2 sticks celery, trimmed

2 carrots

5 ml (1 tsp) salt

3 peppercorns

bouquet garni or sprig of parsley and thyme, bayleaf, blade of mace, etc.

1 Wash the bones. Put in a large pot. If using a pressure cooker add 1.4 litres (2½ pints) water, bring to the boil and skim off any scum. Add roughly chopped vegetables, salt, peppercorns and spices.

2 Bring to High (15-lb) pressure and cook for 1–1¼ hours. If you are using marrow bones, increase the water to 1.7 litres (3 pints) and cook for 2 hours. Reduce pressure at room temperature. (If using an ordinary pan use 2 litres (3½ pints) water. After skimming, add the peppercorns, herbs and spices, vegetables, and simmer, well covered, for 5–6 hours.)

3 Strain the stock thoroughly, discarding the vegetables, and leave to cool. When cold, remove all traces of fat completely.

CHICKEN STOCK

Makes 1.1–1.4 litres (2–2½ pints)

1 roast chicken carcass plus scraps

1.4–1.7 litres (2½–3 pints) water

roughly chopped celery, onions and carrots

bouquet garni (optional)

Put the carcass, bones and scraps in a pan with the water, flavouring vegetables and herbs, if used. Bring to the boil, skim and simmer, covered for 3 hours. (Alternatively, pressure cook at High (15-lb) for 45–60 minutes. Strain the stock and, when cold, remove all traces of fat.)

BASIC WHITE (POURING) SAUCE

Makes 300 ml (½ pint)

15 g (½ oz) butter

15 g (½ oz) plain flour

300 ml (½ pint) milk

salt and freshly ground pepper

1 Melt the butter in a saucepan. Add the flour and cook over low heat, stirring with a wooden spoon, for 2 minutes. Do not allow the mixture (roux) to brown.

2 Remove the pan from the heat and gradually blend in the milk, stirring after each addition to prevent lumps forming. Bring to the boil slowly and continue to cook, stirring all the time, until the sauce comes to the boil and thickens.

3 Once thickened, simmer the sauce very gently for a further 2–3 minutes. Season with salt and freshly ground pepper.

——————— VARIATION ———————

COATING SAUCE

Follow recipe for Pouring Sauce (see above), but increase butter and flour to 25 g (1 oz) each.

QUICK TOMATO SAUCE

Makes about 450 ml (¾ pint)

397 g (14 oz) can tomatoes

5 ml (1 tsp) tomato purée

1 small onion, skinned and chopped

1 clove garlic, skinned and crushed (optional))

pinch of dried basil

pinch of sugar

freshly ground pepper

15 ml (1 tbsp) vegetable oil

1 Put all the ingredients in a blender or food processor and blend until smooth.

2 Heat in a saucepan for 10–15 minutes until slightly thickened. Serve on pasta or use in made-up dishes.

VINAIGRETTE

Makes about 300 ml (½ pint)

75 ml (5 tbsp) red or white wine vinegar*

10 ml (2 tsp) Dijon or made English Mustard

10 ml (2 tsp) salt

5 ml (1 tsp) freshly ground pepper

10 ml (2 tsp) sugar (optional)

2 garlic cloves, crushed (optional)

200 ml (⅓ pint) oil†

For a creamy dressing blend the ingredients in an electric blender or food processor. For a thinner dressing, shake in a screw-topped jar.

——————— VARIATIONS ———————

* Try also **tarragon vinegar** in dressings for tomatoes or potatoes; **thyme vinegar** with eggs or mushrooms; **cider vinegar** with fruits. **Lemon juice** can be substituted for vinegar as well.

† **Sunflower oil** alone or half and half with **olive oil** is pleasant. **Walnut oil** adds interest to strongly flavoured ingredients.

MAYONNAISE

Makes about 400 ml (12 fl oz)

3 egg yolks

7.5 ml (1½ tsp) dry mustard

7.5 ml (1½ tsp) salt

2.5 ml (½ tsp) freshly ground pepper

7.5 ml (1½ tsp) sugar (optional)

450 ml ¾ pint) sunflower oil or
  ½ olive oil and ½ vegetable oil

45 ml (3 tbsp) white wine vinegar
  or lemon juice

1 Put the egg yolks in a bowl with the seasonings and sugar and beat with a whisk. Continue beating and add 150 ml (¼ pint) of the oil about a drop at a time.

2 Once the mixture starts to thicken, continue in a thin stream. Add the vinegar or lemon juice, beating constantly.

3 Add the remaining oil 15 ml (1 tbsp) at a time or in a thin stream, beating continually until it is completely absorbed.

—————— VARIATIONS ——————

Tomato mayonnaise: Prepare as above, but add 2 tomatoes, skinned, seeded and diced; 3 small spring onions, trimmed and chopped; 3.75 ml (¾ tsp) salt and 15 ml (1 tbsp) vinegar or lemon juice.

Garlic mayonnaise: Skin 2 medium-sized garlic cloves and crush with some of the measured salt, add to the finished mayonnaise.

Cucumber mayonnaise: Prepare as above but add 90 ml (6 tbsp) finely chopped cucumber and 7.5 ml (1½ tsp) salt.

CHOCOLATE SAUCE

Makes about 300 ml (½ pint)

175 g (6 oz) plain chocolate in pieces

large knob of butter

45 ml (3 tbsp) milk

45 ml (3 tbsp) golden syrup

1 Put the chocolate in a small bowl with the butter. Add the milk and syrup.

2 Stand the bowl over a pan of warm water and heat gently, stirring, until the chocolate has melted and the sauce is warm.

CREMÈ PATISSIÈRE

Makes 300 ml (½ pint)

2 eggs

50 g (2 oz) caster sugar

30 ml (2 tbsp) plain flour

30 ml (2 tbsp) cornflour

300 ml (½ pint) milk

a few drops of vanilla flavouring

1 Cream the eggs and sugar together until really pale and thick. Sift the flour and cornflour in to the bowl and beat in with a little cold milk until smooth.

2 Heat the rest of the milk until almost boiling and pour on to the egg mixture, stirring well all the time.

3 Return the custard to the saucepan and stir over a low heat until the mixture boils. Add vanilla flavouring to taste and cook for a further 2–3 minutes. Cover and allow to cool before using.

MERINGUES

SMALL MERINGUES

2 egg whites

100 g (4 oz) caster sugar

150 ml (5 fl oz) double cream

1 Line a large baking sheet with non-stick paper. Whisk the egg whites until very stiff.

2 Add half the sugar and whisk again until the mixture regains its former stiffness. Fold the remaining sugar into the mixture very lightly with a metal spoon.

3 Spoon the mixture into a piping bag fitted with a large star nozzle and pipe small mounds on to the prepared baking sheet.

4 Dry out in the oven at 130°C (250°F) mark ½ for 2–3 hours until the meringues are firm and crisp but still white. If they begin to colour, prop the oven door open slightly. Ease the meringues off the paper and leave to cool on a wire rack. Whip cream until stiff and use to sandwich meringues in pairs.

ICING

SEVEN-MINUTE FROSTING

Makes about 175 g (6 oz)

1 egg white

175 g (6 oz) caster sugar

pinch of salt

pinch of cream of tartar

30 ml (2 tbsp) water

1 Put all the ingredients into a bowl and whisk lightly. Then place the bowl over a a pan of hot water and heat, whisking continously, until the mixture thickens sufficiently to stand in peaks. This will take about 7 minutes depending on the whisk used and the heat of the water.

2 Pour the frosting over the top of the cake and spread with a palette knife.

PREPARING AND COOKING VEGETABLES

The choice of vegetables available in shops today is enormous. By importing from different parts of the world at different times of year there is always a wide selection from which to choose. Buy vegetables carefully as quality is important. Bruised, damaged or old, tough vegetables can be picked over and cooked gently into soups, but for boiling and salads you need the best you can buy.

STORING AND PREPARING

Store vegetables in a cool, airy place such as a vegetable rack in a pantry or in the salad drawer of a refrigerator.

Green vegetables should be used as soon as possible after buying, when their vitamin C value is at its highest. Prepare all vegetables as near to their cooking or serving time as possible to retain both flavor and nutrients. Because vitamin C is water-soluble, vegetables should not be put into water until ready to be cooked.

Serve vegetables as soon as they are cooked – they deteriorate through being kept hot. When serving more than one vegetable at a meal try to balance the colors and textures. Slightly under rather than overcook, to preserve nutrients and keep a good texture and color. Steaming and stir-frying are good methods of preserving texture and flavor.

IDEAS FOR SEASONING

Add seasoning to cooked vegetables, especially if they have been steamed or fried without salt. Fresh herbs combine well if sprinkled in just before serving. Try caraway on carrots, tarragon on peas, oregano on zucchini. A little grated nutmeg improves cabbage, spinach and mashed potatoes.

GETTING THE BEST FROM GREENS

Cooked properly, stretched with all manner of ingredients – meat, fish, cheese, rice, vegetables – greens can take pride of place in a varied diet. Prepared greens will keep for a day in a damp plastic bag in the refrigerator. Home-grown greens usually need shorter cooking time than bought ones.

All greens taste better cooked with sea salt. Use about 1 tsp to each $1\frac{1}{4}$ cups water and 1 lb greens. Don't keep greens hot after cooking; if necessary let them cool and reheat when needed. Reheat with a dab of butter and some freshly ground black pepper or grated nutmeg.

Broccoli Never buy broccoli that is yellowing. The stem snaps easily if the vegetable is fresh. To prepare, trim the stems, cut large heads and stems through lengthways and wash. The stem of calabrese (or purple broccoli) can be cut off to 1 inch so that the heads don't overcook. Steam or boil bundles of trimmed broccoli in a little boiling salted water for 10–15 minutes so that the stalks boil and the heads steam. When cooked the broccoli should be crisp to the bite. Drain and serve with melted butter and a squeeze of lemon juice or garnish of toasted flaked almonds. It can also be served with a rich hollandaise sauce.

Brussels sprouts need to be perfectly fresh when bought and don't keep for long. Look for firm, compact sprouts and avoid any that have a trace of yellow or that are open. Good sprouts don't need much trimming. Cut a cross on the stems of larger ones and wash them all in cold water. Use a wide, shallow pan that takes them in one layer, otherwise those underneath will overcook. Cook for 5–8 minutes in about 1 inch of gently boiling salted water and leave the pan lid slightly open to keep a good green color. They should still have a little crunch at the core when done. Drain thoroughly and

toss in melted butter with nutmeg and ground pepper. They are also delicious almost cooked then fried in bacon fat with a few crumbled chestnuts. For a richer dish, turn fully cooked sprouts in gently warmed cream, then garnish with tiny fried croûtons, flaked almonds or buttered crumbs. To accompany roast chicken, purée sprouts with a spoon or two of cream, 2 tablespoons of butter and generous seasoning.

Cabbage Discard rough leaves, quarter and cut away hard core. Shred finely and wash in cold water. Use just enough salted water to cover. Add cabbage to boiling water and cook for about 5 minutes. Drain thoroughly, turn well in butter and season with pepper and nutmeg. Sour cream or natural yogurt make a good finish for cabbage.

Spinach should be young with small leaves. Allow 2 cups per person. Tear away coarse ribs and wash well with plenty of water. Cook over moderate heat in just the water that clings to the leaves after washing and a sprinkling of salt, stirring occasionally for about 5 minutes until tender and reduced. Alternatively, boil small amounts gently in plenty of salted water for about 5 minutes, drain then press with a potato masher. Serve whole or chopped, with melted butter and grated nutmeg. Can be puréed and reheated with cream, pepper, nutmeg and a dusting of grated Parmesan cheese.

Spring greens, kale and curly kale should be bought very fresh. Discard coarse dark leaves, remove any thick ribs, shred roughly, wash. Cook spring greens in a little boiling salted water for 5 minutes; drain well. Serve with butter and nutmeg. Kale needs 10–15 minutes cooking time. To serve, drain well, press out surplus water, chop finely.

POTATOES

All potatoes taste better and keep their shape well if cooked in their skins, which also helps preserve the vitamin C content. The skins can easily be removed after cooking. If you do peel potatoes ahead of time, don't store them in water for long as some vitamins and starch will be lost.

Allow 1 cup per portion.

DUCHESSE POTATOES

2 lb potatoes
salt and freshly ground pepper
4 Tbsp butter or margarine
pinch of grated nutmeg
2 eggs, beaten

1 Boil the potatoes. Drain well, then sieve or mash. Beat in the butter with plenty of seasoning and a pinch of nutmeg. Gradually beat in most of the eggs, reserving a little for glazing.

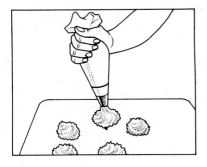

2 Cool the potato mixture then spoon into a piping bag fitted with a large star nozzle. Pipe the mixture in pyramids onto a greased baking sheet.

3 Brush carefully with the remaining egg to which a pinch of salt has been added. Bake in the oven at 400°F for about 25 minutes or until golden brown and set. When cooked, place in a serving dish.

SAUTÉED POTATOES

Serves 4
1½–2 lb potatoes, washed
salt and freshly ground pepper
4 Tbsp butter or 4 Tbsp vegetable oil

1 Cook the potatoes in boiling salted water for 15 minutes or until just tender. Drain well and remove the skins. Cut the potatoes into ¼-inch slices with a sharp knife.

2 Heat the butter or oil in a large frying pan and add the potato slices. Cook until golden brown and crisp all over. Drain well on absorbent paper towels and sprinkle with salt and pepper before serving.

GRATIN DAUPHINOIS

3 lb old potatoes, peeled
1 garlic clove, crushed
1¼ cups light cream
salt and freshly ground pepper
pinch of grated nutmeg
1 cup grated Gruyère cheese
watercress, to garnish

1 Cut the potatoes into small pieces and parboil for 5 minutes; drain well and place in a lightly greased pie pan or shallow casserole.

2 Stir the garlic into the cream, with the salt, pepper and nutmeg. Pour this seasoned cream over the potatoes and sprinkle with the cheese.

3 Cover with foil and bake in the oven at 350°F for about 1½ hours. Remove the foil and run the gratin under the broiler to brown the cheese. Serve garnished with watercress.

HASSELBACK POTATOES

Serves 8
16 small potatoes
vegetable oil
salt and freshly ground pepper

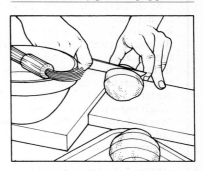

1 Peel and cut the potatoes across their width at ¼-inch intervals three-quarters of the way through.

2 Place in a single layer in an oiled baking pan. Brush with oil and season well.

3 Roast, uncovered, in the oven at 350°F for about 1 hour or until cooked through. Serve immediately.

ROASTED POTATOES

Serves 4
1½–2 lb potatoes, peeled
lard or bacon drippings
chopped fresh parsley, to garnish

1 Cut the potatoes into evenly sized pieces, place them in cold salted water and bring to the boil. Cook for 2–3 minutes and drain.

2 Heat lard in a roasting pan in the oven. Add the potatoes, baste with the fat and cook at 425°F for 45 minutes or until golden brown. Sprinkle with chopped parsley.